T0214056

Lecture Notes of the Institute for Computer Sciences, Social Informatics and Telecommunications Engineering 306

Jun Zheng · Cheng Li · Peter Han Joo Chong ·
Weixiao Meng · Feng Yan (Eds.)

Ad Hoc Networks

11th EAI International Conference, ADHOCNETS 2019
Queenstown, New Zealand, November 18–21, 2019
Proceedings

 Springer

Editors
Jun Zheng
Southeast University
Nanjing, China

Cheng Li
Memorial University of Newfoundland
St. John's, Canada

Peter Han Joo Chong
Auckland University of Technology
Auckland, New Zealand

Weixiao Meng
Harbin Institute of Technology
Harbin, China

Feng Yan
Southeast University
Nanjing, China

ISSN 1867-8211   ISSN 1867-822X   (electronic)
Lecture Notes of the Institute for Computer Sciences, Social Informatics
and Telecommunications Engineering
ISBN 978-3-030-37261-3   ISBN 978-3-030-37262-0   (eBook)
https://doi.org/10.1007/978-3-030-37262-0

This Springer imprint is published by the registered company Springer Nature Switzerland AG
The registered company address is: Gewerbestrasse 11, 6330 Cham, Switzerland

Preface

An ad hoc network is a wireless system for a specific purpose, in which mobile or static nodes are connected using wireless links and dynamically auto-configure themselves into a network without the requirement for any infrastructures such as access points or base stations. Ad hoc networking covers a variety of network paradigms, including mobile ad hoc networks, sensor networks, vehicular networks, unmanned aerial vehicle (UAV) networks, underwater networks, airborne networks, underground networks, personal area networks, device-to-device (D2D) communications in 5G cellular networks, home networks, etc. It promises a wide range of applications in civilian, commercial, and military areas. In contrast to the traditional wireless networking paradigm, this new networking paradigm is characterized by sporadic connections, distributed autonomous operations, and fragile multi-hop relay paths, which have introduced many formidable challenges, such as scalability, quality of service, reliability and security, and energy-constrained operations. Thus, while it is essential to advance theoretical research on the fundamental aspects and practical research on efficient architectures and protocols for ad hoc networks, it is also critical to develop useful applications, experimental prototypes, and real-world deployments to achieve immediate impacts on society for the success of this wireless networking paradigm.

The annual International Conference on Ad Hoc Networks (AdHocNets) aims at providing a forum to bring together researchers from academia as well as practitioners from industry to meet and exchange ideas and recent research work on all aspects of ad hoc networks. As the 11th edition of this event, AdHocNets 2019 was successfully held in Queenstown, New Zealand, during November 18–21, 2019. The conference featured one keynote speech by Prof. Shiwen Mao from Auburn University, USA, who is a leading researcher in the area of ad hoc networks. The technical program of the conference included 28 regular papers that were selected out of 64 submissions through a rigorous review process.

This volume of proceedings includes all the technical papers that were presented at AdHocNets 2019. We hope that it will become a useful reference for researchers and practitioners working in the area of ad hoc networks.

November 2019

Jun Zheng
Cheng Li
Peter Chong
Weixiao Meng
Feng Yan

Organization

Organizing Committee

General Chair

Jun Zheng   Southeast University, China

TPC Co-chairs

Cheng Li	Memorial University, Canada
Peter Chong	Auckland University of Technology, New Zealand
Weixiao Meng	Harbin Institute of Technology, China

Workshop Co-chairs

Kevin W. Sowerby	The University of Auckland, New Zealand
Yifan Chen	University of Waikato, New Zealand

Publication Chair

Feng Yan   Southeast University, China

Publicity Co-chairs

Xiang Gui	Massey University, New Zealand
Lotfi Mhamdi	University of Leeds, UK
Zhifeng Zhao	Zhejiang University, China

Local Arrangement Chair

Saeed Ur Rehman   Auckland University of Technology, New Zealand

Web Chairs

Kai Liu	Southeast University, China
Bingying Wang	Southeast University, China

Conference Manager

Karolina Marcinova   European Alliance for Innovation

Steering Committee

Imrich Chlamtac	University of Trento, Italy
Shiwen Mao	Auburn University, USA
Jun Zheng	Southeast University, China

Technical Program Committee

Rong Chai	Chongqing University of Posts and Telecommunications, China
Peter Chong	Auckland University of Technology, New Zealand
Xiang Gui	Massey University, New Zealand
Shuai Han	Harbin Institute of Technology, China
Cheng Li	Memorial University, Canada
Changle Li	Xidian University, China
Pascal Lorenz	University of Upper Alsace, France
Shiwen Mao	Auburn University, USA
Weixiao Meng	Harbin Institute of Technology, China
Nathalie Mitton	Inria Lille – Nord Europe, France
Symeon Papavassiliou	National Technical University of Athens, Greece
Li Wang	Beijing University of Posts and Telecommunications, China
Pu Wang	University of North Carolina at Charlotte, USA
Yu Wang	Nanjing University of Aeronautics and Astronautics, China
Feng Yan	Southeast University, China
Baoxian Zhang	University of Chinese Academy of Sciences, China
Yuan Zhang	Southeast University, China
Jun Zheng	Southeast University, China
Sun Zhi	The State University of New York at Buffalo, USA
Sheng Zhou	Tsinghua University, China
Kun Zhu	Nanjing University of Aeronautics and Astronautics, China

Contents

Miscellaneous Topics in Ad Hoc Networks

Invited Talk

The 5G Debate in New Zealand – Government Actions and Public Perception

Invited Paper

Syed Faraz Hasan[(⊠)]

Department of Mechanical and Electrical Engineering,
Massey University, Palmerston North, New Zealand
F.Hasan@massey.ac.nz

Abstract. The Fifth Generation (5G) of mobile phone technology is gradually witnessing deployment in many parts of the world. New Zealand is also expected to start 5G deployment by the end of 2019. This paper reviews the progress made to date regarding the introduction of 5G specifically in New Zealand. This paper explores several technical and non-technical issues that relate to the 5G debate that is ongoing across the country. Of particular interest are topics that are associated with government's policy and actions towards 5G, and the perception of the general public about this upcoming technology.

Keywords: 5G · Spectrum allocation · Security · Health impacts

1 Introduction

The Fifth Generation (5G) of mobile phone technology has been introduced in some parts of the world like the US, South Korea, the UK, etc. The early deployment of 5G has mainly been in selected cities in most of the countries. A more ubiquitous and worldwide presence of 5G is anticipated over the next few years. 5G is essentially an improvement on its predecessor 4G. Each 'generation' of mobile phone technology is better than its predecessor at least in terms of network capacity, which may be defined either in terms of the speed each user gets, or in terms of the number of users that can simultaneously connect to the network with a certain Quality of Service. 5G delivers on both definitions of capacity by using the frequency spectra that have never been used for such large scale mobile communication before. The early deployments of 5G are using the 3.5 GHz bands, while the later deployments are expected to use carrier frequencies as high as 28 GHz or 38 GHz. The enormous spectral space that these bands offer enables high speed connections and simultaneous network access to a large user base. Because of this increased capacity, a number of research works are examining the interconnection of devices as diverse as the ground and aerial vehicles [1, 2] with the main 5G network.

In New Zealand, the government has commenced the usual formalities for launching 5G at a national scale. A network service provider called Spark has already launched a 5G lab, which is currently seeking collaborative opportunities with other

J. Zheng et al. (Eds.): ADHOCNETS 2019, LNICST 306, pp. 3–12, 2019.
https://doi.org/10.1007/978-3-030-37262-0_1

industry and academic units. Spark is expected to start deploying 5G from mid-2020, assuming all government processes get completed. In August 2019, another network service operator Vodafone announced its plans of launching 5G as early as December 2019. This has remarkably changed the 5G landscape in New Zealand, which was originally set to be dominated by only one network operator.

The main purpose of this paper is to provide more detail about the progress that is being made in New Zealand in relation to deploying 5G on a national scale. This paper is motivated by the fact that active researchers, not just in 5G but other areas related to technology, often unintentionally neglect some of the non-technical aspects that may affect the overall deployment of technology. By reviewing aspects such as government policy, public perception of 5G, etc., this paper highlights the technical and non-technical state of 5G in New Zealand. The author understands that the New Zealand government is negotiating with the Maori community about their claims to the wireless spectrum. However, the author is not privy to these discussions and therefore cannot make informed comments on this particular subject.

This paper is organized as follows. The key government actions that are pertinent to 5G deployment are reviewed in Sect. 2. Different aspects that relate to the public perception of 5G are examined in Sect. 3. These issues include health implications of 5G, cybersecurity, etc. This paper is concluded in Sect. 4, which is followed by references.

2   Government Actions

2.1   Preparing for 5G in New Zealand

In March 2018, the Government of New Zealand issued a discussion document related to the deployment of 5G in the country. The discussion document [3] set out the government plans and also requested feedback on the same from the general public. The Radio Spectrum Management (RSM) division of the Ministry of Business, Innovation and Employment (MBIE) prepared the draft and also collated the general feedback, which was later published online. Most of the feedback received from the public on the deployment of 5G was related to the health implications of this new technology. The following summarizes the initial plans of the government as described in [3]. The health aspects are discussed separately in Sect. 3.1.

The discussion document pointed out that there is enough frequency spectrum available to support the deployment of three separate 5G networks in New Zealand. Having three separate 5G networks is in contrast with the practice adopted in some countries, which are planning on deploying a single national 5G network. Such a national network would then be shared by the network service providers. The discussion document has indicated that there are enough frequency resources to cater for three separate 5G networks in New Zealand. However, it is not incumbent on all service providers to plan and deploy their own 5G networks. There are three network service providers in New Zealand, but given the size of the country, it is not financially feasible to have three separate 5G networks. In the months that followed, one of the network service providers, Spark, took the lead and announced an ambitious target of rolling out 5G by mid-2020. More recently, another network service provider called Vodafone has announced 5G launch in December 2019. It is expected that Vodafone's 5G network will use the devices provided by Nokia. In terms of access to the 5G spectrum, Vodafone is better positioned to launch 5G because it currently holds the licenses of the concerned frequency bands.

The discussion document also pointed out that the network service providers will likely use their 4G infrastructure to help deploy 5G. This would mean that any equipment that has been in use in 4G will potentially become part of the 5G network. Thus the Huawei equipment present in the 4G infrastructure will inherently affect New Zealand's 5G networks, unless all such devices are carefully removed from the existing network. Huawei is still dealing with the cybersecurity concerns that have been raised about their equipment, which is separately discussed in Sect. 3.2.

The discussion document [3] identified the use of 3.5 GHz and 28 GHz bands for potential use in 5G deployment. A few lower frequency bands were also identified. It has been pointed out in the discussion document that New Zealand will start using the 3.5 GHz band in the first instance, which is in line with the 5G deployments around the world. The government has published another discussion document that focuses entirely on spectral issues specifically in the 3.5 GHz band, which is covered in the following section. The government has proposed four different ways of allocating the 3.5 GHz spectrum: first come first serve, lottery, administrative allocation and auction. The government has apparently chosen to 'auction' the 3.5 GHz spectrum.

2.2   3.5 GHz Band for 5G Deployment

In June 2019, RSM on behalf of MBIE published another discussion document laying out the arrangements for using and making available the 3.5 GHz band. Citing 'international trends', the discussion document [4] has proposed to use Time Division Duplexing (TDD) in the 3.5 GHz band for 5G deployment.

As far as the range of the band is concerned, the discussion document seeks to make the C-band (3800–4200 MHz) available for 5G deployment. The discussion document [4] recommends the use of 3800 MHz to 4200 MHz for 5G transmissions. On the other hand, the table of radio spectrum usage in New Zealand (more specifically PIB21, issue 10 of May 2019 [5]) maintains that the C-band starts at 3700 MHz. It is unclear what the government's plans are for the spectral space that lies between 3700–3800 MHz.

The discussion document [4] maintains that new licenses in the frequency range 3800–4200 MHz band will only be issued selectively. However, it appears that the first 100 MHz of the existing C-band has somehow been excluded from the discussion. In their response to the discussion document, TVNZ has expressed their concerns that this allocation may potentially impact some of the TV transmissions that are ongoing in New Zealand. In any case, the rights to access the C-band are expiring in 2021 but negotiations are allowed to vacate the spectrum sooner.

The frame structure proposed by [4] has been reproduced in Fig. 1, which allows transmission of data in uplink and downlink directions. It is obvious from the figure that significantly larger time resources have been allocated for downlink transmissions.

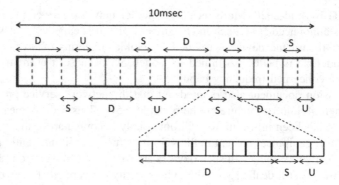

Fig. 1. Frame structure for 3.5 GHz band as proposed in [4].

Table 1. Selected items listed in category II A by the WHO [12].

Selected items	Category	Description
Frying, emissions from high-temperature Red meat (consumption of) Hot beverages about 65 °C (drinking) Indoor emissions from household combustion (wood)	II A	Probably carcinogenic

Notably, the discussion document [4] has not laid out any plans to introduce the discovery frames, which will allow the 5G enabled devices to "discover" each other even in the absence of network coverage. This new feature of discovering other nearby devices does not exist in 4G and pre-4G systems but is expected to be a key feature in 5G. Network-independent device discovery and communication can potentially provide coverage in far-fetch areas (rural townships, etc.) and in emergency situations.

The structure of these discovery frames has been standardized by the 3rd Generation Partnership Project (3GPP), for example in [6]. A number of other research works have modified the legacy discovery frame structure for improved performance [7–9], etc. It is recommended that the entire 3.5 GHz band should be synchronized to a specific "discovery frame structure", in addition to being synchronized to the frame structure shown in Fig. 1. The discussion document has given careful attention to other parameters like the out-of-band emissions and methods for calculating their strength, which are not separately addressed in this paper and can be seen in [4].

3 Public Perception

3.1 Health Implications

The first deployment of 5G around the world and in New Zealand is going to use the 3.5 GHz band, as mentioned earlier in Sect. 2.2. The propagation characteristics of wireless signals in this band are similar to the characteristics of wireless signals that are in common use today, in comparison with that of signals in the 28 GHz or higher bands.

The 28 GHz and higher frequency versions of 5G will use the millimeter-waves [10], which have never been used for wireless communication at this scale. One of the consequences of using mm-waves is that the coverage range of a base station will shrink considerably [11]. Therefore, multiple transmitters will be needed to cover a geographical area that is currently being covered by a single transmitter. The increase in transmission frequency (for example from 2.4 or 2.6 GHz to 28 GHz) and the expected increase in the number of transmitters within our ambient environment has led many to believe that 5G will have adverse effects on human wellbeing.

The World Health Organization (WHO) classifies wireless transmissions as "possibly" carcinogenic [12]. Note that all wireless transmissions in general are deemed possibly carcinogenic by the WHO, not just 5G mm-waves. Possibly carcinogenic is the characterization associated with category IIB, which is a level milder than category IIA that has been labelled as "probably" carcinogenic. The items listed in category IIA are more dangerous than those listed in IIB. Interestingly, a number of items that are in common use are listed as probably carcinogenic (category IIA) by the WHO. Table 1 lists some of such items that are potentially more probable to cause cancer than wireless transmissions, according to WHO.

One of the arguments put forward by the opponents of 5G is that there is no escape from it because it will be everywhere. 5G is indeed expected to interconnect a large number of diverse kinds of devices under the frameworks like Internet of Things [13], Machine-to-Machine communications [14], etc. On the other hand, the proponents of 5G technology claim that despite the widespread use of wireless networks, no concrete links have been established between mobile phone use and different medical conditions [15]. Mobile phones came into commercial use in the 1980s and so have subjected the human beings to electromagnetic radiation ever since. A number of other wireless transmissions have also become ubiquitous over the past e.g. TV and radio transmissions, etc., from which, escape is also not possible. Over the years, the research community has reported works that prove harmful effects of 4G/pre-4G transmissions as well as those that have found none. The work in [16] summarizes both sides of the arguments, including the results obtained by both sides and the conditions in which the results were obtained.

More recently, an article in the New York Times [17] claims to have traced down the research paper that linked the mobile phone transmissions with conditions like brain cancer. Citing active researchers in the field, the article [17] suggests that the work reported in [18], which became a widespread caution against wireless transmissions, did not take into account the shielding effect of the skin when subjected to wireless signals. This shielding effect is known to increase with increasing transmission frequencies, and is therefore expected to result in smaller exposure when high frequency signals are used for mobile telephony.

The study by the National Toxicology Program (NTP) [19] has found that there are some medical effects associated with 4G and pre-4G wireless transmissions. This finding is in contrast with the commonly held belief that non-ionizing radiation (which is used for mobile communication) is completely harmless. The NTP study establishes that non-ionizing radiation may also impart undesirable consequences if appropriate thresholds are not put in place.

The thresholds for wireless transmissions in 4G/pre-4G networks are determined and specified using a metric called the Specific Absorption Rate (SAR). As the name suggests, SAR measures the amount of wireless radiation absorbed per unit mass of the human body. Given that the mm-waves of 5G networks do not penetrate into the human body due to the shielding effect of the skin, the metric that determines the extent of electromagnetic exposure is called Power Density (PD). It appears that PD due to 5G will remain within the permissible threshold [20], which is set at 10 W/m^2 internationally. The same threshold is also enforced in other applications that use wireless signals such as microwave ovens.

However, some works have suggested that exposure to 5G mm-waves will result in temperature elevation across the human skin [21]. A few recent works have even suggested that the thermal effects associated with 5G transmissions may cause permanent damage [22]. Recognizing the fact that all wireless signals (5G or non-5G) are after all bundles of electromagnetic energy, it is important to ensure that the thresholds set by the national and international organizations do not over-expose human users to wireless transmissions.

3.2 Cybersecurity and the Role of Huawei

The public concerns around the security and privacy issues associated with 5G have emerged in the local and international media. While security issues remain linked with all forms of wireless transmissions, 5G poses a new challenge in that it will interconnect not just a users' laptop or a mobile phone, but also appliances that are in everyday use. Therefore, any potential vulnerability in the 5G network may have quite far reaching consequences.

The ban on using Huawei devices, first by the United States and then by other countries, have hinted the existence of security backdoors in the Huawei equipment. A detailed study on the security performance of Huawei devices was conducted in the UK earlier this year. The following briefly reflects on some of the technical aspects of the report published on 28 March 2019 by the Huawei Cyber Security Evaluation Centre (HCSEC) of the UK [23], which covers the assessment of the communication devices that are manufactured by Huawei and deployed in the UK. It must be noted that the technical issues raised by HCSEC will also impact the performance of 4G and 3G networks, and do not specifically relate only to the 5G equipment. Some of the following commentary has come out in a media release [24].

The report published by HCSEC remains largely vague on detail, presumably because publishing too much information about the tests and results may put the Huawei devices at risk. These devices are already in commercial use across the UK and thus must never be comprised. The technical issues that have been highlighted in the report can be broadly classified as software engineering issues and cyber security issues. The issues related to software engineering appear to outnumber those related to cyber security. This may be because many of the cyber security issues stem from the vulnerabilities in the software.

The main issue related to software is concerned with 'binary equivalence' [25], which means that different instances of the same code used in the Huawei devices may build differently. This is problematic because different deployments of the same

Huawei equipment may potentially lead to different performance levels (including the provision of security). Ideally we would want all devices of the same kind to show similar and measurable level of security. Tests performed on four separate Huawei devices have shown that their performance is not repeatable. The report [23] has not identified the devices that have been tested.

On the other hand, one of the main security issues highlighted by HCSEC relates to the cryptographic weaknesses. Cryptography deals with 'hiding' the information transmitted wirelessly so that even when the message is stolen its true contents cannot be retrieved and interpreted. A weak cryptographic solution may lead to the message being decoded by persistent eavesdroppers [26]. Cryptographic weaknesses are addressable too, but the scale of solving this problem may be a potential bottleneck for Huawei. HCSEC has not given any hints on the scale of this problem in the report.

A number of other technical issues have also been highlighted in the report. For example, there are issues around integrating Huawei's operating system with the existing systems. Huawei's OS apparently comes from a third party and uses an outdated code, which is never desirable. There are a few memory safety concerns as well, which, although not explicitly mentioned in the report, typically relate to pushing more data on a memory location than it can actually handle. Such errors result in 'overflows' within the memory units, which may lead to the loss of useful information.

The report did mention that Huawei has offered to invest $2bn over five years to address these issues but HCSEC appears to be looking for a more concrete plan from the company. There are sections within the report that seem to suggest that Huawei has not reasonably addressed the issues raised in the previous audits, which is also a concern for HCSEC. To the best of the author's knowledge, other device manufacturers (Samsung, Ericsson, etc.) have not gone through this kind of security assessment. It would be interesting to see how other manufacturers are doing in terms of the technical issues raised in the Huawei devices. A number of media releases in New Zealand and elsewhere have reported the possibility of security backdoors [27] in the Huawei equipment, which has been denied by the manufacturer.

Previously in 2018, the Government Communications and Security Bureau (GCSB) of New Zealand had rejected Spark's application to use Huawei equipment for deploying the country's 5G network. Spark has not made a resubmission of that application at the time of this writing. Other manufacturers that may provide 5G equipment include Ericsson and Nokia. If Vodafone goes ahead with its plans, the first 5G network of New Zealand will comprise of the devices manufactured by Nokia.

3.3   Unclear Expectations

One of the biggest impediments of 5G in New Zealand is that the general public does not know what it will achieve. Of course there are suggestions that 5G will enable quicker download times, but the existing 4G network in New Zealand is reasonably fast already. A number of urban centers within the country have access to fast fiber optic backbone, which further increases the speed that each user gets. It will be difficult to promote 5G without promoting a strong use-case that solves some of the contemporary problems of New Zealand. One of the only few use-cases that are often talked about is the use of 5G in enhancing the viewership experience of the America's cup [28]. The service provider Spark is the main promoter of this particular application of 5G, which will indeed exploit the real potential of 5G. However, this use-case has an expiry date – it will expire at the end of the competition. What New Zealand really needs is an ongoing use-case that can benefit masses in some meaningful way without an imminent expiry date.

Generally speaking, 5G is great for data hungry applications, just one realization of which is virtual reality. Applications such as online gaming have given rise to lucrative industries in countries like South Korea, Japan, etc. However, in New Zealand, virtually real applications that can enable remote medical consultations might be of more value. There is still a long way to go in that direction but the research community needs to try and address some of the contemporary issues of New Zealand with the help of 5G. A smart combination of 5G with artificial intelligence may support 'predictive maintenance' [29], especially in predicting and averting traffic congestion on New Zealand roads and highways. The 5G technology can also help extend New Zealand's fiber infrastructure to remote communities over wireless links. This would not be possible with the existing 4G networks because of considerable capacity imbalance between fiber cables and the existing 4G technology. However, the high-frequency deployments of 5G will have smaller coverage area, which will make it economically difficult to provide coverage in distant regions that typically have low population density.

3.4   5G and Weather Predictions

The transmission frequencies in the 23.8 GHz band are heavily used in weather monitoring at present. This band is used by the satellite receivers on Earth to estimate the water content in the atmosphere, which then allows a number of other weather predictions to be made. Because the satellite signals are typically low power, any wireless transmission in the adjacent bands may cause loss of information in the 23.8 GHz band [30]. Therefore, 5G deployment in 28 GHz band (or similar) must not leak into the 23.8 GHz band so that the routine weather predictions are not adversely affected by electromagnetic interference. It must be noted that the initial deployment of 5G in the 3.5 GHz band does not pose any significant risks to the weather related transmissions taking place in the 23.8 GHz band.

4   Conclusion

It is an interesting time to be engaged in 5G research and development locally and internationally. In New Zealand, most of the existing issues do not directly relate with the technological foundations of 5G but originate from different concerns, for example security, health and wellbeing, etc. The government and other stakeholders can make a more emphatic case for the deployment of 5G by identifying applications of this new technology that are specific to the New Zealand context. For example, interconnection of health care setups in order to provide medical consultation facilities in areas that typically have few General Practitioners may present a strong use-case of 5G – one that addresses a contemporary problem of New Zealand.

To this end, this paper has provided an updated summary of the state of 5G in New Zealand taking into account a range of technical and non-technical matters.

References

1. Zaidi, K., Hasan, S.F., Gui, X.: Outage analysis of ground-aerial NOMA with distinct instantaneous channel gain ranking. IEEE Trans. Veh. Technol. (2019). https://doi.org/10. 1109/TVT.2019.2938516
2. Jaffry, S., Hasan, S.F., Gui, X.: Effective resource sharing in mobile-cell environments. IET Commun. (2019). [Accepted for publication]
3. Discussion Document: Preparing for 5G in New Zealand. Ministry of Business, Innovation and Employment (2018)
4. Discussion Document: Technical Arrangements of the 3.5 GHz band. Ministry of Business, Innovation and Employment (2019)
5. Table of Radio Spectrum Usage in New Zealand (PIB 21), Issue 10, May 2019. https://www. rsm.govt.nz/assets/Uploads/documents/pibs/ff001f5055/table-of-radio-spectrum-usage-in-new-zealand-pib-21.pdf
6. 3rd Generation Partnership Project: Study on LTE device to device proximity services; Radio aspects. TR 36.843. https://portal.3gpp.org/desktopmodules/Specifications/ SpecificationDetails.aspx?specificationId=2544
7. Jaffry, S., Hasan, S.F., Gui, X.: Neighborhood-aware out-of-network D2D discovery. IET Electron. Lett. **54**(8), 507–509 (2018)
8. Jaffry, S., Zaidi, K., Shah, S.T., Hasan, S.F., Gui, X.: D2D neighborhood discovery by a mobile device. In: IEEE International Communications Conference, pp. 1–6 (2019)
9. Jaffry, S., Hasan, S.F., Gui, X., Kuo, Y.-W.: Distributed device discovery in ProSe environments. In: IEEE Region 10 Conference, pp. 614–618 (2017)
10. Rappaport, T.S., et al.: Millimeter wave mobile communications for 5G cellular: it will work! IEEE Access **1**, 335–349 (2013)
11. Curtis, J., Zhou, H., Hisayasu, P., Sarkar, A., Aryanfar, F.: MM-wave radio: a key enabler of 5G communication. In: IEEE 16th Topical Meeting on Silicon Monolithic Integrated Circuits in RF Systems, pp. 1–3 (2016)
12. International Agency for Research on Cancer: Agents Classified by the IARC Monographs volumes 1–124, July 2019. https://monographs.iarc.fr/agents-classified-by-the-iarc/
13. Lee, C., Fumagalli, A.: Internet of things security - multilayered method for end to end data communications over cellular networks. In: IEEE 5th World Forum on Internet of Things, pp. 24–28 (2019)
14. Tanab, M.E., Hamouda, W.: Machine-to-machine communications with massive access: congestion control. IEEE Internet Things J. **6**(2), 3545–3557 (2019)
15. Science Media Centre NZ.: 5G: Hype vs Reality – Expert Q/A (2019)
16. Yakymenko, I., Tsybulin, O., Evgeniy, S., Henshel, D., Kyrylenko, O., Kyrylenko, S.: Oxidative mechanisms of biological activity of low intensity radiofrequency radiation. Electromagn. Biol. Med. **35**(2), 186–202 (2015)
17. Broad, W.J.: The 5G Hazard that isn't. New York Times (2019)
18. Electromagnetics Science and Technology Consulting. Technical Report to Broward County School Board (2000)

19. National Toxicology Program's Technical Report: Toxicology and Carcinogenesis Studies in B6C3F1/N Mice exposed to Whole-Body RF Radiation at a frequency (1,900 MHz) and Modulations (GSM AND CDMA) used by Cell Phones (2018)
20. Basu, D., Hasan, S.F.: Approximating electromagnetic exposure in dense indoor environ-ments. In: 15th International Symposium on Wireless Communication Systems, pp. 1–5 (2018)
21. He, W., Xu, B., Gustafsson, M., Ying, Z., He, S.: RF compliance study of temperature elevation in human head model around 28 GHz for 5G user equipment application: simulation analysis. IEEE Access **6**, 830–838 (2018)
22. Neufeld, E., Kuster, N.: Systematic derivation of safety limits for time-varying 5G RF exposure based on analytical models and thermal dose. Health Phys. **115**(6), 705–711 (2018)
23. Huawei Cyber Security Evaluation Centre Oversight Board: Annual Report (2019)
24. Griffin, P.: Huawei's 5G future now relies on its ability to clean house. Noted (2019)
25. Wu, B., Ma, Y., Fan, L., Qian, F.: Binary software randomization method based on LLVM. In: IEEE International Conference of Safety Produce Informatization, pp. 808–811 (2018)
26. Fischer, T.: Testing cryptographically secure pseudo random number generators with artificial neural networks. In: 17th IEEE International Conference on Trust, Security and Privacy in Computing and Communications/12th IEEE International Conference on Big Data Science and Engineering (TrustCom/BigDataSE), pp. 1214–1223 (2018)
27. Tien, C.W., Tsai, T.-T., Chen, I.-Y., Kuo, S.-Y.: UFO: hidden backdoor discovery and security verification in IoT device firmware. In: IEEE International Symposium on Software Reliability Engineering Workshops, pp. 18–23 (2018)
28. Arauzo, C.: Emirates Team New Zealand to use Spark's 5G Network in America's Cup Defence Campaign from 2020, November 2018
29. Lin, L., Li, J., Chen, F., Ye, J., Huai, J.: Road traffic speed prediction: a probabilistic model fusing multi-source data. IEEE Trans. Knowl. Data Eng. **30**(7), 1310–1323 (2018)
30. Witze, A.: Global 5G wireless networks threaten weather forecasts. Nature **569**(7754) (2019)

Routing

EL-CRP: An Energy and Location Aware Clustering Routing Protocol in Large Scale Wireless Sensor Networks

Yuehang Bu, Changle Li$^{(\boxtimes)}$, Yao Zhang, and Lina Zhu

State Key Laboratory of Integrated Services Networks,
Xidian University, Xi'an 710071, China
clli@mail.xidian.edu.cn

Abstract. With the development of Internet of Things (IoTs), large-scale wireless sensor networks (WSNs) are widely used in environment monitoring, industrial testing and intelligent transportation. In order to extend the lifetime of WSNs, it is necessary to reduce the energy consumption of sensors. To achieve the large-scale and flexible deployment, the wireless sensors are required to be low memory overhead. The existing WSN routing protocols are difficult to satisfy the requirements for low energy consumption and low memory overhead in those scenarios. This paper proposes an Energy and Location Aware Clustering Routing Protocol (EL-CRP) for large-scale WSN application scenarios. Using an adaptive clustering method, in which the location and energy of cluster members are considered simultaneously, the protocol reduces the energy consumption and memory overhead in the WSNs. Extensive simulations and hardware tests are conducted to evaluate the performance. Results finally verify the advantages of the protocol in large-scale network scenarios.

Keywords: Large-scale WSNs · Energy · Location · Routing protocol · Clustering

1 Introduction

In recent years, with the development of the Internet of Things, WSNs have been widely used. As indicated in [1], from 2019 to 2024, market of global WSNs equipments will maintain a growth rate of 17. 64%. By 2023, the global WSNs market is expected to reach \$9.386 billion, including the fields of environment monitoring, industrial inspection, warehouse storage [2]. In the above scenarios, WSNs typically need to be deployed in a large-scale way.

This work was supported by the National Natural Science Foundation of China under Grant No. U1801266 and No. 61571350, Key Research and Development Program of Shaanxi (Contract No. 2018ZDXM-GY-038, 2018ZDCXL-GY-04-02), the Youth Innovation Team of Shaanxi Universities, and the Science and Technology Projects of Xi'an, China (201809170CX11JC12).

J. Zheng et al. (Eds.): ADHOCNETS 2019, LNICST 306, pp. 15–25, 2019.
https://doi.org/10.1007/978-3-030-37262-0_2

This work focuses on the design of routing protocols in WSNs, in order to meet the requirements of large-scale sensor nodes in low energy consumption with little memory overhead. On the one hand, in large-scale WSNs, sensor nodes have the characteristics of widespread, high deployment density and unknown location. Therefore, in order to establish a stable route, frequent data communications are required between nodes. Through analysis, it is observed that the energy of sensor nodes is mainly consumed in the process of wireless communications [3]. To design an energy-efficient route protocol in large WSNs is an important way to reduce the energy consumption of sensors by reducing the redundant data transmissions. On the other hand, nodes with large-scale deployment in practical scenarios should be low cost and miniaturization. The existing WSN routing protocols are difficult to balance the requirements in low energy consumption and low memory overhead. In response to the above problems in large-scale WSNs, this paper has made the following contributions: (1) Based on the envisaged large-scale WSN application scenarios, a network model and an energy model are constructed. (2) Based on the energy model, an energy and location aware routing protocol is proposed. Using an adaptive clustering method, both the energy consumption and memory overhead at each sensor node are reduced. (3) The performance of the proposed routing protocol is evaluated on a new simulation platform and tested by the developed hardware system.

The structure of this paper is as follows: Sect. 2 describes the system model, and Sect. 3 introduces the design idea of routing protocol with specific steps, including cluster establishment and route establishment. Section 4 evaluates the performance of the protocol through simulations and hardware test. Section 5 summarizes our research work.

2   System Model

In this section, we present the network and energy models of the application scenarios in large-scale WSNs.

2.1   Network Model

The application scenarios envisaged in this paper include environmental monitoring, industrial testing, etc. The network model should cover the following conditions: (1) A WSN consists of multiple normal nodes with routing capabilities and a sink node for data fusion. To simplify the network topology, we assume that the sink node is fixed and there is only one sink node in the network. (2) All the normal nodes are assumed to have identical properties, i.e., same data processing and communication capabilities. (3) Normal nodes are not fixed so that the network has no rigorous requirements in delay. (4) For the sink node, it is assumed that continuous power supply is available to ensure the function achievement. (5) The original location information of all nodes is unknown, there is no auxiliary facility in the network to help the node to obtain location information, and each node can only obtain the required information through communications with neighboring nodes. (6) The network scenario is assumed as sufficiently large so that the sink node can not communicate with all normal nodes directly. For simplicity, we assume that the sink node is located at the center of the scene.

Considering the requirements of low memory overhead, it is necessary to reduce extra function. The traditional methods, i.e., multi-channel communication protocols and adjustment of transmission power require additional hardware overhead, we thus assume that the nodes communicate under a single channel, and the transmission and reception distance of the information is constant.

2.2   Energy Model

The linear energy model is typical method to characterize energy consumption in sensor networks, which is also adopted in our work by referring to [4]. The total energy consumption of a node is denoted as E_i, which is consist of transmission energy consumption E_{Tx}, reception energy consumption E_{Rx}, energy consumption caused in listening state E_l, and energy consumption in sleep state E_s. Specifically, E_i is denoted as:

$$E_i = E_{Tx} + E_{Rx} + E_l + E_s, \tag{1}$$

$$E_{Tx} = lE_{elec} + l, \tag{2}$$

$$E_{Rx} = lE_{elec}, \tag{3}$$

$$E_l = P_l T_l, \tag{4}$$

$$E_s = P_s T_s, \tag{5}$$

where l is the length of the transmitted packet, and the unit is bit. E_{elec} is the energy consumed to process 1 bit of data, and the unit is J/bit. P_l is the power of the node in the listening state. T_l is the time the node is listening. P_s indicates the power of the node in the sleep state. T_s is the time at which the node sleeps.

3   Protocol Design

In large-scale WSNs, the central routing protocol represented by Sensor Protocols for Information via Negotiation (SPIN) [5] can establish routing without excessive memory overhead, but easily causes information congestion in large-scale scenarios, which lead to the deterioration of network performance. The idea to solve this problem is to divide the nodes in the network into different clusters, and select one or more nodes in each cluster as cluster heads. The cluster head undertakes the information interaction of nodes within the cluster and the communications with the sink nodes. The cluster heads are periodically rotated to balance energy consumption. Using the clustering method, the communication efficiency among sensor nodes can be improved so that the network performance could be enhanced.

The routing algorithms using clustering ideas in WSN mainly include Low Energy Adaptive Clustering Hierarchy (LEACH) [6], Power-Efficient GAthering in Sensor Information Systems (PEGASIS) [7], Hybrid Energy-Efficient Reactive protocol (HEER) [8] and Threshold sensitive Energy Efficient sensor Network (TEEN) [9]. LEACH protocol selects the cluster heads based on the random number, which need a sink node control the periodic cluster heads rotation in the network. PEGASIS is a distance-based chain routing algorithm that solves the problem that the LEACH protocol cannot perform multi-hop communications, but in large-scale WSNs, this approach increase the data delay. HEER dynamically selects the cluster head through the information interaction between nodes, and considers the residual energy of the node. TEEN algorithm improves LEACH by adding the hard threshold and the soft threshold to control the time when the node uploads the information data. However, the clustering algorithm of the above protocols relies on the control of a sink node, which increase the data interaction in WSN.

Compared with the clustering process in other WSN routing protocols, the clustering process proposed in EL-CRP does not need to exchange location information with surrounding nodes, which saves the storage space of hardware devices. The self-organizing, adaptive clustering algorithm can flexibly cover the entire network. Since the judgment of whether a node becomes a cluster head depends on the distribution of surrounding nodes, the formed network topology tends to be uniform distribution. Because the application scenario of this paper has low latency requirements, the establishment of routing links refers to PEGASIS. It also provides a route establishment method similar to SPIN for high priority services. The specific processes include cluster establishment and route establishment.

3.1   Cluster Establishment

The cluster establishment algorithm is shown in Algorithm 1. The specific steps are as follows:

Step 1: Node A is powered on, set a random listening time T_{listen}. This step is to avoid network congestion caused by multiple nodes starting and sending broadcasts in close time.

Step 2: Node A enters listening state.

Step 3: If node A hears the beacon frame sent from cluster head B within the time T_{listen}, the node A sends a cluster request to the cluster head B, and waits for the time T_w. If the node A does not receive the reply sent by the cluster head B within the time T_w, step 2 is re-executed. If the node A receives the reply sent by the cluster head B, the node joins the cluster where the cluster head B is located, and sends the interest message to the cluster head B through time division multiple access according to the application requirement. If the node A does not receive the beacon frame within the time T_{listen}, node A itself becomes the cluster head and periodically sends the beacon frame.

Algorithm 1. Cluster Establishment Process.

Require: T_{Min}, T_{Max}, T_w, M, $NodeA$
Ensure: $Cluster_i$
1: Node A power on
2: $T_{listen} = \text{random}(T_{Min}, T_{Max})$, $Timer_1 = T_{listen}$
3: **while** $Timer_1 \mathrel{!=} 0$ **do**
4:    $Timer_1 = Timer_1$ - 1
5:    **if** Node A receives the beacon frame sent by the cluster head B nearby **then**
6:       Node A joins the cluster B
7:    **end if**
8: **end while**
9: **if** $Timer_1 = 0$ **and** Node A does not join any cluster **then**
10:    Node A becomes the cluster head, Node A broadcasts the beacon frame
11: **end if**
12: **if** Node A is cluster head **and** $E_A < Th_{power}$ **then**
13:    **for** i is member id in Cluster A **do**
14:       **if** $E_i > Th_c$ **and** $Node_i$ is the last node communicating with Node A **and** there is no other cluster head around **then**
15:          select $Node_i$ as new cluster head
16:       **end if**
17:    **end for**
18: **end if**

Step 4: If the node A is a cluster head, when the clustering request sent by the node C is detected, determine whether the number of nodes n_c in the current cluster meets the equation: $n_c \leq M - 1$, Where M is the cluster capacity, it means the maximum number of member nodes that a cluster can contain. If equation is met, the reply is sent to the node C, and the cluster head A records the cluster node id; if the condition is not met, no processing will be done.

Step 5: When the energy of cluster head A is lower than the threshold Th_{power} set by us, cluster head A select a member node C as new cluster head. Node C satisfy that the energy of node C is higher than the energy threshold Th_c and node C is the last node to communicated with cluster head A. After that, cluster head A inform all members change the cluster head.

In the above process, the value of T_{Max} depends on the total number of nodes in the network and the transmission delay between adjacent nodes T_{td}, it can be described as: $T_{Max} > NT_{td}$. To ensure that the node can hear at least one beacon frame during the listening period, the following relationships should be met: $T_{Min} > T_{beacon}$, the waiting time meets the relationship $T_w \propto T_{beacon}$. The value of cluster capacity M is related to the density of nodes in the cluster. According to the conclusion of [10], when the cluster capacity M satisfies:

$$M = \sqrt[4]{\frac{3\pi N^2 \varepsilon_{fs}}{2\varepsilon_{amp} L^2}} \qquad (6)$$

the network has the least communications, the total energy consumption of the network is minimum, where L is the length of the area, $\varepsilon_{fs} = 10\,\mathrm{pJ/bit/m^2}$, $\varepsilon_{amp} = 0.0013\,\mathrm{pJ/bit/m^4}$ [11].

3.2 Route Establishment

Since the clustering process proposed in this paper may cause too long communication distance between sensor nodes, which make the direct communications be hard. In order to ensure the communication link work normally, it is necessary to introduce some new routing nodes from the cluster head to sink nodes. The selection of the routing nodes refers to the selection of the cluster head by the LEACH protocol. First, we set a threshold Th_r, the node with routing function generates a random number r after power on, if $r < Th_r$, the node becomes a routing node. The process of establishing route is shown in Algorithm 2. The specific steps are as follows:

Step 1: The sink node A periodically broadcasts routing information to perform routing maintenance.

Step 2: The routing node B which receives the routing broadcast records the address as the parent node. Node B continues to forward the routing broadcast. The routing node C that receives the broadcast and does not have the parent node records the node B as the parent node. This step is repeated until all of the routing nodes in the network have the records of its parent node.

Step 3: The cluster head periodically sends the interest message in the cluster to the parent node according to the application requirements.

The advantage of the route establishment process in EL-CRP is that each routing node only needs to save its own address of parent node, which saves memory overhead. By means of broadcasting, the establishment of a communication link can be realized rapidly in a wide range.

Depending on the application requirements, we design two different modes for this protocol: active mode (EL-CRP/Active) and passive mode (EL-CRP/Passive). In EL-CRP/Active, when there is a message to be sent in the routing node and the parent node is lost, the routing node actively sends a route broadcast within one hop range, and the other routing node that receives the broadcast sends an ACK frame to establish a connection with the routing node. This mode is suitable for scenarios where there is information that needs to be sent urgently. In EL-CRP/Passive, the routing node without parent node does not actively send routing broadcasts, which is suitable for scenarios that do not contain emergency messages.

Algorithm 2. Route Establishment Process.

Require: Th_r
Ensure: $ParentID$
 1: $Node_i$ = Sink Node
 2: **label:** $Node_i$ send routing broadcast
 3: **for** j Within the communication range of $Node_i$ **do**
 4:     **if** $ParentID_j$ == Null **then**
 5:         $ParentID_j$ = i
 6:         i=j
 7:         goto **label**
 8:     **end if**
 9: **end for**

---

4   Simulations and Hardware Tests

Simulations. In order to evaluate the performance of the protocol, we design a simulate platform based on C++. Considering the requirements of the application scenarios, We built a hardware system based on *TI*'s *cc2530* chip [12] for actual testing, for the reason that the performance indicators of the sensor in the simulations refer to the *cc2530* chip. The simulation setting are shown in Table 1.

Table 1. Simulation parameter setting

Parameter	Value
Scene size	$40\,m \times 40\,m$
Number of nodes	1000–10000
Transmission rate	250 kbps
Packet size	1024 bit
Cluster capacity	10–200
Beacon cycle	10 s
Business cycle	10 s
Total simulation time	360 s
Receive power consumption	$24\,mA \times 3.6\,V \times 4\,ms$
Transmit power consumption	$29\,mA \times 3.6\,V \times 4\,ms$
Monitor power consumption	$0.2\,mA \times 3.6\,V \times t$
Sleep power consumption	$0.1\,mA \times 3.6\,V \times t$

We first test the effect of cluster capacity on energy and delivery rate through simulations, as shown in Fig. 1. The x-axis represents the maximum number of each cluster in the network model, and the y-axis represents the average power P_a of each node in the network, the value of P_a is

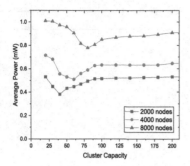

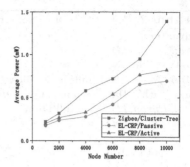

Fig. 1. Relationship between node average power and cluster capacity.

Fig. 2. Relationship between node average power and number of nodes under different protocols.

$$p_a = \frac{E_N}{N \cdot t} \qquad (7)$$

E_N is the sum of energy consumption of all nodes in the network during simulations, N is the total number of nodes in the network, and t is the simulation time. It is obvious in Fig. 1 that there is an optimal value for the cluster capacity in the network, and the optimal value is approximately equal to the result calculated by Eq. 6.

The existing communication technologies widely used in WSNs, mainly include Narrow Band Internet of Things (NB-IoT) [13], LoRaWAN [14] and Zigbee [15]. Since the network construction of NB-IoT or LoRaWAN relies on the establishment of cellular base station or LoRa gateway, the conditions of deployment are demanding. Therefore, NB-IoT and LoRaWAN are not suitable for the application scenario of this paper. We choose Zigbee technology for comparison and testing. Since there is no communication requirement between the terminal nodes in the network model proposed in this paper, the tree topology from the sink node to the terminal node is the most efficient. The Zigbee protocol usually uses the Cluster-Tree routing algorithm [16] to establish a communication link in tree topology. The basic idea of the algorithm is: (1) After receiving the data, the routing node first determines whether the destination address is a child of itself. (2) If the destination node is a child node of the current node, the routing node forwards the data directly to the target node; If the destination node is not a child node of the current node, the data will be send to its parent node for processing. We evaluate the delivery rate and power consumption of EL-CRP/Active, EL-CRP/Passive and Zigbee/Cluster-tree through simulations. The comparison results are shown in Figs. 2 and 3. Obviously, with the increase in the number of nodes in the network, EL-CRP has obvious advantages in energy consumption and delivery rate.

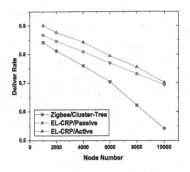

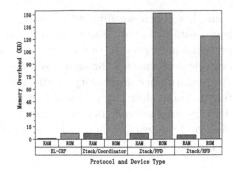

Fig. 3. Relationship between delivery rate and number of nodes under different routing protocols.

Fig. 4. The RAM and ROM overhead of the EL-CRP and Z-stack running on *cc2530* chip.

Hardware Tests. We choose *TI*'s product *cc2530* chip for testing, because the product has the advantages of low power consumption, low cost and supports software programming. *cc2530* chip integrates *TI*'s Z-stack protocol stack to perform basic Zigbee networking and communication. There are three types of devices in the Zigbee protocol, including the coordinator that acts as a sink node, the Full-Function Device (FFD) with routing capabilities, and the Reduce-Fuction Device (RFD) that does not have routing capabilities. We test the memory overhead of running the above three types of nodes in a Zigbee network. At the same time, we replace the original routing protocol in *cc2530* chip with EL-CRP and test the memory overhead under the same conditions. We evaluate the performance of the protocol in memory overhead by the random access memory (RAM) and read only memory (ROM) overhead of the device. By comparing the memory overhead occupied by the z-stack protocol stack and the EL-CRP in actual scenario tests, as shown in Fig. 4. It is obvious that the memory overhead of EL-CRP has significant advantages compared with the Zigbee route protocol, which means that in the same application scenario, devices using the EL-CRP can reduce the size, weight and cost. This result verifies the contribution of EL-CRP on memory overhead.

5   Conclusion

At present, researches on large-scale WSNs mainly focus on reducing energy consumption and extending the lifetime of the network. There is a lack of adequate consideration about how to reduce the memory overhead of sensors in WSNs. This paper designs a energy-efficient WSN routing protocol EL-CRP to meet the requirements of low-energy consumption of nodes and low memory overhead of sensors in large-scale WSN networks. Different from existing routing protocols, our routing protocol is based on a novel clustering scheme, in which clusters are formed by considering both the location and energy of sensor nodes. We first build a network model and an energy model for the application scenarios. Then we divide the routing protocol into cluster establishment and route establishment. Each process is described in detail. Finally, We evaluate protocol performance of EL-CRP on energy consumption and delivery rate in large-scale scenarios through a self-designed software simulation platform, and the performance in memory overhead is achieved through hardware testing. The results show that our protocol has good performance on energy consumption, delivery rate and memory overhead in the scenarios of large number of nodes and high node density, which provides a reference for large-scale WSN application scenarios.

References

1. M Intelligence: Global infrared sensor market-growth, trend, and forecast (2019–2024). Global Information Inc, Technical report (2019)
2. Liu, Y., Mao, X., He, Y., Liu, K., Gong, W., Wang, J.: CitySee: not only a wireless sensor network. IEEE Network **27**(5), 42–47 (2013)
3. Wang, Q., Hempstead, M., Yang, W.: A realistic power consumption model for wireless sensor network devices. In: 3rd Annual IEEE Communications Society on Sensor and Ad Hoc Communications and Networks, vol. 1, pp. 286–295. IEEE (2006)
4. Xu, Z., Chen, L., Chen, C., Guan, X.: Joint clustering and routing design for reliable and efficient data collection in large-scale wireless sensor networks. IEEE Internet Things J. **3**(4), 520–532 (2015)
5. Kulik, J., Heinzelman, W., Balakrishnan, H.: Negotiation-based protocols for disseminating information in wireless sensor networks. Wirel. Netw. **8**(2/3), 169–185 (2002)
6. Zhao, F., Xu, Y., Li, R.: Improved LEACH routing communication protocol for a wireless sensor network. Int. J. Distrib. Sens. Netw. **8**(12), 609–649 (2012)
7. Aliouat, Z., Aliouat, M.: Efficient management of energy budget for pegasis routing protocol. In: 6th International Conference on Sciences of Electronics, Technologies of Information and Telecommunications (SETIT), pp. 516–521. IEEE (2012)
8. Javaid, N., Mohammad, S.N., Latif, K., Qasim, U., Khan, Z.A., Khan, M.A.: HEER: hybrid energy efficient reactive protocol for wireless sensor networks. In: Saudi International Electronics, Communications and Photonics Conference, p. 14. IEEE (2013)
9. Samant, T., Mukherjee, P., Mukherjee, A., Swain, T., Datta, A.: LEACH-V: a solution for intra-cluster cooperative communication in wireless sensor network. Indian J. Sci. Technol. **9**, 48 (2016)
10. Xie, R., Jia, X.: Transmission-efficient clustering method for wireless sensor networks using compressive sensing. IEEE Trans. Parallel Distrib. Syst. **25**(3), 806–815 (2013)
11. Balakrishnan, H., Chandrakasan, A.P., Heinzelman, W.B.: Method for low-energy adaptive clustering hierarchy. US Patent 7,035,240, 25 Apr 2006
12. Li, J.B., Hu, Y.Z.: Design of ZigBee network based on CC2530. Electron. Des. Eng. **16** (2011)
13. Wang, Y.P.E., et al.: A primer on 3GPP narrowband Internet of Things (NBIoT). arXiv preprint arXiv:1606.04171 (2016)
14. Augustin, A., Yi, J., Clausen, T., Townsley, W.: A study of LoRa: long range & low power networks for the Internet of Things. Sensors **16**(9), 1466 (2016)

15. Di Francesco, M., Anastasi, G., Conti, M., Das, S.K., Neri, V.: Reliability and energy-efficiency in IEEE 802.15.4/ZigBee sensor networks: an adaptive and cross-layer approach. IEEE J. Sel. Areas Commun. **29**(8), 1508–1524 (2011)
16. Koubaa, A., Cunha, A., Alves, M.: A time division beacon scheduling mechanism for IEEE 802.15.4/ZigBee cluster-tree wireless sensor networks. In: 19th Euromicro Conference on Real-Time Systems, ECRTS 2007, pp. 125–135. IEEE (2007)

LEER: Layer-Based and Energy-Efficient Routing Protocol for Underwater Sensor Networks

Jianlian Zhu[1,2], Xiujuan Du[1,2(✉)], Duoliang Han[1,2], Lijuan Wang[1,2], and Meiju Li[1,2]

[1] School of Computer Science, Qinghai Normal University, Xining 810008, China
2895025976@qq.com, dxj@qhnu.edu.cn
[2] Key Laboratory of Internet of Things of Qinghai Province, Qinghai Normal University, Xining 810008, China

Abstract. Radio signals attenuate largely when propagating in water, while optical signals have large scattering in water. Therefore, acoustic signals are used for communication in underwater sensor networks (UWSNs). Data transmission in underwater sensor networks is facing challenges due to the characteristics of underwater acoustic channels. In addition, high energy consumption and long latency bring about increased challenges for the design of routing protocols in UWSNs. In this paper, we propose a routing protocol called Layer-based and Energy-efficient Routing (LEER) Protocol to solve the void area routing problem as well as the long end-to-end delay and high energy consumption problems in UWSNs. In LEER, each node extracts the layer field information from Hello messages received and updates its own layer to avoid the void area problem, and all nodes forward packets to the sink node without the need for full-dimensional location information. Simulation results show that the LEER protocol outperforms the depth-based routing (DBR) protocol in terms of delivery rate and end-to-end delay.

Keywords: Underwater sensor networks · LEER · Layer-based routing · Void area

1 Introduction

Underwater Sensor Networks (UWSNs) are usually deployed in an underwater environment such as the ocean, and promise a broad range of applications such as underwater rescuing, offshore mining, offshore exploration, environmental monitoring, and pollutant content detection [1–3]. In UWSNs, radio and optical signals are not suitable for communication as underwater media. Radio signals attenuate greatly when propagating in water, and thus can only propagate over long distances at ultra-low frequencies (30–300 Hz), which requires large wires and high transmission power. Optical signals have a large scattering in water. Therefore, acoustic signals are used for communication in UWSNs. However, UWSNs using acoustic channels have the characteristics of the high latency, high bit error rate (10^{-3}–10^{-7}), low bandwidth,

© ICST Institute for Computer Sciences, Social Informatics and Telecommunications Engineering 2019
Published by Springer Nature Switzerland AG 2019. All Rights Reserved
J. Zheng et al. (Eds.): ADHOCNETS 2019, LNICST 306, pp. 26–39, 2019.
https://doi.org/10.1007/978-3-030-37262-0_3

multi-path effect, and highly dynamic network topology compared with a terrestrial sensor network using radio signals. In addition, underwater nodes move with water current or other underwater activity, and it is difficult to recharge or replace the batteries in the nodes. Due to these characteristics, existing routing protocols for terrestrial sensor networks cannot be directly applied to UWSNs.

This paper proposes a Layer-based and Energy-Efficient Routing (LEER) Protocol for UWSNs, which is independent of the location information on sensor nodes. LEER is a routing protocol based on the layer, the one-hop delay and the residual energy of the node. A sender node does not need to acquire its location prior to sending data packets. In order to balance the energy-consumption of the sensor nodes and maximize the lifetime of the whole network, a receiving node calculates the waiting time for the forwarding timer expires according to its residual energy and one-hop delay. Moreover, LEER can improve the performance in terms the data delivery rate and end-to-end delay, and can effectively solve the void area routing problem.

The rest of the paper is organized as follows. In Sect. 2, we review related work. In Sect. 3, we present the proposed LEER protocol. In Sect. 4, we evaluate the performance of the LEER protocol through simulation experiments. In Sect. 5, we conclude the paper.

2 Related Work

The uniqueness of the underwater acoustic channel brings about some challenges to the design of a routing protocol for UWSNs. To address the characteristics of UWSNs, a variety of routing protocols have been proposed for underwater communication in the literature [3–7].

In [8], Yan et al. proposed a depth-based routing (DBR) protocol. In DBR, a node needs to know the depth information on its own rather than the full-dimensional position information. Data packets are forwarded from the bottom to the water surface, and only the depth is used as the routing metric. The delivery rate with DBR is relatively high in a dense network than in a sparse network, but excessive redundant forwarding would cause additional energy consumption and packet collision. Moreover, the DBR protocol is likely to route a packet to a void area in a sparse network. In [9], Wahid et al. improved DBR and proposed an Energy-Efficient Depth-Based Routing (EEDBR) Protocol. In EEDBR, the selection of forwarding nodes is based on residual energy and depth of the node, which can balance the energy consumption among sensor nodes. In [10], Wahid et al. proposed a multi-layered routing protocol (MRP). In MRP, super nodes are introduced to enhance the battery life of ordinary sensor nodes and increase the delivery rate for data packets. However, MRP is proposed for a network scenario where sensor nodes are deployed in a two-dimensional space, while in the underwater environment sensor nodes are deployed in a three-dimensional space. In addition, the holding time used in the protocol is not correctly defined.

Du et al. proposed a layer-based adaptive geo-routing (LB-AGR) protocol in [11]. LB-AGR introduces layer-based adaptive geo-routing, downstream directed flooding, and downstream routing, needs the full-dimensional location information on each sensor node.

3   LEER Protocol

In this section, we describe the network model and energy consumption model used in this work, and present the proposed LEER protocol.

3.1   Network Model

We consider a three-dimensional UWSN as shown in Fig. 1. The network consists of a sink node located on the water surface and a number of ordinary sensor nodes distributed in an underwater area. In the network, all sensor nodes are divided into several layers based on the hop-count to the sink. Underwater data transmission is directional from bottom to top, i.e., information such as environmental parameters perceived by underwater sensor nodes is subject to be forwarded to the sink node on the surface. The function of the sink is to receive data from underwater nodes and send the received data to the base station on shore. The function of an underwater sensor node is to collect environmental data in water and forward the collected data to the sink node on the water surface in a multi-hop manner. Moreover, we make the following three assumptions:

(1)   Once the sink node is deployed, it's location is fixed;
(2)   All sensor nodes have the same functions and parameters (e.g., initial energy, fixed transmission power, transmission radius) except the sink node;
(3)   All sensor nodes are randomly and evenly deployed in a three-dimensional underwater area in a layered manner.

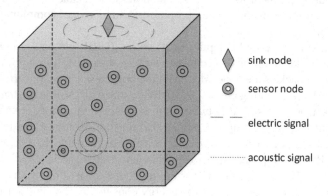

Fig. 1. Three-dimensional UWSNs model

3.2   Energy Consumption Model

In UWSNs, the energy consumption for transmitting data is much larger than that for receiving data. Compared with the energy consumption for transmitting data, the energy consumption for receiving data can be neglected. Thus, in this paper, we define the energy consumption of the whole network as the total energy consumed by all nodes to transmit data. Meanwhile, the energy consumption model proposed in [12] is used as the model. In UWSNs, if the minimum receiving intensity of a signal is P_0 and the signal loss attenuation is $A(x)$, the minimum transmission power P is supposed to be equal to $P_0A(x)$, i.e., $P = P_0A(x)$. According the energy consumption model [12], the attenuation function $A(x)$ is given by

$$A(x) = x^k \partial^x \tag{1}$$

The energy E_l consumed by a sending node to send a data packet of length l to a receiving node is given by

$$E_l = T_{delay}P_0A(x) = T_{delay}P_0x^k\partial^x \tag{2}$$

where x is the transmission distance between the transmitting node and the receiving node, T_{delay} is the data transmission delay for a node to transmit l bits, k is a coefficient related to the underwater acoustic model, and ∂ is a frequency dependent term. For the coefficient k, when the transmitting area is cylindrical, $k = 1$, when it is sphere, $k = 2$. In general, $k = 1.5$. For the frequency dependent term ∂, it is given by $\alpha(f)$

$$\partial = 10^{\alpha(f)/10} \tag{3}$$

where $\alpha(f)$ is the energy absorption coefficient, whose value can be determined using the expression of Throp, i.e.,

$$\alpha(f) = 0.11\frac{f^2}{1+f^2} + 44\frac{f^2}{4100+f^2} + 2.75 \times 10^{-4}f^2 + 0.003 \tag{4}$$

where, the unit of the absorption coefficient $\alpha(f)$ is dB/km, and the unit of the frequency f is KHz.

According to Eqs. (1)–(4), the transmission distance x is exponentially related to the attenuation factor $A(x)$, and the energy consumption E_l is proportional to the attenuation factor $A(x)$. Therefore, when the frequency is constant, the farther the transmission distance is, the more severe the signal attenuation is, and the more energy a node consumes to send data packets.

3.3 LEER Protocol

The LEER protocol is a routing protocol based on a layering strategy. It introduces a layering algorithm to configure all sensor nodes into several layers, and takes into account the residual energy of a node and one-hop delay in packet forwarding. Moreover, it does not need any location information on each sensor node in the network.

The LEER protocol is divided into two phases. In the first phase, the sink node broadcasts a Hello message to the network. The Hello message contains fields of packet type, source node ID, source node layer and other information. After receiving the Hello message, each underwater sensor node extracts the layer field information contained in the Hello message, updates its own layer and the Hello message, and then continues to broadcast the updated Hello message. In the second phase, each underwater sensor node forwards its perceived data to its upper-layer node until the data is transmitted to the sink node on the water surface. In layering based routing, a packet is not forwarded by the nodes at the same layer of the sender, which reduces much redundancy and energy consumption. At the same time, it effectively solves the void area routing problem because after the network initialization phase, each sensor node will have a upper-layer neighbor node. Thus, the next hop node will always be found for forwarding.

3.3.1   Layering Algorithm

The layering algorithm is used by an underwater sensor node to configure their own layers in the network initialization phase. First, the sink node broadcasts a Hello message to the network, and the sink node sets its own layer to layer 0. When a receiving node receives the Hello message for the first time, it will check the value L_Snd of the layer field in the received Hello message, set its own layer to $L\_Rec = L\_Snd + 1$, and start the layer aging timer. Then, the receiving node will update the layer field information of the Hello message with its own layer L_Rec, and continue to broadcast the updated Hello message. After the initialization process is completed, the layer of each sensor node will be fixed until the sink node broadcasts another Hello message.

After a sensor node receives a new Hello message. It has to determine whether it needs to update its own layer. When a sensor node which has acquired its layer and its aging timer is not expired receives a Hello message, it compares the value of its own layer L_Rec with that of the layer L_Snd in the packet. If $L\_Rec > L\_Snd + 1$, the node updates its own layer to $L\_Rec = L\_Snd + 1$, replaces the layer field and the source node ID in the Hello message with its own layer information and the node ID, then broadcasts the updated Hello message. If the aging timer is expired, the receiving node updates its own layer to $L\_Rec = L\_Snd + 1$, and then updates and broadcasts the Hello message. The pseudo code of the layering algorithm is given in Fig. 2.

```
//After receiving a Hello packet
L_self=255;   //Initialization layer of sensor node is 255
L_sink=0; //The layer of the sink node is a fixed value: 0
IF(PacketType= ="Hello Packet")
 IF(L_self= =255)
  L_self=L_snd +1;  //The new node will update the layer.
 Else
  IF(L_self<=L__snd+1)
   Discard  data packet //Nodes have updated their own layer.
  Else
   L_self=L_snd +1;
   Continue to broadcast Hello packet
  End IF
 End IF
End IF
Exit
```

Fig. 2. The pseudo code of the layering algorithm

Figure 3 illustrates a layering example. In this example, the sink node on the water surface first broadcasts a Hello message to the network. After receiving the Hello message, each receiving node (i.e., *N1*, *N2*, *N3*, or *N4*) extracts the value of the layer field in the received Hello message, which is *L_Snd = 0*, the layer of the sender. Then, each receiving node obtains its own layer value, i.e., *L_Rec = 1*, and updates the layer field of the Hello message with "1", and the source node ID with its ID (i.e., *N1*, *N2*, *N3*, or *N4*), and broadcasts the updated Hello message. After a node (i.e., *N5*, *N6*, *N7*, or *N8*) receives the Hello message from an upper-layer node (i.e., *N1*, *N2*, *N3*, or *N4*), it extracts the value "1" of the layer field in the received Hello message, and then obtains its own layer value "2". Next, the node updates the layer field of the Hello message with "2" and the source node ID field with its own ID (i.e., *N5*, *N6*, *N7*, or *N8*), and then continues to broadcast the updated Hello message.

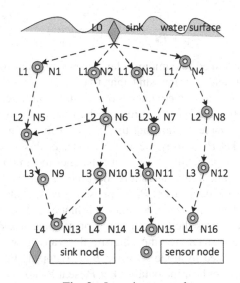

Fig. 3. Layering example

3.3.2 Routing Protocol

In the routing protocol, a receiving node determines whether it is supposed to participate in forwarding a data packet by calculating the forwarding probability. The forwarding probability depends on the one-hop delay and the residual energy of the node. In order to forward the data packet to the sink node along a low-delay path, one-hop delay is considered in calculating the forwarding probability. A waiting time is introduced based on the forwarding probability before the data packet is forwarded. Thus the probability that node k forwards a data packet is given by

$$P_k = \alpha(1 - \frac{Del(k)}{Del_{\max}}) + \beta(\frac{E(k)}{E_{ini}}) \tag{5}$$

where, α and β are weight coefficients that meet $\alpha + \beta=1$, $Del(k)$ is a one-hop delay from a transmitting node to the receiving node k, Del_{max} is a predefined maximum one-hop delay, $E(k)$ is the current residual energy of the receiving node k, and E_{ini} is the initial energy of the node. The weighting coefficients α and β can balance the effect of the minimum delay path and that of the high residual energy. According Eq. (5), the forwarding probability is proportional the residual energy of the node, and inversely proportional to one-hop delay. The more residual energy the receiving node has, the smaller the one-hop delay, and the higher the forwarding probability of the receiving node.

Each receiving node starts a timer after receiving a data packet. The timeout value set by the timer is based on the forwarding probability. The higher the forwarding probability, the earlier the node timer expires. The timeout value T_{out} of the receiving node k timer is defined as

$$T_{out} = \sqrt{\frac{1}{P_k}} \times Del_{max} + Rand() \tag{6}$$

where Del_{max} is the predefined maximum delay in one hop, and $Rand()$ is a random time interval between 0 and 1. Supposing that two nodes have the same remaining energy and one hop delay, their timers may expire at different time, and the two nodes will randomly forward the data packet to reduce the redundant packets.

Figure 4 gives an example to illustrate the role of a timer. In this example, node A receives the data packet P_1 sent by the source node. In this case, node A first calculates its own forwarding probability, and then calculates the timeout value of its timer based on its forwarding probability and starts the timer. After the timer expires, node A immediately forwards the data packet P_1. Meanwhile, node B also receives the same data packet P_1 sent by the source node. Similarly, it first calculates its own forwarding probability, and then calculates the timeout value of its timer based on the calculated forwarding probability and starts the timer. During the waiting period, if node B hears the data packet P_1 forwarded by node A, node B will stop its timer and discard the packet P_1. If node B does not hear the data packet P_1 sent by node A during the waiting period, which implies that node B is not within the transmission range of node A. In this case, node B will also forward the data packet P_1 when its own timer expires. Since the proposed protocol is based on flooding, it belongs to multi-path routing rather than single-path routing. Therefore, each node will forward a data packet immediately when its timer expires. It is equivalent to the case where multiple receivers quasi-simultaneously forward the same data packet.

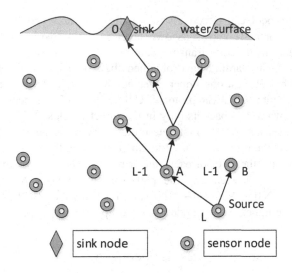

Fig. 4. Example of the role of a timer

3.4   Void Area Routing Problem

In DBR and other greedy routing protocols for UWSNs, a void area is unavoidable when data packets are forwarded in a sparse network. Taking Fig. 5 as an example. After node *N8* receives a data packet, there is no node closer to the sink node to forward the packet upward. In this case, the upper area above node *N8* is called a void area.

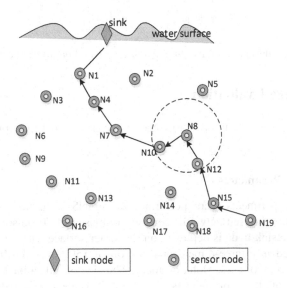

Fig. 5. Void area routing example

The LEER protocol can effectively solve the void area problem. In the LEER protocol, each sensor node knows its own layer in the network initialization phase. When underwater sensor nodes transmit data packets to the sink node, those nodes participating in data forwarding have obtained their own layers. In another word, a forwarding node has at least one upper-layer neighbor node. In this case, there is no void area problem with the LEER protocol. Unlike the DBR protocol, which allows a sensor node to forward data packets only in the direction close to the sink, the LEER protocol allows a sensor node to first determine whether the layer meets the requirements, and then sets the timeout value of its timer based on the forwarding probability.

Figure 6 illustrates the layer of each sensor node in the network after the network initialization phase. It is seen that the path for source node *N19* to the sink is N19→N15→N12→N10→N7→N4→N1→sink. By using the LEER protocol, the void area problem in the upper area of node N8 is completely avoided.

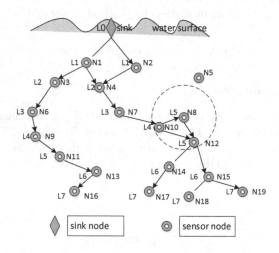

Fig. 6. Illustration of avoiding a void area based on layered routing

4   Performance Evaluation

In this section, we evaluate the performance of the proposed LEER protocol through simulation results.

4.1   Simulation Parameters

The simulation experiments were performed using NS-3. In the experiments, we consider a multi-hop layered network scenario composed of 70 sensor nodes and one sink node. A static sink node is deployed on the water surface. Other sensor nodes are randomly deployed in a three-dimensional region of 1500 m × 1500 m × 2500 m. The MAC layer protocol uses Aloha protocol. The size of a data packet is 134 bytes. The initial energy of all sensor nodes is set to 1000 J. The energy consumed by a node when sending, receiving, and idle is 0.1 J/packet, 0.05 J/packet, and 0.001 J/packet, respectively. The network is divided into three layers, which means that a data source node has at most three hops to the sink node. The simulation parameters are given in Table 1.

Table 1. Simulation parameters

Simulation parameter	Value
Three-dimensional area	1500 m × 1500 m × 2500 m
Number of nodes	21~71
Communication radius R	1000 m
Initial energy	1000 J
Packet size	134 Bytes
Packet frequency	15 S/packet
Topology	Random uniform deployment

4.2   Simulation Results

In the performance evaluation, we use packet delivery rate, end-to-end delay, and energy consumption as the performance metrics. The packet delivery rate (PDR) is defined as the ratio of the total number of packets received by the sink node P_{sucess} to the total number of packets sent by the source node P_{send}, i.e., $PDR = P_{sucess}/P_{send}$. The end-to-end delay is defined as the time taken to deliver a data packet from a source node to the sink node. Energy consumption is defined as the total energy consumed by all nodes during the simulation time.

In Eq. (5), α and β are weight coefficients, where $\alpha + \beta=1$. Table 2 gives the average packet delivery rate for each group of the 21 nodes. When the weight coefficients α and β are different, the average end-to-end delay and energy consumption in the network also have some effects, as shown in Figs. 7 and 8.

Table 2. Effect of different α on PDR

α	β	PDR
0.1	0.9	70.67%
0.2	0.8	72%
0.3	0.7	76.43%
0.4	0.6	78%
0.5	0.5	79.33%
0.6	0.4	78.67%
0.7	0.3	73.33%
0.8	0.2	73.33%
0.9	0.1	76%

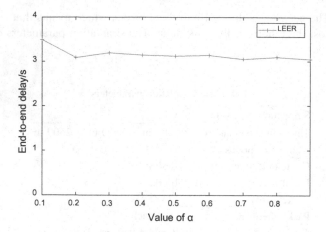

Fig. 7. Effect of different α on end-to-end delay

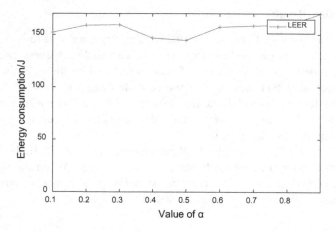

Fig. 8. Effect of different α on energy consumption

In Table 2, it is seen that the highest PDR is generated when the weight coefficient combination is α = *0.5* and β = 0.5. Figure 7 shows the effect of different α on the average end-to-end delay. Figure 8 shows the effect of different α on the total energy consumption in the network. It is observed that the average end-to-end delay decreases with the increase of α.

Figure 9 shows the packet delivery rates with of the LEER routing protocol and the DBR routing protocol, respectively, when the number of nodes are 21, 31, 41, 51, and 71. It is seen that as the number of nodes increases, the packet delivery rate increases. This is because as the number of nodes increases, the number of candidate forwarding nodes for the next hop increases, which increases the data forwarding success rate. As a result, the packet delivery rate from the source node to the sink node increases. On the other hand, the packet delivery rate with the DBR routing protocol decreases from

70.53% to 43.53% with the number of nodes decreasing from around 71 to 21. This is due to the greedy mode of DBR. When the number of nodes is small, the DBR routing protocol sends data packets to the sink node closer to the water surface in a greedy manner. In this case, the nodes at a deeper layer cannot participate in the forwarding of the data packets, which are more likely to be routed to a void area. As a result, it would results in a low packet delivery rate. In contrast, the packet delivery rate with the LEER routing protocol does not change much as the number of nodes decreases, ranging from 79.33% to 82.33%. This is because the LEER routing protocol is based on a layering strategy, which can avoid the void area problem and achieves a relatively stable packet delivery rate. In addition, it is seen that the packet delivery rate of the LEER routing protocol is better than that of the DBR routing protocol.

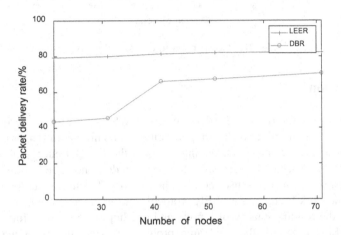

Fig. 9. Comparison in the packet delivery rate

Figure 10 shows the end-to-end delay with the LEER routing protocol and the DBR routing protocol, respectively, when the number of nodes is 21, 31, 41, 51, and 71. It is seen that as the number of nodes increases, the average end-to-end delay with the LEER protocol decreases gradually. This is because with the increase of the number of nodes, the density of nodes in the simulation scenario will increase accordingly. In this case, the number of candidate forwarding nodes will increase, the distance between nodes will decrease, and thus the end-to-end delay will decrease as well. On the other hand, it is seen that the average end-to-end delay with the LEER routing protocol is smaller than that with the DBR routing protocol.

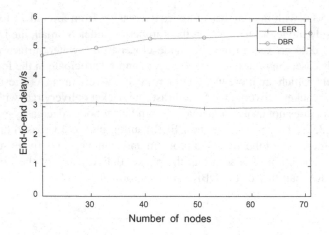

Fig. 10. Comparison in end-to-end delay

5   Conclusion

In the paper, we proposed a LEER protocol for a UWSN based on a layering strategy. The LEER protocol introduces a layering algorithm to configure all sensor nodes in the network into several layers, and takes into account the residual energy of a node and one-hop delay in packet forwarding. Moreover, it does not need full-dimensional location information on each sensor node in the network. To ensure energy balance and prolong the network lifetime, the LEER protocol sets the timer of a sensor node taking into account the residual energy of a node and one-hop delay in data forwarding. By using the LEER protocol, the void area problem can be effectively avoided. The simulation results show that the proposed LEER routing protocol outperforms the DBR routing protocol in terms of the packet delivery rate and average end-to-end delay.

Acknowledgments. This work is supported by the National Natural Science Foundation of China (under grant no.: 61962052), the IoT Innovation Team Foundation of Qinghai Office of Science and Technology, the Key Lab of IoT of Qinghai, Hebei IoT Monitoring Center (under grant no.: 3142016020); and the Key Projects of Hebei Province (under grant no.: 19270318D).

References

1. Javaid, N., Shakeel, U., Ahmad, A., Alrajeh, N., Khan, Z.A., Guizani, N.: DRADS: depth and reliability aware delay sensitive cooperative routing for underwater wireless sensor networks. Wirel. Netw. **25**(2), 777–789 (2019)
2. Ali, T., Jung, L.T., Faye, I.: End-to-end delay and energy efficient routing protocol for underwater wireless sensor networks. Wirel. Pers. Commun. **79**(1), 339–361 (2014)
3. Darehshoorzadeh, A., Boukerche, A.: Underwater sensor networks: a new challenge for opportunistic routing protocols. IEEE Commun. Mag. **53**(11), 98–107 (2015)
4. Ahmed, M., Salleh, M., Channa, M.I.: Routing protocols for underwater wireless sensor networks based on data forwarding: a review. Telecommun. Syst. **65**(1), 139–153 (2017)

5. Zhang, J.N., Du, X.J., Li, M.J., Wang, L.J.: Routing protocol of underwater wireless sensor network based on vector and energy. Comput. Eng. **44**(9), 113–117 (2018)

6. Guan, Q.S., Ji, F., Liu, Y., Yu, H., Chen, W.Q.: Distance-vector based opportunistic routing for underwater acoustic sensor networks. IEEE Internet Things J. **6**(2), 3831–3839 (2019)

7. Shetty, S., Pai, R.M., Pai, M.M.M.: Energy efficient message priority based routing protocol for aquaculture applications using underwater sensor network. Wirel. Pers. Commun. **103**(2), 1871–1894 (2018)

8. Yan, H., Shi, Z.J., Cui, J.-H.: DBR: depth-based routing for underwater sensor networks. In: Das, A., Pung, H.K., Lee, F.B.S., Wong, L.W.C. (eds.) NETWORKING 2008. LNCS, vol. 4982, pp. 72–86. Springer, Heidelberg (2008). https://doi.org/10.1007/978-3-540-79549-0_7

9. Wahid, A., Lee, S., Jeong, H.-J., Kim, D.: EEDBR: energy-efficient depth-based routing protocol for underwater wireless sensor networks. In: Kim, T.-H., Adeli, H., Robles, R.J., Balitanas, M. (eds.) AST 2011. CCIS, vol. 195, pp. 223–234. Springer, Heidelberg (2011). https://doi.org/10.1007/978-3-642-24267-0_27

10. Wahid, A., Lee, S., Kim, D., Lim, K.S.: MRP: a localization-free multi-layered routing protocol for underwater wireless sensor networks. Wirel. Pers. Commun. **77**(4), 2997–3012 (2014)

11. Du, X.J., Huang, K.J., Lan, S.L., Feng, Z.X., Liu, F.: LB-AGR: layer-based adaptive geo-routing for underwater sensor network. J. China Univ. Posts Telecommun. **21**(1), 54–59 (2014)

12. Sozer, E.M., Stojanovic, M., Proakis, J.G.: Underwater acoustic networks. IEEE J. Oceanic Eng. **25**(1), 72–83 (2000)

A Routing Void Handling Protocol Based on Autonomous Underwater Vehicle for Underwater Acoustic Sensor Networks

Yuying Ding[✉], Kun Hao, Cheng Li, Yonglei Liu, Lu Zhao, and Shudong Liu

School of Computer and Information Engineering,
Tianjin Chengjian University, Tianjin 300384, China
1076545117@qq.com, {Kunhao, liushudong}@tcu.edu.cn,
licheng.mum@gmail.com, sanxiong_1@163.com,
zhaolu6892@163.com

Abstract. In underwater acoustic sensor networks (UASNs), efficient packet transmission is essential for monitoring new marine technologies. However, the uneven distribution of nodes and inappropriate selection of forwarding nodes lead to routing voids in adjacent nodes. Aiming at the problem, we propose a routing void handling protocol (RVHP) based on Autonomous Underwater Vehicle (AUV) for UASNs. RVHP effectively detects and avoids void nodes and trap nodes through a void avoidance mechanism, and then uses an AUV-assisted network repair mechanism to timely deal with failure routing in the communication area. AUV adopts a greedily path-finding strategy to visit void nodes, and realizes the void repair of UASNs. Simulation results show that RVHP can effectively improve the packet transmission rate and energy utilization rate.

Keywords: Underwater acoustic sensor network (UASN) · Routing void · Autonomous underwater vehicle (AUV) · Network repair

1 Introduction

With the decrease of land resources, people pay more and more attention to the development of underwater resources [1]. Underwater acoustic sensor network (UASNs) has widely applied in military defense, underwater environment monitoring, disaster prevention and other fields [2–4]. Compared with traditional sensor networks, UASNs communicate through underwater acoustic channels, node deployment is relatively sparse, and battery charging is difficult and expensive [5, 6]. In a harsh underwater environment, UASNs are facing many challenges such as narrow available bandwidth, high deployment cost, and limited energy [7], which lead to large transmission delay, high communication error rate and low network reliability. In addition, the uneven distribution of nodes and improper selection of forwarding nodes, which make it impossible for nodes to find neighbor nodes within the communication range of

J. Zheng et al. (Eds.): ADHOCNETS 2019, LNICST 306, pp. 40–52, 2019.
https://doi.org/10.1007/978-3-030-37262-0_4

nodes, the nodes continue to forward packets, result in routing voids and packet forwarding failures [8]. Therefore, it is very important to find a solution to the routing void problem to improve the communication efficiency of a UASN. The existing routing void processing approaches mainly include decision strategies based on bypassing a void area, power control and mobile assistance [9].

The strategy of bypassing void areas is commonly used in underwater routing void handling protocols. This strategy discovers and maintains another path from an ordinary node to another ordinary nodes, the path can forward packet greedily. However, due to forwarding packets to more nodes, more packet transmission delay is caused. In void-aware pressure routing (VAPR) [10], packets are routed along directional paths to surface sonar buoys. The directional path is determined by a beacon message broadcast by a sonar buoy, which contains a sequence number, a hop number and depth information. When a node receives a beacon message, VAPR updates its forwarding direction based on the depth position of the sender, and detects void nodes through periodic beacons. When routing void occurs in the network, VAPR bypasses the routing void by saving the information of neighbor nodes with a maximum of two hops, and packets are only forwarded up or down according to the directed path, which leads to high network overhead. In vector-based forwarding (VBF) [11], packets are transmitted along virtual "routing pipe". Due to the influence of node density in the pipe, redundant transmission or serious loss of packets is caused. In hop-by-hop vector-based forwarding (HH-VBF) [12], each hop uses different virtual "routing pipes" to transmit packets to sink, which solves the problem of no nodes in a virtual "routing pipe" in a VBF sparse network scenario. Hydraulic pressure based anycast routing (Hydrocast) [13] solves a void by local lower depth recovery. Each local maximum node maintains a recovery routing with a depth lower. When the recovery path is long, the process of finding and maintaining the path makes network expensive.

The void handling protocol based on power control can seek a neighbor node that can continue to forward packets by increasing the communication range of a void node. However, the increase of transmission power leads to the increase of network cost, and the expansion of a void area leads to the conflict of the packet. In adaptive power-controlled routing protocol (APCR) [14], the nodes are deployed in a hierarchical structure, and packets are forwarded to the nearest layer node of the sink until they are transmitted to the sink. The nodes adopt adaptive power control to improve power and ensure network connectivity when the network is sparse. The channel-aware routing protocol proposed in [15] uses power control and link quality in data forwarding, and uses hop information to successfully avoid void areas.

In mobile-based routing protocol for solving the void problem, void nodes are moved to a new location, and the greedy forwarding of nodes is restored, however, the disadvantage is that the energy cost of the mobile void node is high. In the multi-modal communication using the depth adjustment protocol (MMC) [16], according to the size of data transmission, a node decides whether to surface for communication based on network energy consumption and data delay. The depth controlled routing (DCR) [17] utilizes node mobility to reduce the number of void nodes in a UASN by moving nodes. The Geographic and opportunistic routing protocol with the depth adjustment protocol (GEDAR) [18] is based on the topological control of depth adjustment in geographical and opportunistic routing. In GEDAR, a packet is forwarded to the destination node through a greedily opportunity mechanism, and a void node is moved to a new depth position through the depth adjustment of the node so that the node can quickly restore the greedy forwarding.

The above protocols only introduce routing strategies for void nodes, ignoring trap nodes that lead to void nodes in UASNs. A trap node can forward packets to other nodes, but forwarding packets will eventually cause nodes to fall into a void. If trap and void nodes are found before routing and are avoided during packet forwarding, the efficiency of packet transmission can be improved. To this end, we propose a routing void handling protocol (RVHP) based on autonomous underwater vehicle (AUV) for a UASN. RVHP actively detects and effectively avoids void nodes and trap nodes by passive participation. Each ordinary node detects a void node by setting a failure time, and then identifies a trap node by means of controlling packet backward drive so that RVHP finds a void region locally without any increasing overhead. In view of the sudden routing failure of any node within its the communication range, RVHP directly collects data from the failed node by deploying a mobile node AUV. In order to reduce the packet loss, AUV uses a greedy path-finding strategy to access void nodes to adapt the dynamic of the network. Then the AUV sends packets to a sonar buoy through an acoustic channel to repair void in the network. Simulation results show that RVHP not only guarantees an efficient and stable data transmission rate, but also reduces the network energy consumption, and prolongs the network lifecycle.

The remainder of the paper is organized as follows. Section 2 introduces the system model considered in this work. Section 3 describes the design of RVHP. Section 5 evaluates the performance of RVHP. Section 6 concludes the paper.

2 System Model

2.1 Network Model

We consider a UWSN model with different types of network nodes in the network, mainly including ordinary nodes trap nodes, void nodes, AUVs and sonar buoys, as shown in Fig. 1.

In this network model, the ordinary nodes are distributed in the ocean. By sensing and collecting underwater information, each ordinary node sends its monitoring data to the next-hop forwarding node or sonar buoy. The sonar buoys are deployed on the surface as the destinations, which are mainly responsible for underwater and land communication. Data are collected from ordinary nodes through the acoustic link, and the wireless links are used to transmit data to the monitoring center for analysis [19]. An AUV dives into the water by itself, collects sensing data directly from void nodes, and transmits packets to sonar buoys through the acoustic channel, thus minimizing the energy consumption and prolonging the network lifecycle. The main characteristics of these nodes are as follows:

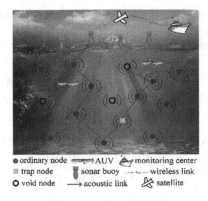

Fig. 1. Network model.

(1) Ordinary nodes are distributed in a discrete, three-dimensional and random manner in the underwater area, and they are responsible for collecting data.

(2) Void nodes are located in a routing void area. The packets lose in this area, ordinary nodes retransmit packets so that the communication efficiency of the acoustic link decreases.

(3) Trap nodes refer to the nodes through which packets can be forwarded to other nodes, but forwarding packets to these nodes will cause these nodes to fall into a void.

(4) AUVs are randomly deployed in underwater areas with unlimited energy [20, 21].

2.2 Underwater Acoustic Channel Model

RVHP adopts the attenuation model of an underwater acoustic signal [22, 23] to estimate the packet transmission rate $p(d, m)$ of transmitted m bits by any pair of nodes with a distance of d. Thus, the attenuation factor without obstacles is

$$A(d,f) = d^k a(f)^d \tag{1}$$

where f is the signal frequency, k is the diffusion factor (cylinder is 1, practical is 1.5, sphere is 2), and k takes 1.5 in the simulation experiment. The absorption coefficient $\alpha(f)$ is

$$\alpha(f) = \frac{0.11f^2}{1+f^2} + \frac{44f^2}{4100+f^2} + 2.75 \times 10^{-4}f^2 + 0.003 \tag{2}$$

The average SNR of distance d is

$$\tau(d) = \frac{E_b/A(d,f)}{N_0} = \frac{E_b}{N_0 d^k \alpha(f)^d} \tag{3}$$

where E_b and N_0 are constants, respectively, representing the average energy consumption per unit bit and noise power density.

We use Rayleigh fading to model small scale fading, where SNR has the following probability distribution:

$$p_d(X) = \int_0^\infty \frac{1}{\tau(d)} e^{-\frac{X}{\tau(d)}} \tag{4}$$

The probability of error can be evaluated as

$$p_e(d) = \int_0^\infty p_e(X) p_d(X) dX \tag{5}$$

This protocol adopts a BPSK modulation mode. The bit error probability of distance d is

$$p_e(d) = \frac{1}{2} \left(1 - \sqrt{\frac{\tau(d)}{1 + \tau(d)}} \right) \tag{6}$$

Therefore, the packet transmission rate $\mathrm{p}(d, m)$ of any pair of nodes with distance d transmitting m bits is

$$\mathrm{p}(d, m) = (1 - p_e(d))^m \tag{7}$$

2.3   Energy Consumption Minimization Model

Since high energy consumption affects the communication performance, RVHP adopts a mathematical model based on linear programming to reduce the energy consumption of each ordinary node [24], i.e.,

$$\mathrm{Min} \sum_{r=1}^{r_{max}} E_{consumption}(r), \forall r \in r_{max} \tag{8}$$

where the constraint condition is

$$E_{trans}, E_{rec} \leq E_{init} \tag{9}$$

$$E_{forw} \leq E_{forw}^{max} \tag{10}$$

$$T_{range} \leq T_{rmax} \tag{11}$$

E_{trans} and E_{rec} are, respectively, the energy consumption when sending and receiving a packet, E_{forw} is the energy consumption of a forwarding node, T_{range} is the communication range of a node.

The total energy consumption of a node during transmission and reception is given by

$$\sum_{r=1}^{r_{max}} E_{consumption}(r) = E_{trans} + E_{rec}, \forall r \in r_{max} \qquad (12)$$

where

$$E_{trans} = P_{trans}\left(\frac{P_{size}}{p(d,m)}\right) \qquad (13)$$

$$E_{rec} = P_{rec}\left(\frac{P_{size}}{p(d,m)}\right) \qquad (14)$$

P_{trans} and P_{rec} are the power consumption when transmitting and receiving a packet, respectively, and P_{size} is the size of a packet.

3 Design of RVHP

3.1 Void Avoidance Mechanism

RVHP actively detects void node and trap node by passive participation, and uses the preventive mechanism to effectively avoid void area, excluding void node and trap node from the candidate set of packets forwarding, which makes RVHP ensure efficient and stable data transmission rate, and reduce network energy consumption.

1. Void Node

RVHP uses a time-based strategy to detect void nodes. Before routing starts, each node sets a void detection timer and waits for a neighboring node with lower depth to transmit a packet. If a node receives the packet within the failure time, the node resets its void detection timer. Otherwise, the node broadcasts a control packet to neighboring nodes, and declares itself as a void node. As shown in Fig. 2, node g and i are void nodes after detection.

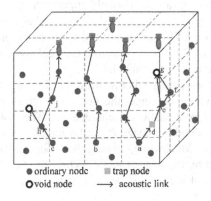

Fig. 2. Schematic diagram of a void avoidance mechanism.

The failure time T_ω^φ of the void detection timer consists of three parts [25]: (1) Packet transmission time $T_h(p)$; (2) The delay difference between the first node and the second node, and the sum $\sum_{k=1}^{\varphi} D(n_k, n_{k+1})/v$ of the delay difference between the $\varphi - 1$ and the φ node; (3) Packet processing time T_{proc}. Thus, the failure time T_ω^φ is given by

$$T_\omega^\varphi = T_h(p) + \sum_{k=1}^{\varphi} \frac{D(n_k, n_{k+1})}{v} + \varphi \cdot T_{proc} \tag{15}$$

The packet transmission time $T_h(p)$ is given by

$$T_h(p) = \frac{R_c - D}{v} \tag{16}$$

where R_c is the communication range, D is the distance between a transmitter and a receiver, and v is the propagation speed of an underwater acoustic signal.

2. Trap Node

After RVHP detects the void nodes in the routing path, it will identify trap nodes using the backward-driven strategy and a control packet. After a node receives the packet, it will update its neighbor table, and check other neighbor nodes whose depth is lower than itself. If the node is a single neighbor in the neighborhood, it is be a trap node.

Similarly, after a node receives a packet from a trap node, the node will first update the state of the trap node in the neighbor table, and confirm own state. If the neighbor does not contain a lower-depth node other than the trap node, that node is also a trap node. This process stops when all trap nodes on the routing path are detected. As shown in Fig. 2, node d is identified as a trap node. Therefore, void nodes and trap nodes at different locations can be detected in the local identification network without any additional overhead.

3.2   Network Repair Mechanism

Due to the water flow, energy consumption of nodes, and high error rate of the propagation channel, a routing failure suddenly appears in the communication range of an ordinary node, resulting in a routing void, which makes a node unable to forward packets to sonar buoys. An AUV can effectively solve the problem. An AUV can dive into the water by itself, directly collect data from the void node, and transmit packets to a sonar buoy through the acoustic channel.

As shown in Fig. 3, during the packet forwarding, if an ordinary node finds itself in a void in a received neighbor message, the node will broadcast a void packet to an AUV through a single hop acoustic communication. The void packet includes the location coordinates L of a node, the size P_{size} of a packet, the attenuation type A, and the degree of emergency T. Meanwhile, all neighbor nodes broadcast the received void packet until it is received by the nearest AUV. When the AUV receives the packet, it will move to the position of the void node, and then transmit the packet directly to a sonar buoy.

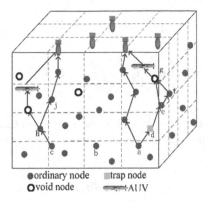

●ordinary node   ▪trap node
○void node   ➞AUV

Fig. 3. Schematic diagram of a network repair mechanism.

In a sparse network, an AUV may receive multiple void packets in a certain period. In order to reduce the packets loss, an AUV uses the greedily pathfinding strategy to access void nodes to adapt to the dynamic of the network. At each decision point, the next void node to be visited by the AUV will be the largest node to transmit packets. If visiting another void node makes an AUV transmit larger packets, the AUV will change its path before reaching the void node.

RVHP decides the routing paths R_{AUV} based on the size P_{size} of packets sent to an AUV by a void node, and the effective transmission time t_{trans} of an AUV is given by

$$R_{AUV} = \frac{P_{size}}{t_{trans}} \tag{17}$$

When an AUV receives a void packet from node i and k, RVHP determines the first void node to visit by comparing the size R_{AUV}. If the value R_{AUV} of void node i is larger, the AUV first visit the void node.

In addition, while an AUV greedily visits the void node with the largest value R_{AUV}, it should also consider the attenuation type A and emergency degree T of packets transmitted by different void nodes. If the exponential attenuation of the packets monitored by node i is smaller, and node k is larger, the two nodes have the same R_{AUV} and T. Then the AUV will first collect the monitoring data of node k, in order to avoid a packet loss, and maximize the transmission of packets to sonar buoys.

4 Complexity Analysis

In terms of complexity, this paper mainly analyzes the computational complexity and communication complexity of RVHP in the routing decision-making process [26].

Assume that l_{ij} represents the link length from node i to node j, and d_{i1} represents the current shortest distance estimation from node i to a given destination node, which is stored in node i. Thus, the routing decision process can be briefly described as follows:

$$d_{i1}^{(0)} = \begin{cases} \infty, & i \neq 1; \\ 0, & i = 1 \end{cases} \tag{18}$$

$$d_{i1}^{(k+1)} = \begin{cases} \min\left[l_{ij} + d_{j1}^{(k)}\right], & j \in N(i), i \neq 1; \\ 0, & i = 1 \end{cases} \tag{19}$$

where $N(i)$ represents the current neighbor set of node i, and k represents the number of iterations. T_1 and T_2 represent the computational complexity and communication complexity, respectively,

$$T_1 = O(\bar{d}\bar{n}_h) \tag{20}$$

$$T_2 = O(\bar{n}_h) \tag{21}$$

where the $\bar{d}$ is the maximum node degree, n is the maximum number of nodes, $\bar{n}_h$ is the biggest hop number, and $1 \leq \bar{n}_h \leq n - 1$. Therefore, the computational and communication time complexity of the RVHP routing decision process should be $O(\bar{d}n)$ and $O(n)$.

5   Performance Analysis

We evaluate the performance of the proposed RVHP using NS-3. For this purpose, we compare RVHP with VAPR and GEDAR in terms of average end-to-end delay, packet transmission rate and average energy consumption. The parameters used in the simulation experimental are given in Table 1.

Table 1. Parameters.

Parameters	Values
Area size of three-dimensional water	1000 m * 1000 m * 1000 m
Number of ordinary nodes	800
Initial energy of a node	100 J
Acoustic signal frequency	25 kHz
Energy consumption of transmitting data	$80*10^{-8}$J/bit
Energy consumption of receiving data	$5*10^{-8}$J/bit
Number of AUVs	2
Packet size	50 Byte
AUV moving speed	2 kn
Simulation running time	2000 s
Number of simulations	50

5.1 Average End-to-End Delay

Figure 4 shows the average end-to-end delay with the three routing protocols as the number of nodes increases. It is seen that VAPR and GEDAR have a higher delay than RVHP. This is because when the nodes are located in the communication void area, VAPR adopts a void recovery mode, which increases the node hops, and GEDAR leads to a high network delay because the node is in a queued waiting state during the void repair. In contract, when the number of nodes increases, the delay of PVHP decreases, and its performance becomes better than those of VAPR and GEDAR. By avoiding local voids and repairing AUV in time, the number of conflicts and retransmission is significantly reduced, thus the network delay being reduced.

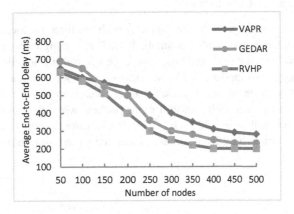

Fig. 4. Average end-to-end delay.

5.2 Packet Transmission Rate

Figure 5 shows the packet transmission rate with the three routing protocols, respectively.

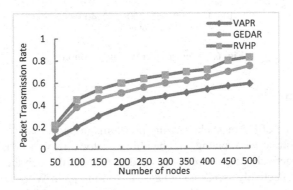

Fig. 5. Packet transmission rate.

It is seen that with the number of nodes increasing, the packet transmission rate increases as well. On the other hand, RVHP has a larger packet transmission rate than both VAPR and GEDAR. This is because RVHP effectively avoids void areas in the routing path by means of local discovery and maintenance. When a routing failure suddenly occurs in the communication area, a node does not discard a packet, but adopts the AUV-assisted network repair mechanism to deal with the routing void. An AUV uses the greedily path-finding strategy to access void nodes to adapt to the dynamic of the network. At each decision point, the next void node to be visited by an AUV is the largest node to transmit packets, which improves the probability for an ordinary node to successfully transmit a packet.

5.3   Average Energy Consumption

Figure 6 shows the average energy consumption with the three protocols, respectively. It is seen that the number of nodes is small, RVHP has a high energy consumption because an alternative path in RVHP may increase the routing length, leading to the increase of energy consumption. With the number of nodes increasing, the energy consumption for a node to send packets decreases. Compared with VAPR and GEDAR, RVHP can successfully transmit more packets when the number of nodes is large. When packets fall into void nodes, RVHP can directly collect and detect data through an AUV, which significantly reduces the energy consumption of a node.

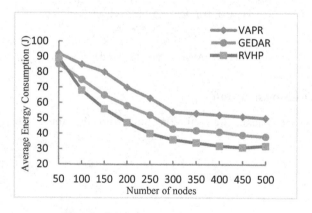

Fig. 6. Average energy consumption.

6   Conclusion

Routing void is one of the most challenging problems in underwater routing. To solve the problem, we proposed a routing void handling protocol (RVHP) based on AUV for a UASN. RVHP actively detects void nodes and trap nodes through the void avoidance mechanism, and effectively avoids a void area in routing path. When an ordinary node suddenly appears routing void in the communication range, RVHP directly collects data from the void node through the AUV-assisted network repair mechanism to realize the void handling of in the network, AUV uses the greedily path-finding strategy to a visit void node, and then sends a packet to a sonar buoy through the acoustic channel to realize void repair of the network. Simulation results show that RVHP can effectively solve the routing void problem, reduce the energy consumption in the network, and improve the packet transmission rate. In the future work, we will consider the link characteristics of a water environment in underwater routing, and effectively prolong the network lifecycle by reducing the communication void area.

Acknowledgments. This research was supported by National Natural Science Foundation of China 61902273, Tianjin Natural Science Fund Project 18JCYBJC85600, Qinghai Key Laboratory of Internet of Things Project 2017-ZJ-Y21, Tianjin Enterprise Science and Technology Commissioner Project 18JCTPJC60500.

References

1. Khan, A., Javaid, N., Latif, G., Karim, O.A., Hayat, F., Khan, Z.A.: Void hole and collision avoidance in geographic and opportunistic routing in underwater wireless sensor networks. In: Barolli, L., Xhafa, F., Javaid, N., Spaho, E., Kolici, V. (eds.) Advances in Internet, Data & Web Technologies. EIDWT 2018. Lecture Notes on Data Engineering and Communications Technologies, vol. 17, pp. 225–236. Springer, Cham (2018). https://doi.org/10.1007/978-3-319-75928-9_20

2. Luo, Y., Pu, L., Zhao, Y., Cui, J.H.: Harness interference for performance improvement in underwater sensor networks. IEEE Syst. J. **99**, 1–12 (2017)

3. Javaid, N., et al.: Delay-sensitive routing schemes for underwater acoustic sensor networks. Int. J. Distrib. Sens. Net. **11**(3), 532676 (2015)

4. Coutinho, R.W.: Topology Control and Opportunistic Routing in Underwater Acoustic Sensor Networks. Doctoral dissertation. Université d'Ottawa/University of Ottawa (2017)

5. Coutinho, R.W., Boukerche, A., Vieira, L.F., Loureiro, A.A.: Geographic and opportunistic routing for underwater sensor networks. IEEE Trans. Comput. **65**(2), 548–561 (2015)

6. Akbar, M., Javaid, N., Khan, A., Imran, M., Shoaib, M., Vasilakos, A.: Efficient data gathering in 3D linear underwater wireless sensor networks using sink mobility. Sensors **16**(3), 404 (2016)

7. Stojanovic, M., Preisig, J.: Underwater acoustic communication channels: propagation models and statistical characterization. IEEE Commun. Mag. **47**(1), 84–89 (2009)

8. Coutinho, R.W., Boukerche, A., Vieira, L.F., Loureiro, A.A.: Design guidelines for opportunistic routing in underwater networks. IEEE Commun. Mag. **54**(2), 40–48 (2016)

9. Coutinho, R.W., Boukerche, A., Vieira, L.F., Loureiro, A.A.: Performance modeling and analysis of void-handling methodologies in underwater wireless sensor networks. Comput. Netw. **126**, 1–14 (2017)

10. Noh, Y., Lee, U., Wang, P., Choi, B.S.C., Gerla, M.: VAPR: void-aware pressure routing for underwater sensor networks. IEEE Trans. Mobile Comput. **12**(5), 895–908 (2012)

11. Xie, P., Cui, J.H., Lao, L.: VBF: vector-based forwarding protocol for underwater sensor networks. In: Boavida, F., Plagemann, T., Stiller, B., Westphal, C., Monteiro, E. (eds.) NETWORKING 2006. Networking Technologies, Services, and Protocols; Performance of Computer and Communication Networks; Mobile and Wireless Communications Systems. NETWORKING 2006. LNCS, vol. 3976, pp. 1216–1221. Springer, Heidelberg (2006). https://doi.org/10.1007/11753810_111

12. Nicolaou, N., See, A., Xie, P., Cui, J.H., Maggiorini, D.: Improving the robustness of location-based routing for underwater sensor networks. In: Oceans 2007-Europe, 18–21 June 2007
13. Noh, Y., et al.: Hydrocast: pressure routing for underwater sensor networks. IEEE Trans. Veh. Technol. **65**(1), 333–347 (2015)
14. Al-Bzoor, M., Zhu, Y., Liu, J., Reda, A., Cui, J.H., Rajasekaran, S.: Adaptive power controlled routing for underwater sensor networks. In: Wang, X., Zheng, R., Jing, T., Xing, K. (eds.) Wireless Algorithms, Systems, and Applications. WASA 2012. LNCS, vol. 7405, pp. 549–560. Springer, Heidelberg (2012). https://doi.org/10.1007/978-3-642-31869-6_48
15. Basagni, S., Petrioli, C., Petroccia, R., Spaccini, D.: CARP: a channel-aware routing protocol for underwater acoustic wireless networks. Ad Hoc Netw. **34**, 92–104 (2015)
16. O'Rourke, M., Basha, E., Detweiler, C.: Multi-modal communications in underwater sensor networks using depth adjustment. In: Proceedings of the Seventh ACM International Conference on Underwater Networks and Systems, p. 31. ACM (2012)
17. Coutinho, R.W., Vieira, L.F., Loureiro, A.A.: DCR: depth-Controlled routing protocol for underwater sensor networks. In: 2013 IEEE Symposium on Computers and Communications, ISCC, pp. 453–458. IEEE (2013)
18. Coutinho, R.W., Boukerche, A., Vieira, L.F., Loureiro, A.A.: GEDAR: geographic and opportunistic routing protocol with depth adjustment for mobile underwater sensor networks. In: 2014 IEEE International Conference on Communications, ICC, pp. 251–256. IEEE (2014)
19. Latif, G., Javaid, N., Sher, A., Khan, M., Hameed, T., Abbas, W.: An efficient routing algorithm for void hole avoidance in underwater wireless sensor networks. In: 2018 IEEE 32nd International Conference on Advanced Information Networking and Applications, AINA, pp. 305–310. IEEE (2018)
20. Gong, Z., Li, C., Jiang, F.: AUV-aided joint localization and time synchronization for underwater acoustic sensor networks. IEEE Sig. Process. Lett. **25**(4), 477–481 (2018)
21. Su, R., Zhang, D., Li, C., Gong, Z., Venkatesan, R., Jiang, F.: Localization and data collection in AUV-aided underwater sensor networks: challenges and opportunities. IEEE Network (2019)
22. Brekhovskikh, L.M., Lysanov, Y.P., Beyer, R.T.: Fundamentals of ocean acoustics. Acoust. Soc. Am. J. **90**, 3382–3383 (1991)
23. Stojanovic, M.: On the relationship between capacity and distance in an underwater acoustic communication channel. ACM SIGMOBILE Mobile Comput. Commun. Rev. **11**(4), 34–43 (2007)
24. Khan, A., Javaid, N., Latif, G., Jatta, L., Fatima, A., Khan, W.: Cluster based and adaptive power controlled routing protocol for underwater wireless sensor networks. In: 2018 21st Saudi Computer Society National Computer Conference, NCC, pp. 1–6. IEEE (2018)
25. Darehshoorzadeh, A., Boukerche, A.: Underwater sensor networks: a new challenge for opportunistic routing protocols. IEEE Commun. Mag. **53**(11), 98–107 (2015)
26. Li, L.Y.: The routing protocol for dynamic and large computer network. Chin. J. Comput. **02**, 137–144 (1998)

Optimal Packet Size Analysis for Intra-flow Network Coding Enabled One Hop Wireless Multicast

Hao Cui[1]([✉]), Yan Yan[1], Baoxian Zhang[1], and Cheng Li[2]

[1] Research Center of Ubiquitous Sensor Networks, University of Chinese Academy of Sciences, Beijing 100049, China
cuihao16@mails.ucas.ac.cn, {yany, bxzhang}@ucas.ac.cn
[2] Faculty of Engineering and Applied Science, Memorial University, St. John's, NL A1B 3X5, Canada
licheng@mun.ca

Abstract. Network coding has received great attention for its ability to greatly improve the performance of wireless networks. However, there still lacks of study to optimize the packet size for maximizing the throughput performance of network coding enabled multicast in wireless networks. In this paper, we study network coding enabled multicast from a base station to multiple receivers using random linear network coding. We build a network throughput model and derive the optimal packet size for maximal multicast throughput. Simulation results verify the high accuracy of our analysis results.

Keywords: Intra-flow network coding · Optimal packet size · Network throughput · Error-prone wireless networks

1 Introduction

It has been known that intra-flow network coding (NC) can significantly improve the multicast throughput. Existing work in this aspect has been mainly focused on designing practical intra-flow multicast protocols. How to improve the intra-flow NC assisted multicast from the perspective of packet size optimization has not been fully investigated. Packet size has big impact on the performance of wireless multicast. In the case of poor channel condition, the larger a packet is, the greater the probability of packet loss; In the case of good channel condition, the smaller a packet is, the bigger the overhead due to fixed packet header will be. Therefore, how to optimize the packet size to maximize the throughput of wireless multicast is a key problem in the study of intra-flow network coding.

This work was supported in part by the NSF of China under Grant Nos. 61872331, 61471339, and the Natural Sciences and Engineering Research Council (NSERC) of Canada (Discovery Grant RGPIN-2018-03792) and InnovateNL SensorTECH Grant 5404-2061-101. Yan's work was also supported by grant from the University of Chinese Academy of Sciences.

J. Zheng et al. (Eds.): ADHOCNETS 2019, LNICST 306, pp. 53–64, 2019.
https://doi.org/10.1007/978-3-030-37262-0_5

In this paper, we focus on studying one-hop networks constituent of one base station and a set of wireless clients. In such a network, we investigate how to maximize the network throughput by optimizing the packet size for single-hop wireless multicast using intra-flow network coding, which adopts random linear network coding (RLNC) for batch forwarding to multiple multicast destinations (receivers). To address this issue, we formulate the network throughput model for our scenario. Based on the network throughput model, we derive the optimal packet size for maximal network throughput for the single-hop wireless multicast scenario. Simulation results verify the high accuracy of our analytical results.

The rest of this paper is organized as follows. In Sect. 2, we briefly introduce related work. In Sect. 3, we build the network throughput model and then derive the optimal packet size for maximal network throughput. In Sect. 4, we conduct simulation results for performance validation. In Sect. 5, we conclude this paper.

2 Related Work

Network coding technology [1] has been proven to have good potential for the enhancement of network throughput. Linear codes are sufficient to achieve the maximum capacity bounds for a multicast traffic [2]. Especially the inherent broadcasting peculiarity makes the network coding more suitable for one-to-many flows in a wireless multi-hop network. Then [3] shows that random linear network coding can take advantage of redundant network capacity for improved packet delivery probability and robustness. Paper [4] studied the integration of opportunistic routing and intra-flow network coding for improved network throughput performance in multi-hop wireless networks.

Packet size optimization has been studied in various aspects. In [5], the authors studied the issue of optimal packet size in energy-constrained wireless sensor networks where optimal packet size is determined for a set of radio and channel parameters by maximizing the energy use efficiency. In [6], Wu et al. built link lifetime models for characterizing the temporal nature of wireless links and subsequently wireless paths by considering node mobility and then computed the optimal packet size as a function of mobility for improving the network throughput. However, none of them have studied the issue of optimal packet size for network coding enabled wireless networks. In [7], Cui et al. studied how to optimize the packet size of unicast packets for maximizing the network throughput of two-hop wireless networks with IEEE 802.11 for medium access. The analysis model in [7] is not suitable for our scenario in this paper due to the following reasons. First, the focus on [7] is on how to introducing various coding/broadcasting gains into a Markov throughput analysis model for establishing the relationship between network throughput and packet size, while in this paper, we focus on allocated wireless channels for transmission, which is quite different from the multi-access channel in [7]. Second, [7] studied unicast traffic while in this paper, we study multicast communications. Third, [7] studied inter-flow network coding while in this paper, we focus on studying intra-flow network coding.

Ref. [8] is a paper relevant to our work in this paper. In [8], the authors studied the throughput performance of RLNC assisted multicast under the requirement of 100%

packet delivery. They derived the normalized throughput in this case, which does not consider the impact of packet size in the throughput calculation, and further its implementation involves operations under asymptotical conditions, paper [8] also derived the upper and lower bounds of throughput of the RLNC assisted multicast with 100% packet delivery with simplified expressions. However, the simplified expressions for the bounds cannot be used to find the optimal packet size leading to maximal throughput. More importantly, achieving 100% delivery may not be necessary in many cases and applications and further it can greatly affect the multicast throughput performance. This happen when different multicast receivers have different packet loss rates since the throughput in this case will be largely determined by the receiver with the worst link loss rate. Different from [8], in this paper, we focus on studying how to optimize the packet size in RLNC assisted multicast while achieving maximal network throughput without considering 100% packet delivery.

3   Optimal Packet Size Analysis

In this section, we first describe the system model, then formulate the problem under study, and finally build our analytical model for optimal packet size analysis.

3.1   System Model

The network under study consists of one base station and multiple clients connected via wireless links. The issue under study is to deliver packets from the base station to N $(N \geq 2)$ multicast receivers $\{R_1, R_2, \ldots, R_N\}$. Assume that each node is equipped with an omnidirectional antenna. All the network nodes have the same communication range. In this paper, we assume that the channel between the source and the multicast receivers is a dedicated broadcast channel (such as 3G/4G/LTE) such that the transmissions from the base station can be received by all the N receivers when no transmission error occurs. We assume transmissions on the wireless channel may suffer from packet loss due to channel fading, multipath effects, etc. We assume a uniform random bit error model although analytical model can also be easily extended to work in other link loss models. The packet receptions at different multicast receivers are assumed to be independent. Table 1 lists the notations used in this paper.

In this paper, we focus on a scenario where the source node S is to multicast a large bulk of data to multiple receivers. The whole data bulk is divided into multiple blocks (batches). The random linear network coding (RLNC) is used to facilitate the batch forwarding such that each batch contains $K + \theta$ coded packets, each of which is a random linear combination of K original data packets to be delivered in the current batch. The coding coefficients are taken from the finite field $GF(q)$. When a receiver receives K linearly independent coded packets, it will be able to decode all the K original data packets of the batch. For the source node, after it sends out the $K + \theta$ coded packets of a batch, it will move to the next batch. This process continues until the source complete the transmissions of all the batches. Therefore, there is no guarantee that a receiver receives all the original packets. This case is of interest for delivering video contents, sensor readings, etc. The value of θ determines the successful delivery probability of the original packets and also has a big impact on the bandwidth efficiency. From the viewpoint of flow rate, if the data flow rate is r, then the actual transmission rate will be $r \times (K + \theta)/K$. Figure 1 illustrates the system model for delivering a batch.

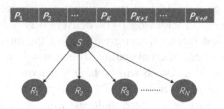

Fig. 1. The multicast scenario using random linear network coding.

Let BER denote the link bit error rate, the packet loss rate between the multicast source and a receiver, denoted by P_e, will be as follows:

$$P_e = 1 - (1 - BER)^{H+h+L} \tag{1}$$

where H is the length of the packet header, h is the length of the encoding vector, and L is the payload length of the packet.

3.2   Problem Formulation

Next, we formulate the problem under study. When a receiver receives a number i $(1 \leq i \leq K + \theta)$ of coded packets of a batch, we are concerned about at which probability the receiver can decode the K original packets of the batch. Note that the possibility of certain linear correlation between received coded packets needed to be considered. Accordingly, we define $P_{i,K}$ as "the probability that a receiver can successfully decode the K code-independent encoded packets of a batch when it successfully receives i coded packets belonging to the batch". Since the theoretical derivation of $P_{i,K}$ involves too many matrix operations and is hard to obtain a closed form, in this paper, the value of $P_{i,K}$ will be obtained empirically via simulations.

The packet decoding at a receiver is as follows. Suppose the source sends out $K + \theta$ coded packets for a batch, for a receiver to decode all the K original packets of the batch, it needs to get K linearly independent coded packets; Otherwise, it will be unable to decode any original packets[1].

[Definition] The batch based multicast transmission problem subject to given transmission redundancy constraint: Given a transmission redundancy θ, for delivering a batch generated by K original data packets, the multicast source will send out a total number $K + \theta$ of RLNC coded packets. For this case, what is the optimal packet size for maximizing the network throughput?

---

[1] Such decoding feature is due to the decoding characteristics of the RLNC package in the NS-3 simulator (i.e., the Kodo-RLNC module developed by Steinwurf) [9].

3.3 Analytical Model

In this subsection, we build our analytical model for deriving optimal packet size for achieving maximal throughput subject to transmission given redundancy.

Consider the lossy nature of wireless channel, when the source sends out $K + \theta$ packets, and the probability that a receiving node receives a number i ($1 \leq i \leq K + \theta$) of packets is as follows:

$$
\begin{aligned}
P_{ri} &= C_{K+\theta}^i (1 - P_e)^i P_e^{K+\theta-i} \\
&= C_{K+\theta}^i (1 - BER)^{i(H+h+L)} \left[1 - (1 - BER)^{H+h+L} \right]^{K+\theta-i}
\end{aligned}
\tag{2}
$$

Therefore, in the transmission of a batch, the source sends out $K + \theta$ coded packets in total, and the probability that a receiving node can decode all the original packets of the batch, denoted by P_{decode}, is as follows:

$$
P_{\text{decode}} = \sum_{i=K}^{K+\theta} P_{ri} P_{i,K}
\tag{3}
$$

In summary, the throughput at a particular receiver can be obtained as follows:

$$
\begin{aligned}
S_{RLNC} &= \frac{L}{H+h+L} \times \frac{K}{K+\theta} P_{\text{decode}} \\
&= \frac{L}{H+h+L} \times \frac{K}{K+\theta} \sum_{K}^{K+\theta} P_{i,K} C_{K+\theta}^i (1 - BER)^{i(H+h+L)} \\
&\quad \left[1 - (1 - BER)^{H+h+L} \right]^{K+\theta-i}
\end{aligned}
\tag{4}
$$

Table 1. Notations used.

Notations	Definitions
H	Data packet header length
L	Payload length
h	Coding vector length
$P_{i,K}$	The probability that a receiving node successfully decodes the K original packets in a batch when it successfully receives i coded packets
P_e	Packet error probability
θ	The number of redundant packets in a batch
K	The number of original data packets in a batch
P_{ri}	The probability that one receiving node receives i packets belonging to a batch
P_{decode}	The probability that a receiver can decode all the original packets belonging to a batch
S_{RLNC}	Normalized throughput at a receiver due to the use of random linear network coding for batch forwarding

It can be seen that S_{RLNC} is a convex function with respect to the payload L. Therefore, there exists an optimal L value within a reasonable range so that S_{RLNC} reaches the maximum. Therefore, let $\partial S_{RLNC}/\partial L = 0$, we can obtain the optimal packet size L^*.

Following (4), for multicast scenario, the mean throughput at an individual multicast receiver (i.e., normalized throughput) can be obtained as follows:

$$
\begin{aligned}
S_{RLNC} &= \frac{1}{N} \times \frac{L}{H+h+L} \times \frac{K}{K+\theta} \sum\nolimits_{j=0}^{N} P_{\text{decode}} \\
&= \frac{1}{N} \times \frac{L}{H+h+L} \times \frac{K}{K+\theta} \\
&\sum_{j=0}^{N} \sum_{K}^{K+\theta} P_{i,K} C_{K+\theta}^{i} \left(1-BER_j\right)^{i(H+h+L)} \left[1 - \left(1-BER_j\right)^{H+h+L}\right]^{K+\theta-i}
\end{aligned}
\tag{5}
$$

where BER_j is the bit error rate of the link between a source node and multicast receiver j. Again, the optimal packet size L^* for this case can be obtained by let the derivative of (5) to be 0 since the sum of convex functions is still convex.

4 Simulation Results

In this section, we conduct simulations using NS-3 to validate the accuracy of our analytical results. Specifically, we use the random linear network coding module Kodo-RLNC developed by Steinwurf to generate batches of packets. Moreover, in the generation of coded packets, we chose finite field $GF(4)$ to generate coding vectors, i.e., the coding coefficients will be random integers in $[0, 2^4-1]$. In the simulations, the source node needs to send a file with a size of 1Mbytes toward multicast destinations like shown in Fig. 1. Each batch contains 10 original data packets. The default number of redundant coded packets for each batch is 5, which will be adjusted later. The topology used in the simulation is shown in Fig. 1. UDP is used for multicast data packet transmission. All links in the network are assumed to have the same BER. In the reported results in terms of network throughput and packet size, only packet payload is counted. The parameter settings are listed in Table 2.

Table 2. Simulation settings.

Parameters	Values
Packet header length	24 bytes
Channel rate	1 Mbps
Packet type	UDP
Payload range L	(0,1500 bytes]
Number of multicast receivers	2, 5
Coding vector length h	4 bytes

In the simulations, we measure the normalized throughput due to different settings. The normalized throughput can be seen as the average number of data bytes from decoded original packets received by an individual multicast receiver when the source node sent out a whole batch of packets over the total number of bytes in all the original data packets in a batch. For example, if the source node sends out 15 coded packets for a batch, and a certain receiver receives some of the packets and decodes all the 10 original packets, then the normalized throughput will be $10 \times L/(15 \times (H + h + L))$, where h is the coding vetch length. Obviously, for $K = 10$ and $\theta = 5$, the upper bound of normalized throughput is 2/3.

4.1 $P_{i,K}$ Training

The first test is to determine (train) the value of each $P_{i,K}$ via simulations (note that $K = 10$ in our case). During the training process, there exist just one source and one receiver. Moreover, the link between the source and the receiver is error free in the training process. In this process, the source has totally 1000 batches to send. Each batch contains 15 coded packets, which are generated based on 10 original data packets. The batch decoding process at receiver works as follows: When the receiver receives i ($i \geq K$) packets belonging to a batch, it will try to decode the K original data packets in the batch; when $i < K$, the Kodo-RLNC module will not produce any original packets (i.e., $P_{i,10} = 0$, $\forall i < 10$). The value of $P_{i,10}$ ($i \geq 10$) is the average ratio between the number of tests that decoding the K original packets when i packets were received and the total number of tests that i packets were received. Table 3 shows the values of $P_{i,10}$ ($i \geq 10$). The obtained $P_{i,K}$ values will be taken into Eqs. (4) (5) for deriving normalized throughput at different bit error rates.

Table 3. Values of $P_{i,K}$.

$P_{i,K}$ ($K = 10$)	Probability
$P_{10,10}$	0.953
$P_{11,10}$	1
$P_{12,10}$	1
$P_{13,10}$	1
$P_{14,10}$	1
$P_{15,10}$	1

Figure 2 shows the packet loss rate with varying bit error rate and payload. It can be seen that the packet loss rate increases with payload and also bit error rate.

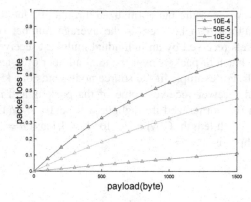

Fig. 2. Packet loss rate with varying payload and bit error rate.

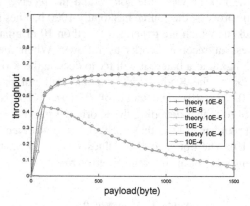

Fig. 3. Comparison of throughput with varying payload and BER. $\theta = 5$.

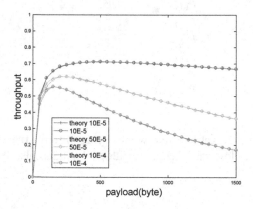

Fig. 4. Comparison of throughput with varying payload and BER. $\theta = 2$.

4.2   Homogeneous BER Case

In this test, the BERs for different multicast receivers were set to be the same. This case is actually equivalent to the unicast case since we are concerned about the normalized throughput performance. That is, the average normalized throughput performance for multicast scenario in this case is the same to the counterpart for unicast scenario under the same BER.

Figure 3 compares the throughput performance by analysis and simulations with varying bit error rate and payload when $\theta = 5$. Figure 4 compares the throughput performance when $\theta = 2$. Other parameters were the same to those used for Fig. 3.

In Fig. 3, it can be seen, in the case of a small BER, the optimal packet size is large. As the BER continues to increase, the channel keeps deteriorating, resulting in lower throughput, and also smaller optimal packet size. However, under the use of random linear network coding, the throughput can still approach the maximum value of 0.66 in the case of lossy channel due to the redundancy introduced by the source node for the delivery of each individual batch. In Fig. 4, when the number of redundant packets θ is reduced to 2. When the BER is low (i.e., 10^{-5}), the channel utilization is increased and the throughput is high, but with BER increasing to 5×10^{-5}, the packet loss rate increases, and the system throughput drops faster (compared to the case of $\theta = 5$). When the BER continues to increase (10^{-4}), the channel conditions are too bad. Even if $\theta = 5$, the receiver may still be unable to successfully receive enough coded packets in many cases. At this time, the case $\theta = 2$ performs better than the case $\theta = 5$. Furthermore, it can be seen from both figures that our analytical results are consistent with the simulation results.

Table 4 shows the optimal packet sizes for different cases. The table shows that the analytical results are very close to the simulation results. The difference between the analysis results and the simulation results is mainly due to the limited granularity of packet size setting in simulations. Table 5 lists the average delivery rates of original packets under different redundancies and bit error rates. The delivery rate is a ratio between the number of original packets received (decoded) and the number of original packets sent out. It is seen that although the bandwidth utilization ratio when $\theta = 5$ is much lower than that when $\theta = 2$, the average delivery rate for the former case is much higher than that for the latter case.

Table 4. Comparison of optimal packet sizes by analysis and simulation.

BER	$\theta = 5$		$\theta = 2$	
	Simulation	Theoretical	Simulation	Theoretical
10^{-5}	1250	1243	459	450
5×10^{-5}	400	370	217	200
10^{-4}	100	123	153	150

Table 5. Average delivery rate of original packets under different redundancies and different bit error rates.

BER	$\theta = 5$	$\theta = 2$
10^{-5}	95%	76%
5×10^{-5}	83%	64%
10^{-4}	41%	32%

Table 6. Comparison of optimal packet sizes due to analysis and simulation.

BER settings	$\theta = 5$		$\theta = 2$	
	Simulation	Theoretical	Simulation	Theoretical
$10^{-4}, 5 \times 10^{-5}, 10^{-5}$	200	179.8	200	203.3
$10^{-5}, 5 \times 10^{-5}, 10^{-6}$	300	303.2	350	334.0

4.3 Heterogeneous BER Case

Next, we extend the multicast scenario to heterogeneous bit error rates. The number of multicast receiver was fixed to three. In the first test in this aspect, the BERs of the links between the source node and each of the three receivers were set to 10^{-4}, 5×10^{-5}, and 10^{-5}, respectively, and the transmission redundancy $\theta = 2, 5$. Figure 5 compares the throughput performance by analysis and simulations for this case. The results show that our analytical results are consistent with the simulation results. In the second test, we fixed the redundancy $\theta = 2$, varied the BERs of different multicast receivers (one case is: 10^{-5}, 5×10^{-5}, 10^{-6}, and another case is 10^{-4}, 5×10^{-5}, 10^{-5}). Figure 6 compares the throughput performance by analysis and simulations. Again, the analytical results are consistent with the simulation results. Table 6 lists the optimal packet sizes for different cases. It is seen that the analytical results are very close to the simulation results.

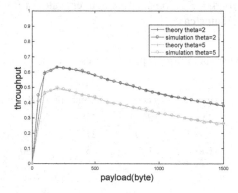

Fig. 5. Comparison of throughput under different θs in heterogeneous BER cases.

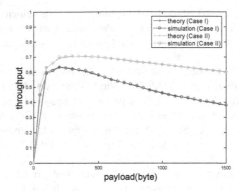

Fig. 6. Comparison of throughput in heterogeneous BER cases. Case I: 10^{-4}, 5×10^{-5}, 10^{-5}, and Case II: 10^{-5}, 5×10^{-5}, 10^{-6}.

5 Conclusion

In this paper, we studied the optimal packet size problem for single-hop wireless multicast using intra-flow network coding with lossy links. Random linear network coding is used for batch forwarding. In this study, we first model the network throughput when given transmission redundancy and then derive the optimal packet size for maximal network throughput. Simulation results verified the high accuracy of our analytical results. The RLNC based throughput-maximization multicast in this paper can also work well with the D2D recovery via localized network coding for further improved delivery performance [10–12].

References

1. Ahlswede, R., Cai, N., Li, S.R., Yeung, R.W.: Network information flow. IEEE Trans. Inf. Theory **46**(4), 1024–1216 (2000)
2. Li, S.Y., Yeung, W.: Linear network coding. IEEE Trans. Inf. Theory **49**(2), 371–381 (2003)
3. Ho, T., et al.: A random linear network coding approach to multicast. IEEE Trans. Inf. Theory **52**(10), 4413–4430 (2006)
4. Zhang, C., Li, C., Chen, Y.: Joint opportunistic routing and intra-flow network coding in multi-hop wireless networks: a survey. IEEE Netw. **33**(1), 113–119 (2019)

5. Sankarasubramaniam, Y., Akyildiz, I., Mchughlin, S.: Energy efficiency based packet size optimization in wireless sensor network. In Proceedings of the first IEEE International Workshop on Sensor Network Protocols and Applications, Anchorage, AK, pp. 1–8. IEEE (2003)

6. Wu, X., Sadjadpour, H.R., Garcia-Luna-Aceves, J.J.: From link dynamics to path lifetime and packet-length optimization in MANETs. Wirel. Netw. (WINET) 15(5), 637–650 (2003)

7. Cui, H., Zhang, B., Yan, Y., Li, C.: Optimal packet size analysis for network coding enabled two-hop error-prone wireless networks. IEEE Commun. Lett. 23(5), 904–908 (2019)

8. Swapna, B.T., Eryilmaz, A., Shorff, N.B.: Throughput-delay analysis of random linear network coding for wireless broadcasting. IEEE Trans. Inf. Theory 59(10), 6328–6341 (2012)

9. http://docs.steinwurf.com/kodo-rlnc/master/quick_start_kodo_rlnc.html

10. Yan, Y., Zhang, B., Li, C.: Opportunistic network coding based cooperative retransmissions in D2D communications. Comput. Netw. 113, 72–83 (2017)

11. Yan, Y., Zhang, B., Li, C.: Network coding aided collaborative real-time scalable video transmission in D2D communications. IEEE Trans. Veh. Technol. 67(7), 6203–6217 (2018)

12. Yan, Y., Zhang, B., Yao, Z.: Space-time efficient network coding for wireless multi-hop networks. Comput. Commun. 73(A), 144–156 (2016)

Access Control

MBA-DbMAC: A Random-Access MAC Protocol for MBAs

Jean-Daniel Medjo Me Biomo$^{(\boxtimes)}$, Thomas Kunz, and Marc St-Hilaire

Department of Systems and Computer Engineering, Carleton University,
Ottawa, ON, Canada
{jemeda,tkunz}@sce.carleton.ca, marc_st_hilaire@carleton.ca

Abstract. Ad hoc networks are infrastructureless and self-organizing networks that consist of static/mobile nodes with limited bandwidth, computing ability and energy. These networks are deployed for civilian/military applications. Having an efficient/reliable routing protocol for communication between the nodes can be critical. A current research avenue involves exploiting Multi-Beam directional Antennas (MBA) to significantly reduce the end-to-end delay in multi-hop ad hoc networks that service multiple traffic flows. To tackle such an issue at the Network level, there is a need for a suitable MAC protocol underneath. In this paper we propose MBA-DbMAC, a MAC protocol for MBAs. MBA-DbMAC is a generic MAC protocol that has the basic functionalities of a MAC protocol and renders possible the basic operation of MBA-equipped nodes in static/mobile ad hoc networks. We adopt a two-tier processing approach whereby the MAC layer is split into two artificial sub-layers: a controller sub-layer (materialized by one node-wide parent process) and a sector sub-layer (materialized by N child processes, 1 child process for each of the N sectors). Other novel aspects of this protocol are the decoupled broadcasting and the time window policy that we adopt to avoid Critical Chain Transmission/Reception. We use Opnet for the implementation/simulations. It is shown that MBA-DbMAC perfectly performs key functions such as unicasting, broadcasting, and concurrent packet transmission/reception.

Keywords: Directional MAC protocol · Multi-beam antenna · Ad hoc networks · Opnet/Riverbed

1 Introduction

As researchers are turning some attention into exploiting Multi-Beam directional Antennas (MBAs) to significantly reduce the end-to-end (E2E) delay in multi-hop ad hoc networks that service multiple traffic flows, the need for a suitable medium-access protocol is growing. In this paper we propose MBA-DbMAC, a generic MAC protocol that has the basic functionalities of a distributed IEEE 802.11 MAC protocol and renders possible the operation of MBA-equipped nodes

© ICST Institute for Computer Sciences, Social Informatics and Telecommunications Engineering 2019
Published by Springer Nature Switzerland AG 2019. All Rights Reserved
J. Zheng et al. (Eds.): ADHOCNETS 2019, LNICST 306, pp. 67–86, 2019.
https://doi.org/10.1007/978-3-030-37262-0_6

both in static and mobile ad hoc networks (MANETs). MBAs represent a major technology improvement over the more traditional single-beam directional antennas (SBAs) whereby only one antenna beam is active at a time. With MBAs, many beams can transmit or receive concurrently; opening up a range of possibilities for network performance improvements.

There is a choice to be made between a TDMA approach and a CSMA/CA approach. We are not going to use TDMA, but rather CSMA/CA. This is because enforcing time synchronization between nodes in MANETs can be very challenging. As noted by Luo et al. in [9], current TDMA-based MAC protocols cannot provide the rapidness and agility to deal with the rapid mobility and varying densities of vehicles in Vehicular Ad hoc NETworks (VANETs)[1] for instance. Among others, Abolhasan et al. [2] also point out the fact that CSMA/CA is a practical MAC protocol for wireless distributed network (WDNs), because it does not require time synchronization and there is no centralized coordination. CSMA/CA has been extensively implemented in WDNs.

In addition to the typical problems inherent to the design of MAC protocols in wireless networks, MBAs introduce new challenges. As already noted, one of these challenges is synchronization. To harness the Concurrent Packet Transmission (CPT) and Concurrent Packet Reception (CPR) capabilities of MBAs, there needs to be some synchronization to ensure that as many transmissions as possible happen while the concerned node is in transmission (Tx) mode before switching to reception (Rx) mode, and vice-versa. Another challenge is Head of Line (HOL) blocking. It needs to be ensured that a packet whose next hop lies in a given beam that is free (medium cleared) is not blocked in a queue behind another packet whose next hop lies in another beam that is waiting for the medium to clear out in that direction. The above challenges and a few more are addressed in the next section.

2   MBA Challenges

2.1   Synchronization for CPT and CPR

Transmitting nodes should start their transmission concurrently so that the common receiver node can simultaneously activate multiple beams pointing toward them. In Fig. 1, assume that nodes A, B, and C need to send data to nodes E, F, and G, respectively, via node D. In the absence of any localized synchronization, the possibility that any two or all three of them will start transmission at the same time using a random access protocol is rare. This is due to the fact that, before initiating transmission, each node waits for a random duration after sensing the channel idle for DIFS duration. Therefore, node D could start receiving a packet from node A. Before that reception is over, nodes B and C could begin their transmissions to D as well. Any of these transmitting nodes might have many packets to transmit and start transmitting those packets before the ongoing transmissions are over. This chain of events would trigger what is

---

[1] Another type of MANETs.

known as transmission starvation on node D which would be locked in successive receptions. To avoid such starvation, [4] proposes that CPR and CPT occur in succession at the bottleneck node (node that is common in two or more routes). To us, even without enforcing that all transmitters start their transmissions at the same time (as is the case in [4]), this scheme would translate into only accepting one packet per transmitter per cycle. That way, after having received packets from all sources, node D would switch to CPT and transmit them all together to their respective destinations, as shown in Fig. 1. We shall present our full strategy on this CPR/CPT issue in a subsequent section.

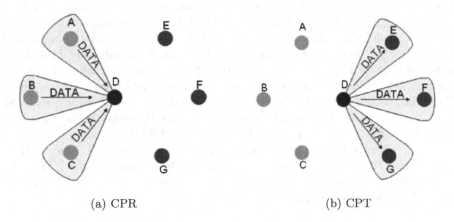

(a) CPR   (b) CPT

Fig. 1. CPR and CPT [4]

2.2 Head-of-Line Blocking

A packet at the head of the data queue may block other packets behind it indefinitely if its intended outbound beam is busy. This phenomenon is known as Head of Line blocking [8,10]. This can be prevented by having a dedicated data queue for each beam as is the case in HMAC [4].

2.3 Deafness

In [4], the authors point out deafness as a problem, invoking beamforming. However, beamforming is not applicable to MBAs. It is only a reality for SBAs. Therefore, we believe that deafness is a non-issue in the context of MBAs. A source node experiences the deafness problem when it fails to communicate with its intended destination node that is pointing towards a different direction for transmission or reception. In fact, we should only consider the case when the intended destination is pointing to another direction for reception. That is because in the case of transmission, even if the destination was pointing to the source, there would be a mode mismatch and the packet from the source would not be received, as the destination cannot be transmitting and receiving at the same time. Now, in the case of MBAs, if the destination node is receiving from a different direction for reception, the beam that is pointing to the source is also able to receive, since the reception mode applies to the entire node (i.e. all beams) and multiple beams can receive concurrently. In SBAs, only one beam can be active at a time.

2.4   Hidden-Terminal

A given scenario experiences the hidden-terminal problem when transmissions from two nodes which cannot hear each other collide at a third node. In the context of directional antennas, all nodes that are located within the destination node's coverage area of interest (covered by a specific beam) and are away from the source node's coverage area of interest are hidden terminals. The shaded area A_h in Fig. 2 indicates the area in which hidden terminals may exist, from the perspective of node S. A node located at any other area where it cannot hear S is not a hidden terminal because, even if it points toward D, its signal either will reach D from a different beam (therefore allowed to be processed thanks to CPR capability) or it will be undetectable (because too far away) by D. Unfortunately, as pointed out in [1], the standard RTS/CTS mechanism fails to completely solve the hidden-terminal problem, as nodes in A_h may initiate transmissions to D during the time the source node S transmits the RTS to D. This problem has not been solved in current literature using a single-channel and single-radio interface [12].

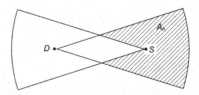

Fig. 2. Hidden-terminal problem [1]

2.5   Exposed-Terminal

A node experiences the exposed-terminal problem if it assumes a busy medium and defers its transmission even though it could be transmitting without impeding ongoing transmissions by other nodes. This is a problem mostly for omni-directional antennas, as pointed out in [7]. In the context of directional antennas, the exposed-terminal problem can easily be solved by taking advantage of directionality. In effect, the exposed-terminal problem happens when a node receives an unintended RTS/CTS and blocks its antenna for the duration of the announced transmission, preventing the node from participating or initiating concurrent transmissions that would not impede the ongoing one. Simply using directional (per sector) NAV timers narrows the scope of this issue, since only the sectors receiving the unintended RTS/CTS will be "blocked". Notice that, even with directional antennas, there is still the possibility of an exposed-terminal if the parallel transmission falls within the blocked beam (See Fig. 3 where the transmission between C and D is prevented by the transmission between A and B that has blocked C's beam that points to D); but we assume that this is infrequent enough to not justify a separate mechanism to deal with it.

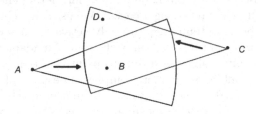

Fig. 3. Exposed-terminal problem with directional antennas

2.6 Random Backoff: Beam-Based or Node-Based

In MBA, each node has several beams, so the problem is how to control the random backoff for each beam after DIFS during transmission or retransmission attempts. One solution is to maintain a separate contention window (CW) for each beam, referred to as beam-based backoff. The other solution is to have a common CW for all beams that increases or decreases depending on the collisions or successful transmissions in the transmitting beams. This scheme is referred to as node-based backoff, where a node can transmit in multiple beams simultaneously. Now all the beams wait for the same random duration after DIFS. This is the approach adopted in HMAC and MMAC-NB [6], where the authors claim that it is conducive to high shares of CPT. This approach implies that if the medium in one beam becomes active, the backoff is suspended in all beams; which, we believe, would not be efficient. Therefore, we do not intend to pursue this approach. Instead, the beam-based backoff approach seems more appropriate.

3 Antenna Model

Similar to the approach proposed in [4], we focus on gains from spatial reuse exclusively and not from range extension of directional beams. Therefore, the range of each beam is constant and is kept equivalent to the omnidirectional range. The antenna is assumed to have a power control mechanism that feeds each beam with a power of P_{TOTAL}/M; M being the total number of beams.

Since the transmission range is kept constant, the implication is that the amount of power used will vary depending on the number of beams that are activated for a given transmission cycle. Broadcasting and multicasting (using multiple beams to send multiple different unicast packets) on all beams will consume the most power while unicasting will consume the least power. In the end, gains in energy efficiency are expected inasmuch as it is anticipated that we will not use all the beams at every single transmission cycle.

The beam shape is assumed to be a disk slice (in 2D). Sidelobes' interferences are not considered for simplicity and simulation tractability. Carrier sensing is performed directionally, that is, before transmission, the medium is sensed only in the desired beam(s). In idle mode, the receiver listens on all its beams (omni mode). A collision occurs only if a node receives interfering energy on the same beam in which it is actively receiving a packet. We use a switched-beam antenna model. A switched-beam antenna requires only activating one of the predefined beams that concentrates in the direction of the user. An adaptive beam antenna requires complex beamforming algorithms to point in the direction of the user. Thus, adaptive beam antennas are more complex to design and are not generally considered for commercial wireless networks [4]. Hence, in the remainder of this work, an MBA refers to a switched-beam antenna capable of switching multiple beams simultaneously. A node can either transmit or receive data, but not both, on multiple beams at the same time.

4 Review of Related Work: A Hybrid MAC Solution

MMAC-NB [6], ESIF [5], and HMAC [4] were all proposed by the same authors. In this section, we summarize only HMAC because it is considered an upgrade of the former two. In effect, although ESIF and HMAC deliver comparable performance, HMAC fares better; owing to its simpler design, reduced cross-layer dependence, and backward compatibility with IEEE 802.11-DCF-based protocols. The reactive mechanism for handling deafness and p-persistent CSMA employed by ESIF requires modifications in the Network layer to store the count of potential transmitters in every beam and message piggybacking among the neighboring nodes, which increases the overhead and complexity of the protocol. On the other hand, MMAC-NB has a poorer Concurrent Packet Reception capability, which leads to the underutilization of multiple beam antennas at the bottleneck (star) nodes.

As discussed in Sect. 2.3, we do dispute the existence of the deafness problem when MBAs are used. In effect, the authors in [4] claim deafness as follows. In Fig. 4, it is assumed that nodes A and B are engaged in communication, and control packets are transmitted directionally. Hence, nodes X and Y are oblivious to the ongoing communication between A and B. The claim is that they continue transmitting RTS messages to node A who is deaf to their messages and hence does not send back any CTS messages to nodes X and Y (which, consequently, go into backoff mode). In fact, in an MBA scenario, A cannot be deaf to the transmissions from X and Y. It will simply receive those transmissions on different beams at the same time as it receives the transmission from B.

HMAC is a cross-layer protocol that uses information from both the Network and the Physical layers for its operation. Similar to MMAC-NB and ESIF, HMAC uses a separate queue for each beam to avoid HOL blocking. It also uses a scheduling (SCH) control packet, which is sent in all desired beams other than the ones being negotiated via RTS/CTS. The purpose of these additional SCH packets is to further mitigate the deafness problem by letting potential transmitters know that the current node is pointing somewhere else. The novel features

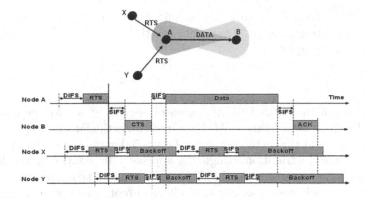

Fig. 4. Illustration of deafness as per [4]

of HMAC include: its channel access mechanism, algorithms for mitigating deafness and contention resolution, as well as jump backoff and role priority switching mechanisms for enhancing throughput. HMAC is also backward compatible with IEEE 802.11 DCF.

To minimize queuing delays in the network by facilitating successive cycles of CPR and CPT, a mechanism similar to hot-potato routing [3] is installed at every node. Thus, depending on the packets in its buffer, a node switches between transmitter and receiver modes. As long as a data packet exists in the queue, the node gives priority to the transmission mode; otherwise, the reception mode supersedes. Moreover, depending on the available neighbor and beam schedules, a node can determine whether it can actually initiate data transmission. If not, the reception mode gets priority.

5   Our Solution: The MBA-DbMAC Protocol

The IEEE 802.11b DCF MAC protocol (omnidirectional) is contention-based. It employs a CSMA/CA mechanism by means of the DCF (Distributed Coordination Function). In [11], this standard MAC protocol was adapted to work with single-beamed directional antennas. The adapted MAC protocol was called the IEEE 802.11b-based Directional MAC (or DbMAC) protocol. DbMAC works mostly like the standard IEEE 802.11b DCF MAC protocol but on a per-antenna-sector basis. At this juncture, we are going to adapt DbMAC to work with MBAs. We call this new protocol the MBA-DbMAC protocol. This new protocol is going to adopt, to a certain extent, some of the approaches of HMAC (thus of MMAC-NB and ESIF as well) to solve some of the MAC protocol challenges that come with the introduction of MBAs as discussed earlier. In the spirit of DbMAC versus existing single-beam directional MAC protocols, MBA-DbMAC combines and/or slightly modifies the common/key features of existing MBA MAC protocols without much of a claim of being a superior protocol. Nevertheless, we do propose a novel decoupled broadcasting scheme whose goal is to give all the beams a chance to transmit when some are not ready during the first broadcasting attempt. The details of MBA-DbMAC are summarized in the next few paragraphs.

5.1 Design

For the design of the MBA-DbMAC protocol, we adopt a two-tier processing approach. In effect, we split the MAC layer into two artificial sub-layers: the controller sub-layer and the sector sub-layer. Figure 5 depicts the contrast between this approach and the traditional single-tier approach. In practice, in the development environment that we use (OPNET), these two sub-layers are materialized with processes: each node has one controller (parent) process that spawns N identical sector (child) processes at run-time; N being the number of antenna sectors. Traditional MAC-layer mechanisms are applied at the sector sub-layer. The controller sub-layer manages: (a) the neighbor table, (b) the assignment of a high-layer packet to the appropriate sector, and (c) the switch between the different operation modes (Tx mode, Idle mode, and Rx mode). The operation mode applies to the whole node. For instance, if a given sector is permitted to transmit at a given time, it is the job of the controller process to instruct all the other sectors via their respective processes to now switch to Tx mode, regardless of whether or not there are packets to be transmitted by these other sectors. Our two-tier design approach is an elegant way of enforcing mode switches in the node while still leaving the full autonomy of medium access to sectors in their respective direction of competence.

5.2 Ensuring CPT and CPR

Unlike DbMAC, we now allow multiple packets to be received or transmitted at the same time. This also means ensuring the processing of such packets by the node, as long as this is happening on different beams. The reception of two or more packets on the same beam at the same time is considered a collision. Likewise, the transmission of two or more packets on the same beam at the same time is forbidden.

We do not enforce that all transmissions on all beams of interest start at the exact same time. However, once a transmission starts on a given beam, the node is now in transmission mode (no reception can occur in any beam at this point). Any other beam that is scheduled to start a transmission while the first is still going on can start its transmission, provided a certain condition that we discuss later in this paragraph. The transmission mode ends when all beams have ended their respective transmissions. To ensure fairness and avoid reception starvation, we limit each beam to only transmit one packet per cycle. Backoff and IFS decisions are made on each beam independently of the others. This means we opt for a beam-based backoff approach, unlike HMAC and ESIF. Once the transmission mode ends, the node goes to Idle mode, or goes to reception mode if a signal is sensed right at that point in time. The node can also start a new transmission cycle if there is no signal sensed and there are packets ready to

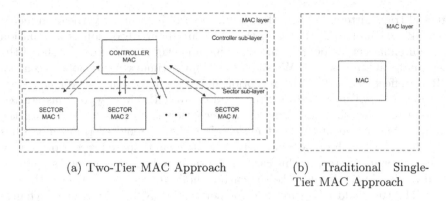

(a) Two-Tier MAC Approach   (b) Traditional Single-Tier MAC Approach

Fig. 5. Two-tier MAC approach vs traditional single-tier MAC approach

be sent instead; with the medium sensed idle long enough (has been clear for an IFS duration). We call Critical Chain Transmission (CCT) a situation where all antenna sectors/beams start transmitting one right before the end of the transmission at another sector. All the sectors are therefore stuck in transmission mode until the last sector of the chain has finished, even though the first transmitting sector has finished its transmission a while ago. CCT might result in spending a disproportionate amount of time in one transmission mode that quickly becomes useless to most sectors. This will then incur some MAC delays. To avoid CCT, we set up the transmission mode such that any sector can only start its transmission within a certain time window after the first sector has started its transmission. Past this time window, no transmission is allowed to start until the next transmission cycle (after the current transmission mode has completed). We set the time window to be half the anticipated transmission time of the first transmitting sector.

We ensure CPR using the same philosophy as with CPT. A node simply stays in Rx mode until all concerned beams have completed their respective receptions. The rule of one packet per beam per cycle also applies to avoid transmission starvation if there are too many packets coming in. Once a given beam has finished receiving one packet, it deactivates itself from further reception for the remainder of that Rx cycle. All packets (unicast and broadcast) arriving during this deactivation period will be lost. The senders of those unicast packets will have to retry sending if applicable. The Rx mode ends when all beams that have sensed a packet before the end of the first reception finish their respective receptions. The node then switches to Tx mode if there is a packet in any of the queues and the medium is ready to be used in the concerned direction. If there is no packet ready to be sent (medium also ready/available), the node goes into Idle mode or a new Rx mode if an incoming signal is sensed right at that time. From Idle mode, a node can go into Tx or Rx mode, depending on which one occurs first: a packet ready to be transmitted and the medium free, or an incoming packet sensed at the Physical layer. We choose to not adopt the approach to synchronize potential transmitters, because that would be a difficult and overhead-inducing undertaking. Similar to the CCT, the Critical Chain Reception is a situation where antenna sectors/beams start receiving a packet right before the end of the reception at another sector. We similarly adopt a time window policy to avoid CCR. In effect, we set up the reception mode such that any sector can start reception only within a certain time window after the first sector has started its reception. Past this time window, no reception is allowed to start until the next reception mode in the next cycle (after the current reception mode has completed). We set the time window to be half the anticipated reception time of the first receiving sector. In this case, the anticipated reception time is approximated to the time it would take the current node to transmit a packet the size of the RTS-threshold (the threshold for performing RTS/CTS frame exchange preceding the transmission of the data frame.) to the neighbor.

5.3   Switch from Tx to Rx Mode

As already mentioned, we set Rx and Tx modes to alternate, with one packet reception/transmission allowed per sector per cycle. The default mode is the Idle mode, where a node is neither transmitting nor receiving on any of its sectors. The switch to Tx/Rx mode is interrupt-driven. In the case of the switching-on of the Tx mode, a node will know when a packet is passed down the protocol stack or has been received and now has to be forwarded. The node checks the medium on the beam of interest. When the medium is ready (after SIFS/DIFS and backoff waiting if applicable) for transmission, a switch to Tx mode occurs, provided that the node is in Idle mode. The node stays in this mode until the transmission is complete and there is no other transmission in progress on any other beam. It then switches back to Idle mode. From the Idle mode, the node can now switch to Rx mode when an incoming packet is sensed by any sector. If no incoming packet signal is sensed at the Physical layer and there is a packet to be transmitted and the medium is free, then a switch to Tx mode occurs. As already mentioned, each node features a controller process that instructs the switch to Rx, Tx, or Idle mode to all the sectors. The state diagram of the controller is depicted in Fig. 6 and the state diagram of the sector/beam is shown in Fig. 7. For instance, while in Idle mode, if an incoming packet is sensed on a sector, that sector starts the reception and immediately reports it to the controller process. The controller process then instructs all the other sectors to switch to Rx mode. At this point, only receptions are allowed. Similarly, while in Idle mode, if the medium becomes available in a certain direction where a packet is waiting to be sent, the concerned sector starts the transmission and informs the controller. The controller then instructs all the other sectors to go into Tx mode. These other sectors can now start their own transmissions, if any, as long as they start within a certain time window as discussed earlier.

Once in Tx mode, all the sectors involved have different transmission end times. The node ends its Tx mode when the latest transmission end time occurs. The same applies to the Rx mode and the different reception end times.

In the special case of a Backoff period ending (for a transmission to start) at the same time as a packet reception starts on a given sector, preference is given to the transmission, and the packet reception is aborted.

5.4 Per-Beam Queues

As is the case for ESIF and HMAC, we set up a separate packet queue for each beam. This prevents HOL blocking. When a higher layer packet arrives at the MAC level, the controller sub-layer, which is hosted by the parent process, checks its address, and forwards it to the appropriate child process (at the sector sub-layer) that then queues the packet on its own queue. For that to be feasible, the parent process maintains a neighbor table as we explain in Sect. 5.8.

5.5 Broadcasting

Broadcasting is performed in a "decoupled" manner as follows. The controller sub-layer makes $N-1$ copies (N being the number of sectors) of the packet to be broadcast. The controller forwards each copy to a different sector process. The latter places the packet copy on its queue. That packet is eventually transmitted when it is its turn (as there might be some other packets ahead of it in the queue) and the medium is free in the concerned direction. No RTS/CTS or IFS are required. With this scheme, we can have broadcast packets be transmitted on some beams while unicast packets are transmitted on other beams during a given Tx mode. We call it "diversity-casting", and it is a novelty of MBA-DbMAC. The mechanism is different than in DbMAC since there is no beam-sweeping involved here, and each beam has its own queue. Moreover, in DbMAC, we provided the nodes with the ability to attempt broadcast packet transmissions twice in a given direction (if the medium was found to be busy the first time around). We do not keep this feature in MBA-DbMAC. Rather, as mentioned, each beam sends its broadcast packet copy independently whenever the medium clears in that direction. With diversity-casting, there is no giving up after one retry as is the case in DbMAC. Therefore, we ensure that all broadcast packets are sent in all directions, unless the normal max retry limit (same as for unicast packets) is reached on a given direction. This should, among others, have a positive impact at the Network layer with route discoveries. The authors of MMAC-NB, ESIF, and HMAC do not specify how broadcasting is handled. But, judging from the emphasis they place on enforcing strict CPT, we can only assume that broadcasting is not decoupled, and that it is done in a synchronous manner; with all the delays that this may impose when confronted with busy medium in certain directions.

The cost of diversity-casting in terms of energy is the same as for broadcasting with omnidirectional antennas when we set the transmission range of the MBAs to be the same[2] as for omnidirectional antennas. MBAs, however, allow spatial reuse. Moreover, diversity-casting ensures that the packet is sent to a specific

---

[2] For fairness in comparison.

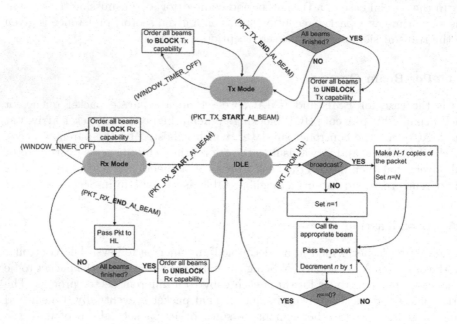

Fig. 6. Controller/parent diagram

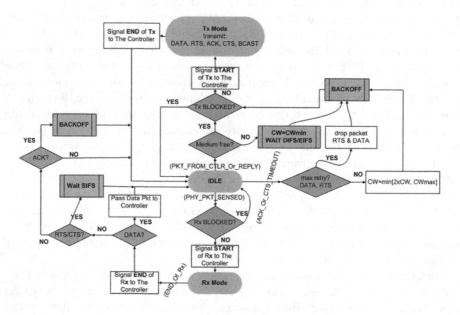

Fig. 7. Beam/child diagram

direction as soon as possible instead of waiting for all directions to be clear. This should have a positive impact in delay reduction.

5.6 RTS/CTS

Similar to DbMAC, RTS and CTS are sent directionally. As the controller sub-layer forwards the packet to the appropriate sector process, the latter takes care of it (including the RTS/CTS exchanges) in its own direction, independently from the other sectors/directions. This mechanism combats the hidden-terminal problem. Moreover, having the RTS/CTS exchange occur directionally solves another problem that might arise in the context of MBAs. A source node might be engaged in an RTS/CTS exchange with a given neighbor in one direction/beam. Another neighbor that can reach this source node on a different beam does not need to know about this exchange since it can engage in a parallel exchange with the same source node thanks to the CPR capability. Having RTS/CTS exchanged omnidirectionally would unnecessarily block exchanges with neighbors from other beams. This can be seen as an exposed-terminal problem in reverse, specific to MBA environments. Restricting RTS/CTS exchanges to occur directionally solves this potential problem.

5.7 DNAV

The Directional Network Allocation Vector (DNAV) is similar to the NAV described in the original IEEE 802.11b DCF MAC; except now the NAV is kept on a per-antenna-beam basis. The exposed-terminal problem is taken care of through the DNAV. Only the sector that receives the unintended RTS/CTS will be "blocked" for transmission for the duration of the neighboring/overheard transmission. Any other sector of the neighbor can engage in a concurrent transmission/reception. As already noted, there is still the possibility of an exposed-terminal if the parallel transmission falls within the blocked beam (Fig. 3). But we assume that this is infrequent enough to not justify a separate mechanism to deal with it. For instance, assuming an N-sector antenna, assuming that the nodes are uniformly distributed in the network, another node (the one sending the unintended RTS/CTS) has to be in the same sector as the one we would transmit in. That cuts down the probability of this occurring by a factor of $1/N$. And the impacted node would need to, presumably, use the impacted sector for its transmission, and that would cause another $1/N$ reduction. Moreover, the sender of the RTS/CTS would also have to use a specific sector (out of its own N) that points to the impacted node. That is yet another $1/N$ reduction. In the end, we can see that would imply a reduction by $1/N^3$ of the probability of occurrence of the exposed-terminal problem. Therefore, that probability drops considerably with an increase in the number of sectors N.

5.8 Neighbor Table

Broadcasting is an important and frequently exploited communication primitive. In the broadcasting mode, nodes send packets on all sectors without having to know where neighbors are. In fact, numerous network layer protocols (routing) do perform neighbor discovery through periodic HELLO message exchanges which are one-hop broadcast messages. Moreover, on-demand protocols broadcast Route Discovery messages before sending unicast packets. Broadcasting messages offer the opportunity to a node to "advertise" itself to all the nodes within its transmission range, and hence be included in their neighbor tables.

Similar to DbMAC, each node maintains a neighbor table. This table is maintained by the controller process with updates coming from individual sector processes. The neighbor table is initially empty and is progressively populated as follows. Whenever a sector receives a frame from the Physical layer, the process responsible for that sector informs the controller sub-layer of the address of the sender of that frame. The controller then updates the neighbor table, if needed, with information that says "Neighbor A lies on beam i". That way, if a frame is later to be sent to that neighbor, the node (controller) knows which antenna sector to use. Therefore, we do not have to calculate the direction of arrival; we know it as soon as the frame arrives on a given sector (that represents a good-enough approximate direction).

6 MBA-DbMAC Functionality Testing

We performed functionality checks of uni-packet transmission (UPT) and broadcasting, and they all worked perfectly as expected. In this section, we show the tests on concurrent-packet transmission and concurrent-packet reception. Furthermore, we examine the time spent in transmit mode and in receive mode. Finally, we assess the performance of our protocol against that of IEEE 802.11b (omnidirectional antenna) and DbMAC (single-beam directional antenna). This performance is evaluated in terms of delay, throughput, and goodput. For these tests, we use the static star-topology scenario depicted in Fig. 8 where node 1 is the central node and all other nodes are peripheral. The default data packet generation rate is set to 5 packets/sec. However, we will increase (and specify) this rate occasionally for some of the tests. All the tests are conducted using OPNET/Riverbed Modeler 16.0. The channel capacity is 11 Mbps, and the default simulation time is 1800 s.

6.1 CPT-CPR Test

To test CPT-CPR, node 1 sends and receives unicast data packets from nodes 2, 3, 4, 5, 6, and 7. These nodes all start sending data packets to node 1 around the same time. For the CPT functionality, the results are as shown in Fig. 9.

The first sub-graph shows that a little over 5 packets per seconds are sent from node 1. This rate is actually the rate at application-layer level. However, in order

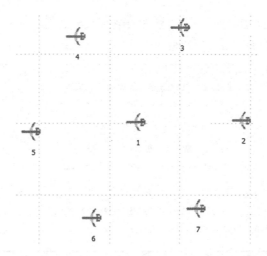

Fig. 8. MAC test scenario topology

to test CPT at MAC level, five copies are made for each application-layer packet (making it a total of 6 packets to be sent at MAC level, one for each sector). For each copy, a different destination address (corresponding to a different neighbor) is set, and the packet is sent via the sector that points to the intended neighbor. Therefore, the application-layer rate becomes the per-sector rate at the MAC level. We implemented this scheme this way because OPNET does not allow us to issue application-layer-level packets with different destination addresses. The remaining sub-graphs clearly show that all nodes, each lying on a different beam of node 1, receive 5 packets per second sent by node 1 on the concerned beam. This is the first step in showing the CPT functionality of MBA-DbMAC.

For the CPR functionality, we obtain the results shown in Fig. 10. The first sub-graph shows that about 35 packets per seconds are received by node 1. The remaining sub-graphs show that nodes 2, 3, 4, 5, 6, and 7 each send a little over 5 packets per second; thus the total of about 35^3 packets received by node 1. This is the first step in showing the CPR functionality of MBA-DbMAC.

6.2 Rx Mode vs Tx Mode

We measure the time spent in Rx and Tx mode in the situation of CPT/CPR. The traffic rate is still 5 packets per second. For a peripheral node, the time spent in Rx mode (18 s) and in Tx mode (18 s) is balanced since only one beam is involved. However, for the central node (node 1), we obtain that more time is spent in Rx mode (79 s) than in Tx mode (48 s). This imbalance can be explained by the fact that, with our current rate of packet generation (5 packets

---

[3] Each of the 6 senders sends a little over 5 pkts/sec, more like a little under 6 pkts/sec, therefore the total received at the common receiver is greater than 30 packets, but still less than 36 packets (as it would be if the senders' rate were exactly 6 pkts/sec).

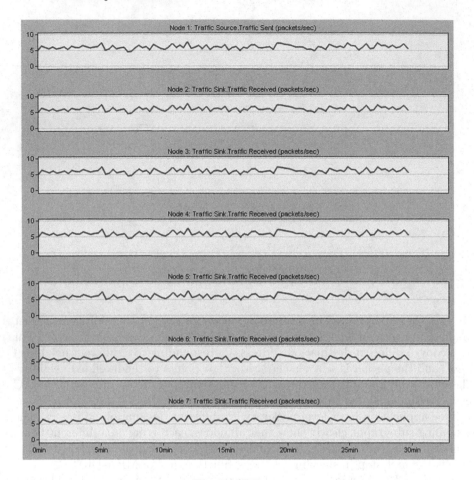

Fig. 9. CPT test

per second), there are more instances of the central node not having packets to transmit than there are instances of at least one of the six peripheral nodes not having packets to transmit (hence the central node not receiving).

One way to address/overcome this asymmetry is to increase data packet generation so that the output buffer of all the nodes is always full. For example, with a higher packet generation rate of 20 pkts/sec, we obtain a more symmetric result for the central node of 304 s spent in Rx mode and 298 s spent in Tx mode.

These time results are the final step in showing that we do, in fact, have CPR/CPT functionality. If the 6 peripheral nodes spend collectively 6 × 18 s to transmit, that is 108 s. But, as we saw earlier, the central receiver (node 1) spends only 78 s receiving. This means that some of the receptions need to happen in parallel; because, after all, all packets are received, as we saw in Fig. 10. This therefore shows the CPR functionality of MBA-DbMAC. Similarly, if the central node sent its packets sequentially (one beam at a time) it would behave as a

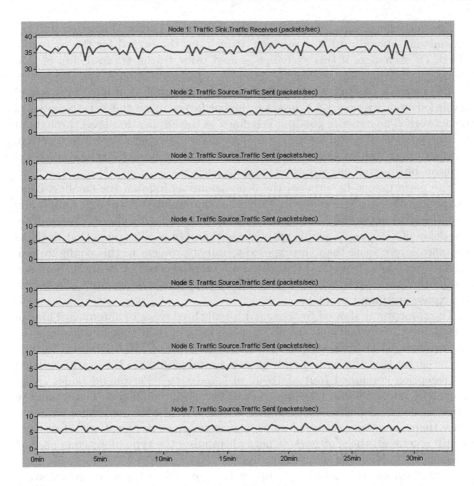

Fig. 10. CPR test

peripheral node (single beam used) in that regard; hence it would take a total of about $18 \times 6 = 108$ s to complete its transmissions. But, as seen earlier, it only takes 47 s, with no packet lost (Fig. 9); which means that some transmissions have been done in parallel. This therefore shows the CPT functionality of MBA-DbMAC.

6.3 Performance Comparison: Delay, Throughput, and Goodput

With the same star topology, we compare the MAC delay, throughput, and good-put when three types of antennas are used: MBAs, SBAs, and omnidirectional antennas. In any given scenario, all nodes are equipped with the same antenna type. MBAs work with the MBA-DbMAC protocol, SBAs work with the DbMAC protocol, and omnidirectional antennas work with the IEEE 802.11b DCF MAC protocol.

The delay here is measured from the time when a packet is inserted into the transmission queue until it is received. It includes the period for the successful RTS/CTS exchange, if this exchange is used prior to the transmission of that frame.

The network throughput is defined as the total number of bits (in bits/sec) forwarded from wireless LAN layers to higher layers in all the WLAN nodes of the network. The network goodput is defined as the application-level throughput (i.e. the number of useful information bits delivered by the network to a certain destination per unit of time). The amount of data considered excludes protocol overhead bits as well as retransmitted data packets.

The performance in terms of the delay comes as follows: the smallest delay is experienced with MBA antennas, 0.5 ms, compared to 3.5 ms for Omni, and 5.5 ms for SBA antennas. MBA antennas reduce the delay by about a factor of 10. The delay of SBA being significantly worse than Omni illustrates that deafness is a more severe issue than the exposed-terminal problem in this configuration. In effect, we know (from [11]) that SBAs are more affected by deafness than any of the other two types, whereas omnidirectional antennas are more affected by the exposed-terminal problem.

The throughput showed to be similar for all three types of antennas. This can be explained by the fact that the nodes spend most of their time in Idle mode (no transmission, no reception). For instance, in the case of MBA-DbMAC testing, we saw earlier that the central node spends a total of about 127 s in transmission and reception combined (out of 1800 s of simulation). Peripheral nodes spend about 36 s out of 1800 in transmission and reception combined. These times in active mode are expected to be higher in the case of SBA and omni antennas (since there is no concurrence of multiple transmissions or receptions). But since we still receive all the sent packets notwithstanding the type of antenna used, it makes sense to have the same throughput.

If we increase the packet generation rate to 105 pkt/sec, we now have a total network load of at least 105 pkt/sec × 1024 Bytes/pkt × 8 bits/Byte × 12 nodes[4] = 10.3 Mbps (recall that the channel capacity is set to 11 Mbps). Throughput-wise, we observed that SBA fails completely with this high packet rate, and that MBA has a lower throughput than Omni. However, MBA actually shows a higher goodput (actual data packets received at the peripheral nodes); even though, in the absolute, both types of antennas (and their corresponding MAC protocols) perform poorly with packet delivery ratios (goodput) of 40% and 50% respectively.

7   Summary

The proposed MBA-DbMAC protocol is a generic MAC protocol that has the basic functionalities of a MAC protocol and renders possible the basic operation of MBA-equipped nodes. MBA-DbMAC is an adaptation/extension of DbMAC

---

[4] 12 nodes = 6 peripheral nodes + 1 central node. However, the central node acts as 6 sources (each of its 6 sectors sends traffic to a neighbor) of traffic.

to the MBA environment. ESIF, HMAC, and MMAC-NB are all MAC protocols designed to work with MBAs. We used the design of these protocols as a starting point in the identification of MBA-specific issues inherent to MAC design. We have adopted some ideas from these protocols, but we are also proposing different, innovative, and fairly simple solutions to some MBA-specific issues. For instance, for the design of the MBA-DbMAC protocol, we adopt a two-tier processing approach whereby the MAC layer is split into two artificial sub-layers: the controller sub-layer (materialized by one node-wide parent process) and the sector sub-layer (materialized by N child processes, 1 child process for each of the N sectors). The sector sub-layer implements traditional MAC-layer mechanisms while the controller sub-layer manages: (a) the neighbor table, (b) the assignment of a high-layer packet to the appropriate sector, and (c) the switch from/to the different operation modes (Tx mode, Idle mode, and Rx mode). This two-tier design approach is an elegant way of enforcing mode switches in the node while still leaving the full autonomy of medium access to sectors in their respective direction of competence. Other novel aspects of our solution are the decoupled-broadcasting or diversity-casting and the time window policy that we adopt in order to avoid Critical Chain Transmission and Critical Chain Reception. In the end, our goal was to have a functional MBA-specific MAC protocol.

References

1. Abdullah, A.A., Cai, L., Gebali, F.: DSDMAC: dual sensing directional MAC protocol for ad hoc networks with directional antennas. IEEE Trans. Veh. Technol. **61**(3), 1266–1275 (2012). https://doi.org/10.1109/TVT.2012.2187082
2. Abolhasan, M., Lipman, J., Ni, W., Hagelstein, B.: Software-defined wireless networking: centralized, distributed, or hybrid? IEEE Netw. **29**(4), 32–38 (2015). https://doi.org/10.1109/MNET.2015.7166188
3. Acampora, A.S., Shah, S.I.A.: Multihop lightwave networks: a comparison of store-and-forward and hot-potato routing. IEEE Trans. Commun. **40**(6), 1082–1090 (1992). https://doi.org/10.1109/26.142798
4. Jain, V., Gupta, A., Agrawal, D.P.: On-demand medium access in multihop wireless networks with multiple beam smart antennas. IEEE Trans. Parallel Distrib. Syst. **19**(4), 489–502 (2008). https://doi.org/10.1109/TPDS.2007.70739
5. Jain, V., Gupta, A., Lal, D., Agrawal, D.P.: A cross layer MAC with explicit synchronization through intelligent feedback for multiple beam antennas. In: GLOBE-COM 2005. IEEE Global Telecommunications Conference, vol. 6, pp. 3196–3200, November 2005. https://doi.org/10.1109/GLOCOM.2005.1578365
6. Jain, V., Gupta, A., Lal, D., Agrawal, D.P.: IEEE 802.11 DCF based MAC protocols for multiple beam antennas and their limitations. In: IEEE International Conference on Mobile Adhoc and Sensor Systems Conference, pp. 8–474, November 2005. https://doi.org/10.1109/MAHSS.2005.1542833
7. Jayasuriya, A., Perreau, S., Dadej, A., Gordon, S.: Hidden vs. exposed terminal problem in ad hoc networks. In: Proceedings of the Australian Telecommunication Networks and Applications Conference (2004)

8. Kolar, V., Tilak, S., Abu-Ghazaleh, N.B.: Avoiding head of line blocking in directional antenna MAC protocol. In: 29th Annual IEEE International Conference on Local Computer Networks, pp. 385–392, November 2004. https://doi.org/10.1109/LCN.2004.30

9. Luo, G., Jia, S., Liu, Z., Zhu, K., Zhang, L.: sdnMAC: a software defined networking based MAC protocol in VANETs. In: 2016 IEEE/ACM 24th International Symposium on Quality of Service (IWQoS), pp. 1–2, June 2016. https://doi.org/10.1109/IWQoS.2016.7590403

10. Luo, Q., Wang, J., Liu, S.: AeroMRP: a multipath reliable transport protocol for aeronautical ad hoc networks. IEEE Internet Things J. 6(2), 3399–3410 (2019). https://doi.org/10.1109/JIOT.2018.2883736

11. Medjo Me Biomo, J.D., Kunz, T., St-Hilaire, M.: Exploiting multi-beam antennas for end-to-end delay reduction in ad hoc networks. Mob. Netw. Appl. 23(5), 1293–1305 (2018). https://doi.org/10.1007/s11036-018-1037-8

12. Subramanian, A.P., Das, S.R.: Addressing deafness and hidden terminal problem in directional antenna based wireless multi-hop networks. Wireless Netw. 16(6), 1557–1567 (2010). https://doi.org/10.1007/s11276-008-0138-x

Blockchain-Aided Access Control for Secure Communications in Ad Hoc Networks

Mingming Wu[✉], Yulan Gao, and Yue Xiao

National Key Laboratory of Science and Technology on Communications,
University of Electronic Science and Technology of China, Chengdu 611731, China
mingmingwuuestc@163.com, yulanggaomath@163.com, xiaoyue@uestc.edu.cn

Abstract. A novel blockchain technology aided peer-to-peer connection (P2P)-based access control protocol is proposed for the distributed ad hoc networks. More specifically, the access process conceived can improve the security performance as an explicit advantage of blockchain technology, which is capable of preventing from the security threatens, e.g., being eavesdropped, being tampered, and malicious access imposed by the lack of the authentication center and the nature of the multi-hop routing. Meanwhile, a reasonable punishment mechanism is integrated into the access protocol that reinforces punishment upon the increase of dishonest or malicious node behaviors and hence, is particularly beneficial for the robustness of the long-term systems. Furthermore, a low-complexity match scheme based on competition access (MCA) is utilized for designing the appropriate multi-hop routings, which considers the min-max delay optimization objective. Numerical results demonstrate that the blockchain-aided access control protocol achieves the lower delay in comparison to the conventional first come, first serve access scheme, random access scheme, and the single-hop access scheme, while improving the security performance of access process in ad hoc networks.

Keywords: Ad hoc networks · Blockchain · Access control · Secure communications

1 Introduction

With thebibliography proliferation of the mobile terminals and the required data [1], ad hoc networks based on peer-to-peer connection and supporting the dynamic topology and self-organization characteristics has attracted extensive research interests in military communications and the industry fields [2]. This is because ad hoc network as an infrastructureless network architecture can improve the robustness and transmission performance without increasing the burden of the base station or other central controllers. More specifically, ad hoc networks can be an independent network architecture, applied to the distributed system [3,4], e.g., wireless sensor network (WSN), vehicular ad hoc

© ICST Institute for Computer Sciences, Social Informatics and Telecommunications Engineering 2019
Published by Springer Nature Switzerland AG 2019. All Rights Reserved
J. Zheng et al. (Eds.): ADHOCNETS 2019, LNICST 306, pp. 87–98, 2019.
https://doi.org/10.1007/978-3-030-37262-0_7

network (VANET), and emergency communications. On the other hand, ad hoc networks can also assist the centralized network [5,6], e.g., the D2D-assisted cellular mobile network, internet of things (IoT), to expand the coverage area, offload the network loads, and improve the performance of devices on the edge of networks. However, in addition to the mentioned advantages, ad hoc networks easily suffer from hostile attacks, e.g., being eavesdropped, being tampered, and malicious access due to the lack of the authentication center and the nature of the multi-hop routing.

To deal with such security risks, it is beneficial to employ effective distributed access control protocols in ad hoc networks [7]. Recently, blockchain as a novel decentralized protocol has gained substantial attention due to its high security performance, owing to the integration of the advanced storage structure, encryption algorithms, and consensus mechanisms [8]. More specifically, blockchain constructs a distributed database shared among nodes that includes data into transactions, stores transactions into blocks, and connects blocks in the form of a chain. Moreover, asymmetric encryption algorithms guarantee the integrity and confidentiality of transactions, and the related consensus mechanisms e.g., proof of work (PoW) and proof of stake (PoS), prevent information recorded in blocks from being tampered. However, the high security performance of blockchain is achieved at the cost of a high delay and a high computation complexity imposed by generating and verifying blocks, which can be tolerated in the field of digital currency but may become particularly challenging in certain communication scenarios, requiring low delays or having limited computation resources. Following this line, [9] proposed a novel blockchain structure called 'Prism', for reducing the delay to the communicable level by deconstructing the entire process into different sub-modules.

Motivated by both the benefits and limitations of ad hoc networks and blockchain technologies, in this paper, we conceive a blockchain-aided access control protocol for ad hoc networks, which is capable of improving the security performance with a tolerable delay level. More specifically, access requests containing the embedded state information are stored in blocks, which allows us to compare the request contracts with the executive results, thereby, punishing the dishonest or malicious node behaviors, with the aid of a reasonable punishment mechanism. Meanwhile, the PoS consensus mechanism is invoked for the balance between the security and delay, with the optimization of the number of alternative relays and verified blocks. Furthermore, a match scheme based on competition access (MCA) is proposed for the design of multi-hop routings, which attains appreciable system delay performance at a low complexity.

The remainder of this paper is organized as follows. In Sect. 2, we detail the system model, which includes the introductions of relay forwarding process and the descriptions of blockchain-aided access control structure. In Sect. 3, the access control problem is formulated into an integer programming model, which considers min-max system delay as the optimization objective. A low-complexity match scheme is proposed for designing multi-hop routings in Sect. 4. Section 5 shows numerical results, which validates the effectiveness and superiority of the proposed scheme. Finally, we conclude in Sect. 6.

2 System Model

Considering an ad hoc network scenario, where several wireless terminals have the requirement of data transmission, denoted as the set of source nodes $S = \{s_1, s_2, \ldots, s_N\}$ and let $D = \{d_1, d_2, \ldots, d_N\}$ as the set of the corresponding destination nodes. We assume that the communication link between nodes is based on P2P connections without the aid of the base station or any access points. Thus, when the source nodes are far away from the destination nodes, the multi-hop transmission mode needs to be employed, and the potential relay nodes set is defined as $R = \{r_1, r_2, \ldots, r_M\}$. To avoid the mutual interference, we assume that different nodes occupy independent bandwidth and the relay forward mode is amplify-and-forward (AF).

2.1 Relay Forwarding

Under the assumption of a multi-hop transmission scenario, we further consider that the connections between source nodes and relay nodes are one-to-one, i.e., each source node only chooses one relay node to forward data at the same time, while a destination node can receive different messages from multiple relay nodes. For simplicity, consider two-hop transmission as the typical example of the multi-hop transmission. The relay rate of two-hop transmission can be expressed as

$$R_{ij} = 0.5B \log(1 + SNR_{ij}), \forall s_i \in S, r_j \in R, d_{\tilde{i}} \in D, \tag{1}$$

where we have

$$SNR_{ij} = \frac{p_i^s p_j^r h_{ij} h_{j\tilde{i}}}{N_0(p_i^s h_{ij} + p_j^r h_{j\tilde{i}} + N_0)}, \tag{2}$$

where p_i^s, p_j^r are the transmit power of the source nodes and the forward power of the relay nodes, respectively, $h_{ij}, h_{j\tilde{i}}$ represent the channel coefficients between the source nodes and the relay nodes, and the relay nodes and the destination nodes respectively, N_0 is the power of the background noise, B is the channel bandwidth. Note that, coefficient 0.5 is attributed to the effect of the two-hop transmission.

The rate of the single-hop transmission is given by

$$R_{i\tilde{i}} = B \log(1 + \frac{p_i^s h_{i\tilde{i}}}{N_0}), \forall s_i \in S, d_{\tilde{i}} \in D, \tag{3}$$

where $h_{i\tilde{i}}$ is the channel coefficient between the source nodes and the relay nodes. When sending a data package whose size is Q, the transmission delay can be derived by

$$T_i^{\text{trans}} = \sum_{j=\tilde{i},1}^{M} x_{ij} \frac{Q_i}{R_{ij}}, \tag{4}$$

subject to

$$\sum_{j=\tilde{i},1}^{M} x_{ij} = 1, \sum_{i=1}^{N} x_{ij} = 1, \tag{5}$$

$$x_{ij} \in \{0,1\}, \forall s_i \in S, r_j \in R, d_{\tilde{i}} \in D,$$

where x_{ij} represents the factor of transmission mode selection and relay node allocation, defined as

$$x_{ij} = \begin{cases} 1, \text{if } s_i \text{ choose } r_j \text{ or single-hop}(j = \tilde{i}) \\ 0, \text{otherwise} \end{cases} \tag{6}$$

In addition to the transmission delay, another kind of delay is the process delay, defined as the delay of processing access requests for the destination node. Because the size of access requests is small, the difference of the transmitting access delays between various nodes can be ignored, thus, the process delay is given by

$$T_i^{\text{proc}} = (t_{\text{Tr}} + t_{\text{Proc}})N_i^{\text{relay}}, \forall s_i \in S, \tag{7}$$

where the constant $t_{\text{Tr}} + t_{\text{Proc}}$ represents the sum of the transmission delay and the process delay of each access request, N_i^{relay} is the number of alternative relay nodes for s_i, ranging from 1 to $M + 1$ (include the single-hop mode). Although the relay node with the best channel condition may be found, when $d_{\tilde{i}}$ receives the access signals from all the relay nodes, the process delay will increase upon the increase of N_i^{relay}.

Due to the randomness of the channel and the mobility of nodes, the system state is not stationary. Thus, the source nodes need to choose and update the transmission modes and relay nodes dynamically, according to the self-demands and system states.

2.2   Blockchain-Aided Access Control

Ad hoc networks without the authentication center are inclined to secure risks, e.g., being eavesdropped, being tampered and malicious access of unauthorized nodes. Thus, for the sake of security performance, effective distributed protocols are needed for secure communications in ad hoc networks. Blockchain as a novel P2P-based decentralized protocol that integrates the specialized storage structure, advanced encryption algorithms and consensus mechanisms, can guarantee reliable, secure information transmissions and records in a distributed network. However, high delay imposed by generating and verifying blocks restricts the applications of blockchain technology in practical communications.

To weaken the influence of blockchain technology on the communication delay, only the part of the access request contracts and the executive results are included into blocks, excluding the transmission data Q out of blocks considering the timeliness of data. A transaction consists of the node states (location,

Fig. 1. The general structure of a transaction in the blockchain.

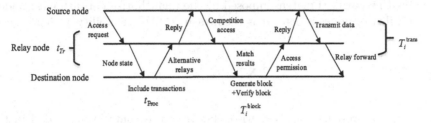

Fig. 2. The general process of the blockchain-aided access control.

achievable rate, power..), the results of multi-hop routings, etc., and its general structure is as shown in Fig. 1.

Such reduction of transaction data contributes to the decrease of the delay and the required storage resources. Moreover, another kind of delay imposed by generating and verifying blocks can be given by

$$T_i^{\text{block}} = t_{\text{generate}} N_i^{\text{verify}}, \forall s_i \in S, \tag{8}$$

where t_{generate} represents the delay of generating a block, N_i^{verify} is the required number of the verified block. To guarantee the security of the storage information in the blockchain, the delay of verifying blocks T_i^{block} needs to be waited before forwarding data Q_i and more verified blocks lead to the higher security but the higher delay. Thus, the size of N_i^{verify} is a key parameter to balance the security and the delay in the blockchain-aided ad hoc networks.

The process of the blockchain-aided secure access control is described as Fig. 2. Firstly, the source nodes transmit the access requests with state information. Next, the relay nodes that receive request signals decide whether to provide relay services and forward the signals to the destination nodes attached with itself information (power, location, trajectory, etc.). Then, the destination node $d_{\bar{i}}$ chooses N_i^{relay} alternative nodes and founds an appropriate routing path for the corresponding source node, according to the proposed match scheme. Afterwards, the match results as a part of transactions are included into blocks and are broadcasted to the whole network. Finally, after the delay of verifying blocks, the source nodes set up the single-hop or multi-hop routing path with the destination nodes according to the match results and start to forward data.

3   Problem Formulation

Considering the mobility of nodes and the randomness of the channel, the performance of the long-term dynamic system is investigated by introducing the definition of frame. A frame τ of s_i is from the beginning of sending access requests to the ending of the $Q_i[\tau]$ data transmission, the length of frame is given by

$$T_i[\tau] = T_i^{\text{trans}} + T_i^{\text{proc}} + T_i^{\text{block}}, \forall s_i \in S. \tag{9}$$

To deal with security threatens imposed by the unauthorized or dishonest nodes, the credibility of nodes is defined as the measure of the reliability, which is given by

$$c_j = \frac{1}{r} \sum_{\tau=1}^{r} w_j[\tau], \forall r_j \in R, \tag{10}$$

where $w_j[\tau]$ represents the comparison between the contracts recorded in the block and the executive results, which are both recorded in the blockchain and can not be modified. Thus, the destination nodes can verify the consistency of the provided request contracts and the real results, such as rate, power, etc., $w_j[\tau]$ is defined by

$$w_j[\tau] = \begin{cases} 1, \text{if contracts match executive results} \\ 0, \text{otherwise}, \forall r_j \in R \end{cases} \tag{11}$$

Based on the credibility of nodes, the punishment mechanism for the dishonest or malicious behaviours is represented by

$$\tilde{p}_j^r[\tau] = c_j p_j^r[\tau], \forall r_j \in R, \tag{12}$$

where $\tilde{p}_j^r[\tau]$ is the destination nodes estimation of r_j power, i.e., if the dishonest nodes break the contract time after time, it will lose the competitiveness of relay access services due to the decrease of relay rate in (1), thereby, the security of the long-term system can be enhanced further.

The system utility function is given by

$$\min_{x_{ij}[\tau]} \max \ \{T_i[\tau], \forall s_i \in S\}, \tag{13.a}$$

$$s.t. \sum_{j=\tilde{i},1}^{M} x_{ij}[\tau] = 1, \sum_{i=1}^{N} x_{ij}[\tau] = 1, \tag{13.b} \tag{13}$$

$$x_{ij}[\tau] \in \{0,1\}, \forall s_i \in S, r_j \in \tilde{R}_i, d_{\tilde{i}} \in D. \tag{13.c}$$

Such optimization model is an integer programming problem, where $\tilde{R}_i$ is a subset of R, whose element includes the N_i^{relay} alternative relay nodes for the source node s_i. The constraints guarantee the one-on-one match between the source nodes and relay nodes.

4 Proposed Algorithm

The above integer programming is an NP-hard problem with complexity $O(M!)$. On the other hand, the optimization model can be considered as a node matching problem and the match priority function is defined as $T_i[\tau]$, i.e., the nodes with the lower delay have the higher priority. To simplify the notation, the singhop mode is seen as the special relay node, whose node number is denoted as 0. Thereby, the priority list of the source node s_i consists of $N_i^{\text{relay}} + 1$ node number, the elements of which are arranged from high to low priority. Assuming all of the source nodes have the same number of alternative relay nodes $N_i^{\text{relay}} = N_{\text{relay}}, \forall s_i \in S$, and the $N \times (N_{\text{relay}} + 1)$ priority matrix is consisted of the preference profile of each source node.

After converting the integer programming into the node matching problem, the problem is not still solved due to the required central structure and the $O(M!)$ complexity when implementing the optimal match algorithm. To solve the above problem in a distributed ad hoc network and at a lower complexity, a suboptimal match algorithm based on competition access (MCA) is proposed. Its main idea is that the source nodes choose the preferred node number according to the priority firstly, which will lead to node collision, when different source nodes choose the same relay node. Then, to avoid the collisions, the relay nodes employ the competition access scheme, where the relay node choose to forward data of the source node having the higher delay based on the consideration of the min -max system utility function. In priority matrix operations, that is, corresponding row of the source node having lower delay rotates left. The details of the MCA algorithm is shown in Algorithm 1.

Note that, MCA does not require the global information, thus, it can be applied to the distributed systems. Moreover, because the node collision will not happen when the different source nodes choose the same number of the node 0 (the single-hop mode), the complexity of the MCA is controlled in $O(N_{\text{relay}} N^2)$. With the number of alternative relay nodes increases, the probability of node collision decreases, thereby the performance of the proposed algorithm can be improved further.

5 Numerical Results

To investigate the performance of the proposed blockchain enabled structure in ad hoc networks, we simulate the system utility value under different parameter settings. And to verify the validity and the advantages of the proposed scheme, the MCA algorithm is compared with the other three schemes: the traditional access scheme (TA), the random access scheme (RA), the only single-hop scheme (SH). More specifically, the TA scheme adopts the rule of first come, first serve, that is, the source node with the higher instantaneous rate can obtain the prior access to the required relay node. And the SH scheme ignores the block delay T_i^{block} due to that the lack of information interactions can avoid certain security threats.

Algorithm 1. The proposed match algorithm based on competition access

---

Input:
  T_i, N_{relay}, N
Output:
  the match results x_{ij}
  for each source node s_i **do**
    Choose N_{relay} relay nodes and sort the priority according to T_i;
  end for
  Construct the priority matrix, the first column as the initial match results;
  for $t = 1;\ t < N_{\text{relay}}; t + +$ **do**
    for $i = 1;\ t < N; i + +$ **do**
      Compare with other node selection;
      if $x_{ij} == x_{i'j} \&\& j \neq 0$ **then**
        node collision happens, then
        if $T_i > T_{i'}$ **then**
          Rotate left the row corresponding to i;
        else
          Rotate left the row corresponding to i';
        end if
      end if
    end for
  end for
  return the first column as the final match results.

In the simulation environment setting, the node mobile model adopts Gaussian-Markov Mobile Model (GMMM) [10], with log-normal shadowing and Rayleigh fading. Without loss of generality, all of the source nodes have the same number of the alternative relay nodes, the required verified blocks and the transmit power, denoted as $N_i^{\text{relay}} = N_{\text{relay}}, N_i^{\text{verify}} = N_{\text{verify}}, p_i^s = P_{\text{max}}^s, \forall s_i \in S$, and all of the relay nodes have the same maximum transmit power P_{max}^r. If not specifically indicated, other parameter settings are as follows: the carrier frequency $f_0 = 2.3\,\text{GHz}$, $B = 0.18\,\text{MHz}$, $P_{\text{max}}^s = 23\,\text{dBm}$, the data size of each frame $Q_i[\tau]$ is subjected to poisson distribution with the mean 1000 kbps, the power spectral density of background noise N_0 is $-174\,\text{dBm/Hz}$, $t_{\text{Tr}} + t_{\text{Proc}} = 0.01\,\text{s}$, $t_{\text{generate}} = 0.5\,\text{s}$.

Figure 3 shows the combined influence of the number of alternative relay nodes and the required verified blocks on the performance of average system delay. It can be observed that as the number of alternative relay nodes N_{relay} increases, the average system delay firstly decreases and then increases slightly, which is attributed to that the smaller number of alternative relay nodes leads to the higher probability of node collision. Thereby, when the number of alternative relay nodes is lower than the number of source nodes ($N_{\text{relay}} < 5$), more source nodes will choose the single-hop mode based on MCA, which results in the higher average system delay. For the sake of the slight increase of the system delay, the increase of the process delay T_i^{proc} with N_{relay} can explain such trend. In addition, more verified blocks can improve the security but incur significant

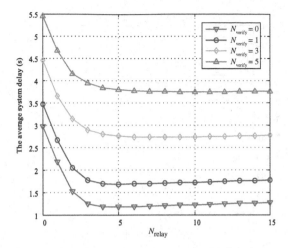

Fig. 3. The average system delay versus N_{relay} under different N_{verify}.

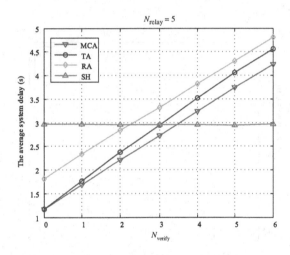

Fig. 4. The comparison of the average system delay of different schemes versus N_{verify}.

delay increase. The number of the verified blocks has important effects on the balance between the security and the delay due to the considerable block delay T_i^{block}, which needs further researches.

Figure 4 compares the delay performance of different schemes versus the number of verified blocks. In general, the SH scheme has the higher delay compared to other three schemes when N_{verify} is small. Then, with the N_{verify} continuing to increase, the delay performance of the SH exceeds other three schemes because of the lack of the block delay. However, it should be pointed out that the impact of block delay on the system delay will be weaken as the data size $Q_i[\tau]$ increases, which can be observed in the following simulations. Besides, the difference of the

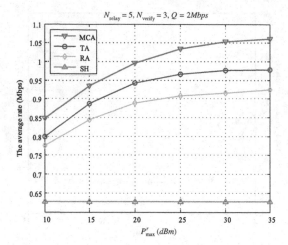

Fig. 5. The comparison of the rate performance of different schemes versus the maximum relay power.

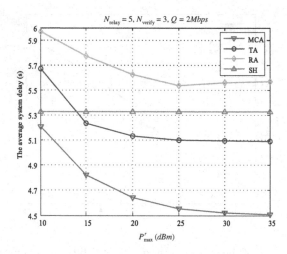

Fig. 6. The comparison of the delay performance of different schemes versus the maximum relay power.

delay between the MCA and the TA scheme gradually grows with the increasing N_{verify}. The reason is that the TA based on the access rule of first come, first serve, only considers the instantaneous rate and ignore the influence of dynamics introduced by the channel randomness, terminal mobility and the data fluctuation, etc., which can be included into the transactions in the MCA scheme. Thus, with the higher waiting time of the block delay, the performance of the TA deteriorates gradually, ultimately close to the RA scheme.

To investigate the rate performance and the delay performance of the different schemes versus the relay node power, the results are shown in Figs. 5 and 6, respectively. Note that, different from the $Q_i[\tau]$ setting in Figs. 3 and 4, the data size in Figs. 5 and 6 is double to show its weakening effect on the role of the block delay in the system delay. We can observe that the rate performance of the multi-hop scheme is superior to the SH scheme and the proposed MCA scheme has the best rate performance. In addition, the TA scheme has the better rate performance than the RA scheme. Although the SH has the worst rate performance, its system delay performance is better than the TA and the RA scheme when the relay power is lower or the data size is smaller, due to the lack of the block delay. Combined Fig. 4 with Fig. 6, it can be observed that with the higher relay power or larger data size, the role of block delay in the system delay is weaken gradually. Consequently, the delay performance of the TA scheme and the MCA scheme exceeds the SH scheme. In general, the proposed MCA scheme has better performance in both delay and rate compared with other schemes, particularly beneficial for larger data and higher relay power scenario.

6   Conclusions

For secure communications in ad hoc networks, we proposed a novel blockchain-aided access control protocol, which integrates the blockchain technology into the multi-hop access process. And the related punishment mechanism was introduced to prevent the access to the dishonest or malicious nodes. Meanwhile, the influences of the number of alternative nodes and the required verified blocks on the system performance were investigated to balance the security and the delay. Furthermore, a low-complexity match scheme based on competition access was proposed to design reasonable routing paths for different source nodes, which minimizes the maximum delay. Numerical results demonstrated that the proposed scheme has significant advantages in the delay performance compared to other conventional access schemes, while improving the security performance in ad hoc networks.

Acknowledgements. This work was supported in part by the National Science Foundation of China under Grant number 61671131, the Fundamental Research Funds for the Central Universities (No. ZYGX2018J092), and Sichuan Science and Technology Program (2018HH0138).

References

1. Chen, S., Zhao, J.: The requirements, challenges, and technologies for 5G of terrestrial mobile telecommunication. IEEE Commun. Mag. **52**(5), 36–43 (2014)
2. Royer, E.M., Toh, C.-K.: A review of current routing protocols for ad hoc mobile wireless networks. IEEE Pers. Commun. **6**(2), 46–55 (1999)
3. Akyildiz, I., Su, W., Sankarasubramaniam, Y., Cayirci, E.: Wireless sensor networks: a survey. Comput. Netw. **38**(4), 393–422 (2002)

4. Hartenstein, H., Laberteaux, L.P.: A tutorial survey on vehicular ad hoc networks. IEEE Commun. Mag. **46**(6), 164–171 (2008)
5. Akyildiz, I.F., Wang, X.: A survey on wireless mesh networks. IEEE Commun. Mag. **43**(9), S23–S30 (2005)
6. Borgia, E.: The internet of things vision: key features, applications and open issues. Comput. Commun. **54**, 1–31 (2014)
7. Zhou, L., Haas, Z.J.: Securing ad hoc networks. IEEE Netw. **13**(6), 24–30 (1999)
8. Christidis, K., Devetsikiotis, M.: Blockchains and smart contracts for the internet of things. IEEE Access **4**, 2292–2303 (2016)
9. Bagaria, V., Kannan, S., Tse, E.A.D.: Deconstructing the blockchain to approach physical limits (2018). https://arxiv.org/abs/1810.08092v1
10. Gao, Y., Xiao, Y., Wu, M., Xiao, M., Shao, J.: Dynamic social-aware peer selection for cooperative relay management with D2D communications. IEEE Trans. Commun. **67**(5), 3124–3139 (2019)

Investigating Mobility Robustness in 5G Networks Using User-Adaptive Handoff Strategies

Masoto Chiputa[1(✉)], Peter Han Joo Chong[1], Saeed Ur Rehman[1], and Arun Kumar[2]

[1] Department of Electrical and Electronic Engineering,
Auckland University of Technology, Auckland, New Zealand
{masoto.chiputa, peter.chong, saeed.rehman}@aut.ac.nz
[2] Department of Computer Science and Engineering, NIT, Rourkela, India
kumararun@nitrkl.ac.in

Abstract. Millimetre Wave (mmWaves) communication is a major capacity booster to the fifth generation (5G) mobile network. However, challenges of significant attenuation and high propagation losses lead to intermittent user connectivity. This limit mmWave applicability in the 5G mobile network. The dual connectivity (DC) architecture with its split control and data plane functionality has proven to be more effective. The DC model uses the less attenuated Long Term evolution (LTE) bands to coordinate mmWave cells while they provide on demand high capacity rates. This guarantees prolonged network association for mmWave links with minimal to no signalling cost at high user data rates. Minimizing signalling cost in LTE bands considering their scarcity is vital too. To that effect, intelligent Handoff (HO) strategies that prolong mmWave link association using minimal signalling cost are vital for a robust DC system. This paper investigates the performances of adaptive HO strategies given a highway multiuser-type mobility scenario on DC systems. Results show that adaptive HO solutions enhance link reliability in mmWaves with minimal signalling cost.

Keywords: 5G · Millimeter wave · Performance evaluation · Dual Connectivity · 3GPP · NR · Adaptive handoffs

1 Introduction

The next generation of cellular networks will need to use macro frequency diversity solutions to overcome the current resource scarcity and meet new capacity demands [1]. Macro frequency diversity allows usage of multiple frequencies with varying propagation capabilities to reduce the effects of user data distortions in wireless transmission [2]. In 5G, the macro frequency diversity is used to mitigate data distortions and boost capacities for mobile network. This is particularly, due to poor propagation characteristics of mmWaves and the scarcity of idle bands in lower frequencies currently deployed for cellular network communication [3].

© ICST Institute for Computer Sciences, Social Informatics and Telecommunications Engineering 2019
Published by Springer Nature Switzerland AG 2019. All Rights Reserved
J. Zheng et al. (Eds.): ADHOCNETS 2019, LNICST 306, pp. 99–112, 2019.
https://doi.org/10.1007/978-3-030-37262-0_8

The Dual Connectivity (DC) model is one example of a macro frequency diversity solution. It has thus far been adopted by 3rd Generation Partnership Project (3GPP) as a 5G mobile network model where it is technically as New Radio (NR) [1] and [5]. Its goal is to provide continuous service guarantees to mmWave mobile network users. The DC system allows non-co-located deployment of PHY and MAC layer of LTE and mmWave networks and a system level 3GPP LTE protocol stack integration [2, 3, 7] for NR1. This NR1 model paves a clean slate to addressing mmWave propagation challenges. Technically, in NR1 also known as 5G, the lower frequencies, such as the Long Term Evolution (LTE) bands, provide oversight links for mmWave link recovery and cell co-ordination. The mmWave links provide on-demand multi-gigabit user rates. To that effect, it is believed that NR will use multi-connectivity solutions with a sub-6 GHz radio overlay for coverage, possibly based on Long Term Evolution (LTE) thanks to a tight internetworking [6], and mmWave links for capacity.

To optimize performance in NR1, longevity of user association to mmWave eNBs overlaid by LTE eNBs as shown by Fig. 1 is vital [3]. The prolonged association reduces HO signalling costs and improves the effective data rates. Thus, intelligent HO strategies are needed to (1) facilitate both intra and inter frequency user data flow without any distortion, (2) minimize resource usage in LTE cells given the scarcity and Low data rates of in lower frequencies plus the additional functionality of LTE bands to provide both fall back [2] and control-plane links [2, 3, 10].

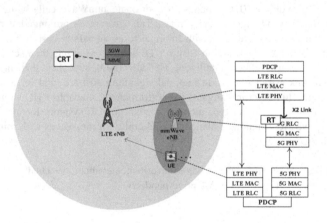

Fig. 1. LTE-mmWave 5G tight integration architecture.

This paper investigates mobility robustness optimization in NR1 given a multi-user mobility perspective in a highway mobility scenario. The objective of mobility robustness is to dynamically improve the network performance using adaptive HO strategies. Ultimately, this enhances Quality of Experience (QoE) for the users and as well as increases the network capacity [9]. This is basically done by automatically adapting appropriate cell parameters to adjust thresholds based on feedback of performance indicators. Thus, we adopt and analyse performance of various adaptive HO strategies from a multi-user type perspective on a highway scenario.

Given the lack of a real end-to-end DC system for system-level analysis in NR1, we use the LTE-mmWave DC module in the ns-3 simulator described in [2] and [3]. The DC framework in ns-3 allows designing network procedures faster than standard standalone hard handover (HH) to improve the mobility management [3]. Besides, it uses a 3GPP antenna array model for mmWave links [1]. This gives it a more practical two-dimensional directional antenna pattern at PHY and MAC layer in mmWaves. Unlike in "flat top" antenna model [1], the main-lobe gain and side-lobe gain of mmWave channels vary with signal changes in the receiving angles.

The principle operations of the ns-3 DC module involves mmWave users directionally broadcasting beaconing messages known as sounding reference signals (SRSs) in time-varying angular spaces. Each potential mmWave eNB in response scans all its angular directions, as it monitors the strength of the received SRSs. It then records the wideband SINR values in the Report Table (RT). The SINR estimates are thereafter transmitted via X2 links to LTE eNB to build a Complete RT (CRT) in the mobile management entity (MME). This data is later used to coordinate mmWave Cells in HO procedures. Figure 1 give a glimpse of the DC module in ns-3, detailed operations can be found in [2, 3] and [10].

2   Related Research

Mobility robustness in the 5G wireless communication is vital to mitigate channel instabilities due to poor propagation characteristics exhibited by mmWaves. For example, the Doppler spread at 60 km/h for 60 GHz band is over 3 kHz [4]. Thus, the mmWave channel changes in orders of hundreds of microseconds faster than today's cellular systems within a small time. Tracking mmWave signal at this rate is a challenge. Moreover, mmWaves are easily blocked by brick, mortar, or even by the human bodies [1]. This makes the quality of the mmWave SINR to exhibit high variability with variations in the order of 30 dB for transitions between Line of Sight (LOS) and Non-Line of Sight (NLOS) [6]. Therefore, mmWave Channel links can turn from being excellent to being unusable within milliseconds

Reducing SINR prediction inconsistences is vital to eliminate short network association and wasteful HOs for mobile users. This will enhance not only link reliability but also reduce signaling. In [2] and [4] where the DC model is used, for example, raw SINR values from SRS are filtered to produce time-averaged SINR trace for HO decisions. Additionally, a much higher averaged SINR threshold value is used to avoid unnecessary HOs and beam switch due to SINR fluctuations. The main objective is to eliminate short-term parameter variation from instigating long HO and beam switching processes. Thus, by time averaging raw SINR values and setting higher threshold values DC systems automatically adjust and adapt practical thresholds that will improve performance.

Additionally, proposed HO strategies show that efficient adjustment of the Time-to-Trigger (TTT) intervals [3], channel and RT updates can enhance effective data rates. In fact, more advanced adaptive strategies HO combining most of the alluded strategies above show significantly prolonged network association and high effective data rate [1, 9]. Given outage is environmentally specific in mmWaves [4], if more network link assessment and mobility support strategies are designed in an intelligent way, robust and efficient network performance can be attained. To that effect, other 5G studies have reinverted interference coordination schemes in 4G, e.g. Almost Blank Sub frames (ABS) to mitigate Radio Link Failure (RLF) and Handover Failure (HOF) occurrence rates [8]. They take advantage of the flexible nature of DC systems by focusing only on mmWave systems. Thus adjust range for non-line of sight (NLOS) and Line of sight (LOS) scenarios. Also, others have integrated DC with of CoMP strategies [10]. They employ prediction algorithms based on user mobility context awareness to predict channel state, or the volume of signaling exchange before reinforcing mobility robustness mechanisms.

Low mobility users are the main interest in most of the works above. Additionally, the focus is on improving load balancing, spectral and energy efficiencies on mmWave cells. Thus, the majority of these works neglect the impact of DC models on LTE cells responsible for coordinating mmWave cells and providing links for fall back and higher-speed users. Thus, a multi-user type mobility analysis is vital because user diversity will stretch both LTE and mmWave networks resource. Ultimately, results obtained from a multi user type gives a truer performance of 5G DC systems.

3   System Model

3.1   Network Model

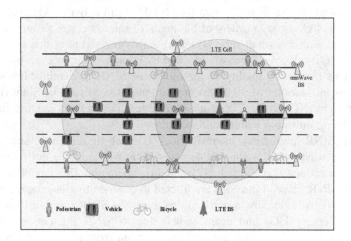

Fig. 2. LTE-5G general user mobility model.

In our scenario, the DC model is assumed and utilized strategically. This is to say, different user type initially connect to which ever cell has the highest Signal to Interference plus Noise Ratio (SINR), before simultaneously connecting to either overlaid LTE-cells or under laid mmWave small cell based on the adaptive HO as explained in Sect. 3.3. LTE operates at 2 GHz while all mmWave cells operate at

28 GHz and connect to LTE's macro cells via the X2 link as illustrated in Fig. 1 based on the NYU and University of Padova DC implementation model [3]. Three LTE eNBs are deployed in the middle of the road stretching over a total length of 1500 m. The coverage radius of the LTE eNB is 250 m and the distance between two LTE eNBs is 500 m. Initially, 20 mmWave primary cells operating at 28 GHz with DC connection are placed over the road as shown in Fig. 2. The source code of the LTE-mmWave DC framework is publicly available in [2] with the ns-3 script (source: mc-example-udp.cc) and is thus used for the simulation scenario here. It features the implementation of the 3GPP channel model for frequencies above 6 GHz and a 3GPP-like cellular protocol stack.

3.2 User Mobility Model

In Users are uniformly distributed and initially associated with the cell providing the highest SINR, that is LTE or mmWave cell. This enables faster initial user access in DC [3]. Three types of users are assumed defined based on their speeds, these include; cars, cyclers and pedestrians. Cars move in four lanes with a length of 1.5 km and each having a width of 3 m. Cycler's paths stretch a width of 1 m from the outermost lanes of the cars on each side of the highway while pedestrians randomly move and change directions on the edges of the cycler's paths also on both sides of the highway. Pedestrian paths have each a width of 1 m. When pedestrians hit the edges of the highway, they bounce back in opposite directions. One third of the total users are pedestrian moving at 3 km/h. They are randomly placed in both walking paths. Another one third are cyclers moving constantly at 10 km/h. The other one third are cars equally distributed in each of the 4 lanes and initially interspaced equally over the length of the highway. They move at a fixed speed 50 km/h. Our assumption on cars is that those in the same lane i.e., in a busy highway are likely to move at similar velocities to avoid crushes. Hence, in each lane, cars' speeds and interspaces are assumed fixed to avoid crushes. The multi-user type mobility model unlike single user type mobility models in [2] and [3], can simultaneously test both LTE and mmWave transmission resources. This is so, given the fact that high speed users in will mostly likely use LTE links due to the band's low Doppler spread. Hence will leave the preferred mmWave links to low speed users despite the higher data rates. This indirectly balances load. Further it gives a fairer assessment of how far the DC network can support users given various adaptive HO strategies. A snap shot of the view of the multi-user type mobility model is as shown in Fig. 2.

3.3 Adaptive Handoff Strategies

The DC framework in ns-3 allows designing network procedures that are fast and dynamic, to improve mobility management in mmWave networks. Particularly in ns-3, it allows designing fast switching mechanisms between the LTE and primary mmWave cells via X2 links at access level as shown in Fig. 1. It further allows HO to Secondary Cells whereby the user does not need to resend SRS signals and incur additional delays before another HO so long as the TTT has not expired [2]. Thus, in our simulation, we investigate three adaptive event triggered fasting switching HO strategies in the DC model for NR1 based on distance, speed, and load, and are as follows:

A. (HO1) Load and SINR only Based HO: In this scenario [3], the, HO decision is based on the data rate, R, and key input information for the HO decision includes (i) instantaneous channel quality based on SINR, (ii) channel robustness based on rate, and (iii) cell occupancy or load [3]. Thus, the rate, R, experienced by the user connected to eNB$_m$ is approximated using the Shannon capacity [2]:

$$R(m) = \frac{W_{mmW}}{N_m} \log_2(1 + SINR(m)),$$ (1)

where N_m is the number of users that are currently being served by eNB$_m$ and W_{mmW} is the available total bandwidth. Unlike traditional procedures where users are not aware of the surrounding cells' current states, the user chooses to connect to a Cell providing the maximum rate, R, taking into account the load of the cell. It is a three phased HO process for DC and is as follows:

First Phase: involves uplink (UL) measurements at mmWave cells, user transmits SRSs to the surrounding mmWave Cells through different antennae directions. mmWave cells performs an exhaustive search to collect the SRSs using different angular directions. Thereafter, based on SRS value, they estimate mmWave cell SINR Once the RTs are filled with the SINR metrics, the second phase is invoked.

Second Phase: involve cell Coordination, at this stage, the mmWave Cell sends its RT to the LTE Cell, via the X2 link in Fig. 1. The overlaid LTE Cell builds a CRT by collecting all the received RTs. The LTE Cell makes HO decisions by selecting optimal mmWave Cell for each user to connect to given (1) before the third phase is evoked.

Third Phase: is decision time, at this stage the LTE Cell forwards the best decision for the transceiver. And the mmWave Cell is informed through the backhaul X2 link.

With respect to the existing algorithms in [2], the use of both the sub-6 GHz and the mmWave control planes in DC is a key functionality to the HO technique. Especially for highly unstable and scarcely dense scenarios, the LTE connectivity ensures a ready backup in case of a failure in mmWave links else will suffer an outage. Furthermore, the handover/beam switch decision is forwarded to the user through the macro Cell, whose legacy link is much more robust and less volatile than its mmWave counterpart, thereby removing possible points of radio link failure (RLF) in the control signaling path [2, 3, 10]. Detailed process is explained in [2] where intra (secondary) cell HO occur if TTT has not expired yet the channel state has changed. Summarily, Inter and intra frequency HO rely on the SINR and the load variation to trigger a handover within TTT. Further, for secondary HOs, they are only processed if the Target cell becomes 3 dB better than that of a serving cell, the HO is cancelled [3]. Secondary HOs are HO that happen between TTT intervals [2, 3, 10].

B. (HO2) Distance Based HO: The second HO algorithm is based HO1 but considers the effect of user distance relative to the target [6] and serving cell besides load and SINR variation in Phase 2 as shown in Fig. 3. The addition of distance is to avoid wasteful HO requests that may arise even when the user is still within the good transmission range of the serving cell. By factoring distance in process HO1, we minimize HO frequencies and prolong network association to one stable cell to enhance the effective rate.

The hypothesis is that if the user displacement relative to the serving eNB is closer than that of the target eNB. The network association with that target cell will be longer so long the correct prediction of a user's direction relative to the target eNB is made. While the initial rate, R, in (1) may be low, so long the SINR with a probability, P, is above a given threshold, the network association to that target cell is likely to be longer. Subsequently, the rate, R, in (1) is likely to improve considering the fact that the user will move closer to the target eNB for the next HO. Thus, we define SINR probability, P, according to dynamic, f_{TTT}, TTT equation in DC model for ns-3 simulator [3] such that:

$$P(SINR_s > t) = \frac{\Delta - \Delta_{min}}{\Delta_{max} - \Delta_{min}}, \tag{2}$$

where Δ is the instantaneous SINR, Δ_{min} is the minimum threshold SINR, t, and Δ_{max} is maximum given the maximum transmission power.

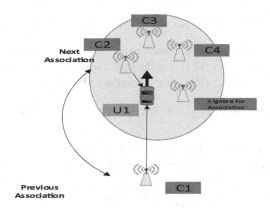

Fig. 3. DC mmWave-LTE-5G distance based HO mechanism.

The concept aims at mitigating radio link failure (RLF) rate and signaling cost due to frequent HOs. It prolongs TTT than in traditional cellular networks. The minimum HO displacement D_{min} is dynamic in our setup. It varies according to user's current displacement relative to the serving eNB at the point the SINR of serving cell falls below 3 dBm. Principally, the HO is evoked, if, within the TTT, the SINR (m) in (1) of another cell becomes 3 dB better than that of the serving mmWave cell and meets the minimum current HO distance at the time the channels update. The user maintains connectivity with serving cell if the serving cell, before the TTT expires, retains the highest SINR again, i.e., the HO process is canceled. Otherwise, the user maintains the HO process to the target cell if the D_{min} condition is met else user connects to the LTE cell before the next mmWave HO is initiate.

Two main direction of users are used (X, −X) representing North and South. eNBs determined to be in a similar direction of the user have at most a 60-degrees variation to serving eNB. This variation accounts for road way anomalies. Besides, users moving in a similar direction stay connected to the same BS longer than users moving in the opposite direction; hence, the eNB may have a stable load prediction in (1). To that effect, the user movement direction (or vector) is crucial when determining neighbors in target eNBs range.

To include the effect of distance on dynamic TTT, we define the Relative distance probability, $P_{TTT}(t)$, such that:

$$P_{TTT}(t) = P(SINR_s > t | D_{\Delta s} > D_{min}),$$ (3)

where $P_{TTT}(t)$ is the coverage approximation [9] given the target eNB distance, $D_{\Delta s}$, is greater than user distance D_{min} relative to serving the cell and the user SINR is greater than the threshold t. The measure of $P_{TTT}(t)$ expresses the network's reliability obtained by improving the reliability of the TTT for handoff timing. In other words, it represents the link reliability loss if the TTT is too unrealistic or short for the user HO, forcing users to engage in wasteful HOs. Thus, the dynamic time, $f_{TTT}(\Delta)$, to trigger HO is defined as

$$f_{TTT}(\Delta) = TTT_{max} - P_{TTT}(t)(TTT_{max} - TTT_{min}),$$ (4)

where the minimum SINR instantaneous Δ expected between the best target cell and of the current serving cell is met. TTT_{min} is the minimum of TTT to trigger HO. Thus, we use (4) instead of (5) used in (HO1) for secondary HOs [4]:

$$f_{TTT}(\Delta) = TTT_{max} - P(SINR_s > t)(TTT_{max} - TTT_{min}).$$ (5)

C. (HO3) User speed Based HO: In this HO, we use user speed and Mobility State Estimation (MSE) with its scaling factor ratio defined as sf_{MSE} [8] and [9];

$$sf_{MSE} = \frac{N_{cell-Change}}{T_{MSE}},$$ (6)

where $N_{Cell-change}$ is the number of HOs and reselections over a specified period of time, T_{MSE}. MSE give the option of scaling up the TTT and SINR Threshold values of a cell. If the user is moving so fast, the HOs can be triggered earlier to avoid RLF. Three MSE scales are used to categories speed; low, medium and high mobility. For high sf_{MSE}, the recommended $N_{cell-Change}$ is 10 and for medium, $N_{cell-Change}$ is 16 [12] over a period T_{MSE} for LTE links. According to 3GPP TS 36.331 [9], the values that high sf_{MSE} or medium sf_{MSE} can take are 0.25, 0.5, 0.75 or 1.0.

Given the DC model, a user connects to more than one band i.e., LTE uses lower carrier frequencies with high transmission range, and has low Doppler spread for high speed users [4]. In contrast, mmWaves have small coverage [4, 11] and high Doppler spread at high speed due to high carrier frequencies. So, even though the user speed on the ground is the same for both LTE eNB and mmWave eNB, for scaling mobility parameters; low, medium and high must be different for the eNBs. Practically, if (6) is used, the user will have crossed over multiple boundaries of the mmWave cells before crossing over the boundary of the overlaid LTE cells. Thus, given the DC network with a dense deployment of mmWave small cells, to allow more resolution in the mobility state estimation, a, second timer [8] is introduced to track mmWave's short-term speed variations. We assume $T_{MSE} = 5$ s to give corresponding mobility states for different cell-type of the network. Hence, the time, T_{HO}, taken to complete HO can be defined as [9]

$$T_{HO} = TTT + HO \ execution \ time(T). \tag{7}$$

The principle operation is done in Phase 3 of the HO1, where the LTE cell passes either the sf-High or sf-medium to the mmWave cell i.e. the factor by which the mmWave cell will scale the TTT and SINR threshold given the user speed. If it doesn't pass any sf value, it is regarded low. By doing passing MSE values, LTE trigger HOs earlier. For instance, if the user is fast moving and high $sf_{MSE} = 0.3$, if normal TTT value is 400 ms and hysteresis value is -2 dB, the new TTT value and the hysteresis will be multiplied by high sf_{MSE}. So, the new value TTT will be 120 ms and -0.6 dB hysteresis. Technically, the MSE procedure just correlates user-type speed defined with a scaling of mobility parameters. It doesn't estimate speed.

Finally, for all HO processes, given the different HO types, channel updates time used, is 200 ms for mmWave HO, and 400 ms for LTE HO. Normal TTT is set at 480 ms. This allows mmWave to initiate a HO event before LTE links can be used as fall backs. RT updates are continuously performed at an interval of 200 ms and with measurements gaps of 6 ms. Based on SRS SINR values, LTE cells trigger the HO procedure.

4 Performance Evaluation

4.1 Tools and Techniques Used

In Simulations were done using ns-3 dual connectivity mmWave-LTE. ns-3 is an open source, C++ based discrete event simulator [2] and [3]. For mmWave SRS, the signals are instantaneous wideband with 10 MHz bandwidth, 1 GHz carrier frequency, a time varying sampling periods of 40 ms and a Doppler frequency varying from 1 to 166 Hz (low, medium and high Doppler frequencies). The radio channel follows the 3 GPP Extended Typical Urban (ETU) environment requirement [13–16]. We consider three classes of user speeds; 3 km/h, 10 km/h and 50 km/h. It is an event-based adaptive HO network simulation with a multi-user road traffic model described and shown in Fig. 2.

4.2 Performance Metrics

The metrics used to assess the performance are the following: average handoff failure (HOF) rates, average delivery ratio, average Handoff number and average throughput per user.

4.3   Baseline Considerations

A hard HO mechanism is considered where macro (LTE) and micro (mmWave) cells do not share the X2 link at access level. Small cells are not coordinated by the LTE cells at access level but share the same core network. Thus, mmWave cells and LTE cells must completely disconnect to one cell prior to choosing a better link as explained in detail in [2, 3, 10].

4.4   Simulation Parameters

Table 1. Simulation parameters.

Parameters	LTE		mmWave
3GPP channel scenario		Urban Micro	
Simulation time		200 s	
Cell transmission power	46 dBm		30 dBm
Carrier frequency	2 GHz		28 GHz
Bandwidth	10 MHz		1 GHz
Number of cells	3		20/LTE cell
Inter cell distance	500 m		[0,125 m]
Path loss		3GPP urban model	
X2 link latency		1 ms	
S1 link latency		10 ms	
TTT		160	
Handoff: Intra - cell delay		10 ms	
Inter - cell delay		[60 ms, 100 ms]	
S1-MME link latency	10 ms		
RLC buffer size B_{RLC}		5 MB	
RLC AM reordering timer		1 ms	
mmWave outage threshold			−5 dB
UDP source rate		100 Mbits	
UE velocity		[3, 60] Km/h	
RLF	0 dB		$- \leq 6$ dB

5   Simulation Results and Discussion

Simulation parameters are shown in Table 1 while results are shown in Figs. 4, 5, 6 and 7 below. To evaluate our adaptive HO model, Fig. 4 shows the HOF rate for hard HO and soft HOs including HO1, HO2 and HO3.

Figure 4 shows the HOF rate for hard HO and soft HOs including HO1, HO2 and HO3. In Fig. 4, results show that the HOF rates are different regardless of user density. The rapid increase of HOF rate in hard HO can be attributed to lack of an access level

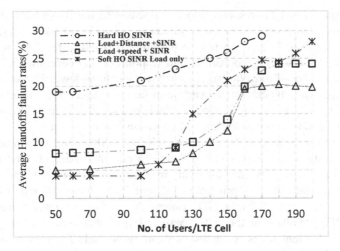

Fig. 4. Comparison of average HOF rate.

coordination resulting into the time increase of a cell selection which ultimately increases the HO latency. Adopting the Soft HO with distance strategy, i.e., (**HO2**), greatly reduces the HOF rate because it corresponds to reduced time needed for HO involvement among involved BSs. Technically, the long network association to one eNB due to distance consideration minimizes the HOF rate. This is proven by the fewer number of HOs when soft HO with distance, **HO2,** consideration is involved as shown in Fig. 5.

It should further be understood that with distance consideration in HO2, a limited number of SRS SINR values is considered at the LTE coordinating cell unlike in hard HO where there is no coordination. Since control plane resources are limited or scarce

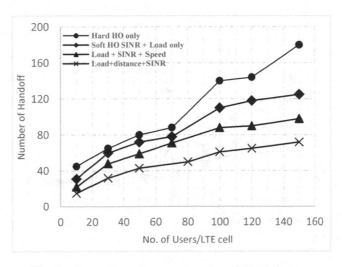

Fig. 5. Comparison of average number of Handoff times.

in lower frequencies, LTE resource blocks allocated to mmWave network requests should be limited to optimize resource availability on LTE fall back links. Since the distance consideration in HO can reduce the number of HOs, the LTE with limited resources can still efficiently coordinate and response to the decentralized SRS even under a large number of mmWave eNBs. At the same time, fewer HO sessions allow enough LTE resource blocks for network association to users that cannot connect to mmWave cells, e.g., due to high velocity which will result into high Doppler spread. This justifies the fewer HO failure rate when distance is considered.

When considering hard HO against soft HO with SINR and Load consideration only, **HO1**, the HOF rate curves in Fig. 4 have a radically different trend from **HO2** and **HO3**; they remarkably increase with increase in user numbers per cell. This attributed to the fact that, in principle, different eNBs have different user service queues, populated with different HO commands at different rates. Therefore, the mmWave eNBs involved in the initial association of the same user may start the association at different times when the network is loaded. There is a high chance (probability) that the HO association begins with non-optimal, but available eNB, because the optimal ones are busy for association with other existing users. As soon as optimal eNBs due to either speed or distance effects in HO assessment have less load or empty their queues, they quickly engage the users well positioned users due to better SINR and less load besides distance and speed estimations for HO2 and HO3. This leads to a more of HOs as seen in Fig. 5 for the Hard HO and HO1 strategies. This becomes worse by the rise in users, where the HO rate keeps raising as seen in Fig. 5 because every well position user in terms of SINR in Hard HO or load in HO1 will be queuing to join the best network. The rise in HOs and HOF is even worse for Hard HO where the user load variation is totally ignored as shown in Fig. 4, and HO complexity keeps increasing due to large number of users. Ultimately, a significant reduction in effective data rate is seen as shown in Fig. 6. For distance and speed-based HOs, HO requests and complexity is minimized by fewer numbers of HOs due to distance and

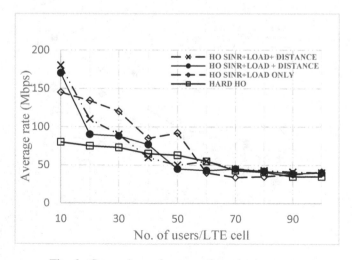

Fig. 6. Comparison of average throughput per user.

speed restrictions. Given a higher number of users, HO2 is able to stabilize HO failure rate better than HO3 as the population grows, this can be attributed to lower number of HOs due to distance consideration unlike speed as shown in Fig. 5.

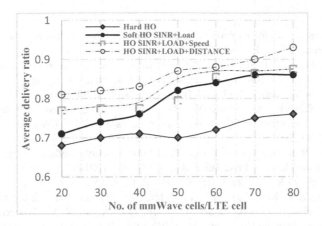

Fig. 7. Comparison of average packet delivery per session.

Finally, results in Fig. 7 clearly show packets generated and successfully received. Thus, the average delivery ratio shows the ability of the HO to transfer data successfully, end-to-end. In Fig. 7, results show that both distance-based, and the speed-based HOs are able to achieve approximately similar average delivery ratio. The average delivery ratios of speed-based and distance-based HO strategies increase by 10% to 15% as compared to that of Load only. Load only HO has also an increased performance compared of about 0.15 to that of Hard HO. Hence, Hard HO has a highest recurring routing overhead while distance-based HO has more reliable dynamic TTT intervals which leads to minimal routing overhead more consistent user rate.

6 Conclusions

We have thoroughly investigated the rich set of network access and HO challenges posed by the introduction of mmWave technologies in the 5G networks with DC capabilities. Results have demonstrated that badly positioned users can severely harm the HO efficiency hence effective user data rates. It requires context aware strategies in HOs and beam switching to sustain user connectivity. Essentially badly positioned users in a network causing multiple handoffs than carefully selected users, thus increase the overhead. While context awareness, such as knowing distance and speed, may increase complexity and signaling, we believe the trade-offs of HO simplicity against HO complexity can be offset by sustained network association or link maintenance. For instance, complexity brought about by considering distance and speed, which requires user and mmWave BS positions to be known by coordinating LTE cells, is offset by fewer HOs and failures. Finally, given the challenges highlighted in HOs, together with the proposed solutions of investigating DC at system level, major contribution that would improve mmWave cell management in 5G networks can be provided.

References

1. Xiao, B.M., et al.: Millimeter wave communications for future mobile networks. IEEE J. Sel. Areas Commun. **35**(9), 1909–1935 (2017)
2. Polese, M., Mezzavilla, M., Zorzi, M.: Performance comparison of dual connectivity and hard handover for LTE-5G tight integration. In: Proceeding of the 9th EAI International Conference on Simulation Tools and Techniques (SIMUTOOLS), pp. 118–123 (2016)
3. Polese, M., Giordani, M., Mezzavilla, M., Rangan, S., Zorzi, M.: Improved handover through dual connectivity in 5G mmWave mobile networks. IEEE J. Sel. Areas Commun. **35** (9), 2069–2084 (2017)
4. Rangan, S., Rappaport, T.S., Erkip, E.: Millimeter-wave cellular wireless networks: potentials and challenges. Proc. IEEE **102**(3), 366–385 (2014)
5. GPP: NR and NG-RAN Overall Description - Rel. 15, TS 38.300 (2018)
6. Park, J., Jung, S.Y., Kim, S., Bennis, M., Debbah, M.: User-centric mobility management in ultra-dense cellular networks under spatio-temporal dynamics. In: Proceeding of IEEE Global Communications Conference (GLOBECOM), Washington, DC, pp. 1–6 (2016)
7. 3GPP: Scenarios and requirements for small cell enhancement for EUTRA and E-UTRAN (Release 14), 3rd Generation Partnership Project (3GPP), TR 36.932, March 2017
8. Joud, M., García-Lozano, M., Ruiz, S.: User specific cell clustering to improve mobility robustness in 5G ultra-dense cellular networks. In: Proceeding of 14th Annual Conference on Wireless On-demand Network Systems and Services (WONS), Isola, pp. 45–50 (2018)
9. Thapliyal, A.: Mobility Robustness in 5G Networks. Ph.D. thesis, Aalto University School of Electrical Engineering, Finland (2016)
10. Gimnez, L.C., Michaelsen, P.H., Pedersen, K.I.: UE autonomous cell management in a high-speed scenario with dual connectivity. In: Proceeding of IEEE International Symposium on Personal, Indoor and Mobile Radio Communications (PIMRC), pp. 1–6, September 2016
11. Lee, S., Jung, J., Moon, J., Nigam, A., Ryoo, S.: Mobility enhancement of dense small-cell network. In: Proceeding of IEEE Consumer Communications and Networking Conference (CCNC), pp. 297–303, January 2015
12. Ibrahim, H., ElSawy, H., Nguyen, U.T., Alouini, M.S.: Mobility aware modeling and analysis of dense cellular networks with CPlane/U-plane split architecture. IEEE Trans. Commun. **64**(11), 4879–4894 (2016)
13. Kuruvatti, N.P., Molano, J.F.S., Schotten, H.D.: Mobility context awareness to improve quality of experience in traffic dense cellular networks. In: Proceeding of International Conference on Telecommunications (ICT), pp. 1–7, May 2017
14. Sun, Y., Chang, Y.: A universal predictive mobility management scheme for urban ultra-dense networks with control/data plane separation. IEEE Access **5**, 6015–6026 (2017)
15. Bassoy, S., Farooq, H., Imran, M.A., Imran, A.: Coordinated multi point clustering schemes: a survey. IEEE Commun. Surv. Tutor. **19**(2), 743–764 (2017)
16. Kurda, R., Boukhatem, L., Kaneko, M., Yahiya, T.A.: Mobility-aware dynamic inter-cell interference coordination in HetNets with cell range expansion. In: Proceeding of IEEE International Symposium on Personal, Indoor and Mobile Radio Communications (PIMRC), pp. 1115–1119, September 2014

The Effect of Propagation Models on IEEE 802.11n Over 2.4 GHz and 5 GHz in Noisy Channels: A Simulation Study

Sonia Gul$^{(\boxtimes)}$ and Nurul I. Sarkar

Department of IT and Software Engineering,
Auckland University of Technology, Auckland, New Zealand
{Sonia.gul, nurul.sarkar}@aut.ac.nz

Abstract. IEEE 802.11 wireless local area networks (also called Wi-Fi) are widely used as Internet access technologies due to its availability, high-speed, low-cost, and standardization world-wide. While the performance of Wi-Fi has been studied and reported extensively in the network literature, the effect of radio propagation models on system performance in noisy channels has not been fully explored yet. This paper, therefore, investigates the effect of propagation models (two ray ground, path loss shadowing, and overall shadowing) over 2.4 GHz and 5 GHz on the performance of a typical 802.11n network in noisy channels. A campus-wide 802.11n network simulation model is developed for the said study using the Riverbed (OPNET) Modeler 18.7. We consider both real-time (e.g. voice and video) and non-real time (e.g. FTP) applications to generate traffic on the network. Simulation results show that FTP download time and FTP upload response times have significant effect on radio propagation models as well 2.4- and 5 GHz channels. However, the effect of propagation models on VoIP packet delays, jitter as well as video delays is found to be insignificant. The findings reported in this paper provide some insights into Wi-Fi performance under noisy channels that can help network researchers/engineers to contribute further towards developing next generation Wi-Fi networks capable of operating in noisy channels.

Keywords: IEEE 802.11n · Radio propagation models · Noisy channel

1 Introduction

Wireless Local Area Networks (WLANs) are one of the profound components of today's communications network of any organization. Regardless of the various backbone network technologies, the network access layer should support wireless technologies to keep pace with the current and upcoming wireless devices. Various WLAN standards have been standardized by IEEE including 802.11n operating either on 2.4 GHz or 5 GHz channels.

In this paper we investigate the impact of radio propagation models on 802.11n over 2.4 GHz and 5 GHz noisy channels. Riverbed Modeler 18.7 [1] is used as simulation tool to develop network models for performance study.

© ICST Institute for Computer Sciences, Social Informatics and Telecommunications Engineering 2019
Published by Springer Nature Switzerland AG 2019. All Rights Reserved
J. Zheng et al. (Eds.): ADHOCNETS 2019, LNICST 306, pp. 113–121, 2019.
https://doi.org/10.1007/978-3-030-37262-0_9

The rest of the paper is organized as follows. Section 2 provides an introduction to 802.11n standard and focuses on both 2.4 GHz and 5 GHz channel implementations. Section 3 describes the simulation environment and network model for two scenarios based on operating frequencies of 2.4 GHz and 5 GHz. Section 4 discusses the simulation results and model validation. Section 5 concludes the paper.

2 Background and Related Work

With increase in the demand of high throughput applications; the accessibility of these applications over wireless network has also escalated. This started the discussions and technological research to come up with solutions to increase the data rate over wireless channels. IEEE 802.11n standard [2] came into the horizon from the aspect of high throughput and data rate in mind. The said standard is designed using the Multiple Input Multiple Output (MIMO), incorporating with improved security and frame aggregation. The details on the process and design of 802.11n standard can be found in [3]. From this paper's point of view we are interested in mainly 802.11n implementations over 2.4 GHz and 5 GHz channels. The channel characteristics of 802.11n is highlighted in Table 1.

Table 1. IEEE 802.11n channel characteristics (2.4 GHz and 5 GHz channel)

Parameters	802.11n 2.4 GHz	802.11n 5 GHz
Frequency	2.4 GHz	5 GHz
Modulation	MIMO-OFDM	MIMO-OFDM
Bandwidth	20 MHz	40 MHz
Data rate	Up to 288.8 Mbps	Up to 600 Mbps

We have simulated 802.11n campus network over 2.4 GHz and 5 GHz to investigate the effect of radio propagation models on system performance in noisy channels. The details of simulation environment and network model is discussed next.

2.1 Noisy Channels

In real life environment, the communication channel possesses some characteristics that will either lost some frames completely or introduce errors in data being communicated over the channel. These errors may be identified and in some cased corrected or rectified at the receiving end; such channels are called noisy channels. However, we can simulate an environment with the channel which is not introducing any errors or any packet losses; such channels are known as perfect channels.

In this paper, we simulated both perfect and noisy channels to observe the effect of radio propagation models. Perfect channel is being simulated using the default settings of the Riverbed Modeler. However, the noisy channel is simulated by increasing the noise figure of Riverbed Modeler default values from 1 to 5.

2.2 Radio Propagation Models Used in the Simulation

We considered three well-known indoor propagation models (two-ray ground, shadowing path loss, and the overall shadowing) in the Riverbed Modeler-based simulation study to find out the effect of these propagation models on system performance. A brief description of each of the propagation model is given below.

Two-Ray Ground Reflection Model: The two-ray ground model is a single line-of-sight path between two mobile nodes is seldom the only means of propagation. The model considers both the direct path and a ground reflection path. This model provides more accurate prediction at a long distance than the free space model [9].

$$P_r(d) = \frac{P_t G_t G_r h_t^2 h_r^2}{d^4 L} \tag{1}$$

where:

- P_r = received signal power
- d = separation between transmitter and receiver
- P_t = transmitted signal power (in Watts)
- G_t = transmitter antenna gain (Set to '1' in the simulation)
- G_r = receiver antenna gain (Set to '1' in the simulation))
- L = System 'Loss' factor (loss of signal waves that weren't captured by the receiver. $L = 1$ means no loss was noted by the hardware)
- h_t = Height of the transmitting antenna (meters)
- h_r = Height of the receiving antenna (meters)

Shadowing Path Loss Model: One of the two shadowing models is known as the path loss model. The path loss model predicts the mean received power at distance d, denoted by Pr(d). It uses a close-in distance d_0 as a reference. While two-ray model predicts the received power as a deterministic function of distance but the received power at a certain distance is a random variable due to multipath propagation effects, which is also known as fading effects [9].

$$\left[\frac{P_r(d)}{P_r(d_0)}\right]_{dB} = -10\beta \log\left(\frac{d}{d_0}\right) \tag{2}$$

where:

- β = path loss exponent, and is usually empirically determined by field measurement.

The path loss exponent (β) for two ray ground (line-of-sight) varies from 1.6 to 1.8, Shadowed urban area varies from 2.7 to 5, and the Overall shadowing (Obstructed office) varies from 4 to 6. Larger values correspond to more obstruction and hence faster decrease in average received power as distance increases [9].

Overall Shadowing Model: The shadowing model reflects the variation of the received power at certain distance. It is a log-normal random variable, that is, it is of Gaussian distribution if measured in dB (ns 2010). The overall shadowing model is represented by:

$$\left[\frac{P_r(d)}{P_r(d_0)}\right]_{dB} = -10\beta \log\left(\frac{d}{d_0}\right) + X_{dB} \tag{3}$$

where:

- X_{dB} = a Gaussian random-variable with zero mean and standard deviation σ_{dB}. σ_{dB} is called the shadowing deviation and is also obtained by measurement.

The typical values of shadowing deviation (σdB) for an office (hard partition) is 7, for office (soft partition) is 9.6, and for factory (line-of-sight) varies from 3 to 6 [4].

3   Simulation Study

The simulation study explores the effect of radio propagation models on 802.11n performance over 2.4 GHz and 5 GHz in noisy channels. For the purpose of investigation, we consider Auckland University of Technology (AUT) south campus network environment having various subnets for each building ensuring that traffic flows and inter-subnet communication taking place. The 802.11n infrastructure network is modeled using Riverbed Modeler 18.7 [1]. This section describes in detail the simulation models and parameter settings.

3.1   Modelling the Network

The network model is based on the logical topology of AUT South Campus Network as shown in Fig. 1. We have simulated 25 wireless nodes of mixed traffic across 6 subnets linked to a Gigabit Ethernet backbone.

The characteristics of simulated voice and video traffic at the packet level is investigated. For modeling voice and video traffic, a Voice over Internet Protocol (VoIP) and Video-conferencing applications were chosen, respectively. The simulation environment is designed to investigate the impact of radio propagation channels on 802.11n 2.4 GHz and 5 GHz over noisy channels. We develop an AUT South Campus Network simulation model containing various subnets for each building. The subnets are wirelessly linked to access points (APs) which are connected to a wired Gigabit Ethernet backbone network. Riverbed Modeler (Previously OPNET Modeler) is used as simulation tool for network performance study. We work on two simulation scenarios; one for 2.4 GHz channel and the other one for 5 GHz channel. The parameters used in the simulation are listed in Table 2.

The Server (FTP) is located in the center of the network infrastructure building (MB), and five buildings/subnets (MA, MD, ME, MH and MC) are connected through a backbone Gigabit Ethernet switch.

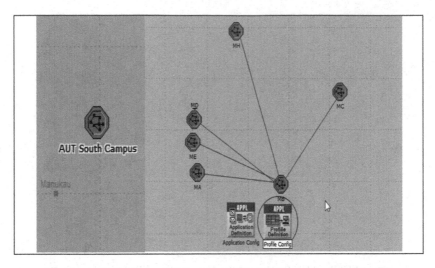

Fig. 1. High-level view of the simulated AUT South Campus Network

Table 2. Parameters used in the simulation

Parameter	Value
AP transmit power	32 mW
No. of wireless nodes	25
Application/Traffic	FTP, VoIP, Video-conferencing
FTP	High load
VoIP encoder	PCM quality
Video-conferencing	Low resolution
Propagation models	Two ray ground, Shadowing pathloss, Overall shadowing
Wireless node mobility	0
Length of simulation	60 min

Figure 2 shows the simulation topology of the MB subnet. The parameters we have investigated are FTP Download and Upload response times, VoIP delay and jitter, Video delay and throughput, and WLAN Throughput.

Figure 3 shows the screen shoot of a wireless node configuration where FTP traffic was set to high loads. We ran our simulation models in noisy channels. We also ran simulation under perfect channel condition for comparison purposes.

3.2 Validating Simulation Model

To validate the results, we have used two validation techniques discussed in [5]. Firstly, we have used the concept of face validation, which is when the model's behavior is expected and reasonable. Second, we compare our results with the work already published in the literature [6–8]. We have also checked the simulation log file ensuring

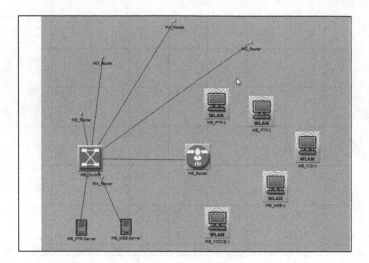

Fig. 2. AUT South Campus subnet in the MB building

Fig. 3. Node configuration in which FTP traffic set to high loads

that models run smoothly without unexpected errors. Moreover, we have also simulated our network on multiple machines and for varied period of times to rectify any anomalies in the simulation.

4   Results and Discussion

We observe the effect of three radio propagation models (two ray ground, Shadowing Path Loss, and overall shadowing) on 802.11n 2.4 GHz and 5 GHz in noisy channels. The results for perfect channel are also presented for comparison purposes. Using Riverbed Modeler simulator, we measure FTP download and upload response times, VoIP packet delays and Jitter, Video packet delays and Throughput, and WLAN Throughput. The summary of research findings is presented in Table 3.

Table 3. Summary of simulation results for noisy channel (2.4 GHz and 5 GHz)

Performance metric	802.11n performance in noisy channel					
	Two ray ground		Shadowing path loss		Overall shadowing	
	2.4 GHz	5 GHz	2.4 GHz	5 GHz	2.4 GHz	5 GHz
FTP download (s)	0.31 (0.31)	7.3 (5.9)	0.14 (0.33)	24 (11.9)	0.41 (0.36)	27 (4.8)
FTP upload (s)	0.33 (0.33)	10.9 (23)	0.58 (0.44)	32 (24)	0.45 (0.33)	28 (21)
VoIP delay (s)	0.1 (0.1)	0.11 (0.1)	0.1 (0.1)	0.11 (0.1)	0.1 (0.01)	0.11 (0.11)
VoIP jitter (s)	0.0000007 (0.023)	0.0000024 (0.0000034)	0.001 (0.012)	0.0000026 (0.0000035)	0.011 (0.014)	0.0000026 (0.0000027)
Video delay (s)	0.028 (0.28)	0.89 (0.09)	0.28 (0.22)	0.088 (0.09)	0.28 (0.034)	0.089 (0.09)
Video throughput (Mbps)	0.14 (1.85)	1.4 (1.4)	10.78 (1.78)	1.4 (1.4)	10.78 (1.78)	1.4 (1.4)
WLAN throughput (Mbps)	16 (16)	18 (17)	24 (25)	18 (17)	25 (26)	18 (19)

Note: Values in the bracket () represent the perfect channel.

4.1   Effect of Radio Propagation Model

The two ray ground model is used in the simulation as default setting for Riverbed Modeler where a connection represents off a surface and "Bounces" to a different connection. In our findings we observe that there are small differences in Jitter and Video Throughput while there is not much differences in any of the other parameter. These differences are observed at 1.0 noise level which is "Perfect" and at a 100-noise level which is "Noisy". We also observe that there is a difference of 16 s in Jitters and a difference of 450,000 s in Video Throughput.

Shadowing Path Loss model is simulated by considering an object between the transmitter and destination addresses which interfere with the transmissions. Results obtained show that there are significant differences between Path Loss and Two Ray Ground models.

The overall Shadowing is a model in which the topology is outside of the specified terrain causes interference in the transmissions causing larger delays than Shadowing Path Loss. We also observe FTP (upload and download response), Video (delay and throughput) and WLAN throughput performance deteriorates for overall shadowing model over 5 GHz channel. This is due to its distance from the specified terrain.

4.2   Effect of 2.4 GHz and 5 GHz

Another interesting observation of our simulation study is the effect of 2.4 GHz and 5 GHz channel on system performance. For FTP traffic, 2.4 GHz channel performs much better than 5 GHz channel for all three propagation models. Moreover, the system performance changes to overall shadowing. Our simulation results (Table 3) show network throughput increase over 5 GHz channel (using two ray ground model) as compared to that of 2.4 GHz channel.

The summary of our research findings is presented in Table 4. We observe the effect of three propagation models on system performance in noisy channels for mixed traffics including FTP, VoIP, and Video. Our findings show that the shadowing path loss model performs best for FTP downloads whereas two ray ground model performs well for FTP uploads, Video throughput, and WLAN throughput over 2.4 GHz. The effect of propagation models on VoIP and Video delay performance is found to be insignificant. The overall shadowing over 5 GHz channel performs worst in all traffics investigated including FTP, VoIP, Video, and WLAN throughput.

Table 4. Summary of findings

Metrics	Good performance with	Worse performance with
FTP download (s)	Shadowing path loss (2.4 GHz)	Overall shadowing (5 GHz)
FTP upload (s)	Two ray ground (2.4 GHz)	Overall shadowing (5 GHz)
VoIP delay (s)	Impact on propagation model is not significant	
VoIP jitter (s)	Impact on propagation model is not significant	
Video delay (s)	Impact on propagation model is not significant	
Video throughput (Mbps)	Two ray ground (2.4 GHz)	Overall shadowing (5 GHz)
WLAN throughput (Mbps)	Two ray ground (2.4 GHz)	Overall shadowing (5 GHz)

5   Conclusion

In this paper we investigated the effect of radio propagation models on the performance of an 802.11n campus network over 2.4 GHz and 5 GHz in noisy channels. In the investigation, we considered three well-known radio propagation models such as two ray ground, shadowing path loss and overall shadowing. Simulation results obtained have shown that the shadowing path loss model over 2.4 GHz performed excellent for FTP download. However, the two-ray ground model performed the best for FTP (upload), VoIP and Video traffics over 2.4 GHz. The overall shadowing model over 5 GHz performed worst for all traffics investigated. An investigation of the impact of radio propagation models on a wide-area network is suggested as future work.

References

1. Riverbed Modeler. https://www.riverbed.com/sg/products/steelcentral/opnet.html. Accessed 10 Aug 2019
2. IEEE 802.11n standard. https://standards.ieee.org/standard/802_11n-2009.html. Accessed 10 Aug 2019
3. Perahia, E.: IEEE 802.11 n development: history, process, and technology. IEEE Commun. Mag. **46**(7), 48–55 (2008)
4. He, R., Zhong, Z., Ai, B., Xiong, L., Ding, J.: The effect of reference distance on path loss prediction based on the measurements in high-speed railway viaduct scenarios. In: 6th IEEE International ICST Conference on Communications and Networking in China (CHINACOM), pp. 1201–1205 (2011)
5. Sargent, R.G.: Verification and validation of simulation models. In: Proceedings of the 2010 IEEE Winter Simulation Conference, pp. 166–183 (2010)
6. Sarkar, N.I., Sowerby, K.W.: Wi-Fi performance measurements in the crowded office environment: a case study. Presented at the 10th IEEE International Conference on Communication Technology (ICCT 2006), Guilin, China, 27–30 November 2006, pp. 37–40 (2006)
7. Sarkar, N.I., Lo, E.: Indoor propagation measurements for performance evaluation of IEEE 802.11 g. Presented at the IEEE Australasian Telecommunications Networks and Applications Conference, Adelaide, Australia, 7–10 December 2008, pp. 163–168 (2008)
8. Sarkar, N.I., Lo, E.: Performance studies of 802.11 g for various AP configuration and placement. Presented at the 2011 IEEE Symposium on Computers and Informatics (ISCI 2011), Kuala Lumpur, Malaysia, 20–22 March 2011, pp. 29–34 (2011)
9. Henderson, T.: 18.1 Free space model (2011). http://www.isi.edu/nsnam/ns/doc/node217.html. Accessed 16 July 2019

Medium Access Control for Flying Ad Hoc Networks Using Directional Antennas: Challenges, Research Status, and Open Issues

Lingjun Liu, Laixian Peng[✉], Renhui Xu[✉], and Wendong Zhao

College of Communication Engineering, Army Engineering University of PLA,
Nanjing, China
chaconne2013@foxmail.com, lxpeng@hotmail.com,
xurenhui@aa.seu.edu.cn, nj_mouse@163.com

Abstract. As flying ad hoc networks (FANETs) are increasingly used in military and civilian scenarios, and the utilization of directional antennas can significantly increase the communication distance between UAVs and anti-interception capability of transmission, the research on media access control (MAC) protocols using directional antennas has become a new research hotspot. In this paper, we first summarize the design elements and requirements of directional MAC protocols for FANETs are summarized considering the characteristics of FANETs and the challenges brought by directional antennas. Based on the classification of channel access mechanisms, contention and scheduling based MAC protocols for FANETs with directional antennas are then reviewed. Finally, the characteristics and performance of various typical protocols are compared and analyzed. Problems that need to be further addressed are summarized, expecting to provide some illumination for those researchers engaged in this field.

Keywords: FANET · Directional antenna · MAC protocol

1 Introduction

In recent years, the advantages of relatively low cost, easy deployment and flexible networking have enabled unmanned aerial vehicles (UAVs) to be applied in both civilian and military tasks such as emergency rescue, intelligence gathering, target monitoring and tracking, etc. Ad hoc networks composed of UAVs are called flying ad hoc networks (FANETs). This concept was originally proposed by Temel in [7]. FANETs have also several other names in the literature, such as unmanned aeronautical ad hoc networks (UAANETs) [29], network of UAVs [8], and airborne networks [9]. For the sake of unity, this paper uses the term FANETs. FANETs use the architecture of mobile ad hoc networks (MANETs), which have the characteristics of no infrastructure, distributed control, dynamic networking flexibility, self-healing and strong invulnerability. The special ad hoc networks of UAVs can enhance the interoperability between UAVs and has become a research hotspot.

Currently, the research on FANETs mainly focuses on network management, mobility model [23] and control [10], and network protocols [21]. As part of the

© ICST Institute for Computer Sciences, Social Informatics and Telecommunications Engineering 2019
Published by Springer Nature Switzerland AG 2019. All Rights Reserved
J. Zheng et al. (Eds.): ADHOCNETS 2019, LNICST 306, pp. 122–132, 2019.
https://doi.org/10.1007/978-3-030-37262-0_10

network protocol stack, medium access control (MAC) protocols provide fair and fast access mechanisms for nodes to ensure time efficient, reliable and stable data transmission. The functionality of MAC protocols directly affects the channel utilization and the network throughput, playing a decisive role in the performance of FANETs. However, owing to high dynamics of UAVs, frequent three-dimensional topology changes, and unreliable wireless communication links, existing MAC protocols for MANETs cannot be fully applied to FANETs. Modification or developing new MAC protocols are necessary to meet the communication needs of FANETs.

Different from existing surveys in the literature [7, 20, 22, 24], which provide general networking frameworks for FANETs, this review aims at the research progress and prospects of MAC protocols using directional antennas in FANETs. The reasons why emphasize the implementation of directional antennas are as follows: available bandwidth below 3 GHz is narrow and frequency interference is severe, causing difficulty in enhancing channel capacity. Therefore, the high frequency becomes the choice when designing communication systems in the future. However, the attenuation of high frequency signal is more serious than that of lower frequency together with limited transmission distance of omnidirectional antennas, while directional antennas can effectively alleviate transmission loss of high frequency signals, expand the communication distance and reduce the number of hops. Directional transmission also reduces mutual interference of neighboring nodes, increasing the chance of spatial reuse and network capacity [5, 18]. Additionally, directional communication can enhance the concealment of transmission and enhance anti-interference ability of networks.

This paper is organized as follows. Section 2 describes the characteristics of FANETs, and discusses the challenges and key points for designing MAC protocols with directional antennas. Section 3 reviews MAC protocols for FANETs using directional antennas. Section 4 summarizes and compares the characteristics and performance of several typical MAC protocols. Section 5 concludes this paper with open issues in future research.

2 Challenges and Design Requirements

2.1 Characteristics of FANETs

FANETs not only have the problems of the limited bandwidth and frequent topology changes faced by MANETs, but also face other challenges, such as more dramatic topology changes in 3D space and link failures caused by high node mobility, and poor network environment as a result of communication in open air. FANETs have the main characteristics as follows:

1. **Low node density**
   Currently, the mainly used UHF frequency band has enabled single-hop communication distance up to several hundred kilometers, resulting in high transmission delay. In a real network scenario, the number of nodes in a network is small and thus the network density is relatively low, which may cause poor network connectivity.

2. **Wide distribution in 3D space**

   When UAVs are on missions, they tend to be far away from neighboring UAVs. Therefore, the coverage of FANETs in 3D space can reach tens or even hundreds of cubic kilometers, which poses a great challenge to the neighbor discovery in the initialization of the network.

3. **High node mobility**

   The speed of UAVs is usually between 30–460 km/h [26]. High-speed mobile nodes would cause dramatic topology changes, making mobility models especially important in protocol design.

4. **Unstable communication links**

   Since the transmission space of FANETs is open air with bad channel conditions such as high fading and Doppler effects, resulting in unreliable communication links between UAVs. High bit error rate, transmission delay and communication interruption may also occur especially when the distance between UAVs is large.

5. **Network heterogeneity**

   In addition to the communication between UAVs, communication with fixed nodes such as ground stations may also be needed. Therefore, both UAV-to-UAV and UAV-to-infrastructure connections may exist concurrently, making the FANET as a heterogeneous network.

2.2 Problems Brought by Directional Antennas

Directional antennas may bring several particular problems when they are used in a FANET.

1. **Hidden terminal problem**

   A hidden terminal is a phenomenon in which a node does not know that its target node is communicating, and a collision occurs at its target node after the node sends out the RTS packet. In this case, this node is called a hidden terminal of its target node. An ad hoc network using directional antennas may have 2 kinds of hidden terminal problems: unheard RTS/CTS and asymmetry in gain when both directional and omnidirectional transmission are adopted in the protocol [6].

2. **Deafness problem**

   When a node transmits the RTS packet to its target node which is communicating with other nodes directionally, the targeted node cannot hear the RTS packet and thus the transmitting node cannot receive the CTS reply. In this case, the targeted node is called a deaf node. And the transmitting node will retry the RTS transmission repeatedly until it receives the CTS reply. In the worst case, the transmitting node may drop the packet when the number of retries exceeds a certain value. Through the above illustration, it can be concluded that the transmission of redundant RTS packets makes the transmitting node suffer from low transmission efficiency and high delay.

3. **Header-of-Block (HOL) problem**

   The HOL problem occurs as a result of using the first-in-first-out (FIFO) queuing policy in the MAC layer. The HOL problem is a phenomenon that a node detects that the channel in a certain direction is idle and thus it can send packets to the targeted node located in this direction, but if the packet at the top of the queue is destined to a busy direction, the subsequent packet will be blocked due to the FIFO policy. As a result, nodes suffering from the HOL problem fail to fully utilize the spatial multiplexing function of directional antennas, and thus the network throughput is reduced.

2.3 MAC Design Elements

Considering the characteristics of FANETs, the design requirements for FANETs using directional antennas are described as follows.

1. **Flexible networking ability**
   In FANETs, the network nodes are organized in a peer to peer manner. Meanwhile, a node may join or leave the network dynamically. A MAC protocol needs to realize rapid establishment of communication links of incoming nodes and optimize channel access mechanism to achieve fair and efficient resource allocation.
2. **Stable and reliable QoS guarantee**
   FANETs are expected to provide a variety of network services. Different applications or different types of user traffic have diverse quality of service (QoS) requirements in terms of transmission delay, data loss, etc. For instance, low transmission delay and non-collision data delivery is of vital importance for command and control information, while voice and video services require high throughput. In addition, the high propagation delay and potential link failure need the MAC layer to achieve stable services.
3. **Cross-layer interaction capability**
   Geographic information is of vital importance in a FANET because a node in the network may move beyond the beam coverage. A MAC protocol needs to obtain the latest neighbor information from the upper layers frequently to ensure reliable transmission.

3 Classification and Research Status

Currently, there is no uniform classification of MAC protocols using directional antennas for FANETs. There are many classification criteria, such as contention and scheduling mechanism; distributed or centralized mechanism; single channel or multichannel, and whether or not a protocol is based on a busy tone mechanism, etc. A MAC protocol may belong to different classifications. Next we present a review of MAC protocols proposed for FANETs using directional antennas according to contention and scheduling mechanism.

3.1 MAC Protocols Based on a Contention Mechanism

In the contention mechanism, when a node has a packet to send, it will first detect whether the channel is idle. If the channel is idle, it will immediately send the packet. Otherwise, it will wait for a period of time, referred to as backoff time. After the waiting process is completed and the channel is detected idle, the packet will be sent out, then the sending node will wait for an acknowledgement packet from its target node. If the sending node successfully receives the acknowledgement packet, the communication is completed. Otherwise, the sending node will retry the transmitting process, that is, it will repeat the aforementioned process. If the number of retries exceeds a certain value, the node will drop the packet. This mechanism does not need to allocate time slots for each node in advance. It can effectively deal with a dynamically changing number of nodes and burst services. The IEEE 802.11 DCF is the most representative contention mechanism widely used in wireless networks. Many benchmark MAC protocols with directional antennas are based on this mechanism [5, 17].

1. Adaptive MAC Protocol for Unmanned Aerial Vehicle

In [2, 4], Alsbatat et al. proposed a MAC protocol named Adaptive Medium Access Control Protocol for Unmanned Aerial Vehicle (AMAC_UAV). The antenna model used in the AMAC_UAV protocol is an antenna array consisting of two omnidirectional antennas and two adaptive antennas. One omnidirectional antenna and directional antenna pair are installed on the UAV, responsible for communication in the airspace above the UAV, and the other pair is responsible for transmission in the airspace under the UAV. The protocol uses an omnidirectional antenna to broadcast periodic heartbeat information to frequently update node's location information. In order to avoid the hidden terminal problems, the protocol transmits an RTS/CTS/DATA/ACK packet in an omnidirectional mode by default, and switches to a directional transmission mode when the distance between two nodes exceeds the omnidirectional transmission range. In the directional antenna mode, if the packet error rate and the number of retransmissions are higher than the predefined threshold, the antenna mode is switched to the omnidirectional transmission mode. The OPNET simulation results show that average end-to-end delay is nearly quartered and the throughput is increased more than fivefold with the protocol when compared to IEEE 802.11.

However, some problems still exist in the protocol. Firstly, after switching to the omnidirectional transmission mode, the communication requirement of the nodes whose distance is between OO (omnidirectional transmission and omnidirectional reception) and DO (directional transmission and omnidirectional reception) cannot be satisfied. Secondly, the collision problem in the heartbeat information broadcasting process is not considered. Thirdly, this protocol cannot handle the hidden terminal problems caused by gain asymmetry. Based on the above MAC protocol, the authors further proposed a cross-layer structure of FANETs called IMA_UAV in [3]. This protocol merges the lower three layers of the OSI model into one layer to provide a OLSR protocol modified under directional transmission conditions, of which the routing related information can be provided directly by the lower layers.

2. Location Oriented Directional MAC Protocol

In [27], Temel et el. proposed a location-oriented MAC protocol (LODMAC). The core of this protocol is to use two transceivers with different working frequencies to separate the control channel from the data transmission channel. The authors point out that there is a problem in existing MAC protocols where location information is somehow obtained from the upper layer. To solve this ambiguity, the proposed MAC protocol uses transceiver T1 to detect the location of neighbor nodes. The duration of each probing phase lasts for one second. GPS update, called location estimation, is performed at the beginning of each probing phase, and the remaining time is used for communication control. Additive to RTS/CTS interactions in the 802.11 DCF mechanism, in order to solve the well-known deafness problem, the transceiver T2 of a busy node, which works at a different frequency from T1, is used to send the busy-to-send (BTS) packet to inform the current transmitting node of the busy time of the busy? node. Moreover, the protocol also cooperates well with near space high altitude platforms [25].

However, this protocol still has several problems. Firstly, the hidden terminal problem is not alleviated. Secondly, in the process of location estimation, which is actually the process of neighbor discovery, it is stated that the nodes in the network take turns to become the only sender to inform the neighbors of its own location without collision. But at the beginning of location estimation period, since the node does not know the IDs of the remaining nodes, this process is difficult to achieve without collision. Thirdly, in the directional broadcasting process, the article does not give the way of scheduling antenna beam in a 3D scenario.

3.2   MAC Protocols Based on a Scheduling Mechanism

In MAC protocols based on the scheduling mechanism for FANETs, Time Division Multiple Access (TDMA) mechanism is most widely used. The basic idea of TDMA is to divide the time into frames, and each frame is divided into multiples time slots. A time slot is assigned to transmission links, so that the packets in the transmission queue are sent in the corresponding time slots. When an appropriate slot allocation algorithm is adopted, packets can be transmitted without any conflicts. Compared with MAC protocols based on the contention mechanism, the TDMA mechanism reduces flexibility of networking to a certain extent, but more reliable transmission of packets is guaranteed.

1. Distributed Spatial TDMA MAC Protocol
In [13], Huba et al. proposed a cross-layer protocol based on directional antennas, called D-STDMA. In network layer, the authors propose a meshed tree clustering algorithm [1] that creates multi-hop clusters of configurable cluster size. For cluster clients (CCs) and cluster heads (CHs), multiple proactive routes are established. Furthermore, the overlap among neighboring clusters, which can be used for reactive routing establishment, is supported. In MAC layer, a distributed TDMA scheduling algorithm is proposed, which allows nodes in the cluster to schedule their own transmission and reception time slots with their neighbors. Besides, the cluster formation process is utilized to determine when nodes join to establish a new link scheduling. However, D-STDMA lacks support for multi-priority services.

2. MAC Protocol for FANETs Using Directional Antennas
In [11], Guo proposed a MAC protocol for FANETs using directional antennas (DAMAC). In DAMAC protocol, one time slot consists of two sub time-slots. One of the sub-timeslots is fixed, which is used for the transmission of high-priority services, while the other is called additional sub-timeslot with variable frame length. The timeslot allocation algorithm is as follows: when the fixed sub-timeslot is insufficient to satisfy the transmission of high-priority services, the unsent high-priority services are

transmitted in the additional sub-timeslot, which can dynamically change the frame length according to the queue buffer of high-priority services. If there are more caches, the frame length is doubled. Otherwise, the frame length is compressed to half of the original length. After the transmission of the high priority services is satisfied, the remaining additional sub-timeslots are used to transmit the low-priority services. The advantage of DAMAC protocol is that it is oriented to the QoS requirements of multi-priority services, and can adaptively adjust the slot allocation strategy according to the network traffic load. The disadvantage is that the transmission fairness of DAMAC protocol is poor. When the network traffic load is large, low-priority services will suffer from severe packet loss problem to guarantee the transmission of high-priority services.

Note that since there are only few studies on directional MAC protocols for FANETs and whether omnidirectional antennas or directional antennas are utilized, MAC protocols need to solve common problems such as multi-priority service sup-port and dynamic network topology, so MAC protocols with omnidirectional antennas for FANETs using TDMA mechanism will also be briefly described below.

1. A TDMA MAC Protocol with Piggybacking ACK

   In [14], Jang points out that existing protocols need two guard times in a time slot because an aircraft node will wait an ACK packet after it sends data in a time slot, thus two guard times in one time slot are needed. To overcome this problem, the author proposes a TDMA MAC Protocol using a novel piggyback mechanism, where data and ACK are not sent to the same destination different from traditional piggyback mechanism where node sends both of data and ACK together in one frame. The proposed MAC make the data sent to the next relaying aircraft, while the ACK is sent to the previous relaying aircraft. This proposed protocol provides better network utilization because only one guard time is required in a time slot compared with traditional MAC protocols.

2. Location-based TDMA MAC Protocol

   In [15], Jang proposed a Protocol Termed Location-Based TDMA (LTTM). The proposed LTTM protocol uses location information to solve the ACK guard interval problem. Moreover, it can effectively support various broadcast modes. With LTTM, a receiving node calculates the propagation delay of the transmitting node based on the location information. It can effectively reduce the guard interval of ACK to achieve collision-free transmission, thus achieving better delay performance.

3. Interference-based Distributed TDMA MAC Protocol

   In [16], Li et al. proposed an interference-based Distributed TDMA Algorithm (IDTA) aiming at the frequent changes of the network topology and link state in a FANET. The degree of a link interference and the structure of a time frame are defined. With the link interference, the time slot allocation for neighbor nodes and traffic priorities, a node selects the communication link. The simulation results show that IDTA can achieve better delay performance than STDMA when the network topology changes more dramatically. However, time slot allocation can be further optimized by using a dynamic allocation mechanism and a variable frame length for different traffic priorities.

3.3   MAC Protocols Based on a Hybrid Access Mechanism

The hybrid mechanism is a combination of the contention mechanism and the scheduling mechanism. In the hybrid mechanism, according to the network load, one mechanism is set as the main mechanism while the other mechanism serves as the supplementary mechanism, which is beneficial to the global optimization of the network. A typical idea is to use the contention mechanism when the network load is low to reduce the delay and improve the channel utilization. When the network load becomes high, the protocol switched to the TDMA mode to reduce the collision probability.

In [28], Li et al. proposes a Multi-beam Smart Antennas based MAC Protocol (MBSAs_MAC). The MBSAs_MAC protocol divides the MAC layer into two sub-layers. The upper sub-layer uses TDMA-like scheduling mechanism to alleviate the packet collision in multi-beam data transmissions. In the lower sub-layer, an enhanced PCF/DCF mechanism compatible with conventional IEEE 802.11 protocols is introduced. In addition, a Hierarchical Dirichlet Process (HDP) enhanced hidden Markov model (HMM) is used for mobility prediction in each beam of a node. However, in the enhanced PCF phase, this protocol uses a star node to transmit a QoS query message to its neighbor nodes, which is quite centralized and thus cannot support flexible networking well.

4   Analysis and Comparisons

Tables 1 and 2 give a comparison of the characteristics and performance of different types of MAC protocols for FANETs using directional antennas.

Table 1. Characteristic comparison.

Name	Type	Antenna model	Number of channels	Cross-layer design	Centralized control
AMAC_UAV	Contention-based	2 adaptive arrays and 2 omni-directional antennas	Single	Not considered	Not needed
IMAC_UAV	Contention-based	2 adaptive arrays and 2 omni-directional antennas	Single	Considered	Not needed
D-STDMA	TDMA-based	4-phased array antenna	Single	Considered	Not needed
LODMAC	Contention-based	Switched beam antenna	Multi	Not considered	Not needed
MBSAs_MAC	Hybrid	Multi-beam antenna	Single	Considered	Needed
DAMAC	TDMA-based	Switched beam antenna	Single	Not considered	Not needed

Table 2. Performance comparison.

Name	Delay	Throughput	Multi-priority	Networking flexibility	Disadvantages
AMAC_UAV	One quarter of IEEE 802.11	Fivefold than IEEE 802.11	Not supported	Relatively high	Lack of addressing hidden terminal problems caused by asymmetry in gain
IMAC_UAV	Slightly better than IEEE 802.11	Not mentioned	Not supported	Mediocre	Lack of addressing the deafness problems
D-STDMA	Relatively low	Not mentioned	Not supported	Poor	Lack of supporting multi-priority services
LODMAC	Low	Relatively high	Not supported	Relatively high	The hidden terminal problems are not considered and the contention in location estimation is ignored
MBSAs_MAC	Relatively high	High	Supported	Relatively poor	The protocol runs in a centralized manner
DAMAC	Mediocre	High	Supported	High	The performance degrades obviously under high load

Due to the real-time and randomness of contention approach, this kind of MAC protocols can dynamically and flexibly set up the network, while providing relatively low end-to-end delay. These features are consistent with features of FANETs, but due to random packet delivery, even with multiple mitigation methods, collisions cannot be completely avoided. Thus, this method is difficult to provide a stable and reliable QoS guarantee, and it is difficult to ensure system stability when the load is heavy.

The TDMA-based MAC protocols statically or dynamically allocate time slots to each user in a certain manner, which can ensure fair scheduling, an average delay with an upper bound, and a robust system once the network size is determined. However, the requirements for synchronization are extremely demanded. Furthermore, it is difficult to effectively cope with dynamic changes of the number of nodes and burst traffic. Dynamic TDMA protocols have improved in flexibility, but the mechanism of time division multiplexing is difficult to be applied to occasions with high delay requirements. Additionally, the implementation is of high complexity.

5 Open Issues and Conclusion

Comparing and analyzing different types of MAC protocols for FANETs with directional antennas can provide guidance for further studies. In the next step, the key technologies of directional MAC protocols for FANETs still need to be further addressed in terms of stability, flexibility and scalability:

The assumptions in current theoretical studies on traffic models, communication links, and mobility models are too ideal and simplified. For instance, most work uses a Poisson arrival to model traffic, which is not suitable for burst traffic. The disparity between a theoretical model and the actual situation limits the proposed MAC protocols from theory to practice.

In most cases, UAVs' trajectory is not random but predefined. Adding a node's speed information on the next time interval to the control information can largely alleviate the link failure of beamforming towards wrong direction caused by a node's mobility. In addition, location prediction has been merged into protocols in both MANETs and VANETs [12, 19]. FANETs can also utilize some effective techniques such as artificial intelligence to predict nodes' location and reduce poor connectivity.

The existing MAC protocols do not fully consider dynamic changes of node members and link failures, which limits the flexibility and reliability of the network.

Providing reliable information transmission is the major goal of the design of MAC protocols. In actual scenarios, however, it is also necessary to focus on the delay and successful transmission of multi-priority packets as well as the system throughput.

Acknowledgement. Special thanks for Professor Zheng for his helpful and detailed comments. The work is supported by the National Natural Science Foundation of China (No. 61671471).

References

1. Al-Mousa, Y., Huba, W., Shenoy, N.: An integrated TDMA-based MAC and routing solution for airborne backbone networks using directional antennas. In: The Seventh International Conference on Networking and Services (2011)
2. Alshbatat, A.I., Dong, L.: Adaptive MAC protocol for UAV communication networks using directional antennas. In: International Conference on Networking (2010)
3. Alshbatat, A.I., Dong, L.: IEEE 2010 international conference on networking, sensing and control (ICNSC) - Chicago, USA (2010.04.10–2010.04.12) - Cross layer design for mobile ad hoc unmanned aerial vehicle. In: International Conference on Networking (2010)
4. Alshbatat, A.I., Dong, L.: Performance analysis of mobile ad hoc unmanned aerial vehicle communication networks with directional antennas. Int. J. Aerosp. Eng. **2010**(14) (2010)
5. Andryeyev, O., Artemenko, O., Mitschele-Thiel, A.: Improving the system capacity using directional antennas with a fixed beam on small unmanned aerial vehicles. In: European Conference on Networks and Communications (2015)
6. Bazan, O., Jaseemuddin, M.: A survey on MAC protocols for wireless ad hoc networks with beamforming antennas. IEEE Commun. Surv. Tutor. **14**(2), 216–239 (2012)
7. Bekmezci, I., Sahingoz, O.K., Temel, Ş.: Flying ad-hoc networks (FANETs): a survey. Ad Hoc Netw. **11**(3), 1254–1270 (2013)
8. Bok, P.B., Tuchelmann, Y.: Context-aware QoS control for wireless mesh networks of UAVs. In: International Conference on Computer Communications & Networks (2011)
9. Cheng, B.N., Moore, S.: [IEEEMILCOM 2012 - 2012 IEEE Military Communications Conference - Orlando, Fl, USA (2012.10.29–2012.11.1)] MILCOM 2012 - 2012 IEEE Military Communications Conference - a comparison of MANET routing protocols on airborne tactical networks (2012)
10. Cheng, X., Dong, C., Dai, H., Chen, G.: [IEEE 2018 IEEE 19th International Symposium on a World of Wireless, Mobile and Multimedia Networks (WoWMoM) - Chania, Greece (2018.6.12–2018.6.15)] 2018 IEEE 19th International Symposium on a World of Wireless, Mobile and Multimedia Networks (WoWMoM), pp. 14–22 (2018)
11. Guo, B.: Study on MAC protocol of aeronautical ad hoc networks using directional antenna. Master's thesis, Chongqing University (2017)

12. Hajiyev, C., Soken, H.E.: Robust adaptive Kalman filter for estimation of UAV dynamics in the presence of sensor/actuator faults. Dialogues Cardiovasc. Med. DCM **28**(1), 376–383 (2013)
13. Huba, W., Martin, N., AlMousa, Y., Orakwue, C., Shenoy, N.: A distributed scheduler for airborne backbone networks with directional antennas. In: Third International Conference on Communication Systems & Networks (2011)
14. Jang, H.: Airborne TDMA for high throughput and fast weather conditions notification. Int. J. Comput. Netw. Commun. **3**(3), 206–220 (2011)
15. Jang, H., Kim, E., Lee, J.J., Lim, J.: Location-based TDMAMAC for reliable aeronautical communications. IEEE Trans. Aerosp. Electron. Syst. **48**(2), 1848–1854 (2012)
16. Li, J., Gong, E., Sun, Z., Li, L., Xie, H.: An interference-based distributed TDMA scheduling algorithm for aeronautical ad hoc networks. In: International Conference on Cyber-Enabled Distributed Computing & Knowledge Discovery (2013)
17. Ko, Y.B., Shankarkumar, V., Vaidya, N.H.: Medium access control protocols using directional antennas in ad hoc networks (1999)
18. Li, P., Zhang, C., Fang, Y.: The capacity of wireless ad hoc networks using directional antennas. IEEE Trans. Mob. Comput. **10**(10), 1374–1387 (2011)
19. Liu, C., Zhang, G., Guo, W., He, R.: Kalman prediction-based neighbor discovery and its effect on routing protocol in vehicular ad hoc networks. IEEE Trans. Intell. Transp. Syst. **PP** (99), 1–11 (2019)
20. Mukherjee, A., Keshary, V., Pandya, K., Dey, N., Satapathy, S.C.: Flying ad hoc networks: a comprehensive survey. In: Satapathy, S.C., Tavares, J.M.R.S., Bhateja, V., Mohanty, J.R. (eds.) Information and Decision Sciences. AISC, vol. 701, pp. 569–580. Springer, Singapore (2018). https://doi.org/10.1007/978-981-10-7563-6_59
21. Rosati, S., Kruzelecki, K., Traynard, L., Rimoldi, B.: Speed-aware routing for UAV ad-hoc networks. In: GLOBECOM Workshops (2013)
22. Sahingoz, O.K.: Networking models in flying ad-hoc networks (FANETs): concepts and challenges. J. Intell. Robot. Syst. **74**(1–2), 513–527 (2014)
23. Sharma, V., Kumar, R.: G-FANET: an ambient network formation between ground and flying ad hoc networks. Telecommun. Syst. **65**, 1–24 (2016)
24. Sharma, V., Kumar, R.: Cooperative frameworks and network models for flying ad hoc networks: a survey. Concurr. Comput. Pract. Exp. **29**(4), 1–36 (2017)
25. Temel, S., Bekmezci, I.: On the performance of flying ad hoc networks (FANETs) utilizing near space high altitude platforms (HAPs). In: International Conference on Recent Advances in Space Technologies (2013)
26. Temel, S., Bekmezci, I.: Scalability analysis of flying ad hoc networks (FANETs): a directional antenna approach. In: IEEE International Black Sea Conference on Communications & Networking (2014)
27. Temel, S., Bekmezci, I.: LODMAC: location oriented directional MAC protocol for FANETs. Comput. Netw. **83**, 76–84 (2015)
28. Li, X., Hu, F., Hu, L., Kumar, S.: Airborne networks with multi-beam smart antennas: towards a QOS-supported, mobility-predictive MAC. In: Latifi, S. (ed.) Information Technology: New Generations. AISC, vol. 448, pp. 47–57. Springer, Cham (2016). https://doi.org/10.1007/978-3-319-32467-8_5
29. Li, Y., St-Hilaire, M., Kunz, T.: Enhancements to reduce the overhead of the reactive-greedy-reactive routing protocol for unmanned aeronautical ad-hoc networks. In: International Conference on Wireless Communications (2012)

Resource Allocation

Fair Resource Allocation Based on Deep Reinforcement Learning in Fog Networks

Huihui Xu[1(✉)], Yijun Zu[2], Fei Shen[3,4], Feng Yan[2], Fei Qin[5],
and Lianfeng Shen[2]

[1] Wuhan University, Wuhan 430072, China
xuhuis@whu.edu.cn
[2] National Mobile Communications Research Laboratory,
Southeast University, Nanjing 210096, China
zyj@seu.edu.cn
[3] Key Lab of Wireless Sensor network and Communication, Shanghai Institute
of Microsystem and Information Technology, Chinese Academy of Sciences,
Shanghai 200050, China
fei.shen@mail.sim.ac.cn
[4] Shanghai Research Center for Wireless Communications, Shanghai 201210, China
[5] The School of Electronic and Electrical Communication Engineering,
University of Chinese Academy of Sciences, Beijing 100049, China

Abstract. As the terminal devices grow explosively, the resource in a
fog network may not satisfy all the requirement of them. Thus scheduling the resource reasonably becomes a huge challenge in the future 5G
network. In the paper, we propose a fair resource allocation algorithm
based on deep reinforcement learning, which makes full use of the computational resource in a fog network. The goal of the algorithm is to
complete processing the tasks fairly for all the user nodes (UNs). The
fog nodes (FNs) are expected to assign their central processing unit
(CPU) cores to process offloading tasks reasonably. We apply the Deep
Q-Learning Network (DQN) to solve the problem of resource scheduling.
Firstly, we establish an evaluation model of a priority to set the priority
for the offloading tasks, which is related to the reward in the reinforcement learning. Secondly, the model of reinforcement learning is built by
taking the situation of UNs and resource allocation scheme as the state
of environment and the action of the agent, respectively. Subsequently,
a loss function is analysed to update the parameters of a deep neural
network. Finally, numerical simulations demonstrate the feasibility and
effectiveness of our proposed algorithm.

This work is supported in part by the National Natural Science Foundation of China
(No. 61871370, No. 61601122 and No. 61773266), the Natural Science Foundation of
Shanghai, China (No. 18ZR1437500 and No. 19ZR1423100), the Hundred Talent Program of Chinese Academy of Sciences (No. Y86BRA1001), the Fundamental Research
Funds for the Central Universities (No. 2242019K40188), the Key Research & Development Plan of Jiangsu Province (No. BE2018108), and the Postdoctoral Science Foundation of China (No. 2019M651476).

J. Zheng et al. (Eds.): ADHOCNETS 2019, LNICST 306, pp. 135–148, 2019.
https://doi.org/10.1007/978-3-030-37262-0_11

Keywords: Fog computing · Deep reinforcement learning · Resource allocation

1 Introduction

As thebibliography 5G era comes, there are an increasing number of terminal devices connecting to the network [1]. In addition, most of mobile applications generate massive data, such as augmented reality and autopilot. This brings a heavy burden on the transmission link to the cloud data server. Therefore, the fog computing is proposed to relieve the pressure of link delay and congestion in the network [2]. In a fog network, fog nodes (FNs) are expected to be deployed in the whole network and help process the data tasks offloaded from user nodes (UNs). However, as the data tasks grow explosively in the fog network, the FNs with limited resources, such as computational resources, storage resources and network resources, can not process the tasks in time, which will cause some tasks to be unprocessed for a long time. Therefore, in order to guarantee the data tasks to be processed effectively and fairly [4], it is essential to allocate the resources reasonably in the fog network.

In past few years, numerous researches focusing on resource allocation have been carried out. For example, among them, a double-matching strategy for the resource allocation problem in fog computing network is proposed [6]. The strategy analyses the utility and cost of resource allocation to maximize the cost efficiency, which is an extension of classic matching algorithm. A novel mechanism named Gaussian Process Regression for Fog-Cloud Allocation (GPRFCA) is introduced [3]. The GPR method is utilized to predict the future requests to improve the utilization of limited resource in the FNs and the Power Usage Effectiveness is considered as the metric to improve the energy efficiency of FNs. The joint radio and computational resource allocation in fog networks is formulated as a mixed integer nonlinear programming problem [5], with the constraints including transmission power, service delay and so on. To improve the user experience, the authors propose a matching game framework to solve the resource allocation problem.

Although there exist a large amount of literatures about resource allocation in fog networks, few literatures solve the resource allocation problem with deep reinforcement learning [9]. In this paper, we focus on the computational resource allocation and solve the problem of fair computational resource allocation with a classic deep reinforcement learning algorithm, Deep Q-Learning Network (DQN) [7]. After modeling computational resource allocation problem into Markov decision process, we propose a fog computing resource allocation strategy based on DQN. The strategy first sets priorities for different tasks, and then utilizes the deep reinforcement learning framework to perceive dynamical resource environments. Finally, computational resources are reallocated to different tasks in real time according to the task priorities. The strategy can not only alleviate the computing pressure of the UNs and dynamically sense the environment but also realize the automatic allocation of resources and determine the optimal resource allocation scheme.

Therefore, our work can be concluded as follows:

(1) We determine the user priorities and define different task states. The task priority model is established according to different user priorities and task states. Under the model of task priority, resource utilization and task execution rate are improved, which meets the quality of experience (QOE) of different users.
(2) We solve the resource allocation problem in the fog network with deep reinforcement learning. The state and reward of environment and the action of agent are set to establish the model of resource allocation reinforcement learning. The value function is defined to update the neural network and the analysis of the update is provided.
(3) The algorithm based on deep reinforcement learning is realized, and the resource allocation simulation experiment is completed. The effectiveness and feasibility of our proposed algorithm are verified.

The remainder of this paper is organized as follows. The preliminary, including system model and task priority, is introduced in Sect. 2. We formulate the problem in Sect. 3, where we transform the resource allocation in the fog network into the problem of deep reinforcement learning. In Sect. 4, we apply the classic deep reinforcement learning DQN to solve the problem. Numerical simulations are provided to evaluate the performance of our proposed strategy in Sect. 5. At last, the paper is concluded in Sect. 6.

2   Preliminary

2.1   System Model

We consider a fog network consisting of the cloud data server, a FN and multiple UNs, as depicted in Fig. 1. The FN is available with M total central processing unit (CPU) cores for processing the offloading tasks. The computational capacity of each CPU core is denoted as C, measured in [bit/s]. We denote the set of UNs as $\mathcal{U} = \{U_1, \ldots, U_n, \ldots, U_N\}$. The operating time of the fog network system is slotted and we denote the index of time slot as k with $k \in \mathcal{K} = \{1, 2, 3, \ldots\}$. Each time slot is denoted by t_s (in seconds). For the UNs, the possibility of data generation satisfies discrete-time On/Off Markov arrival model [8]. At each time slot, the data from UN U_n is transmitted to the FN and cached in the buffer n, where the queues in the buffer are first-in-first-out (FIFO) queues. Subsequently, the FN allocates the computational resources (CPU cores) to the cached data in the buffer. At the beginning of time slot, the CPU cores are reallocated to the different buffers according to the size of data to be processed in the different buffers. After processed by the FN, the result of the data is transmitted back to the UNs or forwarded to the cloud data server.

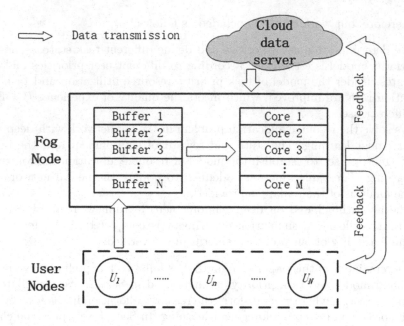

Fig. 1. System model.

2.2   Task Priority Model

Due to the multi-source nature of the UNs and the large number of data tasks, there exists the competition between the UNs. To prevent the link congestion problem caused by resource competition, it is especially essential to arrange the order of task processed by the FN reasonably. Therefore, it is considered to set a priority level for the data task from UNs before the data tasks are processed. The data tasks with higher priority are assigned computational resources preferentially.

We take the UN priority, the waiting time and the size of data tasks to be processed into consideration. The specific priority strategy are as follows. The U_n priority is represented as ζ_n. Different UNs have different user priority levels. For example, a car node has a higher user priority than a sensor node. Additionally, considering the task response speed, too long waiting time is not allowed, which results in the link congestion and poor quality of experience (QoE). Therefore, the longer the waiting time, the higher the task priority. We denote W_n^k, W_{max}^k as the waiting time of the data task from U_n, the maximum of the waiting time among the data tasks during the time slot k, respectively. At last, the quantity of the cumulative tasks in the buffer should be considered. Similarly, the more the cumulative tasks in the buffer, the higher the task priority. We denote D_n^k, D_{max}^k as the cumulative tasks from U_n, the maximum of cumulative tasks during the time slot k, respectively.

Above all, we can obviously obtain the priority of the data task from U_n as follow.

$$\theta_n^k = \left(\left\lfloor \frac{D_n^k}{D_{\max}^k} \right\rfloor \times \alpha + \left\lfloor \frac{W_n^k}{W_{\max}^k} \right\rfloor \times \beta \right) \times \zeta_n, \tag{1}$$

where α, β represent the weight coefficient of the cumulative tasks and the waiting time, respectively.

Under consideration of fair resource allocation, the priority θ_n^k is adjusted dynamically according to the state of the fog network, including the cumulative tasks and the waiting time.

3 Problem Formulation

Resource allocation in the fog network is a decision-making process where to allocate computational resources to process the data tasks from the UNs during each time slot. Thus, we model this decision-making process into a Markov decision process. Because the data tasks generate randomly in the UNs, the Markov transition probabilities are uncertain. The environment's dynamics are unknown when the agent selects the action, thereby we use model-free reinforcement learning to obtain the best policy. Therefore, the fog computing resource allocation strategy based on deep reinforcement learning is to continuously sample by interacting with the external environment, and to find the optimal strategy by maximizing the cumulative reward. The resource allocation model based on reinforcement learning is established as follows.

3.1 State Vector

At the beginning of each slot time, the FN caches the data tasks, which generates at the previous time slot, to the corresponding buffers. The system state can be obtained as follows.

- D^k: D^k is the vector of the cumulative tasks in the buffers and can be represented as $[D_1^k, \ldots, D_n^k, \ldots, D_N^k]$, where D_n^k is the cumulative tasks in the nth buffer during the time slot k.
- W^k: W^k is the vector of the waiting time. And W^k can be represented as $[W_1^k, \ldots, W_n^k, \ldots, W_N^k]$, where W_n^k is the waiting time of data tasks from U_n in the time slot k.

Finally, the state of the fog network can be denoted as

$$s^k = \{D^k, W^k\}. \tag{2}$$

3.2 Action Vector

After sensing the state of the fog network, the agent selects the action from the action set $\mathcal{A}$ according to the strategy π, namely, $a^k = \pi\left(s^k\right)$. a^k is the vector of action and can be expressed as

$$a^k = \left[a_1^k, \ldots, a_n^k, \ldots, a_N^k\right], \tag{3}$$

where $\sum_{n=1}^{N} a_n^k = M$ and a_n^k represents the number of CPU cores allocated to process the data tasks from U_n.

After determining $\boldsymbol{a}^k$, if there exists $a_n^k = 0$, meaning the data tasks from U_n are not processed during the time slot k, the waiting time increases. The waiting time state of U_n can be expressed as

$$W_n^{k+1} = \begin{cases} W_n^k + 1, & \text{if } a_n^k = 0 \\ 0, & \text{if } a_n^k \neq 0 \end{cases} \tag{4}$$

3.3   Reward Function

Taking the action $\boldsymbol{a}^k$ under the state of $\boldsymbol{s}^k$, the agent can obtain a reward from the environment. Effectively setting the reward function is very important for deep reinforcement learning to achieve the desired goal. In order to maximize the execution rate of the task and the satisfaction of the user, we set the reward function as follows.

$$r^k = \sum_{n=1}^{N} \theta_n^k \times \phi_n^k, \tag{5}$$

where ϕ_n^k represents the data tasks from UN U_n processed during the time slot k, and can be expressed as

$$\phi_n^k = a_n^k C t_s. \tag{6}$$

At the time slot k, the agent obtains the immediate reward r^k. Our goal is to maximize the total reward, which can be expressed as follows.

$$R^k = \sum_{i=0}^{\infty} \gamma^i r^{k+i}, \tag{7}$$

where the discount factor $\gamma \in (0,1)$ weighs the myopic or foresighted decisions.

3.4   Value Function

The action $\boldsymbol{a}^k$ is drawn from a stochastic policy $\pi(\boldsymbol{a}|\boldsymbol{s}) = \Pr(\boldsymbol{a}^k = \boldsymbol{a}|\boldsymbol{s}^k = \boldsymbol{s})$, which is a mapping from the state of the fog network to the probability of taking actions. The value function is the expected value of cumulative discounted rewards received over the entire process following the policy. The process of reinforcement learning contains two phases: (a) policy evaluation and (b) policy improvement. In the first phase, the agent samples data according to the stochastic policy $\pi(\boldsymbol{a}|\boldsymbol{s})$. In the second phase, the agent updates the policy $\pi(\boldsymbol{a}|\boldsymbol{s})$ according to the value function.

There are two definitions of value function: (a) the state value function $V(\boldsymbol{s})$ and (b) the state-action value function $Q(\boldsymbol{s}, \boldsymbol{a})$. The relationship between $V(\boldsymbol{s})$ and $Q(\boldsymbol{s}, \boldsymbol{a})$ satisfies $V(\boldsymbol{s}) = \sum_{\boldsymbol{s}} \Pr(\boldsymbol{a}^k = \boldsymbol{a}|\boldsymbol{s}^k = \boldsymbol{s}) Q(\boldsymbol{s}, \boldsymbol{a})$. $Q(\boldsymbol{s}, \boldsymbol{a})$ can be expressed as

$$Q(\boldsymbol{s}, \boldsymbol{a}) = E\left[\sum_{i=0}^{\infty} \gamma^i r^{k+i}|\boldsymbol{s}^k = \boldsymbol{s}, \boldsymbol{a}^k = \boldsymbol{a}\right]. \tag{8}$$

The optimal $Q(s, a)$ is denoted as $Q^*(s, a)$ and can be calculated by the Bellman optimality equation as follows.

$$Q^*(s^k, a^k) = E\left[r^k + \gamma \max_{a^{k+1}} Q\left(s^{k+1}, a^{k+1}\right)\right]. \tag{9}$$

To optimize the long-term performance, the Eq. (9) is adopted to update the value function in the Q-learning algorithm. However, when the space of action is very high or even continuous, it is almost impossible to calculate all $Q(s, a)$. Consequently, neural network can be used as the function approximator to approximate the value function.

3.5   Q-Value Approximation

We apply deep neural network (DNN) to approximate the value function. Therefore, the Q-value can be represented as $Q_w(s, a)$, which uses a fully-connected DNN that is parameterised by a set of weights $w = \{w_1, w_2, \ldots, w_n\}$. DNN is comprised of input layer, output layer and hidden layers. The calculation of each layer consists of three parts: weight, bias and activation (e.g., sigmoid, tanh, ReLU). For example, let y_{ij} and x_i denote the output value of the jth neuron in the layer i and the input values, respectively. Therefore, we can obtain

$$y_{ij} = f_{act}\left(w_i \cdot x_i + b_{ij}\right), \tag{10}$$

where f_{act} is the activation function, w_i is the weights in the layer i and b_{ij} is the bias.

The network parameters will be updated by minimizing the loss function, which can be expressed as

$$L(w) = E\left[r^k + \gamma \max_{a^{k+1}} Q_w\left(s^{k+1}, a^{k+1}\right) - Q_w\left(s^k, a^k\right)\right]^2. \tag{11}$$

4   Solution with DQN

DQN is an improvement on Q-learning, which replaces Q-value function with a deep neural network. Additionally, experience replay and target network are introduced in the DQN, making the neural network more stable and well-trained.

4.1   Target Network

In order to make the performance of the algorithm more stable, two structurally identical neural networks are established: a network with continuously updated network parameters (evaluation network) and a neural network for target value update (target network). At the initial moment, the parameters of the evaluation network are assigned to the target network, and then the evaluation network continues to update the neural network parameters, while the parameters of the target network are fixed. After several rounds of updates for the evaluation network, the parameters of the evaluation network are assigned to the target network. The setting of the two networks makes the target Q value stable over a period of time, thereby improving the stability of the algorithm update.

Therefore, the loss function in Eq. (11) can be reexpressed as follows.

$$L(w) = E\left[Q_t - Q_w\left(s^k, a^k\right)\right]^2, \tag{12}$$

where Q_t is the Q-value generated in the target network and can be expressed as $Q_t = r^k + \gamma \max_{a^{k+1}} Q_{w^t}\left(s^{k+1}, a^{k+1}\right)$. w^t is the weight parameters in the target network.

When the loss function is continuously differentiable with respect to parameters w, the parameters w of the evaluation network can be updated with the gradient of the loss function. Therefore the update of w is as follows:

$$\Delta w = \alpha_l \left[Q_t - Q_w\left(s^k, a^k\right)\right] \nabla_w Q_w\left(s^k, a^k\right), \tag{13}$$

where α_l is the learning rate of the evaluation network.

4.2 Experience Replay

In DNN, the data used to train the neural network needs to be guaranteed be independent. However, the data sampled from each episode is related to each other. The experience replay is proposed to break up the temporal correlations within different data in the episode. The main idea of the experience replay is to store the agent's own experience from different episodes and then build a data set to train the neural network.

The data stored in the replay buffer is a tuple of (s^k, a^k, r^k, s^{k+1}). DNN samples a mini-batch of I tuples from the replay buffer and utilizes the stochastic gradient descent (SGD) method to update parameters. Therefore, the parameters w updated in Eq. (13) can be reexpressed as follows:

$$\Delta w = \alpha_l \frac{1}{I} \sum_{i=1}^{I} \left[Q_t^i - Q_w\left(s_i^k, a_i^k\right)\right] \nabla_w Q_w\left(s_i^k, a_i^k\right), \tag{14}$$

where $Q_t^i = r_i^k + \gamma \max_{a^{k+1}} Q_{w^t}\left(s_i^{k+1}, a^{k+1}\right)$. The index i refers to the ith sample.

4.3 DQN Based Resource Allocation Algorithm

The architecture of DQN is depicted in Fig. 2. In the process of reinforcement learning, the interaction between the agent and environment generates a large amount of data like (s^k, a^k, r^k, s^{k+1}), which are stored in the replay buffer. The data set in replay buffer D is used to train the evaluation neural network.

The main steps of the DQN based resource allocation algorithm with target network and experience replay are as follows.

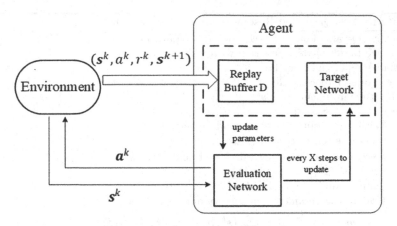

Fig. 2. The architecture of DQN

(1) The evaluation network initializes the parameters. The target network is built with the same parameters as that of the evaluation network. The replay buffer is cleared.

(2) The agent observes the state s^k of the environment and generates action a^k according to the current ϵ-greedy policy.

(3) The agent observes the next state s^{k+1} and the reward r^k. The transition (s^k, a^k, r^k, s^{k+1}) is stored in the experience replay buffer.

(4) Sample random mini-batch of I tuples from replay buffer.

(5) The evaluation network is updated with the mini-batch from replay buffer according to Eq. (14).

(6) The target network is updated with the parameters of the evaluation network every X steps.

The specific algorithm is shown in Algorithm 1.

5 Simulation Results

In order to verify the feasibility and efficiency of tasks offloading algorithm based on deep reinforcement learning, we use the task execution rate and waiting time as the evaluation indicators of the simulation experiment. We define task execution rate as follows.

$$ER_n = \frac{O_n}{O_{total}}, \tag{15}$$

where O_n, O_{total} indicate that the processed data size offloaded by U_n and the size of data generated by U_n in a certain period of time. All parameters are provided in Table 1.

For convenience, in Figs. 3, 4 and 5, the number of CPU and UN is 5 and 3, respectively. And the priority of U_1, U_2, U_3 is set as 0.5, 0.3, 0.2.

Figure 3 compares the performance of the random allocation scheme, the Fair and Energy-Minimized Task Offloading (FEMTO) [10] scheme and our

---

Algorithm 1. DQN based Resource Allocation Algorithm

1: Initialize Q-value function with random weights w
   Initialize target Q-value function with weights $w^- \leftarrow w$
   Initialize replay memory D
2: **for** episode=1 to $E_{\max}$ **do**
3:    Reset environment state s^1.
4:    **for** $k = 1$ to $k_{\max}$ **do**
5:       With probability ϵ select a random action a^k,
          otherwise select $a^k = \arg\max_a Q_w\left(s^k, a^k\right)$.
6:       Execute a^k, observe reward r^k and next state s^{k+1}.
7:       Store (s^k, a^k, r^k, s^{k+1}) in D.
8:       Sample random mini-batch of I tuples from D.
9:       Update the parameters of the evaluation network:

$$w \leftarrow w + \alpha_l \frac{1}{I} \sum_{i=1}^{I} \left[Q_t^i - Q_w\left(s_i^k, a_i^k\right)\right] \nabla_w Q_w\left(s_i^k, a_i^k\right).$$

10:      Every X steps, update target network parameters:
          $w^- \leftarrow w$.
11:   **end for**
12: **end for**

Table 1. Simulation parameters

Parameter	Value
Discount factor γ	0.9
Capacity of replay memory D	300
Number of CPU cores M	$4-10$
Number of UNs N	$2-8$
Time slot t_s	$5\mu s$
Mini-batch I	30
Weight coefficiency α	2
Weight coefficiency β	5
Computational capacity C	200bit/s
Explore probability ϵ	0.1
Learning rate of network α_l	0.01
Priority of UN ζ_n	$0-1$

proposed scheme. For the random allocation scheme, the fog node randomly assigns the computing resources of the node in each step size. For the FEMTO schemeit uses the fair scheduling metric mechanism to optimize the allocation of resources with the objective of fair and energy minimization. As shown in Fig. 3, the average task execution rate of our proposed algorithm is significantly higher than the random allocation. In addition, as total step increases, the average task execution rate of our proposed algorithm increases gradually while the execution rate of the FEMTO scheme decreases.

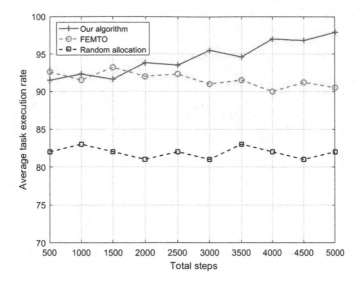

Fig. 3. Comparison between our algorithm and random allocation.

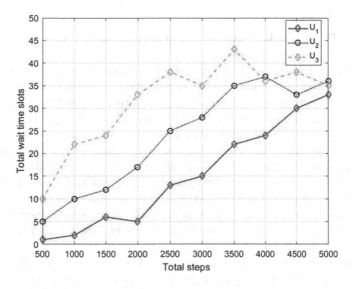

Fig. 4. Relationship between steps and waiting time in different UNs.

As shown in Fig. 4, U_1 with the highest user priority has the least total number of tasks waiting, and U_3 with the lowest user priority has the most waiting time slots, namely, U_3 has the highest probability of not being allocated computing resources in the time slot. As total step increases, the waiting time slots of UNs increase gradually. After reaching a certain peak value, the growth slows down, and the number of waiting time slots of different users gradually approaches.

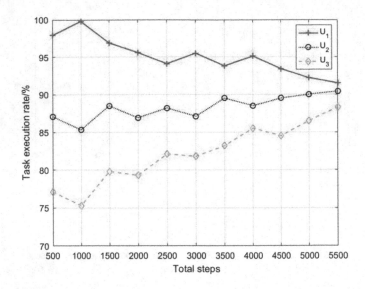

Fig. 5. Relationship between steps and task execution rate in different UNs.

In Fig. 5, U_1 has the highest task execution rate and U_3 has the lowest at the initial moment. As the total number of time slots increases, the task execution rate of different UNs gradually approach. The analysis demonstrates that the task with high priority has a high task execution rate, namely, the task with higher priority is allocated computational resources firstly for task processing such that the task is processed faster. The task with higher priority has higher service satisfaction. As the number of time slots increases, the accumulation of data tasks from UN with low priority and the waiting time of tasks increase such that the task priority of them gradually increases, resulting that the priority of UN has little effect on task execution. From Figs. 4 and 5, we observe that whatever the priority of the UN is, the computational resources are allocated fairly finally, which results in the increment of the average task execution rate in Fig. 3. Additionally, the fluctuation of the curves in Figs. 4 and 5 indicates the learning process of reinforcement learning.

As shown in Fig. 6, when the number of UNs increases, the total waiting time slots of each UN increases obviously. Additionally, we observe that when the number of UNs is twice more than that of CPU cores, the waiting time increases rapidly, which reduces the performance of our proposed algorithm. Therefore, it will be better that there exist enough CPU cores to schedule.

In Fig. 7, we can observe the trend of loss function $L(\boldsymbol{w})$. As the training steps increase, the loss function tends to converge, which satisfies our expectation.

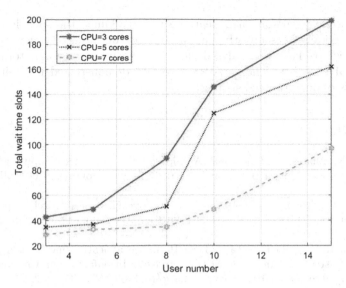

Fig. 6. Relationship between the number of UNs and waiting time with different CPU cores.

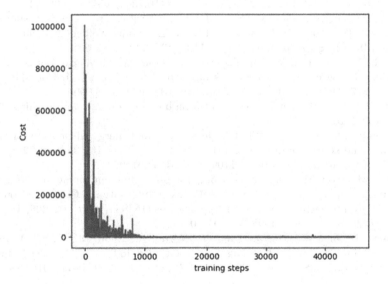

Fig. 7. Trend of loss function.

6   Conclusion

In this paper, we applied deep reinforcement learning to allocate computational resource in fog networks. At the beginning of each time slot, the computational resource is reallocated to process the data tasks. We transformed the process into a Markov decision process. And then, we introduced the state, reward and action of the deep reinforcement learning and explained the specific algorithm of DQN in detail. Subsequently, the analysis of updating the neural network was provided. At last, we analysed the task execution rate and total waiting time slots of each UN. The simulation results demonstrated the fairness and effectiveness of our proposed strategy.

References

1. Abbas, N., Zhang, Y., Taherkordi, A., Skeie, T.: Mobile edge computing: a survey. IEEE Internet Things J. **5**(1), 450–465 (2018). https://doi.org/10.1109/JIOT.2017. 2750180
2. Chiang, M., Zhang, T.: Fog and IoT: an overview of research opportunities. IEEE Internet Things J. **3**(6), 854–864 (2016). https://doi.org/10.1109/JIOT.2016. 2584538
3. da Silva, R.A.C., da Fonseca, N.L.S.: Resource allocation mechanism for a fog-cloud infrastructure. In: 2018 IEEE International Conference on Communications (ICC), pp. 1–6, May 2018. https://doi.org/10.1109/ICC.2018.8422237
4. Ghazy, A.S., Selmy, H.A.I., Shalaby, H.M.H.: Fair resource allocation schemes for cooperative dynamic free-space optical networks. IEEE/OSA J. Opt. Commun. Netw. **8**(11), 822–834 (2016). https://doi.org/10.1364/JOCN.8.000822
5. Gu, Y., Chang, Z., Pan, M., Song, L., Han, Z.: Joint radio and computational resource allocation in IoT fog computing. IEEE Trans. Vehicular Technol. **67**(8), 7475–7484 (2018). https://doi.org/10.1109/TVT.2018.2820838
6. Jia, B., Hu, H., Zeng, Y., Xu, T., Yang, Y.: Double-matching resource allocation strategy in fog computing networks based on cost efficiency. J. Commun. Netw. **20**(3), 237–246 (2018). https://doi.org/10.1109/JCN.2018.000036
7. Mnih, V., et al.: Human-level control through deep reinforcement learning. Nature **518**(7540), 529 (2015)
8. Ozmen, M., Gursoy, M.C.: Wireless throughput and energy efficiency with random arrivals and statistical queuing constraints. IEEE Trans. Inf. Theory **62**(3), 1375–1395 (2016). https://doi.org/10.1109/TIT.2015.2510027
9. Sarigl, M., Avci, M.: Performance comparision of different momentum techniques on deep reinforcement learning. In: 2017 IEEE International Conference on INnovations in Intelligent SysTems and Applications (INISTA), pp. 302–306, July 2017. https://doi.org/10.1109/INISTA.2017.8001175
10. Zhang, G., Shen, F., Liu, Z., Yang, Y., Wang, K., Zhou, M.: FEMTO: fair and energy-minimized task offloading for fog-enabled IoT networks. IEEE Internet Things J. **6**(3), 4388–4400 (2019). https://doi.org/10.1109/JIOT.2018.2887229

Multi-agent Reinforcement Learning for Joint Wireless and Computational Resource Allocation in Mobile Edge Computing System

Yawen Zhang[✉], Weiwei Xia, Feng Yan, Huaqing Cheng, and Lianfeng Shen

National Mobile Communications Research Laboratory,
Southeast University, Nanjing 210096, China
{220170890,wwxia,feng.yan,220170869,lfshen}@seu.edu.cn

Abstract. Mobile edge computing (MEC) is a new paradigm to provide computing capabilities at the edge of pervasive radio access networks in close proximity to intelligent terminals. In this paper, a resource allocation strategy based on the variable learning rate multi-agent reinforcement learning (VLR-MARL) algorithm is proposed in the MEC system to maximize the long term utility of all intelligent terminals while ensuring the intelligent terminals' quality of service requirement. The novelty of this algorithm is that each agent only needs to maintain its own action value function so that the computationally expensive issue with the large action space can be avoided. Moreover, the learning rate is changed according to the expected payoff of the current strategy to speed up convergence and get the optimal solution. Simulation results show our algorithm performs better than other reinforcement learning algorithm both on the learning speed and users' long term utilities.

Keywords: Mobile edge computing · Joint resource allocation · Multi-agent reinforcement learning · Variable learning rate

1 Introduction

With the development of Internet, mobile intelligent terminals are becoming more and more popular and its function is more and more various. New applications such as face recognition, image recognition, automatic driving, video chat and augmented reality (AR) keep emerging [8]. However, these emerging applications require that mobile devices should have abundant computational resources and storage resources, while the resources of intelligent terminals are limited.

Mobile edge computing (MEC) has developed rapidly in recent years, as it provides a large amount of computational resources to bridge the gap between

This work was supported by the National Natural Science Foundation of China (No. 61741102, 61601122, U1805262).

J. Zheng et al. (Eds.): ADHOCNETS 2019, LNICST 306, pp. 149–161, 2019.
https://doi.org/10.1007/978-3-030-37262-0_12

the demands of applications and the restricted capacity of intelligent terminals. MEC servers are deployed at the base stations (BSs) in close proximity to mobile subscribers to execute latency-sensitive services, thereby extending computing, storage and data processing capabilities of intelligent terminals [5].

The joint computational and wireless resources allocation in mobile edge computing systems has been a key point attracting great interests in the MEC system in recent years [7]. To address the problem that the users in the MEC system typically suffer from unfair resource allocation, an approach is proposed in [17] to maximize the overall network throughput under the constraint of each user's minimum transmission rate. In [16], the offloading selection, radio resource and computational resource allocation are jointly optimized to minimize the energy consumption on smart mobile devices in a multi-mobile-users MEC system. In [9], three models, namely local compression, edge cloud compression and partial compression offloading are studied and compared. However, in their papers, the MEC servers need to know the global information.

Reinforcement Learning (RL) interacts with the environment and improves the behavior through trial and error to obtain the optimal solution. RL algorithm is a learning method that requires less prior knowledge and has been widely studied in the artificial intelligence community [1]. Therefore, there are also some literatures on the use of RL to solve the problem of resource allocation. In [14], an intelligent agent is designed to develop a real-time adaptive policy for computational resource allocation in order to improve the average end-to-end reliability by employing a deep reinforcement learning method. In [15], a dynamic offloading framework was formulated as a multi-label classification problem and the deep supervised learning method is developed to minimize the computational overhead. The Q-learning based and deep reinforcement learning based schemes are proposed respectively in [6] to tackle the resource allocation in wireless MEC system. However, the literatures above only study the situation after offloading without considering the necessity of offloading. Besides, Q-learning algorithm will cause the large state and action spaces, which leads to high computational complexity.

In this paper, variable learning rate multi-agent reinforcement learning (VLR-MARL) algorithm is proposed and the main contributions of this paper are as follows:

(1) Wireless and computation resources are jointly allocated in this paper in order to maximize the utility by increasing the throughput and reducing the cost of each user. Moreover, the necessity of offloading is also considered in this paper.
(2) Multi-agent reinforcement learning (MARL) method is used to reduce the learning time and speed up the search for the optimal strategy through multiple agents parallel processing.
(3) The learning rate is changed according to the expected payoff of the current policy and each agent only needs to maintain its own action value function, which reduces the complexity of this algorithm.

The rest of paper is organized as follows: in Sect. 2, the system model is described in detail. In Sect. 3, the VLR-MARL based resource allocation policy is proposed. Section 4 presents the simulation results. Finally, we conclude the paper in Sect. 5.

2   System Model

The MEC system studied in this paper is illustrated in Fig. 1, which includes a base station, MEC Servers and intelligent terminals. The intelligent terminals are connected to the BS through the wireless links and the MEC server is deployed inside the BS or connected to the BS through the optical fiber. The MEC server is a relatively small pool of resources with limited communication and computational resources.

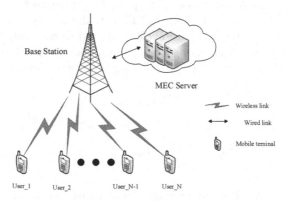

Fig. 1. System model.

In this paper, we consider that there are N users as $\mathcal{N} = \{1, 2, 3, \cdots, N\}$. Each user has computational intensive tasks that need to be offloaded to the MEC server. We can divide the wireless channel into K subcarriers, where $\mathcal{K} = \{1, 2, 3, \cdots, K\}$. Assuming that the subcarriers are orthogonal to each other, the users that choose different subcarriers do not interfere with each other. The connection between the user n and the subcarrier k is defined as c_n^k. When the user n utilizes the subcarrier k, $c_n^k = 1$, and $c_n^k = 0$ otherwise. Each user can only access to no more than one subchannel, which means

$$\sum_{k=1}^{K} c_n^k \leq 1, \forall n \in N \tag{1}$$

2.1   Communication Model

Since many users share the same channel, we need to take channel interference into account when transferring computing tasks to the MEC server through the wireless channel. The uplink data rate of each user can be expressed as follows:

$$r_n = \omega \log_2 \left(1 + \frac{p_n c_n^k g_{n,s}}{\sigma_0 + \sum_{i \in N, i \neq n} p_i c_i^k g_{i,s}} \right) \tag{2}$$

where ω and σ_0 represent channel bandwidth and background noise power, p_n is the transmission power of user n which is determined according to some power control algorithms such as [13] and [3]. Further, $g_{n,s}$ is the channel gain between user n and BS s, which is written as

$$g_{n,s} = l_{n,s}^{-\alpha} \tag{3}$$

where $l_{n,s}$ is the distance between user n and BS s and α is the path loss factor.

We assume that each user n has a computation-intensive task $J_n = \{b_n, d_n\}$. Here b_n denotes the size of input data (including task code and input parameters) and d_n denotes the numbers of CPU cycles required to complete the task J_n. A terminal can apply the methods in [4] to obtain the information of b_n and d_n. In order to offload the task to the MEC server, additional wireless transfer time is required as

$$t_n^{up} = b_n / r_n \tag{4}$$

The energy consumption generated during this period can be expressed as

$$e_n^c = p_n \frac{b_n}{r_n} + L_n \tag{5}$$

where L_n represents the energy consumption generated for a period of time after the completion of data uploading. After the MEC server receives the computational task, it will execute the task.

2.2 Computation Model

We assume that f_n^c is the computational resources (the number of CPU cycles per second) allocated to user n from the MEC server, so the task execution time for user n can be expressed as

$$t_n^{exe} = d_n / f_n^c \tag{6}$$

Therefore, the total overhead of user n can be given as

$$K_n^c = \lambda_n^t (t_n^{up} + t_n^{exe}) + \lambda_n^e e_n^c \tag{7}$$

The time it takes for the MEC server to transmit the results back to the user is negligible because the results are usually much smaller than the uplink data.

If the user does not upload the task to the MEC server, but decide to compute it locally, the cost only includes the computational time and energy consumption.

Let f_n^m be the computational capability of the user n. The local computational time of the task $J(n)$ can be given as

$$t_{n,local}^{exe} = d_n / f_n^m \tag{8}$$

Then the local energy consumption can be denoted as

$$e_n^{local} = \gamma_n d_n \tag{9}$$

where γ_n is the coefficient denoting the consumed energy per CPU cycle, which can be obtained by the measurement method in [12].

According to the Eqs. (8) and (9), then the local overhead can be expressed as

$$K_n^{local} = \lambda_n^t t_{n,local}^{exe} + \lambda_n^e e_n^{local} \tag{10}$$

where $\lambda_n^t, \lambda_n^e \in [0,1]$ represents the weighting parameters of computational time and energy consumption for intelligent terminal n.

The utility function for each user should be related to the data transfer rate and resource overhead. Therefore, the utility function for the nth user can be given as:

$$u_n = \rho_i r_n - v_i(\lambda_n^t(t_n^{up} + t_n^{exe}) + \lambda_n^e e_n^c) \tag{11}$$

The first item in the above formula represents the data transmission rate provided to the user, and the second item represents the total cost incurred in offloading the task to the MEC server. ρ_i and v_i are coefficients of both items.

2.3 Problem Formulation

The resource allocation in MEC system is formulated as an optimization problem. The objective of this paper is to maximize the utility function of all agents. When the cost of offloading is less than the cost of local computing, it can be considered that the resource allocation is reasonable and can meet users overhead requirement, otherwise the offloading is unreasonable. Each user can only choose one subcarrier. Under this constraint, the problem is formulated as

$$\max U = \sum_n u_n \tag{12}$$

$$s.t. K_n^{exe} < K_n^{local} \tag{13}$$

$$\sum_{k=1}^{K} c_n^k = 1, \forall n \in N \tag{14}$$

3   Multi-agent Reinforcement Learning Based Resource Allocation Algorithm

In this section, reinforcement learning is applied to solving the problem (12)–(14) to obtain the joint strategy of wireless and computational resource allocation. In the following, we first present the basic model of RL, then propose MARL to speed up the rate of convergence by parallel computation, and at last add variable learning rate to reduce the complexity of state and action space.

3.1   Basic Model

In the MEC network, each user acts as an agent. In each time slot, the agent chooses an action from action space. After applying an action, the agent receives a reward or punishment from the environment.

(1) State Space: The degree of satisfaction of user n can be defined as $s_n(t)$, so state space is expressed as

$$\mathcal{S}(t) = \{s_1(t), s_2(t), \ldots, s_N(t)\} \tag{15}$$

where $s_n(t) = \{0, 1\}$, when $s_n(t) = 0$, it means that the offloading cost of the user is more expensive than the local computation. On the contrary, if it is $s_n(t) = 1$, it means that the offloading is reasonable and the user meets the needs of overhead costs.

(2) Action Space: Each user selects computational and wireless resources, so the action space can be represented as:

$$a_n(t) = \{b_n(t), c_n(t)\} \tag{16}$$

where $c_n(t)$ represents computational resources obtained from the server and $b_n(t)$ represents wireless resources. The computational resources provided by the server have been decentralized as $\{4000, 4500, 5000, 5500\}$, therefore $c_n(t)$ represents the computing resource arbitrarily selected on behalf of the user. Besides, $b_n(t) = \{b_n^1(t), b_n^2(t), \ldots, b_n^K(t)\}$, $b_n^k(t) = 1$ represents that user n chooses subchannel k.

(3) Reward: When the user chooses the action $a_n(t)$ by observing the state $s_n(t)$, it will obtain an immediate reward $r_n(t)$ as

$$r_n(t) = u_n(t) - \Phi \tag{17}$$

where $\Phi > 0$ is a fixed cost when the user chooses an action. Multiple agents collectively explore the environment and refine wireless and computational resource allocation based on their own observations of the environment state. While the resource allocation problem may appear a competitive game, in order to make all agents cooperate with each other, the same reward is used for all agents. As such, the reward includes the instantaneous utilities of all intelligence terminals. In the meantime, to achieve the objective that all users offload successfully as much as possible, the reward is set to add a constant number Ω, that is greater than the largest utility. The reward of the user at each time step t is defined as

$$R_n(t) = \begin{cases} \sum_n r_n(t), if \sum_n s_n(t) < N \\ \sum_n r_n(t) + \Omega, f \sum_n s_n(t) = N \end{cases} \tag{18}$$

3.2 Multi-agent Reinforcement Learning Policy

Reinforcement learning often has the characteristics of delay in return, so a function is defined to indicate the long-term influence on the strategy chosen in its current state. This function is called the value function [10]. The expression of value function is

$$V^\pi(s) = \mathbb{E}_\pi[\sum_{i=0}^\infty \gamma^i r_i | s_0 = s] \tag{19}$$

where $\mathbb{E}(x)$ denotes the expectation of x. The above formula represents a cumulative expectation of the reward value obtained by the strategy in the initial state s, and γ^i is the discount factor to measure the importance of the reward in the value function. In general, the further away from the current state, the smaller the effect of the reward.

The current value function can be estimated by the value function of the subsequent state and the formula can be obtained as

$$V^\pi(s) = \pi(s) \sum_{s' \in S} p(s, s')[r_0 + \gamma V^\pi(s')] \tag{20}$$

where $p(s, s')$ represents the state transition probability from state s to state s' and $\pi(s)$ denotes the policy of agent i at state s. All subsequent states can be obtained from the model formula $\pi(s)$ and action set. When these conditions are unknown, the subsequent state can be obtained only by trials and sampling.

A policy usually corresponds to multiple execution actions. The value function can be decomposed into the expression related to each action, and the action value function can be obtained as

$$Q(s, a) = r_s^a + \gamma \sum_{s \in S} p(s, s') \sum_{a' \in A} \pi(a|s') Q(s', a') \tag{21}$$

where r_s^a denotes the reward when agent i chooses action a at state s, $p(s, s')$ represents the state transition probability from state s to state s' and $\pi(a|s')$ denotes the policy of agent i at state s' choosing action a.

In order not to get stuck in a locally optimal solution, we adopt $\varepsilon - greedy$ strategies [2] to explore the environment. ε is a very small number, as the probability of picking a random action and $1 - \varepsilon$ denotes the probability value of selecting the optimal action.

$$\pi(a|s) = \begin{cases} 1 - \varepsilon + \frac{\varepsilon}{|A(s)|}, a = \arg\max Q(s, a) \\ \frac{\varepsilon}{|A(s)|}, a \neq \arg\max Q(s, a) \end{cases} \tag{22}$$

One popular reinforcement learning method is Q-learning [11]. In Q-learning, the optimal Q-value function can be obtained from the Bellman's equation. The Q-value of the current state can be calculated using the Q-value of the next state. There is a difference between the calculated Q-value and the original value in this state, which is called incremental Q-value. Then, we can use it to update the Q-value, which is given as:

$$Q(s,a) \leftarrow Q(s,a) + \alpha \left(r + \gamma \max_{a'} Q(s',a') - Q(s,a) \right) \qquad (23)$$

where α represents the learning rate and usually $\alpha = 0.1$, $\max_{a'} Q(s',a')$ represents the maximum Q-value of all possible actions in the next state.

In this paper, all users are assumed to be agents. All the actions of agents constitute the joint action space set $A = a_1 \times a_2 \times \ldots a_n$. The return function of each Agent is calculated based on the joint action space and all agents' policies are combined into joint strategy h. The Q-value of each Agent in state s is

$$Q_n^h(s,a) = \mathbb{E}\{\sum_{k=0}^{\infty} \gamma^k r_{i,k+1} | s_0 = s, a_0 = a, h\} \qquad (24)$$

This Q-value iteration algorithm is guaranteed to converge to the optimal point with $Q(s,a) \rightarrow Q^*(s,a)$ as $iteration \rightarrow \infty$ [10]. Because Q-learning is off-policy, which means the agent learning and interacting with the environment are different. The behavior policy is used to interact with the environment to generate datas in order to make decisions in the training process. The target policy is constantly studying and optimizing using the datas generated by the behavior policy. The target policy is greedy while choosing behavior uses $\varepsilon -$ *greedy* strategy. The maximum action value is used to calculate the expected return of the next state, however the current policy does not always select the optimal action. The strength of the off-policy is that by separating the target policy from the behavior policy, the global optimal value can be obtained while maintaining exploration.

3.3   Variable Learning Rate-MARL Algorithm

To reduce the space complexity of multi-agent problem and improve convergence, we propose a VLR-MARL algorithm. The learning rate changes by the principle that learn fast while losing and learn slowly while winning. The principle helps convergence by giving other agents more time to adapt to strategy changes that initially seem beneficial, while allowing agents to adapt more quickly to other agents' harmful strategy changes. This algorithm requires two learning parameters δ_{lose} and δ_{win}. If the agent is currently determined to be winning, δ_{win} is used, otherwise, δ_{lose} is used. It is based on virtual game, and replaces the unknown equilibrium strategy with the approximate equilibrium average greedy strategy.

The agent will explore action a_k when it transfers from stage s_k to s_{k+1} and has the reward function R. Then its average estimation strategy update can be expressed as:

$$\bar{\pi}_i(s_k, a_k) = \bar{\pi}_i(s_k, a_k) + \frac{1}{C(s)}[\pi_i(s_k, a_k) - \bar{\pi}_i(s_k, a_k)] \qquad (25)$$

where $C(s)$ denotes the number of occurrences of state s. The strategy can be given as

$$\pi_i(s_k, a_k) = \pi_i(s_k, a_k) + \Delta_{sa_i} \tag{26}$$

$$\Delta_{sa_i} = \begin{cases} -\delta_{sa_i} a_i \neq \arg\max_{a'} Q(s, a') \\ \sum_{a' \neq a_i} \delta_{sa'}, others \end{cases} \tag{27}$$

The learning rate that is used to upgrade the policy depends on whether the agent is currently determined to be winning or losing. This is determined by comparing whether the current expected value is greater than the current expected value of the average strategy. If the expectation of the current policy is smaller, then the larger learning rate δ_{lose} is used.

$$\delta_{sa_i} = \min(\pi(s_k, a_k), \frac{\delta}{|A_i| - 1}) \tag{28}$$

$$\delta = \begin{cases} \delta_{win}, \sum_{a_i \in A_i} \pi_i(s_k, a_k)Q_i > \sum_{a_i \in A_i} \bar{\pi}_i(s_k, a_k)Q_i \\ \delta_{lose}, others \end{cases} \tag{29}$$

The detailed procedure of the proposed VLR-MARL algorithm is presented in Algorithm 1.

4   Performance Evaluation

In this section, we evaluate the performance of our VLR-MARL algorithm and provide the numerical results compared with other algorithms.

In this simulation, we suppose that there are $20, 30$ or 40 users within a radius of $100\,m$, randomly distributed around the base station. The total number of channels is $K = 5$ with channel bandwidth $W = 5\,MHz$. The user's transmitted power is $100\,mW$. The path loss coefficient of the channel gain is $\alpha = 4$ and the background noise power σ_0 is $-100\,dBm$. The size of all users' input data b_n for the computation task J_n is $5000\,kB$ and the number of CPU cycles d_n required to complete the task is $1000\,Mc$. The available computational resources in MEC servers is $f_n^c = \{5000, 8000, 10000, 12000\}\,M/s$. The local computational capability of each user is $500\,M/s$.

4.1   Convergence of Proposed Algorithm

The convergence of the proposed VLR-MARL algorithm is shown in Fig. 2. The initial action is chosen randomly and the stable state is achieved within 20 iterations. Figure 2 also shows the performance with different learning rate δ_{win} and δ_{lose}. When the $\frac{\delta_{win}}{\delta_{lose}} = \frac{1}{2}$, VLR-MARL algorithm reaches the optimal utility a bit faster. Therefore, the learning rate is chosen to be $\delta_{win} = 0.005$ and $\delta_{lose} = 0.0025$ in the next simulation.

Figure 3 shows the offloading success rate of different numbers of users. The state function of the users shows the offloading situation. When $s_n(t) = 1$, the task offloading is known as successful. When the number of users increases, the rate of convergence will slow down.

Algorithm 1: VLR-MARL Algorithm for Resource Allocation in MEC Network

---

    Input: The number of populations $\mathcal{N}$, the distance d between each user and MEC Server, Max_iteration, the number of wireless channel $\mathcal{K}$

    Output: Optimal sequence of actions required to maximize the users' utility

1 Initialize: $Q_i(s, a_k) = 0$, $\pi_i(s, a_k) = \frac{1}{|A_i|}$, $\bar{\pi}_i(s, a_k) = \frac{1}{|A_i|}$, δ_{lose}, δ_{win}, $C(s) = 0$,

    $\alpha, \gamma, \varepsilon \in [0, 1]$; **for** $iteration = 1$ to $Max\_iteration$ **do**

2 | **for** $user_i$ to $user_N$ **do**

3 | $user_i$ take $\varepsilon - greedy$ policy to choose action a_k based on the current state s

4 | Calculate the next reward value r_i

5 | Calculate the next state s'

6 | Update $Q_i(s, a_k)$

$$:Q_i(s, a_k) \leftarrow Q_i(s, a_k) + \alpha\left(r + \gamma\max_{a'} Q(s', a') - Q_i(s, a_k)\right)$$

7 | Update $C(s) = C(s) + 1$

8 | Update the average estimation strategy $\bar{\pi}_i(s, a_k)$

$$= \bar{\pi}_i(s_k, a_k) + \frac{1}{C(s)}[\pi_i(s_k, a_k) - \bar{\pi}_i(s_k, a_k)]$$

9 | Determine whether the agent is wining and choose

$$\delta = \begin{cases} \delta_{win}, \sum_{a_i \in A_i} \pi_i(s_k, a_k)Q_i > \sum_{a_i \in A_i} \bar{\pi}_i(s_k, a_k)Q_i \\ \delta_{lose}, others \end{cases}$$

10 | Update the strategy function $\pi_i(s, a_k)$

11 | $iteration = iteration + 1$

12 Return the action space of all users

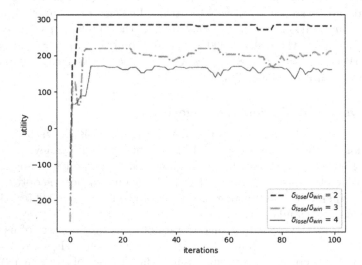

Fig. 2. Utility of users

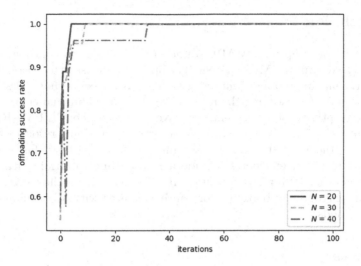

Fig. 3. Offloading success rate

4.2 Comparison to Other Algorithms

Then, the convergence efficiency are analyzed with various MARL algorithms. Figure 4 shows the learning curves of centralized single agent Q-learning algorithms in [6], Q-learning MARL algorithms and VLR-MARL algorithms proposed in this paper. As can be seen, Q-learning reaches the optimal solution more slowly than the proposed VRL-MARL algorithm. Moreover, the utility of Q-learning single agent reinforcement learning (SARL) and Q-learning-MARL are lower than VRL-MARL. Therefore, the VRL-MARL algorithm performs better both on the learning speed and users' utilities.

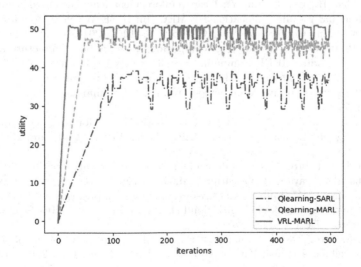

Fig. 4. Learning curves of different algorithms

5   Conclusion

In this paper, we propose a MARL framework to obtain the optimal resource allocation strategy in the MEC system. The optimization issue has been designed to obtain the maximum long-term reward while guaranteeing that users' offloading is reasonable. Considering the non-convex and combinatorial characteristics of this joint optimization problem, we have proposed the VLR-MARL strategy by jointly choosing channels and allocating computational resource to users. Based on the theory that learn slowly while winning and learn fast while losing, our strategy can efficiently provide a near-optimal solution with a small amount of iterations. Simulation results are given to indicate the convergence of the proposal method and better performance compared with other reinforcement learning methods.

References

1. Arulkumaran, K., Deisenroth, M.P., Brundage, M., Bharath, A.A.: A brief survey of deep reinforcement learning. arXiv preprint arXiv:1708.05866 (2017)
2. Bu, L., Babu, R., De Schutter, B., et al.: A comprehensive survey of multiagent reinforcement learning. IEEE Trans. Syst. Man Cybern. Part C (Appl. Rev.) **38**(2), 156–172 (2008)
3. Chiang, M., Hande, P., Lan, T., Tan, C.W., et al.: Power control in wireless cellular networks. Found. Trends® Networking **2**(4), 381–533 (2008)
4. Cuervo, E., et al.: MAUI: making smartphones last longer with code offload. In: Proceedings of the 8th International Conference on Mobile Systems, Applications, and Services, pp. 49–62. ACM (2010)
5. Lan, Z., et al.: A hierarchical game for joint wireless and cloud resource allocation in mobile edge computing system. In: 10th International Conference on Wireless Communications and Signal Processing (WCSP), pp. 1–7. IEEE (2018)
6. Li, J., Gao, H., Lv, T., Lu, Y.: Deep reinforcement learning based computation offloading and resource allocation for MEC. In: IEEE Wireless Communications and Networking Conference (WCNC), pp. 1–6. IEEE (2018)
7. Mach, P., Becvar, Z.: Mobile edge computing: a survey on architecture and computation offloading. IEEE Commun. Surv. Tutorials **19**(3), 1628–1656 (2017)
8. Mao, Y., You, C., Zhang, J., Huang, K., Letaief, K.B.: A survey on mobile edge computing: the communication perspective. IEEE Commun. Surv. Tutorials **19**(4), 2322–2358 (2017)
9. Ren, J., Yu, G., Cai, Y., He, Y.: Latency optimization for resource allocation in mobile-edge computation offloading. IEEE Trans. Wireless Commun. **17**(8), 5506–5519 (2018)
10. Sutton, R.S., Barto, A.G.: Reinforcement Learning: An Introduction (2011)
11. Watkins, C.J., Dayan, P.: Q-learning. Mach. Learn. **8**(3–4), 279–292 (1992)
12. Wen, Y., Zhang, W., Luo, H.: Energy-optimal mobile application execution: taming resource-poor mobile devices with cloud clones. In: Proceedings IEEE Infocom, pp. 2716–2720. IEEE (2012)
13. Xiao, M., Shroff, N.B., Chong, E.K.P.: A utility-based power-control scheme in wireless cellular systems. IEEE/ACM Trans. Networking **11**(2), 210–221 (2003)

14. Yang, T., Hu, Y., Gursoy, M.C., Schmeink, A., Mathar, R.: Deep reinforcement learning based resource allocation in low latency edge computing networks. In: 15th International Symposium on Wireless Communication Systems (ISWCS), pp. 1–5. IEEE (2018)
15. Yu, S., Wang, X., Langar, R.: Computation offloading for mobile edge computing: a deep learning approach. In: IEEE 28th Annual International Symposium on Personal, Indoor, and Mobile Radio Communications (PIMRC), pp. 1–6. IEEE (2017)
16. Zhao, P., Tian, H., Qin, C., Nie, G.: Energy-saving offloading by jointly allocating radio and computational resources for mobile edge computing. IEEE Access 5, 11255–11268 (2017)
17. Zhu, Z., et al.: Fair resource allocation for system throughput maximization in mobile edge computing. IEEE Access 6, 5332–5340 (2018)

Cooperative Transmission with Power Control in the Hyper-cellular Network

Dan Zhang[1], Xin Su[2], Huanxi Cui[1], Bei Liu[2], Lu Ge[2], and Jie Zeng[2(✉)]

[1] School of Communication and Information Engineering,
Chongqing University of Posts and Telecommunications, Chongqing, China
zhdan@tsinghua.edu.cn
[2] Beijing National Research Center for Information Science and Technology,
Tsinghua University, Beijing, China
suxin@tsinghua.edu.cn, zengjie@mail.tsinghua.edu.cn

Abstract. In response to the challenge of no difference coverage in seamless wide-area coverage scenarios, the 5G hyper-cellular network (HCN) is proposed to ensure user mobility and traffic continuity. In this network, Control Base Station (CBS) is responsible for control coverage, and the traffic base stations (TBSs) take care of high-speed data transmission. Firstly, this paper analyzes the spectral efficiency of different users by dividing the center region and edge region based on Poisson Voronoi Tessellation (PVT) model. For central users, a power control scheme is used to optimize the transmit power of TBSs. For edge users, a cooperative transmission technology and a power control scheme are employed to increase the spectral efficiency. In addition, the TBS sleeping strategy is used to further reduce inter-cell interference. Then, the analytical expressions of the spectral efficiency are derived by using random geometry. The simulation results illustrate that this scheme has a good effect on improving the spectral efficiency of the users with constant mobile velocity.

Keywords: Hyper-cellular network · Random model · Cooperative transmission technology · Power control · Spectral efficiency

1 Introduction

In order to make full use of spectral resources and the ever-increasing capacity demand, a new hyper-cellular network (HCN) architecture is proposed, which has the advantage of being able to cope with the differentiated service requirements of users, flexibly configuring network resources. The core idea is moderately separate the control signaling and service data transmission on the coverage [1]. The control base station (CBS) manages the user's access request and is the global information master of the network; the traffic base station (TBS) is used for high-speed data transmission to the user, which is flexible and efficient. With

This work was supported by the National S&T Major Project (No. 2018ZX03001011).

J. Zheng et al. (Eds.): ADHOCNETS 2019, LNICST 306, pp. 162–173, 2019.
https://doi.org/10.1007/978-3-030-37262-0_13

the separation architecture, CBS can wake up the corresponding TBS when there is service demand, achieving joint optimization of energy efficiency and resources.

However, as the number of base stations increases, inter-cell interference is a key obstacle to achieve higher spectral efficiency. As a solution to the green cellular network, a cooperative transmission technique is proposed that converts interference into the useful signal by neighbor cell cooperation according to changes in the environment [2]. It ensures less disruption to the user experience, allowing for spectrum reuse in dense areas with interference limited. The power control scheme can better control mutual co-channel interference by optimizing the transmit power between multiple base stations.

Cooperative transmission technology and power control scheme are extensively studied in literature. In [3], a power control algorithm based on the average channel gain matrix is proposed. This algorithm minimizes the transmit power of the base station, while ensuring the signal to interference plus noise ratio (SINR) and increases the system capacity, but this scheme is too singular and does not fully optimize user performance. To increase system capacity and cell edge capacity, [4] proposes a scheme that combines cooperative transmission with quality of service guaranteed and multi-cell coordinated power control, but does not give specific implementation details. [5] is an adaptive modulation scheme that defines three different joint transmission modes based on the number of cooperative base stations, which increases the flexibility of cooperative transmission, but did not consider the power consumption.

Considering the randomness and density of distribution of users and base stations in actual scenarios, random geometry is a novel and useful method to provide instructive results for SINR and the spectral efficiency [6]. Both base stations and users are modeled as a Poisson Point Process (PPP) in [7], comparing the average spectral efficiency of conventional distributed antenna systems (DAS) and user-centric DAS. Further considering cooperative transmission to improve network performance, [8] comprehensively analyzed the average spectral efficiency of uplink transmission and downlink transmission. In addition, [9] obtains the capacity expression under cooperative transmission considering the change of user distribution density. In [10], a partitioning method suitable for the edge user and the central user is proposed in random networks, and analyze the impact of user density on coverage probability by two resource allocation methods. In [11], the edge users are divided based on the method of [10], and a cooperative cluster is formed by Voronoi diagram to improve the throughput of the edge users.

From the research results in the introduction, it can be found that on the one hand, some cooperation schemes are relatively simple, the spectral efficiency improvement is limited or the implementation details of the scheme are not given in the actual topology of the network, on the other hand, performance analysis is not performed for users who are moving at high speed for actual scenarios. Therefore, this paper mainly studies the downlink edge spectral efficiency and average spectral efficiency in HCN. The power control scheme related to the distance is applied to optimize the transmit power of the TBS and improve the received signal quality of the central user. The edge users further eliminate serious interference from neighboring TBSs by cooperative transmission technique to improve edge spectral efficiency. The new expressions for downlink spectral efficiency are obtained by random distribution features. Finally, simulation analysis demonstrates that this scheme can greatly improve the spectral efficiency of users.

The rest of this paper is organized as follows. Section 2 describes the system model of the HCN and establishes the average spectral efficiency expression of the central user and the edge user. Section 3 defines the center user and the edge user, the analytical expressions for edge spectral efficiency and average spectral efficiency are obtained. In Sect. 4, numerical simulation evaluates the edge spectral efficiency and the average spectral efficiency. In the end, this paper is summarized in Sect. 5.

2   System Model

Considering a PVT model in HCN which consists of a CBS and multiple TBSs, the active state and transmit power of TBSs are controlled by CBS, and the whole space is divided by voronoi diagram. The TBS set and the user set are denoted by Φ_b and Φ_u, and the corresponding respectively Poisson distribution densities are λ_b and λ_u. In this paper, cooperative transmission technology is only used to enhance the receiving power of the edge users. Furthermore, CBS selects the cooperative TBSs for the edge user according to the distance between TBSs and the edge user (Fig. 1).

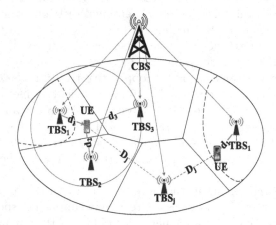

Fig. 1. Downlink cooperative transmission for central users and edge users in HCN, where the red solid line represents the desired signal, the red dotted line is the interference signal, the blue line is the backhaul link, and the black dotted line denotes the boundary line of the center area and the edge area. (Color figure online)

Assuming that a randomly selected edge user is at the origin, there are n cooperative TBSs to provide services, the cooperative TBSs are sequentially sorted according to the distance $(d_1 < d_2 < \cdots < d_n)$, where the distance between the edge user and the i-th cooperative TBS is d_i, and the distance from the j-th interfering TBS is D_j. The channel gain experienced by the users from the serving TBS is assumed to follow Rayleigh distribution with mean 1. In order to optimize the transmission power of the TBSs, which is expressed in a functional form proportional to the distance between the user and the serving TBS i.e., $P = pd^{\rho\alpha}$, where d is distance between service TBS and the user, p is the initial power of each TBS and ρ is the power control factor.

According to the above conditions, the $SINR_c$ of the central user with non-cooperative transmission and the $SINR_e$ of the edge user with cooperative transmission are

$$SINR_c = \frac{P_d}{I_d + N} = \frac{ph_1 d_1^{\rho\alpha} d_1^{-\alpha}}{\sum\limits_{j \in \Phi_b, j \neq 1} ph_j d_j^{\rho\alpha} D_j^{-\alpha} + \sigma^2} \tag{1}$$

and

$$SINR_e = \frac{P_d}{I_d + N} = \frac{\sum\limits_{i \in B_0} ph_i d_i^{\rho\alpha} d_i^{-\alpha}}{\sum\limits_{j \in \Phi_b \setminus B_o} ph_j d_j^{\rho\alpha} D_j^{-\alpha} + \sigma^2} \tag{2}$$

where d_1 is the distance between the user and the local service TBS, and h follows the exponential distribution with μ^{-1}. P_d is the total received power of the desired signal, I_d is the received power of the interference signal, and σ^2 is the variance of Gaussian white noise. B_o denotes a circular area with the user as the origin and the distance d_n as a radius. Assuming each TBS transmitting signal is the Gaussian signal, the spectral efficiency of the center user and the edge user are derived from (1) and (2), respectively,

$$SE_c' = E_{\Phi_b, h} \left[In\left(1 + SINR_c\right) \right] \tag{3}$$

$$SE_e' = E_{\Phi_b, h} \left[In\left(1 + SINR_e\right) \right] \tag{4}$$

Next, (3) and (4) are transformed by the Laplace transform to find more exact expressions. Then, we get the integral expression of the spectral efficiency of the edge user and the central user according to the definition of Laplace transform [7]

$$SE_c' = \int_0^\infty \frac{e^{-s\sigma^2/p}}{s} L_{c\_I}(s)\left(1 - L_{c\_S}(s)\right) ds \tag{5}$$

$$SE_e' = \int_0^\infty \frac{e^{-s\sigma^2/p}}{s} L_{e\_I}(s)\left(1 - L_{e\_S}(s)\right) ds \tag{6}$$

3   The Spectral Efficiency

It can be seen from (5) and (6) that only the Laplace transform of the desired signal P_d and the interference signal I_d is required, and the corresponding spectral efficiency expression can be obtained. Further considering the selection probability of the central user and the edge user in the cell and the distance distribution function between the users and the TBSs, the average spectral efficiency expression of the final central user and the edge user can be obtained.

$$SE_c = P_c \int\limits_{d_1>0} SE_c' f_c(d_1) dd_1 \tag{7}$$

$$SE_e = P_e \int\limits_{d_1>0} ... \int\limits_{d_n>d_{n-1}} SE_e' f_e(d_1)...f_e(d_n) dd_1...dd_n \tag{8}$$

Therefore, this paper is divided into four parts to solve these two expressions.

3.1   Selection Probability of the Central User and the Edge User

Assume that only one user is scheduled in a given time slot. The user selection probability indicates the probability that a randomly selected user is allocated a corresponding resource and served by the TBS. Since the distance between TBSs is random, the fixed distance threshold cannot be used to define edge users and central users. Considering the cell is voronoi structure, the distance d_1 and d_2 between the user and the nearest two TBSs have a specific ratio, and the central user and the edge user can be divided according to the proportional threshold R. If $d_1/d_2 > R$, the user is defined as the edge user, otherwise it is the central user [10]. We can get the joint probability density function (PDF) of the distance between the user and the nearest two TBSs is [12] (Fig. 2)

$$f(d_1, d_2) = (2\pi\lambda_b)^2 d_1 d_2 \exp\left(-\pi\lambda_b d_2^2\right) \tag{9}$$

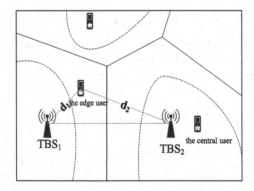

Fig. 2. An example of dividing edge users and central users

The selection probability of the edge user is obtained

$$P_e = 1 - P\left[d_1/d_2 \leq R\right]$$

$$= 1 - \int_0^\infty \int_0^{d_2 R} f(d_1, d_2) dd_1 dd_2 \qquad (10)$$

$$= 1 - R^2$$

The selection probability of the central user is $P_c = R^2$.

3.2   Distance Distribution Function Between the User and TBSs

The central user uses the nearest TBS as the service TBS. Thus, the PDF of d_1 can be obtained

$$f_c(d_1) = 2\pi\lambda_b d_1 e^{-\lambda_b \pi d_1^2}, \ d_1 > 0 \qquad (11)$$

The edge user has n closer TBSs to provide service. Let the distance of the i-th cooperative TBS and the selected edge user be ς_i, no other TBSs can be closer than ς_i, so the cumulative distribution function (CDF) of d_i is [8]

$$F_{\varsigma_i}(d_i) = 1 - P(d_i \leq \varsigma_i)$$

$$= 1 - \sum_{t=0}^{i-1} e^{-\pi\lambda_b d_i^2} \frac{\left(\pi\lambda_b d_i^2\right)^t}{t!} \qquad (12)$$

and the expression of the PDF of d_i can be obtained as

$$f_e(d_i) = 2\pi\lambda_b d_i e^{-\pi\lambda_b d_i^2} \frac{\left(\pi\lambda_b d_i^2\right)^{i-1}}{(i-1)!}, \ i \in [1, ..., n] \qquad (13)$$

3.3   Laplace Transform of Desired Signal

We can obtain $P_i \sim E(d_i^{\alpha(\rho-1)}\mu)$ by $h_i \sim E(\mu)$, then the Laplace transform of the desired signal of the central user is

$$L_{c\_S}(s) = \int_0^\infty e^{-sP_i} d_i^{\alpha(\rho-1)} \mu e^{-d_i^{\alpha(\rho-1)}\mu P_i} dP_i$$

$$= \frac{1}{1 + s\mu^{-1} d_1^{\alpha(1-\rho)}} \qquad (14)$$

The edge user receives signals from n cooperative TBSs in a maximum ratio combining manner, i.e. $P_d = \sum_{i=1}^n h_i d_i^{\alpha(\rho-1)}$. The Laplace transform of the desired signal of the edge user can be obtained by Eq. (14) as follows

$$L_{e\_S}(s) = \prod_{i=1}^n L_{c\_S}(s) \qquad (15)$$

3.4   Laplace Transform of Interference Signal

In a given time slot, there may be no users who need services in the neighboring cells and the TBSs can be controlled to be in a sleep state. Therefore, the sleeping probability that the TBS does not have any user in need of service in its coverage in a time slot. This probability can sparse the λ_b of the interference TBSs. Assuming the number of users in the cell is M, the sparse TBS density λ' can be obtained from the proposition 1 in [9]

$$\lambda' = \lambda_b \left(1 - P\left(M = 0\right)\right)$$

$$= \lambda_b \left[1 - \left(1 + 3.5^{-1}\frac{\lambda_u}{\lambda_b}\right)^{-3.5}\right] \tag{16}$$

Therefore, the Laplace transform of the interference signal is

$$L_{e\_I}(s) = E_{\Phi_b^I, h}\left[\exp\left(-s\sum_{j\in\Phi_b^I} h_j d_j^{\rho\alpha} D_j^{-\alpha}\right)\right]$$

$$= E_{\Phi_b^I}\left\{\prod_{j\in\Phi_b\backslash\beta_o} E_h\left[exp(-sh_j d_j^{\rho\alpha} D_j^{-\alpha})\right]\right\} \tag{17}$$

$$= \exp\left(-\pi^2\lambda'\lambda_b \int_{d_n^2}^{\infty}\int_0^{\infty} \frac{e^{-\pi\lambda_b x}}{1+\mu s^{-1}x^{-\rho\alpha/2}y^{\alpha/2}}dxdy\right)$$

where (17) is derived from the probability generating function of PPP and h following the exponential distribution.

For the central user, laplace transform of the interference signal is

$$L_{c\_I}(s) = \exp\left(-\pi^2\lambda'\lambda_b \int_{d_1^2}^{\infty}\int_0^{\infty} \frac{e^{-\pi\lambda_b x}}{1+\mu s^{-1}x^{-\rho\alpha/2}y^{\alpha/2}}dxdy\right) \tag{18}$$

After the above series of calculations, we can respectively obtain the spectral efficiency of the central user and the spectral efficiency of the edge user.

Combining with the selection probability of the central user and the edge user, the average spectral efficiency of the user is

$$SE = (1 - P_e)SE_c + P_e SE_e. \tag{19}$$

4   Simulation Results and Performance Evaluation

To simplify the analysis, consider a microcell coverage scenario in the HCN in a time slot i.e., $\lambda_b > \lambda_u$. In this paper, we use the derived edge spectral efficiency (ESE) and average spectral efficiency (ASE) mathematical expressions and numerical simulation methods to discuss user's performance. The setting of the simulation parameters is generally $\lambda_b = 0.2$, $\lambda_u = 0.1$, $\alpha = 4$, $\mu = 1$ and

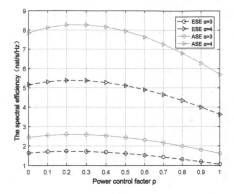

Fig. 3. Downlink edge spectral efficiency and average spectral efficiency as a function of ρ.

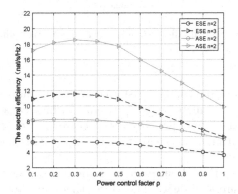

Fig. 4. Downlink edge spectral efficiency and average spectral efficiency as a function of n.

$\sigma^2 = \sqrt{2}$. The central user and the edge user partition threshold R of the edge user is set to $2/3$ [12].

Figure 3 shows the effect of the power control factor on spectral efficiency. First, as the ρ increases, the edge spectral efficiency and the average spectral efficiency both increase first and then decrease. Therefore, the transmit power of the TBS has an optimal value $\rho = 0.2$ and is obtained at $\lambda_b = 0.2$. The reason for the increase is transmission power of the TBSs increases as the ρ increases, leading to increased spectral efficiency, but the transmission power of interference TBSs also increases sharply and causes the SINR to decrease drastically, and the spectral efficiency shows the descending trend.

Comparing the two curves with different α, the spectral efficiency shows an upward trend. That is because the interference TBSs are farther away from the user and the interference power is attenuated faster so that the spectral efficiency shows an overall upward trend. As shown in Fig. 4, as the number n

of cooperative TBSs increases, inter-cell interference further decreases, and the edge spectral efficiency and the average spectral efficiency are improved.

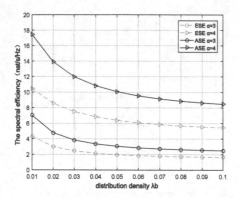

Fig. 5. Downlink edge spectral efficiency and average spectral efficiency as a function of λ_b.

In Fig. 5, we can find that the distance between the user and the TBSs decreases and interference increase as λ_b increase, which causes the spectral efficiency to decline. In the later stage, because received power of the desired signal and interference signal simultaneously increase, the spectral efficiency eventually shows a steady decline.

Since the user may bring about frequent handover during the mobile process, resulting in the transmission delay. Therefore, this paper evaluates the spectral efficiency of mobile users by describing the switching cost due to users moving at high speed. The handover cost is defined according to the normalized handover delay and it is given [13]

$$D = \min\left(H_t \times T, 1\right) \qquad (20)$$

where H_t is the handover rate per unit time and T is the delay time in each handover. For the general trajectory and moving model, the handover rate of the homogeneous network based on the PPP is verified as $H_t = 4v\sqrt{\lambda_b}/\pi$ [13], where v is the mobile velocity. Then, by quantifying the effect of the handover cost on the spectral efficiency, it is expressed as

$$SE_i = SE_i \times (1 - D), i = \{c, e\} \qquad (21)$$

Figures 6 and 7 are the comparison of the spectral efficiency of the three schemes when velocity is 120 km/h and T = 1 ms. The first scheme only considers power control. The second traditional cooperative transmission scheme, all cooperative TBSs are transmitted with the initial power, and the third is the proposed scheme. Comparing the three curves, it can be clearly seen that when $\lambda_b < 0.2$, the second scheme is better than the other two schemes. This is

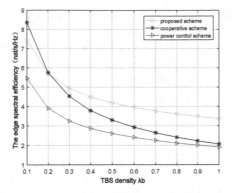

Fig. 6. Comparison of the edge spectral efficiency under three schemes.

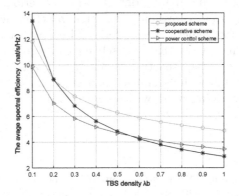

Fig. 7. Comparison of the average spectral efficiency under three schemes.

because when λ_b is small, the transmission power of the TBS is larger, and the quality of the received signal of the user is better. Thus, the spectral efficiency is also increased. However, when $\lambda_b \geq 0.2$, as the density of TBSs increases, the inter-cell interference is larger as transmission power increases. The power control scheme can be used to select the optimal transmission power to reduce the interference and the cooperative transmission can increase receiving quality of the signal, improving the spectral efficiency of the user, so the proposed scheme is best.

In Fig. 7, it can be observed from the simulation of average spectral efficiency that the second scheme is better than the second scheme when $\lambda_b < 0.6$, indicating that the cooperative scheme has a significant effect on improving the edge spectral efficiency and the average spectral efficiency, However, when the λ_b continues to increase, more users are concentrated in the central area of the cell. At this time, the power control scheme is more conducive to the improvement of the average spectral efficiency than the cooperative transmission scheme.

It can be calculated that the edge spectral efficiency of the third scheme is increased by 60% compared with the first scheme, and the average spectral efficiency is improved by 34%. The third scheme has an improvement of 29% in the edge spectral efficiency and an improvement of 32% in average spectral efficiency compared to the second scheme.

5   Conclusion

Aiming at the serious inter-cell interference problem in seamless wide-area coverage scenarios, this paper proposes a joint power control and cooperative transmission technology based on the PVT model under HCN. For the cell center user, the power control scheme and the sleeping scheme are applied to reduce the interference from the neighboring TBSs. For the cell edge user, we joint cooperative transmission and power control to reduce serious inter-cell interference. Then, the analytical expression of the spectral efficiency of the edge user and the average spectral efficiency are derived by the random geometry. The simulation results demonstrate that this scheme can significantly improve edge spectral efficiency and average spectral efficiency compared to other schemes. It is suitable for high mobility and seamless connectivity in the seamless wide-area coverage scenario, providing users with comprehensive coverage of high-speed service experience.

References

1. Niu, Z., Gong, J., Zhou, S.: Research on hyper cellular mobile communication system based on energy efficiency and resource optimization. Telecommun. Sci. **30**(12), 34–47 (2014)
2. Maxwell, C.: A Treatise on Electricity and Magnetism, 3rd edn. Clarendon, Oxford (1892)
3. Jacobs, S., Bean, P.: Fine particles, thin films and exchange anisotropy. Magnetism **3**, 271–350 (1963)
4. Hoshino, K., Fujii, T.: Multi-cell coordinated power control with adjacent cell cooperative transmission considering actual environment. In: 2011 IEEE 73rd Vehicular Technology Conference (VTC Spring), pp. 1–5. Yokohama (2011)
5. Cui, Q., Song, H., Wang, H., Valkama, M., Dowhuszko, A.: Capacity analysis of joint transmission CoMP with adaptive modulation. IEEE Trans. Veh. Technol. **66**(2), 1876–1881 (2016)
6. ElSawy, H., Hossain, E., Haenggi, M.: Stochastic geometry for modeling, analysis, and design of multi-tier and cognitive cellular wireless networks: a survey. IEEE Commun. Surv. Tutorials **15**, 996–1019 (2013)
7. Lin, Y., Yu, W.: Downlink spectral efficiency of distributed antenna systems under a stochastic model. IEEE Trans. Wirel. Commun. **13**(12), 6891–6902 (2014)
8. Cai, J.: Application of random geometry theory in cellular networks. Nanjing University of Posts and Telecommunications, Doctor (2016)
9. Yu, M., Kim, L.: Downlink capacity and base station density in cellular networks. In: 2013 11th International Symposium and Workshops on Modeling and Optimization in Mobile, Ad Hoc and Wireless Networks (WiOpt), Tsukuba Science City, pp. 119–124 (2013)

10. Mankar, D., Das, G., Pathak, S.: Load-aware performance analysis of cell center/edge users in random HetNets. IEEE Trans. Veh. Technol. **67**(3), 119–124 (2018)
11. Park, J., Lee, N., Heath, W.: Cooperative base station coloring for pair-wise multi-cell coordination. IEEE Trans. Commun. **64**(1), 402–415 (2016)
12. Moltchanov, D.: Distance distributions in random networks. Ad Hoc Netw. **10**(6), 1146–1166 (2012)
13. Arshad, R., Elsawy, H., Sorour, S., et al.: Handover management in 5G and beyond: a topol-ogy aware skipping approach. IEEE Access **4**, 9073–9081 (2016)

Energy-Efficient Power Allocation for Fading Device-to-Device Channels in Downlink Resource Sharing Communication

Fengfeng Shi, Jiaheng Wang, Hong Shen$^{(\boxtimes)}$, and Chunming Zhao

National Mobile Communications Research Laboratory,
Southeast University, Nanjing 210096, China
{sff,jhwang,shhseu,cmzhao}@seu.edu.cn

Abstract. Green wireless communications have received increasing attentions from researchers, who committed to improving energy efficiency for the ubiquity of wireless applications. This paper deals with the power allocation strategies for nearby users' high speed download services to effectively address the energy consumption of D2D communications underlying cellular systems. Energy efficiency maximization problems are analyzed with respect to ergodic sum capacity under different power constraint cases, relating to average power thresholds over all the fading stations and instantaneous power thresholds over each fading station of D2D transmission links and frequency-shared interference links. By applying the Dinkelbach method and the Lagrange duality method, the original intractable problems are decomposed into sub-dual functions that are lower complexity and solvable. Accordingly, we infer closed-form solutions of the proposed optimal problems, which resemble "water-filling" solutions for the parallel fading channels. Simulation results verify that the proposed strategies provide effective uses of limited energy.

Keywords: Device-to-Device · Green communication · Energy efficient · Power allocation

1 Introduction

Wireless communication usage has reached new heights over the past decade and will continue to grow in the upcoming years in the field of medium of choice. A major issue for wireless communication system design is the continuing consumption of the energy. The green low-power wireless communication is an inevitable trend for the oncoming 5G or 6G network. As a promising technology, D2D communication technology has been regarded as an effective technique to provide better wireless services in local areas [1] and D2D standard is ready for products [2].

In a D2D underlaid mobile communication system, to satisfy the quality of service (QoS) of the cellular user, we should consider the interference causes

© ICST Institute for Computer Sciences, Social Informatics and Telecommunications Engineering 2019
Published by Springer Nature Switzerland AG 2019. All Rights Reserved
J. Zheng et al. (Eds.): ADHOCNETS 2019, LNICST 306, pp. 174–186, 2019.
https://doi.org/10.1007/978-3-030-37262-0_14

to the cellular user while managing wireless resource for the D2D link. The introduction of D2D should not only effectively improve spectrum efficiency, but also well control the interference to the normal cellular users. Relying on this premise, many optimal power allocation strategies have been well designed for both uplink [3] and downlink [4] D2D communication.

While the cellular users (CUs) are interference-limited, the D2D users (DUs) are power-limited, whose energy are generally produced by battery. Evaluating power control in cellular networks involves the use of a number of metrics, of which energy efficiency (EE) is the most common one. The previous works also have launched some investigations into the energy efficiency problems of D2D communication, such as [5] in uplink and [6] in downlink resources sharing. To prolong the lifetime of networks, energy harvesting has also been applied to D2D underlaying networks [7]. All of these works for the energy efficiency considered static optimization on the basis of instantaneous channel state information (CSI). Since the system performance should be based on all the fading states to protect the cellular users' quality of services, the investigations of average energy efficiency and the protection of the QoS are necessary.

Different from these previous works on energy efficiency, our goal is to design energy efficient power allocation strategies over fading channels. The ergodic sum capacity can be a relevant measure for the maximum achievable throughput of the D2D link, when the D2D transportation has a sufficiently large delay tolerance [8,9]. The maximum ergodic sum capacity problems of secondary links are considered in [8] for cognitive radio network, but in which the interference from primary links to secondary links didn't be considered. In [9], the energy efficiency maximization problems are analyzed in both delay-insensitive cognitive radio and delay-sensitive cognitive radio.

In this paper, we investigate the energy efficiency of the D2D links sharing downlink spectrum resource with cellular system. We take an information theoretic approach to characterize the maximum achievable rate of D2D links averaged over the channel fading states. The energy efficiency maximization problems are formulated under the statistical average or instantaneous transmit power constraints. As for the cellular users, the performance metrics of the QoS are considered under both the instantaneous and the average interference power too. The formulated problems are nonlinear fractional programming problems, which are intricate and difficult to find their globally optimal solution. Despite the difficulty, we decouple the original problems into sets of independent concave problems which can be solved separately. Hence the problems can be solved bia standard optimization methods, such as Dinkelbach iterative methods and sub-gradient methods. Finally, the effect of the proposed energy efficient optimal power allocation strategies is verified by proper numerical examples.

2   System Model

We consider D2D communication as an underlay downlink resource sharing of cellular systems. Let $\mathfrak{K}$ and $\mathfrak{J}$ represent the sets of downlink cellular users and

D2D pairs, respectively, $|\mathfrak{R}| = K$ and $|\mathfrak{J}| = J$. Each user k occupies a dedicated orthogonal resource block (RB). We assume each CU's RB can be used by at most one D2D link, which is constraint has been widely used [3, 4, 10, 11]. Denote the instantaneous transmission channel gain at fading state v from the BS to CU k by $h_k(v)$, and the D2D link j which reuse the resource of the CU k by $h_j(v)$. The interference channels from BS to D2D link and from the D2D link to CU are represented by $g_{kj}(v)$ and $g_{jk}(v)$, respectively. These channel gains are assumed to be independently drawn from a vector random process, which to be ergodic over the transmission blocks.

It is assumed that the BS and D2D transmit signals in the same narrow-band frequency channel. Let x_k and x_j represent the transmitted signals of the CU k and D2D link j respectively. Then, the received signals of the user k and the inband D2D link j are

$$y_k^C(v) = h_k(v)x_k + g_{jk}(v)x_j + n_k$$

$$y_j^D(v) = h_j(v)x_j + g_{kj}(v)x_k + n_j$$

where n_k and n_j are the additive zero mean Gaussian noise with variances δ_k^2 and δ_j^2, respectively.

Assume that both the CUs and DUs use Gaussian codes on each frequency band with transmit power $p_k = E|x_k|^2$ and $p_j = E|x_j|^2$. Due to the coexistence of cellular and D2D users on the same frequency band, the throughput of the D2D link j are given by

$$R_j^D(v) \triangleq log\left[1 + \frac{p_j(v)\tilde{h}_j(v)}{1 + p_k(v)\tilde{g}_{kj}(v)}\right] \tag{1}$$

where $\tilde{h}_j(v) = l_j|h_j(v)|^2/\delta_j^2$, and $\tilde{g}_{kj}(v) = l_{kj}|g_{kj}(v)|^2/\delta_k^2$ are normalized channel gains which integrate with the path-loss.

Since the energy consumption of D2D transmitters are generally produced by battery, our work is mainly focused on allocating the transmit power of D2D to raise the energy efficiency of mobilizable devices. If we use $\eta(p_j(v))$ to denote the energy efficiency of the D2D link, the energy efficiency maximization problem over all the fading states can be formulated as

$$\begin{aligned}\max_{\{p_j(v)\in\mathfrak{F}\}}\eta &= \frac{R^D(p_j(v))}{P^D(p_j(v))} \\ &= \frac{E\left\{log_2\left(1 + \frac{p_j(v)\tilde{h}_j(v)}{p_k(v)\tilde{g}_{kj}(v)+1}\right)\right\}}{E\{p_j(v)/\zeta + P_c^D\}}\end{aligned} \tag{2}$$

where ζ and P_c^D denote the amplifier and the constant consumption of circuit power of D2D link, which is a power offset derived from signal processing, as well as batter backup, etc. According to the definition, the energy efficiency is affected by not only the transmit power allocation of D2D link but also the interference power from the cellular system.

Assuming the cellular system will communicate without concerning the interference to D2D link, which means it transmits with the quota power

$$p_k(v) = P_{th}^C, \forall v. \tag{3}$$

The condition set $\mathfrak{F}$ is the different cases of power constraints, in addition to the default nonnegative condition,

$$p_j(v) \geq 0, \forall v \tag{4}$$

more details of power constraints will describe in the following Sects. 3 and 4.

The energy efficient problems considered in problem (2) are correlated to the ergodic capacity of D2D link, which is averaged over all the channel fading states. The ergodic capacity can be a relevant measure for the maximum achievable throughput of the communication system when the data traffic has a sufficiently large delay tolerance. As an optional service introduced to the cellular systems, the D2D links generally have lower priorities than the cellular users. The D2D communication is typically implemented as a complement to the cellular systems. Therefore, the QoS target should be imposed to ensure the normal cellular communications. The BS transmit power allocation $p_k(v)$ and the power allocation of D2D link $p_l(v)$ lead to a theoretical limit of the cellular users' performance.

3   Average Transmit Power Constraints

As we optimize the performance of the D2D link, some protections to the cellular user are necessary. The D2D link should reuse the resource of cellular user without exceeding the maximum transmit power,

$$E\{p_j(v)\} \leq \bar{P}_{th}^D, \forall v \tag{5}$$

where the expectation is taken over v with respect to its cumulative distribution function(CDF). The power threshold $\bar{P}_{th}^D$ is the average transmit power budget for the D2D link.

The average interference power constraints should be imposed on the D2D link in order to protect the cellular from tolerable average interference to noise power ratio

$$E\{p_j(v)\tilde{g}_{jk}(v)\} \leq \gamma_I^D, \forall v \tag{6}$$

or more restrictive instantaneous power constraints

$$p_j(v)\tilde{g}_{jk}(v) \leq \gamma_I^D, \forall v. \tag{7}$$

The optimal problem defined in (2) seems intractable. Fortunately $P^D(p_j(v))$ and $R^D(p_j(v))$ are both differentiable and concave in $p_j(v)$ under the power constraints (3), (4), (5), (6) and (7). Therefore the nonlinear concave fractional programming can be related to nonlinear parametric programming by using Dinkelbach algorithm [12].

Let η^* denote the maximum $\eta(p_j(v))$, the optimization objection function can be written as

$$\eta^* = max\frac{R^D(p_j(v))}{P^D(p_j(v))} \tag{8}$$

Since the denominator of η^* is positive with $P^D(p_j(v)) \geq 2P_c^D$, the fractional programming problem (2) can be transformed into a corresponding subtractive form

$$\max_{\{p_j(v)\in\mathfrak{F}\}} E\left\{log_2\left(1+\frac{p_j(v)\tilde{h}_j(v)}{p_k(v)\tilde{g}_{kj}(v)+1}\right)\right\} - \eta^* E\left\{p_j(v)/\zeta + P_c^D\right\}. \tag{9}$$

The equivalence of (8) and (9) can be easily verified at $p_j^*(v)$ with corresponding maximal η^*. With an strictly concave numerator and convex denominator, the η can be updated by Dinkelbach's method [12]. In a concave fractional programming problem, local maximum is a global maximum [13]. Then, motivated by the works in [8,9], we transform the problem into an equivalent subtractive mixed integer programming problem under condition set $\mathfrak{F}$

$$\max_{\{p_j(v)\in\mathfrak{F}\}} f(p_j(v),\eta), \tag{10}$$

where

$$f(p_j(v),\eta) = E\left\{log_2\left(1+\frac{p_j(v)\tilde{h}_j(v)}{p_k(v)\tilde{g}_{kj}(v)+1}\right)\right\} - \eta E\left\{p_j(v)/\zeta + P_c^D\right\}.$$

Finally, the optimal solution can be found by using classical Lagrange multipliers.

3.1   Average Interference Power Constrains

Under the average transmit power and the average interference power constrains, the condition set $\mathfrak{F}$ is the combination of (3), (4), (5) and (6).

All the power constraints in current section and following sections are affine and so do their combinations. It is easy to prove that the problem (9) is a strictly quasi-convex problem [9], which can be solved by using the Lagrange duality method [13]. Here we introduce the non-negative Lagrange multipliers λ and μ for the inequality constraints. The Lagrangian with respective to the transmit power $p_j(v)$ is

$$L(p_j(v),\lambda,\mu) = E\left\{log_2\left(1+\frac{p_j(v)\tilde{h}_j(v)}{p_k(v)\tilde{g}_{kj}(v)+1}\right)\right\}$$
$$- \eta E\left\{p_j(v)/\zeta + P_c^D\right\} - \lambda\left\{E\left\{p_j(v)\right\} - P_{th}^D\right\}$$
$$- \mu\left\{E\left\{p_j(v)\tilde{g}_{jk}(v)\right\} - \gamma_I^P\right\} \tag{11}$$

We can get the Lagrange dual function as

$$G(\lambda,\mu) = \max_{0\leq p_j(v)} L(p_j(v),\lambda,\mu) \tag{12}$$

The dual function serves as an upper bound on the optimal value of the original problem, denoted by γ^*, that is $\gamma^* \leq G(\lambda, \mu)$ for any nonnegative λ and μ. The dual problem is then defined as $\min_{\lambda \geq 0, \mu \geq 0} G(\lambda, \mu)$.

Let the optimal value of the dual problem be denoted by d^*, which is achievable by the optimal dual solutions λ^* and μ^*, that is $d^* \leq G(\lambda^*, \mu^*)$. For a convex optimization problem with a strictly feasible point as in our problem, the Slater's condition is satisfied and thus the duality gap $r^* - d^* \leq 0$ is indeed zero. So the problem (9) can be equivalently solved from its dual problem, i.e. by first maximizing its Lagrangian to obtain the dual function for some given dual variables, and then minimizing the dual function over the dual variables.

Firstly, obtain $G(\lambda, \mu)$ with given λ and μ,

$$G(\lambda, \mu) = E\left\{\tilde{G}(v)\right\} - \eta P_c^D + \lambda P_{th}^D + \mu \gamma_I^D \tag{13}$$

where

$$\tilde{G}(p_j(v)) = \max log_2\left(1 + \frac{p_j(v)\tilde{h}_j(v)}{p_k(v)\tilde{g}_{kj}(v) + 1}\right)$$
$$- \eta p_j(v)/\zeta - \lambda p_j(v) - \mu p_j(v)\tilde{g}_{jk}(v). \tag{14}$$

The dual function can be obtained via solving for sub-dual-functions $\tilde{G}(p_j(v))$, each for one fading state with channel realization.

Note that the maximization problem with different (v) all have the same structure and can be solved using the same computational routine. For conciseness, we drop the index (v) for the maximization problem at each fading state in the expression below. For a particular fading state, the associated subproblem can be defined as

$$\max_{0 \leq p_j} log_2\left(1 + \frac{p_j\tilde{h}_j}{p_k\tilde{g}_{kj} + 1}\right) - \eta p_j/\zeta - \lambda p_j - \mu p_j\tilde{g}_{jk} \tag{15}$$

The problems (9) has been transformed into sets of independent concave problems which can be solved separately.

Proposition 1. *The energy efficient optimal power allocation strategy to problem (15) can be given as a quasi-water-filling form*

$$p_j^* = \left[\frac{1}{(\eta/\zeta + \lambda + \mu\tilde{g}_{jk})ln2} - \frac{p_k\tilde{g}_{kj} + 1}{\tilde{h}_j}\right]^+, \forall v \tag{16}$$

where $[a]^+ = max(a, 0)$ and $max(a, 0)$ denotes the maximum between a and 0.

Proof. Since the objective function is concave function related to p_j and the constraints are linear, the problem (15) is convex. Hence the problems can be solved bia standard optimization methods. To satisfy the KKT conditions, the following dual solution need to be satisfied

$$\frac{1}{ln2} \frac{\tilde{h}_j}{p_k \tilde{g}_{kj} + 1 + p_j^* \tilde{h}_j} - (\eta/\zeta + \lambda + \mu \tilde{g}_{jk}) + \vartheta^* = 0, \forall v \tag{17}$$

$$\vartheta^* p_j^* = 0, \forall v$$

With $\vartheta^* \geq 0$ and $p_j^* \geq 0, \forall v$, from the KKT optimality conditions, it is easy to obtain that the energy efficient optimal power allocation strategy can be given as in (16).

3.2 Instantaneous Interference Power Constraints

When the interference constraints are more strict on each fading state, the problem can also be proven to be a concave fractional programming problem. Similar to the above subsection, the condition set $\mathfrak{F}$ is now the combination of (3), (4), (5) and (7).

The Lagrangian with respective to the transmit power $p_j(v)$ is

$$L(p_j(v), \lambda, \mu) = E \left\{ log_2 \left(1 + \frac{p_j(v) \tilde{h}_j(v)}{p_k(v) \tilde{g}_{kj}(v) + 1} \right) \right\}$$
$$- \eta E \{ p_j(v)/\zeta + P_c^D \} - \lambda \{ E \{ p_j(v) \} - P_{th}^D \} \tag{18}$$

Let $\mathfrak{B}$ denote the set of $p_j(v)$ specified by the constrains in (5) and (7), $\mathfrak{B} = \{ p_j(v) \mid p_j(v) \geqslant 0, p_j(v) \tilde{g}_{jk}(v) \leq \gamma_I^D, \forall v \}$. We can get the Lagrange dual function as

$$G(\lambda) = \max_{p_j(v) \in \mathfrak{B}} L(p_j(v), \lambda) \tag{19}$$

The dual problem is then defined as $\min_{\lambda \geq 0} G(\lambda, \mu)$. Similar to problem 9, this dual problem can be decomposed into individual sub-dual-functions. Firstly, obtain $G(\lambda)$ with given λ,

$$G(\lambda) = E \left\{ \tilde{G}(v) \right\} - \eta P_c^D + \lambda P_{th}^D \tag{20}$$

where

$$\tilde{G}(p_j(v)) = \max_{p_j(v) \in \mathfrak{B}} log_2 \left(1 + \frac{p_j(v) \tilde{h}_j(v)}{p_k(v) \tilde{g}_{kj}(v) + 1} \right) - \eta p_j(v)/\zeta - \lambda p_j(v). \tag{21}$$

The dual function can be obtained via solving for sub-dual-functions $\tilde{G}(p_j(v))$, each for one fading state with channel realization. Drop the index (v) for the maximization problem at each fading state in the expression below. For a particular fading state, the associated subproblem can be defined as

$$\begin{aligned} max \ & log_2 \left(1 + \frac{p_j \tilde{h}_j}{p_k \tilde{g}_{kj} + 1} \right) - \eta p_j/\zeta - \lambda p_j \\ s.t. \quad & p_j \geqslant 0 \\ & p_j \tilde{g}_{jk} \leq \gamma_I^D \end{aligned} \tag{22}$$

Proposition 2. *The energy efficient optimal power allocation strategy to problem (22) can be given as*

$$p_j^* = min\left(\left[\frac{1}{(\eta/\zeta + \lambda)\,ln2} - \frac{p_k \tilde{g}_{kj} + 1}{\tilde{h}_j}\right]^+, \frac{\gamma_I^D}{\tilde{g}_{jk}}\right) \tag{23}$$

where min(a,b) denotes the minimum between a and b, $[a]^+ = max(a,0)$ and max(a,0) denotes the maximum between a and 0.

Proof. Since the objective function is concave function related to p_j and the constraints are linear, the problem (22) is convex. Hence the problems can be solved bia standard optimization methods. To satisfy the KKT conditions, the following primal and dual solution need to be satisfied

$$
\begin{aligned}
\frac{1}{ln2}\frac{\tilde{h}_j}{p_k\tilde{g}_{kj}+p_j^*\tilde{h}_j+1} - (\eta/\zeta + \lambda) - \mu^*\tilde{g}_{jk} + \vartheta^* &= 0 \ , \forall v \\
\vartheta^* p_j^* &= 0 \qquad\qquad ,\forall v \\
\mu^*\left(p_j^*\tilde{g}_{jk} - \gamma_I^D\right) &= 0 \qquad\qquad ,\forall v
\end{aligned}
\tag{24}
$$

With $\mu^* \geq 0$, $\vartheta^* \geq 0$ and $p_j^* \geq 0, \forall v$. Suppose that $p_j^* \geq 0, \forall v$, it follows that $\vartheta^* = 0$. Unlike in the (17), where μ^* is fixed, the μ^* in (24) is different for each fading state. As we consider an egoistic cellular, the base station transmits at maximum power $p_k(v) = P_{th}^C, \forall v$. To satisfy the KKT optimality conditions, we analyze the following two cases, sinceμ^*, ϑ^* and p_j^* are strictly positive.

Firstly, consider the case where $\mu^* = 0$. Since $\vartheta^* \geq 0$, the following must be true:

$$\frac{1}{ln2}\frac{\tilde{h}_j}{p_k\tilde{g}_{kj} + p_j^*\tilde{h}_j + 1} - (\eta/\zeta + \lambda) \leq 0$$

Thus the power allocation follows

$$p_j^* = \left[\frac{1}{ln2\,(\eta/\zeta + \lambda)} - \frac{p_k\tilde{g}_{kj} + 1}{\tilde{h}_j}\right]^+$$

Secondly, consider the case where $\mu^* > 0$. It follows that $p_j^* = \frac{\gamma_I^D}{\tilde{g}_{jk}}$ and $p_j^* < \frac{1}{ln2(\eta/\zeta+\lambda)} - \frac{p_k\tilde{g}_{kj}+1}{\tilde{h}_j}$. Then the following condition must be satisfied:

$$\frac{\gamma_I^D}{\tilde{g}_{jk}} < \frac{1}{ln2\,(\eta/\zeta + \lambda)} - \frac{p_k\tilde{g}_{kj} + 1}{\tilde{h}_j}$$

The energy efficient optimal power allocation strategy in (23) can achieved by summing up the above analysis.

4   Instantaneous Transmit Power Constraints

Similar to the interference power, more strict instantaneous transmit power constraint for the D2D link can be given as

$$p_j(v) \leq P_{th}^D, \forall v \tag{25}$$

As we maximum the $f(p_j(v), \eta)$ under the instantaneous transmit power and the average interference power constraints, the condition set $\mathfrak{F}$ in (10) is the combination of (3), (4), (6) and (25).

Proposition 3. *The energy efficient optimal power allocation strategy for instantaneous transmit power and average interference power constraints can be given as*

$$p_j^* = min\left(\left[\frac{1}{(\eta/\zeta + \mu\tilde{g}_{jk})\,ln2} - \frac{p_k\tilde{g}_{kj} + 1}{\tilde{h}_j}\right]^+, P_{th}^D\right) \tag{26}$$

where min(a, b) denotes the minimum between a and b, $[a]^+ = max(a, 0)$ and max(a, 0) denotes the maximum between a and 0.

Finally, while both the transmit and interference power constraints are instantaneous, the condition set $\mathfrak{F}$ is the combination of (3), (4), (7) and (25).

Proposition 4. *The energy efficient optimal power allocation strategy for instantaneous transmit and interference power constraints can be given as*

$$p_j^* = min\left(\left[\frac{1}{ln2\eta/\zeta} - \frac{p_k\tilde{g}_{kj} + 1}{\tilde{h}_j}\right]^+, \frac{\gamma_I^D}{\tilde{g}_{jk}}, P_{th}^D\right) \tag{27}$$

The two propositions in this section can be solved by using proving process similar to Propositions 1 and 2. For brevity, the details are not given here.

In the Proposition 3, only μ is required to be updated. In an extreme case of $\mu = 0$, the ergodic capacity of the D2D user is achieved with the maximum available power, which is consistent with no interference constraints (6).

5   Simulation Results and Discussion

In this section, simulation results are presented to evaluate the energy efficiency of the D2D link with the proposed optimal power allocation strategies. An power allocation algorithms based on classical Dinkelbach's iterative method and subgradient method can be applied to solve the energy efficient optimal problems. Main system parameters are listed in Table 1.

Table 1. Simulation parameters

Parameter	Value
Carrier frequency	2 GHz
Cell radius	500 m
BS transmit power	43 dBm
D2D transmit power	20 dBm
Circuit power of D2D	600 mW
Path loss factor α_l in urban environments	1.75
Path loss factor α_l of D2D links	1.5
Log-Normal Shadowing standard deviation	4 dB
Noise variance	−120 dBm

The large scale path-loss is calculated by $L = 32.45 + 20log_{10}f_c + \alpha_l 20log_{10}d$, where f_c and d are united by GHz and meters. The channels of the D2D links follow the Rician fading while other channels follow the Rayleigh fading. In the following simulations, we set the cell radius 500 m, and the CUs and D2D links are uniformly distributed within the cell. While not involving with distance change, the distances are identically set to $d_j = 50$ m, $d_k = 200$ m, $d_{kj} = 350$ m, $d_{jk} = 400$ m.

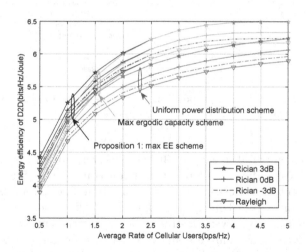

Fig. 1. Energy efficient performance comparison.

Figure 1 shows the average energy efficiency of D2D versus the average interference to noise power ratios γ_I^D, which restrict the degree of resource sharing between the CUs and D2D links. The different degrees of Rician factor of the D2D links ($K = 3, 0, -3$ dB) are investigated. Three power allocation strategies are compared, that is the proposed energy efficient optimal power allocation, the ergodic capacity maximization allocation and the baselines, in which uniform power distribution scheme are employed. In the schemes of propositions, the power amplifier coefficients of D2D are set to $\zeta = 1$. We compare the simulation result with the ergodic capacity maximization problems, which is approximately in consistent with schemes [8]. As for frequency sharing interferences, not only the sharer to the provider, but the provider to the sharer, are considered in our propositions, which are an improvement over the ergodic capacity maximization schemes in [9]. The higher transmit power of D2D link means the high interference to the CUE. As is indicated in the graph, the energy efficiency of D2D increases with the transmit power. But, as Shannon principle reveals that the spectrum efficiency and power efficiency cannot infinitely increase with the power, the energy efficiency approaches to the limit as well.

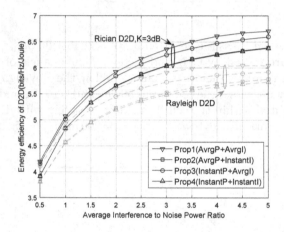

Fig. 2. Energy efficiency of four propositions with different transmit power and interference power constraints.

In Fig. 2, we compare the energy efficiency of D2D link of the four proposed propositions corresponding to different power constraints. The simulation parameters are consistent with those of Fig. 1. The black full lines depict the D2D links with Rician factor of $K = 3$ dB and the dotted blue lines depict Rayleigh D2D links. The instantaneous power constrains are more stringent explicitly over the average power constrains. Through analyzing the result, the interference power constraints are more dominant than the transmit power constraints. Therefore the energy efficiency of D2D under the average interference power constraints is much larger than that under the instantaneous interference power constraints.

As we considering the average spectral efficiency, the reduction of CUE rate with the invasive spectral sharers and the increment of D2D rate are compared in Fig. 3. The admission of D2D link causes only modest loss of CUE rate, therefore there are significant increases in spectral efficiency. The proposed energy-efficient

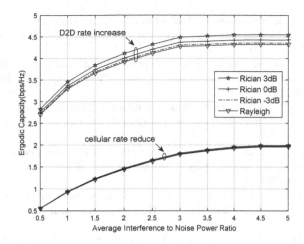

Fig. 3. Rate performance with the introduce of D2D in cellular system

optimal power allocation strategies not only improve the energy efficiency of the D2D links but also on the premise that cellular communication performance is guaranteed.

6   Conclusions

In this paper, the energy-efficient power allocation strategy has been studied for D2D communications underlaying downlink cellular networks. The energy efficiency maximization problem was formulated under both average and instantaneous power constraints. The numerical results proved the proposed strategies of better performance at both energy and spectrum efficiency with the D2D underlaying normal cellular communication.

Acknowlegment. This work was supported in part by the National Natural Science Foundation of China under Grants 61601115, 61871108, 61971130, 61571107, 61711540305, and 61720106003, in part by the National Science and Technology Projects of China under grant 2018ZX03001002, and in part by the Natural Science Foundation of Jiangsu Province under Grant BK20160069.

References

1. Gandotra, P., Jha, R., Jain, S.: Green communication in next generation cellular networks: a survey. IEEE Access **5**(6), 11727–11758 (2017)
2. David, K., Berndt, H.: 6G vision and requirements: is there any need for beyond 5G. IEEE Veh. Technol. Mag. **13**(3), 72–80 (2018)
3. Wang, J., Zhu, D., Zhao, C., et al.: Resource sharing of underlaying device-to-device and uplink cellular communications. IEEE Commun. Lett. **17**(6), 1148–1151 (2013)

4. Zhu, D., Wang, J., Swindlehurst, A.L., et al.: Downlink resource reuse for device-to-device communications underlaying cellular networks. IEEE Signal Process. Lett. **21**(5), 531–534 (2014)

5. Wu, D., Wang, J., Hu, R.Q., et al.: Energy-efficient resource sharing for mobile device-to-device multimedia communications. IEEE Trans. Veh. Technol. **63**(5), 2093–2103 (2014)

6. Hu, J., Heng, W., Li, X., et al.: Energy-efficient resource reuse scheme for D2D communications underlaying cellular networks. IEEE Commun. Lett. **21**(9), 2097–210 (2017)

7. Dai, H., Huang, Y., Xu, Y., et al.: Energy-efficient resource allocation for energy harvesting-based device-to-device communication. IEEE Trans. Veh. Technol. **68**(1), 509–524 (2018)

8. Zhang, R., Cui, S., Liang, Y.C.: On ergodic sum capacity of fading cognitive multiple-access and broadcast channels. IEEE Trans. Inform. Theory **55**(11), 5161–5178 (2009)

9. Zhou, F., Beaulieu, N.C., Li, Z., et al.: Energy-efficient optimal power allocation for fading cognitive radio channels: ergodic capacity, outage capacity, and minimum-rate capacity. IEEE Trans. Wirel. Commun. **15**(4), 2741–2755 (2016)

10. Dominic, S., Jacob, L.: Distributed resource allocation for D2D communications underlaying cellular networks in time-varying environment. IEEE Commun. Lett. **22**(2), 388–391 (2018)

11. Nguyen, H.H., Hasegawa, M., Hwang, W.J.: Distributed resource allocation for D2D communications underlay cellular networks. IEEE Commun. Lett. **20**(5), 942–945 (2016)

12. Dinkelbach, W.: On nonlinear fractional programming. Manage. Sci. **13**(7), 492–498 (1967)

13. Boyd, S., Vandenberghe, L.: Convex Optimization, 5th edn. Cambridge University Press, Cambridge (2004)

Delay Based Wireless Scheduling and Server Assignment for Fog Computing Systems

Yuan Zhang[1]([✉]), Mingyang Xie[1], Qiang Guo[1], Wei Heng[1],
and Peng Du[2]

[1] National Mobile Communications Research Laboratory,
Southeast University, Nanjing 210096, China
{y.zhang, qguo, wheng}@seu.edu.cn, 1090492123@qq.com
[2] College of Automation and College of Artificial Intelligence,
Nanjing University of Posts and Telecommunications, Nanjing 210023, China
dupeng@njupt.edu.cn

Abstract. To further reduce the delay in fog computing systems, new resource allocation algorithms are needed. Firstly, we have derived the recursive expressions of the communication and computing delays in the fog computing system without assuming the knowledge of the statistics of user application arrival traffic. Based on these analytical formulas, an optimization problem of delay minimization is formulated directly, and then a novel wireless scheduling and server assignment algorithm is designed. The delay performance of the proposed algorithm is evaluated via simulation experiments. Under the considered simulation parameters, the proposed algorithm can achieve 13.5% less total delay, as compared to the traditional algorithm. The impact of the total number of subcarriers in the system and the average user application arrival rate on the percentage of delay reduction is evaluated. Therefore, compared with the queue length optimization based traditional resource allocation algorithms, the delay optimization based resource allocation algorithm proposed in this paper can further reduce delay.

Keywords: Fog computing · Resource allocation · Delay · Lyapunov

1 Introduction

Recent years have seen a trend of users needing to run computation-intensive applications. To meet this requirement, the idea of fog computing is introduced [1, 2]. That is, computing servers (also known as fog nodes) are located near users, then users' applications are offloaded to fog nodes to execute. In fog computing systems, the problem of resource allocation has two aspects. Firstly, how to schedule wireless resource among users? For example, as illustrated in Fig. 1, both U1 and U2 want to offload applications to F1. How to schedule wireless resource between U1 and U2? Secondly, how to assign servers to users? For example, as illustrated in Fig. 1, U3 can offload applications to F2, F3, or F4. How to assign servers to U3? This paper studies these two aspects of resource allocation and proposes wireless scheduling and server assignment algorithms for fog computing systems.

© ICST Institute for Computer Sciences, Social Informatics and Telecommunications Engineering 2019
Published by Springer Nature Switzerland AG 2019. All Rights Reserved
J. Zheng et al. (Eds.): ADHOCNETS 2019, LNICST 306, pp. 187–198, 2019.
https://doi.org/10.1007/978-3-030-37262-0_15

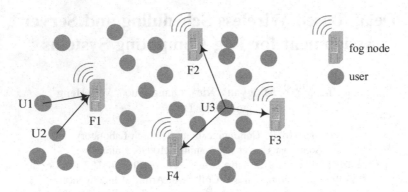

Fig. 1. Wireless scheduling and server assignment in fog computing systems.

There are many related studies in the literature (e.g., [3–15]). According to the assumptions of delay, there are three categories of resource allocation algorithms. For the first category of resource allocation algorithms (e.g., [3–7]), only the time of communicating data bits from user to fog node and the time of running application are considered. However, the time wasted in the user queues waiting to communicate or the time wasted in the fog node queues waiting to run is not considered. For the second category (e.g., [8–11]), in addition to communication time and running time, the delays of queueing are also included. However, this category assumes the queues can be modelled as M/M/1 or M/G/1 queues so that those formulas of delay in the queueing theory can be re-used. For the third category (e.g., [12–15]), the queueing delays are also included. For this category, the resource allocation algorithm is derived in the following manner. Firstly, according to Little's Law, the average delay and queue length can be considered equivalent; then, the queue length based Lyapunov function is introduced and the bound of the conditional drift of this Lyapunov function is esti-mated; finally, using the Lyapunov optimization framework established in [16, 17], the resource allocation algorithm is design to minimizes the drift.

In this work, we focus on the category of Lyapunov optimization technique based resource allocation algorithms. This category of algorithms does not need any assumptions about the statistics of traffic. Consequently, the formulas of delay in the queueing theory cannot be used. Thus, since there is no formula of delay, this category of resource allocation algorithms cannot directly attack the problem of delay mini-mization but have to address the problem of queue length stability as an alternative. Therefore, this work will extend the category of Lyapunov optimization technique based resource allocation by designing algorithms which can directly minimize the delay and at the same time does not need assumptions on the statistics of traffic. The work in [18] is our first step toward this direction which focused on the single access-point scenario. Compared with our previous work in [18], this work focuses on the multi-access-point scenario, in which in addition to the need to decide to schedule subcarriers, it is also necessary to decide which access point to transfer the computation application to. The contributions of this work are summarized as following. Firstly, the recursive expressions of queueing delays in fog computing systems are derived. During the derivations, no assumptions on the statistics of traffic is needed. Secondly, a resource allocation algorithm for fog computing systems is proposed which can minimize the total delay directly. Finally, simulation results are reported which show that the proposed delay based resource allocation algorithm provides better delay performance than the traditional queue length based Lyapunov allocation algorithm.

The organization of this paper is as follows. Section 2 derives the queueing and delay models. Section 3 proposes a resource allocation algorithm which minimizes delay directly. Section 4 reports the results of simulation experiments. Section 5 gives concluding remarks. The summary of the main notations used in this paper is provided in Table 1.

Table 1. Summary of notations.

Notation	Description
T	The duration of a slot
I	User number
E_i	The number of cycles needed by the application of user i
J	Fog node number
F_j	The number of cycles provided by fog node j per second
Ψ_i	The set of neighbor fog nodes of user i
Ω_{ij}	The set of competitor users of user i for fog node j
$U_i[n-1]$	The number of queued applications of the ith user sampled at the start of the nth slot
$X_i[n]$	The number of applications leaving the queue of the ith user during the nth slot
R	The number of subcarriers in the air interface
$R_{ij}[n]$	The number of subcarriers to transfer an application from the ith user to the jth fog node in the nth slot
$W_i[n]$	The virtual queue of the normalized communication delay of user i
ε_n	Smoothing coefficient
$x_{ij}[n]$	The number of applications from the ith user to the jth fog node which is decided at the end of the nth slot
α_{ij}	The value of E_i/F_jT
$S_j[n]$	The normalized value of the number of cycles needed by all the applications which are still in the jth computing queue at the end of the $(n+1)$th slot
$d_{ijh}[n]$	The normalized value of the computing delay of the hth application which comes from the ith user and is executed by the jth fog node
$D_{ij}[n]$	The value of $\sum_{h=1}^{x_{ij}[n]} d_{ijh}[n]$
$Z_{ij}[n]$	the virtual queue of the normalized computing delay of user i in fog node j
$L[n]$	The Lyapunov function
$\Delta[n]$	The conditional drift of the Lyapunov function

2 System Models

Consider a time-slotted fog computing system. Let T represent the duration of a slot. Let I and J represent the number of users and fog nodes, respectively. For any application of user i, it will need E_i cycles to execute. For each fog node j, it can provide F_j per second. Applications are offloaded to fog nodes to execute. Therefore, if an application of user i is transferred to the jth fog node to execute, it need E_i/F_j seconds to finish the execution.

Given a pair of fog node j and user i, if the fog node can receive the signal from user i with a SINR (i.e., the signal to interference plus noise ratio) exceeding a given threshold, user i is a *neighbor* of fog node j. Let Ψ_i denote the set of neighbor fog nodes of user i. Further, for any two users i and k, if there exists a fog node which is accessible by both i and k, we say user k is a *competitor user*. For any user i, let Ω_i be the set of all his competitor users.

2.1 Communication Delay Model

Firstly, we derive the equation describing the evolution of communication queues. For the ith user, let $U_i[n-1]$ denote the number of queued applications which is sampled at the start of nth slot. Then, let $X_i[n]$ denote the number of applications which is transferred to some fog node (i.e., depart the queue) during the nth slot. Finally, let $A_i[n]$ denote the number of applications which newly arrives to this queue during the nth slot. Although $X_i[n]$ is the number of applications which leave the ith communication queue during the nth slot, its value is actually decided at the start of the nth slot. The value of $X_i[n]$ should not be greater than the number of applications which are still staying in the ith communication queue when the decision is made, that is, at the start of the nth slot. Then we have:

$$0 \leq X_i[n] \leq U_i[n-1]. \tag{1}$$

Additionally, the value of $X_i[n]$ is constrained by the capability of wireless transmission resource. Let R represent the number of all possible subcarriers which can be used. Then for each fog node $j \in \Psi_i$, we have:

$$\sum_{j \in \Psi_i} R_{i,j}[n] + \sum_{k \in \Omega_i} \sum_{h \in \Psi_k} R_{k,h}[n] \leq R, \tag{2}$$

where $R_{ij}[n]$ represents the number of subcarriers which are required to transfer a user i's application to the jth fog node in the nth slot. Hence, the recursive equation describing the communication queue of the ith user is:

$$U_i[n] = U_i[n-1] - X_i[n] + A_i[n], \tag{3}$$

where $X_i[n]$ satisfies the constraints in (1) and (2).

Next, we derive the recursive expression of the communication delay (including transmitting time and waiting time) of the ith user. Let $\Gamma_{\text{tot},i}[n]$ be the total communication delay that has been experienced by all applications of the ith user until the $(n + 1)$th slot. Thus, we have that:

$$\Gamma_{\text{tot},i}[n] = \sum\nolimits_{k=1}^{n} U_i[k]T. \tag{4}$$

Let $\Gamma_i[n]$ denote the time-average of $\Gamma_{\text{tot},i}[n]$, that is:

$$\Gamma_i[n] = \frac{\Gamma_{\text{tot},i}[n]}{n}. \tag{5}$$

In this paper, $\Gamma_i[n]$ is used to indicate length of the communication delay of the ith user. We further express $\Gamma_i[n]$ as a virtual queue:

$$\Gamma_i[n] = \Gamma_i[n - 1] - \varepsilon_n \Gamma_i[n - 1] + \varepsilon_n U_i[n]T, \tag{6}$$

with $\varepsilon_n = 1/n$. Let $W_i[n]$ be the value of $\Gamma_i[n]$ normalized to the slot length, that is, let $W_i[n] = \Gamma_i[n]/T$. Thus, we have that:

$$W_i[n] = W_i[n - 1] - \varepsilon_n W_i[n - 1] + \varepsilon_n U_i[n]. \tag{7}$$

2.2   Computing Delay Model

Firstly, we derive the equation describing the evolution of computing queues. Since there are J fog nodes, there are J computing queues to be modeled. At the end of the nth slot, there are $\sum_{1 \le i \le I} X_i[n]$ applications arriving to fog nodes. Let $x_{ij}[n]$ be the number of applications which are transferred from the ith user to the jth fog node. Thus, at the start of the $(n + 1)$th slot, there will be $\sum_{1 \le i \le I} x_{ij}[n]$ applications arriving to the jth fog node. These applications require $\sum_{1 \le i \le I} E_i x_{ij}[n]$ cycles. Obviously, $x_{ij}[n]$ must satisfy the following constrain:

$$\sum\nolimits_{j=1}^{J} x_{ij}[n] = X_i[n]. \tag{8}$$

Let $\Phi_j[n]$ be the cycle number of all the applications staying in the jth computing queue by the end of the $(n + 1)$th slot. Hence, the recursive equation of the computing queue is:

$$\Phi_j[n] = \left(\Phi_j[n - 1] + \sum\nolimits_{i=1}^{I} E_i x_{ij}[n] - F_j T \right)^+, \tag{9}$$

where $(\cdot)^+ = \max(\cdot, 0)$ and $x_{ij}[n]$ satisfies the constraint in (8). Similarly, let $S_j[n]$ be the value of $\Phi_j[n]$ normalized to the cycle number provided by fog node in one slot, that is, $S_j[n] = \Phi_j[n]/F_j T$. Thus, we have that:

$$S_j[n] = \left(S_j[n-1] + \sum_{i=1}^{I} \alpha_{ij} x_{ij}[n] - 1\right)^+, \tag{10}$$

where $\alpha_{ij} = E_i/F_j T$.

Next, we derive the formula of computing delay (including execution time and waiting time) of user i. Let $Z_{\text{tot},ij}[n]$ be the normalized version of the total computing delay which is experienced by all applications of the ith user in the jth fog node until the $(n+1)$th slot. Thus, we have that:

$$Z_{\text{tot},ij}[n] = \sum_{k=1}^{n} \sum_{h=1}^{x_{ij}[n]} d_{ijh}[k], \tag{11}$$

where $d_{ijh}[n]$ is the normalized version of the computing delay of the hth application and $1 \leq h \leq x_{ij}[n]$. The expression of $d_{ijh}[n]$ is derived as follows, which have three terms. For the first term, on the arrival of the hth application, if the queue is not null, it has to wait the applications queued before it to complete their executions. Therefore, $d_{ijh}[n]$ includes the term of $S_j[n-1]$. For the second term, let $Bef_{ijh}[n] = \{(k, l)$: the lth application of user k is executed before the hth application of user i on fog node j in slot $n+1\}$. Therefore, $d_{ijh}[n]$ includes the term of α_{kj} for each (k, l) in $Bef_{ijh}[n]$. For the third term, the running time of the application itself should also be considered. Thus, we have that:

$$d_{ijh}[n] = S_j[n-1] + \sum_{(k,l)\in Bef_{ijh}[n]} \alpha_{kj} + \alpha_{ij}. \tag{12}$$

Let $Z_{ij}[n]$ denote the time-average of $Z_{\text{tot},ij}[n]$, that is:

$$Z_{ij}[n] = \frac{Z_{\text{tot},ij}[n]}{n}. \tag{13}$$

In this paper, we use $Z_{ij}[n]$ to indicate length of the computing delay which is experienced by the applications of the ith user in the jth fog node. We express $Z_{ij}[n]$ as a virtual queue:

$$Z_{ij}[n] = Z_{ij}[n-1] - \varepsilon_n Z_{ij}[n-1] + \varepsilon_n D_{ij}[n], \tag{14}$$

where

$$D_{ij}[n] = \sum_{h=1}^{x_{ij}[n]} d_{ijh}[n]. \tag{15}$$

3 Algorithm Design

First of all, the Lyapunov function defined in this paper is:

$$L[n] = \sum_{i=1}^{I} W_i[n]^2 + \sum_{i=1}^{I} \sum_{j=1}^{J} Z_{ij}[n]^2 \qquad (16)$$

According to the Lyapunov optimization technique established in [16, 17], we need to estimate the value of the conditional drift $\Delta[n] = \mathrm{E}\{L[n] - L[n-1]|\mathbf{W}[n-1], \mathbf{Z}[n-1]\}$, where $\mathrm{E}\{\cdot\}$ is the expectation operation, $\mathbf{W}[n-1] = [W_1[n-1],\dots, W_I[n-1]]$, and $\mathbf{Z}[n-1] = [Z_{11}[n-1],\dots, Z_{IJ}[n-1]]$. Substituting (16), we have $\Delta[n] = \mathrm{E}\{\Sigma_{1 \le i \le I}\varepsilon_n^2 W_i[n-1]^2 + \Sigma_{1 \le i \le I}\Sigma_{1 \le j \le J}\varepsilon_n^2 Z_{ij}[n-1]^2 + \Sigma_{1 \le i \le I}\varepsilon_n^2 U_i[n]^2 + \Sigma_{1 \le i \le I}\Sigma_{1 \le j \le J}\varepsilon_n^2 D_{ij}[n]^2 - \Sigma_{1 \le i \le I}2\varepsilon_n W_i[n-1]^2 - \Sigma_{1 \le i \le I}\Sigma_{1 \le j \le J}2\varepsilon_n Z_{ij}[n-1]^2 + \Sigma_{1 \le i \le I}2\varepsilon_n(1-\varepsilon_n)W_i[n-1]U_i[n] + \Sigma_{1 \le i \le I}\Sigma_{1 \le j \le J}2\varepsilon_n(1-\varepsilon_n)Z_{ij}[n-1]D_{ij}[n]|\mathbf{W}[n-1], \mathbf{Z}[n-1]\}$, where the first six terms can be upper bounded by a constant under the expectation operation. According to the Lyapunov optimization technique established in [16, 17], this expression can be minimized by an algorithm which obtains the values of $\mathbf{W}[n-1]$ and $\mathbf{Z}[n-1]$ and chooses $X_i[n]$ and $x_{ij}[n]$ to minimize $\Sigma_{1 \le i \le I}W_i[n-1] U_i[n] + \Sigma_{1 \le i \le I}\Sigma_{1 \le j \le J}Z_{ij}[n-1]D_{ij}[n]$. Further, substituting (3), the objective can be written as $\Sigma_{1 \le i \le I}W_i[n-1]U_i[n-1] + \Sigma_{1 \le i \le I}W_i[n-1]A_i[n] - \Sigma_{1 \le i \le I}W_i[n-1] X_i[n] + \Sigma_{1 \le i \le I}\Sigma_{1 \le j \le J}Z_{ij}[n-1]D_{ij}[n]$, where the first two terms can also be upper bounded by a constant. Thus, this expression can be minimized by the algorithm that minimizes $-\Sigma_{1 \le i \le I}W_i[n-1]X_i[n] + \Sigma_{1 \le i \le I}\Sigma_{1 \le j \le J}Z_{ij}[n-1]D_{ij}[n]$. Substituting (15), the final form of the programming to be solved for each slot n is:

$$\min_{\{X_i[n],\, x_{ij}[n]\}} -\sum_{i=1}^{I} W_i[n-1]X_i[n] + \sum_{i=1}^{I}\sum_{j=1}^{J}\left(Z_{ij}[n-1]\sum_{h=1}^{x_{ij}[n]} d_{ijh}[n]\right)$$

$$\text{s.t.}\quad X_i[n] \le U_i[n-1] \qquad (17)$$

$$R_{ij}[n]X_i[n] + \sum_{k\in\Omega_{ij}} R_{kj}[n]X_k[n] \le R, \ j \in \Psi_i$$

$$\sum_{j=1}^{J} x_{ij}[n] = X_i[n]$$

where $d_{ijh}[n]$ is provided in (12) and $X_i[n]$ and $x_{ij}[n]$ are integers.

Before describing the algorithm, the concept of feasible user is needed to be introduced. Specifically, for the ith user, if the following judging criteria are true, one more application can be allowed to be transferred from this user to some fog node. For the first criteria, according to the constraint in (1), if $X_i[n] < U_i[n-1]$, then one more application can be allowed to be transferred from the ith user to some fog node; otherwise, if $X_i[n] = U_i[n-1]$, then no application is allowed to be transferred from the ith user to some fog node. For the second criteria, if the constraint in (2) holds with equality, then no application is allowed to be transferred from the ith user to some fog node. Thus, the set of feasible user is define as:

$$C[n] = \{i : X_i[n] < U_i[n-1] \text{ and}$$
$$\sum_{j \in \Psi_i} R_{i,j}[n] + \sum_{k \in \Omega_i} \sum_{h \in \Psi_k} R_{k,h}[n] \leq R - 1\} \tag{18}$$

Then, the proposed resource allocation algorithm works as following. Initially, we have $X_i[n] = 0$, $x_{ij}[n] = 0$, $TW_i = (1 - \varepsilon_n)W_i[n-1]$, $TZ_{ij} = (1 - \varepsilon_n)Z_{ij}[n-1]$, $TS_j = S_j[n-1]$ for each i and j. The steps of the proposed algorithm are as follows.

Step 1: Determine the value of the feasible user set $C[n]$. If $C[n]$ is null, the algorithm halts.

Step 2 (Wireless Scheduling): Select the user $i^* = \arg \max TW_i$ over all feasible users in $C[n]$. Update $X_{i*}[n] \leftarrow X_{i*}[n] + 1$ and $TW_{i*} \leftarrow TW_{i*} + \varepsilon_n$.

Step 3 (Server Assignment): Determine the fog node $j^* = \arg \min TZ_{i*j}$ over all fog node $j \in \Psi_{i*}$. Update $x_{i*j*}[n] \leftarrow x_{i*j*}[n] + 1$, $TS_{j*} \leftarrow TS_{j*} + \alpha_{i*j*}$, and $TZ_{i*j*} \leftarrow TZ_{i*j*} + \varepsilon_n TS_{j*}$. Go to Step 1.

3.1 The Traditional Queue Length Based Algorithm

For convenience, the traditional queue length based Lapunov resource allocation algorithm is outlined in this subsection. The queue length based Lyapunov function is defined as follows:

$$L[n] = \sum_{i=1}^{I} U_i[n]^2 + \sum_{j=1}^{J} S_j[n]^2 \tag{19}$$

We need to estimate the bound of the conditional drift of this Lyapunov function, which can be written as $\Delta[n] = E\{L[n] - L[n-1]|U[n-1], S[n-1]\}$, where $U[n-1] = [U_1[n-1],\ldots, U_I[n-1]]$, and $S[n-1] = [S_1[n-1],\ldots, S_J[n-1]]$. After similar derivations [16, 17], the optimization problem to be solved by the traditional queue length based algorithm is:

$$\min_{\{X_i[n], x_{ij}[n]\}} - \sum_{i=1}^{I} U_i[n-1]X_i[n] + \sum_{i=1}^{I} \sum_{j=1}^{J} \left(S_j[n-1] \sum_{h=1}^{x_{ij}[n]} \alpha_{ij} \right)$$
$$\text{s.t.} \quad X_i[n] \leq U_i[n-1] \tag{20}$$
$$R_{ij}[n]X_i[n] + \sum_{k \in \Omega_{ij}} R_{kj}[n]X_k[n] \leq R, \, j \in \Psi_i$$
$$\sum_{j=1}^{J} x_{ij}[n] = X_i[n]$$

where $X_i[n]$ and $x_{ij}[n]$ are integers. Since this optimization problem is similar to the one in (17), we can use the similar procedure to address this problem. Initially, set $X_i[n] = 0$, $x_{ij}[n] = 0$, $TU_i = U_i[n-1]$, and $TS_j = S_j[n-1]$. Then steps of the traditional queue length based algorithm are as follows.

Step 1: Calculate the value of the feasible user set $C[n]$. If $C[n]$ is null, the algorithm halts.

Step 2 (Wireless Scheduling): Select the user $i^* = \arg \max TU_i$ over all $i \in C[n]$. Update $X_{i^*}[n] \leftarrow X_{i^*}[n] + 1$ and $TU_{i^*} \leftarrow TU_{i^*} - 1$.

Step 3 (Server Assignment): Determine the fog node $j^* = \arg \min TS_j$ over all fog node $j \in \Psi_{i^*}$. Update $x_{i^*j^*}[n] \leftarrow x_{i^*j^*}[n] + 1$ and $TS_{j^*} \leftarrow TS_{j^*} + \alpha_{i^*j^*}$. Go to Step 1.

4 Performance Evaluation

Consider a time-slotted fog computing system. Assume there are $J = 4$ fog nodes. We set the geographical locations of fog nodes as (400, 400), (400, 800), (800, 400) and (800, 800) in meter. The default value of F_j is 2×10^9. Set $I = 25$ users. We set the geographic locations of user to be evenly distributed within 1200×1200 in meter. For each user i, the applications arrive according to a Poisson distribution with the average inter-arrival time of T_i. The default value of T_i is 1.5 slots. The value of R_{ij} is set to be 2 and the value of E_i is set to be 3×10^6 for each i. Let d_{ij} represents the distance between user i and fog node j. If $d_{ij} < 1.1 \times (\max_{1 \leq k \leq I} (\min_{1 \leq h \leq J} d_{kh}))$, user i is a neighbor of fog node j. Then the set Ψ_i and Ω_{ij} can be determined for each user i and fog node j. Selected simulation results are reported as follows. The performance considered in this paper is the total delay which is the sum of the average communication delay and computing delay. Two different algorithms are considered in simulations: the first is the proposed delay based resource allocation algorithm, the second is the traditional queue length based resource allocation algorithm. The outline of the traditional queue length based scheduling algorithm can be found Sect. 3.1. Given the parameter configuration, the simulation experiment is repeated 100 times and then averaged as the final result.

Figure 2 shows the normalized value of the total delay (i.e., measured in slot time) with different R (i.e., the total number of subcarriers in the system) for different resource allocation algorithms. The curve with square represents the proposed delay based resource allocation algorithm and the curve with triangle represents the traditional queue length based resource allocation algorithm. We can observe that, as the value of R increases, the value of the delay increases. Specifically, for the proposed delay based resource allocation algorithm, when R increases from 20 to 26, the delay decreases from 1.95 to 1.50 slots. Further, it can be observed that, the proposed delay based resource allocation algorithm has better delay performance than that of the traditional queue length based one. Specifically, when $R = 22$, the delay of the queue length based resource allocation algorithm is 1.63 slots, while the delay of the proposed delay based resource allocation algorithm is 1.83 slots, with a drop of 12.45%. The main reason is that the proposed delay based resource allocation algorithm minimizes delay directly, while the traditional queue length based one does not. Therefore, the proposed delay based resource allocation algorithm has better delay performance that the traditional queue length based one.

Figure 3 shows the normalized value of the total delay (i.e., measured in slot time) for different values of $1/T_i$ (i.e., the average arrival rate of applications). In this experiment, we set $R = 25$. For the curves in the figure, we can observe that, with the increase of $1/T_i$ (i.e., with the decrease of T_i), the delay also increase. Specifically, for the delay based resource allocation algorithm, when the value of $1/T_i$ increases from $1/1.8$ to $1/1.2$ (i.e., T_i decreases from 1.8 to 1.2), the delay increases from 1.42 to 2.17 slots. Further, it can be observed that, the proposed delay based resource allocation algorithm can provide better delay performance than the traditional queue length based resource allocation algorithm. Specifically, when the value of $1/T_i$ is $1/1.2$ (i.e., the value of T_i is 1.2), the delay of the traditional queue length based resource allocation algorithm is 2.46 slots, while the delay of the proposed delay based resource allocation algorithm is 2.17 slots, with a drop of 13.5%. The reason is also that the proposed delay based resource allocation algorithm minimizes delay directly, while the traditional queue length based resource allocation algorithm does not.

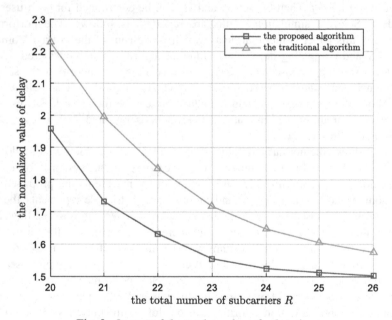

Fig. 2. Impact of the total number of subcarriers.

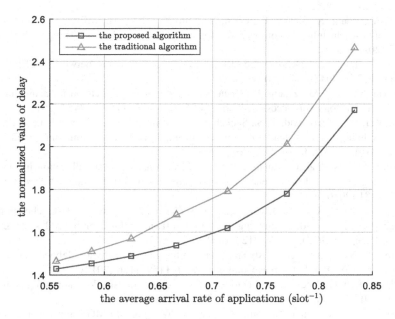

Fig. 3. Impact of the average arrival rate of applications.

5 Conclusions

In this work, the recursive expressions of the communication and computing delays in fog computing systems were derived in which the assumptions on the statistics of traffic is not needed at all. Using the framework of Lyapunov optimization, a novel delay based wireless scheduling and server assignment algorithm was proposed to stabilize the virtual queues of communication and computing delays. Simulation results were reported which showed that the average delay of the proposed delay based resource allocation algorithm can be 13.5% lower as compared to the traditional queue length based one.

Acknowledgments. This work was supported by the National Natural Science Foundation of China (No. 61571111 and No. 61771132) and the NFSC Incubation Project of NUPT (No. NY219106).

References

1. Chiang, M., Zhang, T.: Fog and IoT: an overview of research opportunities. IEEE Internet Things J. **3**(6), 854–864 (2016)
2. Aazam, M., Zeadally, S., Harras, K.: Fog computing architecture, evaluation, and future research directions. IEEE Commun. Mag. **56**(5), 46–52 (2018)
3. Bittencourt, L., Diaz-Montes, J., Buyya, R., Rana, O., Parashar, M.: Mobility-aware application scheduling in fog computing. IEEE Cloud Comput. **4**(2), 26–35 (2017)

4. Yang, Y., Wang, K., Zhang, G., Chen, X., Luo, X., Zhou, M.: MEETS: maximal energy efficient task scheduling in homogeneous fog networks. IEEE Internet Things J. **5**(5), 4076–4087 (2018)
5. Jiang, Y., Tsang, D.: Delay-aware task offloading in shared fog networks. IEEE Internet Things J. **5**(6), 4945–4956 (2018)
6. Rahman, S., Peng, M., Zhang, K., Chen, S.: Radio resource allocation for achieving ultra-low latency in fog radio access networks. IEEE Access **6**, 17442–17454 (2018)
7. Alameddine, H., Sharafeddine, S., Sebbah, S., Ayoubi, S., Assi, C.: Dynamic task offloading and scheduling for low-latency IoT services in multi-access edge computing. IEEE J. Sel. Areas Commun. **37**(3), 668–682 (2019)
8. Deng, R., Lu, R., Lai, C., Luan, T., Liang, H.: Optimal workload allocation in fog-cloud computing toward balanced delay and power consumption. IEEE Internet Things J. **3**(6), 1171–1181 (2016)
9. Zeng, D., Gu, L., Guo, S., Cheng, Z., Yu, S.: Joint optimization of task scheduling and image placement in fog computing supported software-defined embedded system. IEEE Trans. Comput. **65**(12), 3702–3712 (2016)
10. Misra, S., Saha, N.: Detour: dynamic task offloading in software-defined fog for IoT applications. IEEE J. Sel. Areas Commun. **37**(5), 1159–1166 (2019)
11. Josilo, S., Dan, G.: Decentralized algorithm for randomized task allocation in fog computing systems. IEEE/ACM Trans. Netw. **27**(1), 85–97 (2019)
12. Zhao, S., Yang, Y., Shao, Z., Yang, X., Qian, H., Wang, C.: FEMOS: fog-enabled multitier operations scheduling in dynamic wireless networks. IEEE Internet Things J. **5**(2), 1169–1183 (2018)
13. Yang, Y., Zhao, S., Zhang, W., Chen, Y., Luo, X., Wang, J.: DEBTS: delay energy balanced task scheduling in homogeneous fog networks. IEEE Internet Things J. **5**(3), 2094–2106 (2018)
14. Deng, Y., Chen, Z., Zhang, D., Zhao, M.: Workload scheduling toward worst-case delay and optimal utility for single-hop fog-IoT architecture. IET Commun. **12**(17), 2164–2173 (2018)
15. Li, L., Guan, Q., Jin, L., Guo, M.: Resource allocation and task offloading for heterogeneous real-time tasks with uncertain duration time in a fog queueing system. IEEE Access **7**, 9912–9925 (2019)
16. Tassiulas, L., Ephremides, A.: Stability properties of constrained queueing systems and scheduling policies for maximum throughput in multihop radio networks. IEEE Trans. Autom. Control **37**(12), 1936–1948 (1992)
17. Neely, M.: Stochastic Network Optimization with Application to Communication and Queueing Systems. Morgan & Claypool, San Rafael (2010)
18. Zhang, Y., Du, P., Wang, J., Ba, T., Ding, R., Xin, N.: Resource scheduling for delay minimization in multi-server cellular edge computing systems. IEEE Access **7**, 86265–86273 (2019)

Localization and Tracking

High Precision Indoor Positioning Method Based on UWB

Janyong Yan, Donghai Lin, Kai Tang, Guangsong Yang[(⊠)],
and Qiubo Ye

Jimei University, Xiamen 361021, Fujian, China
gsyang@jmu.edu.cn

Abstract. In order to meet the increasing requirement of indoor positioning, a high precision positioning method based on Ultra Wide Band (UWB) is designed and implemented. Firstly, the ranging method and its improvement are discussed. Secondly, by combining a median filter and Kalman filter algorithm, the collected data are processed by a smooth method to obtain stable ranging data. Finally, an indoor real-time positioning system is realized by using a weighted least square positioning algorithm. Experiment results show that when the refresh frequency is 10 Hz, the ranging accuracy between the base station and the tag can reach 5 cm.

Keywords: Ultra Wide Band · Kalman filtering · Indoor positioning

1 Introduction

A Real Time Location System (RTLS) [1] describes a class of systems that provide information in real-time about the location of objects, animals, people, or just about anything you can imagine. There are many applications of RTLS, for example, tracking and locating assets and patients in healthcare [2]; tracking and locating pallets, packages and items in warehousing and logistics [3]; tracking and monitoring farm animals; and tracking of inventory, work in progress and finished goods in manufacturing environments.

With the development of computer technology and the need of people's quality of life, the demand for positioning accuracy is increasing. Although GPS satellite positioning technology has high accuracy, it is limited by the characteristics of high cost, high power consumption and poor expansibility, neither can it provide effective positioning in indoor and other special areas. Therefore, we need to adopt some mechanisms to achieve precise indoor positioning.

Ultra Wide Band (UWB) [4] is a kind of radio technology based on IEEE 802.15.4a and 802.15.4z standards [5], and the physical properties of the UWB RF signal were specifically defined to achieve real-time, ultra-accurate, ultra-reliable location and communication. The use of complex modulation and demodulation is conducive to reducing costs. UWB uses pulses with nanosecond, which can measure the arrival time of radio waves with high precision and locate the distance with high precision. Because

J. Zheng et al. (Eds.): ADHOCNETS 2019, LNICST 306, pp. 201–207, 2019.
https://doi.org/10.1007/978-3-030-37262-0_16

of the low radiation power density of UWB, it has little effect on a human body. UWB can be widely used in indoor ranging, BAN (Body Area Network) and others fields.

The rest of the paper is organized as follows. In Sect. 2, we describe a ranging method and its improvement. In Sect. 3, we present a smoothing method to smooth the experiment data. Numerical results are given in Sect. 4. Finally, Sect. 5 concludes the paper.

2 Ranging Method and Improvement

There are a number of different methods for implementing RTLS [6], and they usually devolve into two basic types. One is the scheme based on signal strength, which is commonly referred to as RSSI (Received Signal Strength Indication). Another is the time-based method, which is based on the measurement of time it takes for the radio signal to travel between transmitter and receiver. UWB can enable the very accurate measurement of the radio signal propagation time, leading to centimeter accuracy distance/location measurement.

2.1 Two-Way Ranging

Two-way ranging is depicted in Fig. 1. Device A transmits a radio message to Device B and its transmission time (transmit timestamp) t1 is recorded. Device B receives the message and transmits a response (a radio message) back to Device A after a particular delay T_{reply}. Device A then receives this response and records a receive timestamp t2.

Now using the timestamps t1 and t2, Device A can calculate the round trip time T_{round} and know the reply time in the tag, T_{reply}, so $\hat{T}_{\text{prop}}$ can be determined by

$$\hat{T}_{\text{prop}} = \frac{1}{2}\left(T_{\text{round}} - T_{\text{reply}}\right) \tag{1}$$

T_{reply} and T_{round} are independently measured using the crystal oscillator of Device A and Device B. Thus, there are offset errors e_A of Device A and e_B of Device B, respectively. The dominant error in the ranging accuracy of this scheme is given by

$$\text{error} = \hat{T}_{\text{prop}} - T_{\text{prop}} \approx \frac{1}{2}\left(e_B - e_A\right) * T_{\text{reply}} \tag{2}$$

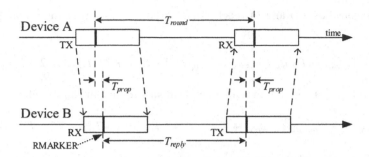

Fig. 1. Two-way ranging

2.2 Symmetric Double-Sided Two-Way Ranging

In the case of two-way ranging, there are a number of error sources due to clock drift and frequency drift. The error in ranging accuracy in the simple two-way ranging scheme is large even with small frequency offsets. An alternative scheme [7] to minimize the error by introducing another message in the ranging transaction is shown in Fig. 2. It reduces the error due to the clock and frequency drift.

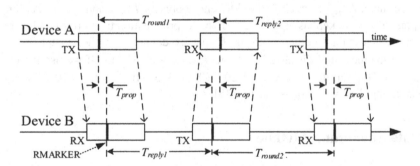

Fig. 2. Symmetric double-sided two-way ranging

In Fig. 2, Device A starts the first round-trip ranging and device B starts the second round-trip ranging. The receiving and transmitting timestamps are recorded and transmitted to device A in the form of data packets for aggregate calculation. Propagation delay can be calculated as

$$T_{round1} = T_{reply1} + 2 * \hat{T}_{prop} \tag{3}$$

$$T_{round2} = T_{reply2} + 2 * \hat{T}_{prop} \tag{4}$$

Multiplying Eqs. (3) and (4) each other on both sides with simple manipulation yields

$$\mathrm{T}_{round1} * \mathrm{T}_{round2} - T_{reply1} * T_{reply2} = \hat{T}_{\mathrm{prop}} * (4 * \hat{T}_{\mathrm{prop}} + 2 * T_{reply1} + 2 * T_{reply2}) \quad (5)$$

Adding Eqs. (3) and (4) on both sides with simple manipulation yields

$$\mathrm{T}_{round1} + \mathrm{T}_{round2} + T_{reply1} + T_{reply2} = 4 * \hat{T}_{\mathrm{prop}} + 2 * T_{reply1} + 2 * T_{reply2} \quad (6)$$

Combining (5) and (6), we can obtain $\hat{T}_{\mathrm{prop}}$ below,

$$\hat{T}_{\mathrm{prop}} = \frac{\mathrm{T}_{round1} * \mathrm{T}_{round2} - T_{reply1} * T_{reply2}}{\mathrm{T}_{round1} + \mathrm{T}_{round2} + T_{reply1} + T_{reply2}} \quad (7)$$

The dominant error in the ranging accuracy of this scheme is given by

$$\mathrm{error} = \frac{1}{4}(\mathrm{e}_B - \mathrm{e}_A) * \Delta T_{\mathrm{reply}} \quad (8)$$

Now we can see that dependence on T_{reply2} has been eliminated. The error is now dependent upon $\Delta T_{\mathrm{reply}}$, which is the difference between T_{reply1} and T_{reply2}. As long as T_{reply1} and T_{reply2} are kept as equal as possible, the propagation time error can be greatly reduced, which mainly comes from the frequency deviation of the crystal oscillator. Assuming the measured distance is 100 m, $\hat{T}_{\mathrm{prop}}$ will be 333 ns. If we use the crystal oscillator of 20 ppm, the error will be $20 * 10^{-6} * 333 * 10^{-9} = 6.7 * 10^{-12}$ s and the corresponding distance error is 2.2 mm [8].

3 Data Smoothing Method

In order to ensure sensitivity and obtain smoother data, a filtering algorithm is proposed combining a median filter and a Kalman filter. Before the data are sent to the Kalman filter for processing, the median filter is used to eliminate the jitter in order to obtain stable data quickly.

Firstly, we set 3 storage spaces (s_1, s_2, s_3) in memory and save three data d_{i-1}, d_i, d_{i+1} in these spaces, and then select the median among d_{i-1}, d_i and $, d_{i+1}$. But the refresh rate of this scheme is reduced by three times, from 20 samples per second to only 6–7 samples per second. To solve this problem, we put the median value of each output back into the storage space as data for the next comparison. Thus, the refresh rate is reduced by 10 samples per second.

Secondly, we designed a Kalman filter. Assume that the variables in the optimal estimation matrix $\hat{x}_k$ are random and obey the Gaussian distribution with mean μ and variance σ^2. We predict the next state (k moment) from the current state (k-1 moment), and the prediction process is shown as

$$\hat{x}_k = F_k * \hat{x}_{k-1} \tag{9}$$

where F_k is a prediction matrix representing the state of the next moment, in which the variables are usually correlated. It can be expressed by covariance matrix P_k shown in Eq. (10) below. Each element in the matrix represents the correlation between the ith and the jth state variables.

$$P_k = F_k * P_{k-1} * F_k^T \tag{10}$$

If external interference is taken into account, the noise with covariance of Q_k should be added and Eq. (10) can be expressed as

$$P_k = F_k * P_{k-1} * F_k^T + Q_k \tag{11}$$

Because the sensor has noise, its uncertainty is expressed by covariance R_k and its mean value $\vec{z}_k$ is the sensor data we read.

Thus we have two Gaussian distributions, one near the predicted value (μ_0, σ_0^2) and the other near the sensor reading value (μ_1, σ_1^2). In order to find the optimal estimation in these two distributions, it is necessary to multiply the two Gaussian distributions to obtain the output of Kalman filter (μ', σ'^2).

$$k = \frac{\sigma_0^2}{\sigma_0^2 + \sigma_1^2} \tag{12}$$

$$\mu' = \mu_0 + k*(\mu_1 - \mu_0) \tag{13}$$

$$\sigma'^2 = \sigma_0^2 - k*\sigma_0^2 \tag{14}$$

According to Eqs. (12), (13), and (14) we can obtain $(\hat{x}_k, P_k)$ and $(\vec{z}_k, R_k)$.

$$K = P_k * (P_k + R_k)^{-1} \tag{15}$$

$$\hat{x}_k' = \hat{x}_k + K * (\vec{z}_k - \hat{x}_k) \tag{16}$$

$$P_k' = P_k - K*P_k \tag{17}$$

All in all, $\hat{x}_{k-1}$ and P_{k-1} are the optimal estimate of the previous moment. The estimate values $\hat{x}_k$ and P_k are obtained by the prediction process matrix F_k, and then updated to the optimal estimate value $\hat{x}_k'$ and P_k' by the measured readings. The optimal estimate can be iterated in the next prediction and updating equation.

4   Experiments and Analysis

We design UWB nodes based on DW1000 UWB chip [7] of DecaWave company in Ireland, using 2 nodes as base stations which are fixed on the support frame and 30 cm apart. With a node as label (target object) in hand, the experimenter moves away from the base station for 0.5 m to 6 m. At this time, the original data will generate 20–30 cm fluctuation. After the filter processing, relatively smooth data can be obtained. The experiment results are shown in Fig. 3.

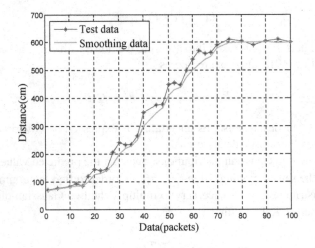

Fig. 3. Experiment data for 0.5 m to 6 m

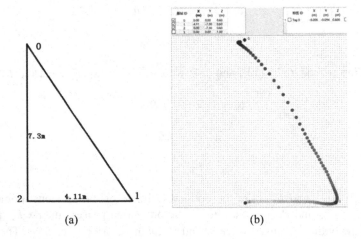

(a)   (b)

Fig. 4. Position of base stations and trajectories of the label

The indoor location test environment is shown in Fig. 4, including three base stations and one label. The coordinates of base stations 0, 1, and 2 are (0 m, 0 m), (4.11 m, −7.3 m) and (0.00 m, −7.3 m), respectively. Three base stations constitute a right triangle.

The hand tag moves straight from base station 2 to base station 1, and then goes straight to base station 0. The location trajectory is shown in Fig. 4. The indoor positioning experiment shows that the accuracy of the indoor positioning system can reach 10 cm except for the sloshing caused by walking.

5 Conclusion

In this paper, we design a high precision positioning method based on UWB technology. First, the symmetric double-sided two-way ranging method is used to reduce test error. Then, the algorithm combining a median filter and a Kalman filter is proposed to smooth data. The indoor real-time positioning system is realized by using weighted least square positioning algorithm at last.

In our future work, we will optimize the Kalman filter to process the system noise and measurement noise adaptively so as to improve the prediction accuracy. The scheme in this paper needs 2-way handshakes for positioning, and the number of target tags is limited. Next, TDOA will be adopted to further increase the number of object labels and reduce the power consumption of nodes.

References

1. Koyuncu, H., Yang, S.H.: A survey of indoor positioning and object locating systems. IJCSNS Int. J. Comput. Sci. Network Secur. **10**(5), 121–128 (2010)
2. Najera, P., Lopez, J., Roman, R.: Real-time location and inpatient care systems based on passive RFID. J. Network Comput. Appl. **34**(3), 980–989 (2011)
3. Zhang, D., et al.: Real-time locating systems using active RFID for Internet of Things. IEEE Syst. J. **10**(3), 1226–1235 (2014)
4. Fontana, R.J.: Recent system applications of short-pulse ultra-wideband (UWB) technology. IEEE Trans. Microwave Theory Tech. **52**(9), 2087–2104 (2004)
5. Salman, N., Rasool, I., Kemp, A.H.: Overview of the IEEE 802.15.4 standards family for low rate wireless personal area networks. In: 2010 7th International Symposium on Wireless Communication Systems, IEEE (2010)
6. Dardari, D., Closas, P., Djurić, P.M.: Indoor tracking: theory, methods, and technologies. IEEE Trans. Veh. Technol. **64**(4), 1263–1278 (2015)
7. DecaWave Ltd.: The implementation of two-way ranging with the DW1000. https://www.decawave.com/application-notes/. Accessed 23 Aug 2018
8. DecaWave Ltd.: Sources of Error in Two Way Ranging, https://www.decawave.com/application-notes/. Accessed 23 Aug 2018

Improvement of a Single Node Indoor Localization System

Yang Li, Weixiao Meng[⊠], Yingbo Zhao, and Shuai Han

Harbin Institute of Technology, Harbin, China
wxmeng@hit.edu.cn

Abstract. With the development of wireless communication technologies and the Internet, the application scenarios of positioning technologies are becoming more and more abundant. Therefore, the demand for location-based services is increasing greatly. Moreover, due to the widespread deployment of commercial WIFI devices, a WIFI-based localization system is very promising. This paper focuses on the localization algorithms utilizing Channel State Information (CSI) based on a conventional MUSIC algorithm in a single-node indoor localization system. However, the conventional MUSIC algorithm searches all the peaks in spatial spectrum. It requires enormous computation and thus is unsuitable for accurate positioning applications. This paper is intended to improve the algorithm in terms of positioning accuracy and computational complexity. Numerical results show that the proposed algorithm can improve the positioning accuracy and reduce computational complexity.

Keywords: Single-node indoor localization · Band splicing · Direct search

1 Introduction

As indoor environment become more and more complex, the demand for location-based services is increasing greatly. At present, indoor positioning systems mainly use wireless sensor networks for positioning, including Bluetooth, Zigbee, WIFI and so on. With the promotion of the IEEE 802.11 protocol, the WIFI has been widely used thanks to the features of low cost, high transmission rate and convenient connection [1]. Therefore, the design of indoor positioning system based on WIFI protocol has gradually become a research hotspot.

At present, the positioning technology based on WIFI can be mainly divided into two parts: position resolution based on geometry and matching positioning based on position fingerprint [2]. The positioning algorithm based on geometric model needs to calculate the time of arrival (TOA) or angle of arrival (AOA) transmitted by the terminal to AP, and then use the geometric model for positioning. The position fingerprint algorithm can be mainly divided into two stage. The first stage is called the offline stage. In this stage, we need to place several APs in the location area, then divide the location area into several subareas, measure the received signal strength indication (RSSI) in each subarea, and map all the RSSI to the location information. The second stage is called the online stage. In this stage, receive RSSI message online and find out the most similar fingerprint location as a result of the positioning. However, the

J. Zheng et al. (Eds.): ADHOCNETS 2019, LNICST 306, pp. 208–219, 2019.
https://doi.org/10.1007/978-3-030-37262-0_17

position fingerprint algorithm requires large number of APs and needs to collect information offline, which brings inconvenience to system deployment. And no matter which position fingerprint algorithm, RSSI is generally used as the basis for positioning. But, RSSI is susceptible to many factors in a typical indoor environment [3]. This may cause a large error in the positioning result. We need to use channel state information (CSI), which can carry detailed information, instead of RSSI [4].

The channel state information is the channel attribute in communication, and can describe the signal amplitude and phase information of each subchannel of the OFDM modulated signal. So, the CSI contains more fine-grained information than the RSSI and get accurate results in indoor positioning.

From the perspective of system construction and maintenance, traditional indoor positioning systems require more than one APs, and some systems require pre-deployment. Indoor positioning systems are limited for scenarios where multiple APs cannot be placed and the environment changes rapidly over time.

Based on the problems existing in conventional indoor positioning systems, this paper proposes a single node indoor localization system use channel state information. Select the phase of the received CSI to calculate the position. Using the Multiple Signal Classification (MUSIC) algorithm to estimate the AOA in TOA [5]. Finally, it is proposed that band splicing and direct search algorithm respectively improve the positioning accuracy and reduce the computational complexity of the algorithm.

2   System Model

2.1   Single Node Indoor Localization System Model

In a single node indoor localization system, in order to calculate the position of the terminal, it is necessary to know the distance d and angle of the θ AP to terminal [6]. The estimation of the angle can be obtained by estimating the spatial spectrum of the antenna array, and in order to calculate the distance, it is necessary to obtain the signal transmission time, and then multiply by the propagation speed of the electromagnetic wave. The single node indoor localization model is shown in Fig. 1.

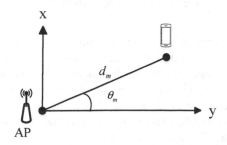

Fig. 1. Single node indoor localization model

2.2 Theoretical Derivation

In the indoor environment, the transmitted signal will be reflected and scatter through the wall to reach the receiving AP with multipath signals of different delays and amplitudes. Therefore, the frequency response of the channel is shown in Eq. (1).

$$H_i = \sum_{p=1}^{L} a_{i,p} e^{-j2\pi f_i \tau_{i,p}} \tag{1}$$

By performing discrete Fourier transform, the channel impulse response (CIR) in the corresponding time domain can be obtained, and the power delay distribution (PDP) can be obtained by squared, as shown in Eq. (2).

$$P_i(\tau) = E\left[|h_i(\tau)|^2\right] = E\left[\left|\sum_{p=1}^{L} a_{i,p}\delta(\tau - \tau_{i,p})\right|^2\right] \tag{2}$$

The power delay distribution calculated by using the received channel state information matrix is as shown in Fig. 2.

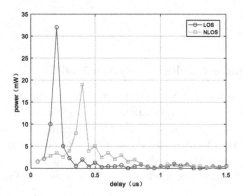

Fig. 2. Power delay distribution

The first peak in the power delay can be found as the direct path, and the corresponding delay time can be used as the transmission delay to calculate the distance. However, since multiple signal peaks overlap together in a complicated indoor environment, which causes the first peak to be indistinguishable, the performance of the transmission delay calculation based on the power delay is poor. Given the above reasons, in this paper, we use the phase of the channel state information to calculate the signal transmission delay.

Compared to RSSI, the channel state information contains amplitude and phase information of the subcarrier. Assuming that there is no multipath signal, the phase of subcarrier i is as shown in Eq. (3).

$$\phi_i = \xi + \tau \cdot (f_0 + \Delta f \cdot k_i) \tag{3}$$

Where ξ represents the initial phase and τ represents the transmission delay. For any two subcarriers, the phase difference is as shown in Eq. (4).

$$\Delta\phi = \tau \cdot \Delta f(k_i - k_j) \tag{4}$$

It can be seen that the phase difference of the subcarriers is proportional to the transmission delay, so the transmission delay can be solved by the phase difference. However, due to the multipath effect in the indoor environment, it is necessary to identify the multipath of the received phase, and the same problem exists for the calculate the angle of arrival. This paper proposes using the MUSIC algorithm to calculate the transmission delay and angle of arrival.

3 MUSIC Algorithm

3.1 Theoretical Basis

The basic idea of MUSIC is to decompose the covariance matrix of the array to obtain the signal subspace and the noise subspace, and use the orthogonality of the two subspaces to estimate the parameters of the signal. The theoretical model is shown in Fig. 3.

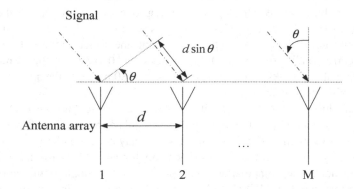

Fig. 3. The model of MUSIC algorithm

In the figure, the number of antennas is M, and the spacing between two adjacent antennas is d. The number of OFDM subcarriers is 30. It is assumed that the signal is reflected and scatter by the wall and becomes L multipath to reach the positioning AP. For different received signals, their phase offsets on different receiving antennas are related to the carrier frequency and the transmission distance to different antennas, while the difference of transmission distance is determined by the angle of arrival. Therefore, the phase difference due to the difference between the AOA and the carrier frequency is shown in Eq. (5).

$$a_{m,i}(\theta_p, \tau_p) = \Phi_{\theta_p}^{m-1}\Omega_{\tau_p}^{i-1} = e^{-j2\pi(m-1)d\sin\theta_p \cdot f/c}e^{-j2\pi(i-1)\Delta f \cdot \tau_p} \tag{5}$$

As long as $a(\theta, \tau)$ can be calculated based on the phase information of the received CSI, the angle θ and delay τ can be obtained. The steering matrix can be solved by using the orthogonality of the signal subspace and the noise subspace. Angles and delays are obtained by constructing a spatial spectrum and searching for peaks in the spatial spectrum. The definition of spatial spectrum is shown in Eq. (6)

$$P(\theta, \tau) = \frac{1}{a^H(\theta, \tau)E_N E_N^H a(\theta, \tau)} \tag{6}$$

The denominator part of the equation is the product of the steering matrix and the noise matrix. When the steering matrix is orthogonal to the noise matrix, the denominator is zero, but there is a minimum due to the presence of noise. By changing the angle and delay, we can find the peak of the spatial spectrum, and then obtain the arrival angle and transmission delay of the multipath signal. Detailed solution process in [7].

3.2 Insufficient in the Algorithm

3.2.1 Computational Complexity of the Algorithm

In the MUSIC algorithm introduced in Sect. 3.1, in addition to the calculation of the matrix, it is necessary to search the angle and delay peak in spatial spectrum. In order to ensure that the peaks of different multipaths can be accurately distinguished, it is necessary to reduce the search step size to improve the resolution of the spatial spectrum. It is assumed that the AOA is 1° in steps and the search range is from −90° to 90°. The transmission delay is in steps of 1 ns, and the search range is from 0 ns to 100 ns (the corresponding distance is 0.3 m in steps, and 0 to 30 m is the search range). In order to find all the peaks, it at least calculates 18, 180 points in the spatial spectrum and make thousands of comparisons.

Moreover, during the positioning, it is only necessary to find the peak with the smallest transmission delay as the direct path to calculate the position. Generally, it is not necessary to know the AOA and transmission delay corresponding to all peaks, so it is unnecessary to perform the two-dimensional peak search for all the peaks. Therefore, reducing the computational complexity of the single-point indoor positioning algorithm based on MUSIC and reducing the time of spatial spectrum search is an urgent problem to be solved.

3.2.2 Positioning Accuracy of the Algorithm

Although the resolution of the peak can be increased by reducing the search step size, the resolution is limited by this method, so it is necessary to look for the factors affecting the peak resolution from the algorithm itself.

We take the derivative of Eq. (5) and then get Eqs. (7) and (8).

$$\frac{\partial \Phi_\theta^{m-1}}{\partial \theta} = -j2\pi d(m-1) \cdot \frac{\cos \theta}{c} \cdot f \cdot \Phi_\theta^{m-1}, m \in [1, M] \tag{7}$$

$$\frac{\partial \Omega_\tau^{i-1}}{\partial \tau} = -j2\pi(i-1) \cdot \Delta f \cdot \partial \Omega_\tau^{i-1}, i \in [1, N_{sub}] \tag{8}$$

It can be seen that the resolution of the spatial spectrum depends on factors such as the number of antennas in the antenna array, adjacent antenna spacing, subcarrier frequency and number of subcarriers. Since the wireless network card capable of receiving CSI only has an Intel 5300 network card, and its antenna interface has only three, it is impossible to increase the spatial spectral resolution by increasing the number of antennas. Meanwhile, in the actual antenna array, the interval between the antennas is fixed. Therefore, it is also impossible to increase the spatial spectral resolution by increasing the spacing between the antennas. Therefore, the spatial spectrum resolution can be improved by increasing the carrier frequency, subcarrier frequency interval and the number of acquired subcarriers.

4 Improvement of Accuracy and Complexity

4.1 Band Splicing Improve Accuracy

4.1.1 Band Splicing
Section 3.2 analyzes how to improve the resolution of the spatial spectrum. Whether increasing the subcarrier frequency interval or increasing the number of acquired subcarriers, it is necessary to increase the bandwidth of the received CSI, that is, to get more phase information of CSI in continuous frequency bands. Under the 802.11n protocol, the channel division corresponding to the 2.4 GHz band is shown in Fig. 4.

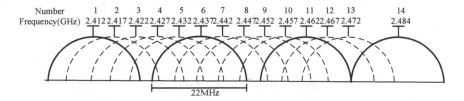

Fig. 4. Channel division at 2.4 GHz

Receive the phase of 1, 4, 7, and 10 channels by changing the receiving center frequency of the WIFI. And splice the phase information of four channels by using frequency band splicing. The method of spectrum splicing is shown in the Fig. 5.

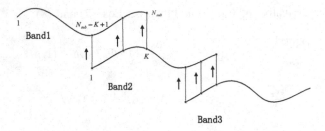

Fig. 5. The method of spectrum splicing

Band splicing can be divided into 3 steps:

(1) Change the channel where the AP is located, and receive 4 sets of channel state information under the channels with the center frequency of 2.412 MHz, 2.427 MHz, 2.442 MHz, 2.457 MHz, respectively.
(2) Calculate the relative phase difference of the subcarriers overlapping in the adjacent channel, and use the average value of the difference as the upward translation value of the latter channel phase information, wherein the phase of the overlapping portion takes the mean of the two channel phase values.
(3) Repeat step 2 until all phase are stitched together and phase band splicing is shown in the Fig. 6.

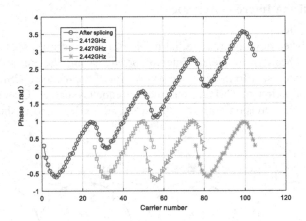

Fig. 6. Phase after band splicing

4.1.2 Spatial Spectrum

After band splicing, the bandwidth is increased from 20 MHz to 65 MHz. There are two ways to increase the resolution of the spatial spectrum. The first is to increase the number of subcarriers, and to use the phase information of all 105 subcarriers; the second is to increase the subcarrier spacing, extract 30 subcarriers from 105 subcarriers at equal intervals, and use the phase information of the extracted subcarriers. Detailed mathematical derivation can refer to the literature [8]. The spatial resolution after band spliced are shown in the Figs. 7, 8 and 9.

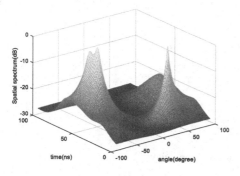

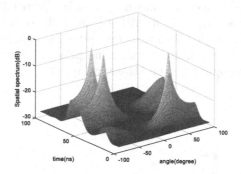

Fig. 7. Spatial spectrum without band splicing   **Fig. 8.** Increasing the number of subcarriers

Fig. 9. Increase subcarrier frequency spacing

As can be seen from the figure, after the band is spliced, the resolution of the spatial spectrum is improved, more peaks can be discerned, and positioning error can be also reduced.

4.2 Reduce Computational Complexity

In the single-node indoor positioning system based on the MUSIC algorithm, the angle and delay of the multipath signal are mainly estimated by using the phase difference of the received CSI. The transmission delay is estimated by using the phase difference of different frequency subcarriers in the same antenna, while. The angle is estimated by the phase difference of the same frequency subcarriers received by adjacent antennas in the antenna array. Therefore, the angle and time delay estimates can be split, and one of the variables can be estimated by constructing a one-dimensional spatial spectrum. Calculate another variable by substituting the estimated value into a two-dimensional spatial spectral formula. In short, the meaning of direct search is to use one part of information to estimate one of the two variables, than to estimate another variable in the spatial spectrum of all the information.

First, estimate the transmission delay by using 30 subcarriers which received by the same antenna. The method of estimating the delay is the same as that introduced in 3.1, except that the dimension of the spatial spectrum is one-dimensional.

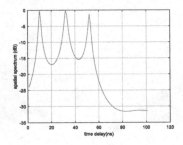

Fig. 10. Spatial spectrum of time delay

There are three peaks that can be clearly distinguished in the Fig. 10, and the corresponding delay is the multipath transmission delay. After selecting the minimum delay as the transmission delay of the direct path, multiply it by the speed of the electromagnetic wave to get the distance. For the receiving angle, we need to substitute the delay into the formula (5), and calculate the peak to get the angle. The spatial spectrum after substituting the delay is shown in Fig. 11.

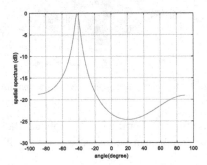

Fig. 11. Spatial spectrum of angles

The direct search algorithm decomposes the two-dimensional spatial spectrum and reduces the computational complexity. However, for the estimation of the delay, a one-dimensional peak search is still needed. In this paper, the Root-MUSIC algorithm and the ESPRIT algorithm are used to avoid the peak search.

The Root-MUSIC algorithm mainly obtains delay by constructing and solving high-order polynomials. The ESPRIT algorithm needs to construct two equally spaced sub-arrays and then use the rotation invariance of the sub-array to calculate the delay. Both methods avoid peak search and reduce computational complexity. However, the positioning accuracy may be affected when the amount of calculation is reduced. However, when the amount of calculation is reduced, the positioning accuracy may be affected. Figure 12 shows the variation of the positioning error of different algorithms with the change of SNR.

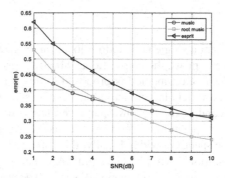

Fig. 12. Positioning error varies with SNR

It can be seen that under the low SNR, the positioning error of the MUSIC algorithm is relatively small, and under the high SNR, the positioning error of the Root-MUSIC algorithm is relatively small. But overall, the MUSIC algorithm is relatively stable.

This paper selects a test point which is located at a distance of 7 M. The following are the test results.

As shown in

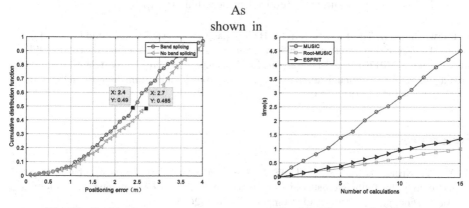

Fig. 13. Positioning error

Fig. 14. Time required for operation

Fig. 13, the positioning error is about 2.4 m when there is no band splicing, and the positioning error after band splicing is about 2.7 m. Figure 14 shows the time required for the three algorithms to run as the number of calculations increases. Therefore, the positioning error of the single-point indoor positioning system is about 2.7 m. The positioning accuracy of single-node indoor positioning system can be improved by frequency band splicing and algorithm complexity can be reduced by direct search.

5 Conclusion

In this paper, we implement a single node indoor localization system based on MUSIC algorithm. Moreover, we improve the conventional MUSIC algorithm in three aspects. Firstly, a phase error elimination method is proposed in this paper. For the linear and nonlinear phase error, the interpolation method and the least squares scheme are proposed, respectively. Secondly, for the low spatial resolution problem in the conventional single point WIFI positioning system, we use a frequency band splicing technology to expand the spectrum width. Finally, this paper reduces the computational complexity of the conventional MUSIC algorithm. A direct search algorithm is proposed, which decomposes the two-dimensional spatial spectrum into angle spatial spectrum and time spatial spectrum. This method avoids two-dimensional search. Moreover, we further reduce the computational complexity of one-dimensional spatial spectrum by using Root-MUSIC algorithm and ESPRIT algorithm.

The simulation result shows that the phase error elimination method can effectively eliminate the phase error of channel state information. The measurement results in various indoor scenes and the simulation results on the MATLAB platform show that the system can achieve a positioning error of 2.7 m. Compared with conventional algorithm, the computational complexity of the proposed algorithm is reduced by 70% while the positioning accuracy is reduced by less than 0.2 m.

Acknowledgment. This topic is from the Heilongjiang Provincial Science Fund Project. Project Name: High-precision single-point indoor positioning theory and method based on OFDM-MIMO (No. ZD2017013) and from the national Science Fund Project: Wide-area space-based broadband wireless communication theory and air-ground multi-beam high-throughput transmission method (No. 61871155).

References

1. Xu, Y., Xiang, G., Sun, Z., et al.: WSN node localization algorithm design based on RSSI technology. In: Fifth International Conference on Intelligent Computation Technology and Automation, pp. 556–559. IEEE Computer Society (2012)
2. Gu, Y., Lo, A., Niemegeers, I.: A survey of indoor positioning systems for wireless personal networks. IEEE Commun. Surv. Tutorials 11(1), 13–32 (2009)
3. Wu, K., Xiao, J., Yi, Y., et al.: FILA: fine-grained Indoor Localization. In: Proceedings - IEEE INFOCOM vol. 131, no. 5, pp. 2210–2218 (2012)
4. Xiao, J., Wu, K., Yi, Y., et al.: Pilot: passive device-free indoor localization using channel state information. In: International Conference on Distributed Computing Systems, pp. 236–245. IEEE Computer Society (2013)
5. Kotaru, M., Joshi, K., Bharadia, D., et al.: SpotFi: decimeter level localization using WiFi. In: ACM SIGCOMM Computer Communication Review, vol. 45, no. 5, pp. 269–282 (2015)
6. Vasisht, D., Kumar, S., Katabi, D.: Decimeter-level localization with a single WiFi access point. In: 13th USENIX Symposium on Networked Systems Design and Implementation (NSDI 16), pp. 165–178. USENIX Association (2016)

7. Han, S., Li, Y., Meng, W., et al.: Indoor localization with a single Wi-Fi access point based on OFDM-MIMO. IEEE Syst. J. **13**(1), 964–972 (2019)
8. Zhuo, Y., Zhu, H., Xue, H., et al.: Perceiving accurate CSI phases with commodity WiFi devices. In: IEEE Conference on Computer Communications INFOCOM 2017, pp. 1–9. IEEE (2017)

An Efficient Approach for Rigid Body Localization via a Single Base Station Using Direction of Arrive Measurement

Shenglan Wu[1], Lingyu Ai[1], Jichao Zhan[1], Le Yang[2], Qiong Wu[1,3], and Biao Zhou[1(✉)]

[1] IoT Engineering School, Jiangnan University, Wuxi 214122, China
zhoubiao@jiangnan.edu.cn
[2] Department of Electrical and Computer Engineering, University of Canterbury, Christchurch 8020, New Zealand
[3] Department of Electronic Engineering, Tsinghua University, Beijing 100084, China

Abstract. Rigid bodies are objects whose profile will not change after moving or being forced. A framework of rigid body localization (RBL) is to estimate the position and the orientation of a rigid object. In a wireless node network (WSN) based RBL approach, a few wireless nodes are mounted on the surface of the rigid target. Even though the position of the rigid body is unknown, we know how the nodes are distributed, which means that the topology of the nodes is known. Recently, a novel RBL scheme is studied, in which the rigid target is localized with just one single base station (BS) by measuring the angles between the BS and the positions of wireless nodes in the current frame, i.e., direction of arrival (DOA). However, the DOA-based RBL model is highly nonlinear and existing heuristic algorithms are generally time-consuming. In this paper, we intend to find the optimal solution of the 3-D positions of wireless nodes by fusing the topology information and DOA measurements with Newton's Iteration algorithm (NIA). Then, the rotation matrix and the translation vector can be obtained by the unit quaternion (UQ) method with the 3-D positions of wireless nodes, which completes the RBL task. Finally, we evaluate the proposed NIA-based RBL performance in terms of the root mean squared error (RMSE), as well as the computation costs.

Keywords: Rigid body localization · Single base station · Direction of arrival · Newton's iteration algorithm · The unit quaternion method

1 Introduction

1.1 Background

Generally, a rigid target is the object whose deformation of the moving object can be ignored when we consider the object as a rigid body. Compared with general positioning models, rigid body localization (RBL) considers not only the position of the object but also the attitude [1].

© ICST Institute for Computer Sciences, Social Informatics and Telecommunications Engineering 2019
Published by Springer Nature Switzerland AG 2019. All Rights Reserved
J. Zheng et al. (Eds.): ADHOCNETS 2019, LNICST 306, pp. 220–230, 2019.
https://doi.org/10.1007/978-3-030-37262-0_18

The RBL plays an important role in many fields. With its maturity, RBL can be used to the small-scale instruments such as virtual reality (VR) helmets, video games and smart robots. For example, the three-dimensional (3-D) position and posture of VR helmets are essential to provide more realistic virtual images. RBL is also applied to large-scale appliance such as vehicles, ships, aircraft and spacecraft. In unmanned systems, the position and orientation information are absolutely necessary, and unmanned systems require high precision to ensure safety [2]. In addition, RBL can also be applied to monitor and estimate the oblique of buildings in real time.

Global Positioning System (GPS) is a system for positioning and navigating globally by satellites which can provide navigation information including the absolute position and the speed of users. GPS can also be used for RBL and has been applied widely in many fields such as transportation, marine exploration, aerospace, and so on. However, it has to consider the problems of period ambiguity in phase measurement and the costs of the antenna mounted on the object. Besides, GPS cannot be applied in many sheltered scenarios such as indoor positioning. The source localization in wireless node networks (WSNs) compensates well for the vacancy of GPS in accurate scenarios [3], since the position of rigid object can be estimated by the physical characteristics of the signal from the distributed wireless nodes in a WSN with relatively low cost.

1.2   Related Work

In order to estimate the position of an object in WSNs, there are many processing methods for the information which is obtained from wireless nodes, such as time of arrival (TOA), time difference of arrival (TDOA), direction of arrival (DOA) and so on. In the framework of RBL based on TOA and TDOA, several wireless nodes have to be mounted on the rigid object and then TOA and TDOA between nodes and each base station (BS) can be measured [4, 5].

The TOA method realizes the localization by converting the time of propagating signals between the wireless nodes and the BSs to a distance. However, it is obvious that most of the existing TOA-based positioning methods have limitations. It is generally difficult to measure absolute arrive time of signals and then the TDOA method is proposed. The TDOA method is an improvement to the TOA method. Instead of directly utilizing the time of signal arrival, the TDOA method determines the location of the moving object using the time difference between the signals received by multiple BSs, which reduced time synchronization requirements of TOA between wireless nodes and BSs. Even though the TDOA method relatively improves the accuracy of position, both of the TOA and TDOA method need three BSs in WSNs at least and have to make sure the positions of BS are fixed and known.

In the framework of RBL based on DOA, there likewise are wireless nodes mounted on the rigid object and DOA between these nodes and the single BS can be measured. The DOA method estimates the position of a rigid object with the angles of arrival. It means that the method does not need to know the position of the BS, and it can determine the position of the object by using just a single BS because of the 2-dimensional DOA information, including the azimuth and pitch angles. The locating measurement of object is using multi-station positioning system mostly which makes sure the position of an object by three to five BSs. Multi-station positioning system requires several BSs to synchronize data transmission, while single-station positioning system requires only one observation BS. And it does not need to transmit information actively, the only requirement is to receive information of the wireless nodes to achieve the localization of the target. Compared with multi-station positioning system, the single BS positioning system greatly reduces the consumption of resources.

Recently, several heuristic search positioning algorithms based on the evolutionary algorithm paradigm are studied for the DOA-based RBL scheme, such as particle swarm optimization (PSO) [6] and participatory searching algorithm (PSA) [7]. They all realized the RBL purpose of the DOA-based single BS method, starting from the random solution and achieving the optimal solution through iterations. PSO is to initialize a bunch of random particles (random solution) and to follow the current searched optimal value to find the global optimal. The method uses PSO to optimize the target cost function to obtain the true distance of the object and achieves accurate solution. PSA is a population-based search procedure derived from the participatory learning paradigm. The algorithm is forming search as a pool with individuals, reserving the one nearest to the current best individuals and adding new random individuals in each step.

The PSO algorithm is easy to be accomplished and does not need to adjust too many parameters. It has great development value and can be applied to multiple fields such as pattern recognition, image processing and neural network training. Even though the methods of PSO and PSA are superior for their easy to implement in practical problems, they also have shortcomings of slow running speed and low success rate. The two methods run slowly because they are both heuristic algorithms. And they are easy to fall into a local optimum when the model to be optimized is highly non-linear, so that the global optimum solution cannot be obtained.

In this paper, the rigid object is located by DOA with single BS, and the position of wireless nodes in the current frame is estimated by Newton's iteration algorithm (NIA). The reference frame is a preset system of information about the position and attitude of wireless nodes in the 3-D space, and the current frame is the position and attitude of wireless nodes after transforming relative to the reference frame. The algorithm is used to linearize the nonlinear equation to find the approximate root. When the positions of wireless nodes in the reference frame and current frame are known, we can obtain the rotation matrix and the translation vector by the unit quaternion (UQ) method [9].

The remainder of the paper is organized as follows. The model of positioning system and the considered problems are introduced in Sect. 2. Section 3 discusses the relative process about determining location information of rigid object by NIA and solving transformation information of object by the UQ method. In Sect. 4, the performance of proposed method is analyzed by contrast results based on simulations. Finally, a conclusion of the paper is drawn in Sect. 5.

For clarity, the notations used in this paper are shown as below. Uppercase or lowercase bold letters are used to represent matrix and vectors. $\mathbf{X}^T$ is the transpose of $\mathbf{X}$, $\otimes$ is the notation of the Kronecker product, and $\mathbf{I}_n$ is the identity matrix of $n \times n$. $\|*\|$ means the Euclidian norm and $\text{vec}(\mathbf{X})$ denotes a column vector by stacking the columns $\mathbf{X}$.

2 DOA-Based RBL Model

As mentioned above, a framework of network that K wireless nodes are mounted is built to determine the position and orientation of a rigid object in the 3-D space. These wireless nodes are mounted on the rigid object with a certain accuracy and their topology is known. As illustrated in Fig. 1, the coordinate system is set to make the single BS as the origin O of and a reference frame is assumed at the origin O to be the starting point of the rigid object. After a series of transformations, the object arrives at another position which defined as the current frame.

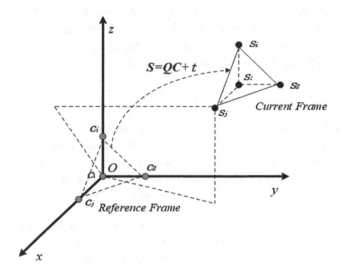

Fig. 1. DOA-based RBL framework

In the reference frame, the coordinate of the kth wireless node is denoted as 3-D vector $\mathbf{c}_k = \left[c_{k,x}, c_{k,y}, c_{k,z}\right]^T$ and the wireless nodes topology is determined by the matrix $\mathbf{C} = [\mathbf{c}_1, \mathbf{c}_2, \ldots, \mathbf{c}_K] \in \mathbb{R}^{3 \times K}$. The position of wireless node $\mathbf{c}_k$ is determined because of the known topology. Let the absolute coordinate of the kth wireless node in the current frame be denoted as 3-D vector $\mathbf{s}_k = \left[s_{k,x}, s_{k,y}, s_{k,z}\right]^T$ and the absolute coordinates of these wireless nodes are collected in $\mathbf{S} = [\mathbf{s}_1, \mathbf{s}_2, \ldots, \mathbf{s}_K] \in \mathbb{R}^{3 \times K}$. The current frame is transformed from the reference frame by rotation and translation, mathematically $\mathbf{S}$ can be expressed by $\mathbf{C}$ that

$$\mathbf{S} = \mathbf{RC} + \mathbf{t} \otimes \mathbf{1}_{1 \times K}, \tag{1}$$

where $\mathbf{t} = [x, y, z]^T \in \mathbb{R}^{3 \times 1}$ is the unknown translation vector, and $\mathbf{R} \in \mathbb{R}^{3 \times 3}$ is the unknown rotation matrix which is orthogonal matrix with determinant is 1, i.e. $\mathbf{R}^T\mathbf{R} = \mathbf{R}\mathbf{R}^T = \mathbf{I}_3$.

Specifically, the 3-D vector c_k is the known coordinate of the kth wireless node in the reference frame while the s_k is the unknown coordinate of the kth wireless node in the current frame that we need to solve. The unknown orthogonal matrix $\mathbf{R}$ actually represents how the rigid object rotates from the reference frame. It means that the rotation matrix $\mathbf{R}$ refers to the orientation of the transformation of the rigid target. And the unknown vector $\mathbf{t}$ represents the moving position of the rigid target. When the rigid object does not experience rotation, the rotation matrix $\mathbf{R} = \mathbf{I}_3$.

In order to obtain the positions of the wireless nodes in the current frame, two conditions are needed in the RBL estimation. The first one is the Euclidean distances between the node pairs on the rigid target. We denote the distance between the ith and jth wireless nodes in the reference frame as $d_{i,j}$. The distance $d_{i,j}$ can be obtained since the topology of wireless nodes is known. The known distance $d_{i,j}$ can be calculated by the position of wireless nodes in the reference frame that $d_{i,j} = \left\| c_i - c_j \right\| = \left\| s_i - s_j \right\|$. Collecting the distance $d_{i,j}$, and we obtain a column vector

$$\mathbf{d} = \left[d_{1,2}, \ldots, d_{i,j}, \ldots, d_{K-1,K} \right]^T, i,j = 1, \ldots, K, i > j. \tag{2}$$

The second condition for RBL is not known information, it need the single BS to measure. Assuming that the BS is equipped with phased array radar (PAR), which is used to measures the DOA of wireless nodes signals in 3-D space for RBL. In the phased array, signals can be used for both reception and transmission. The angles between nodes signals and the x- and z-axes can be obtained and we denote the kth node's DOA as α_k and β_k corresponding to the x- and z-axes.

The distance of wireless nodes pairs $d_{i,j}$ can be rewritten by the coordinates of nodes in reference frame. Combining with the DOAs, α_k and β_k, the equation of the nonlinear system can be obtained according to the spatial geometric:

$$\begin{cases} \alpha_k = \arccos \frac{x_k}{\sqrt{x_k^2 + y_k^2 + z_k^2}}, \\ \beta_k = \arccos \frac{z_k}{\sqrt{x_k^2 + y_k^2 + z_k^2}}, \\ d_{i,j} = \sqrt{\left(x_i - x_j \right)^2 + \left(y_i - y_j \right)^2 + \left(z_i - z_j \right)^2}. \end{cases} \tag{3}$$

Usually, there is no root formula to solve the nonlinear system exactly in most cases. So, it is difficult or even impossible to find the exact solution. In order to obtain the position of wireless nodes in current frame, it is particularly important to find the approximate solution of the nonlinear equation. The method proposed to solve the problem is given in the next section.

3 Proposed RBL Algorithm

3.1 Newton's Iteration Method

Newton's iteration is one of the important methods to find the root of the nonlinear model and it is a classical method of optimization. The advantage of the method is that there is performance of square convergence around the single root of the equation. Newton's method is the process of using the iteration to continuously recur the new value with the old value of the variable. Therefore, it is necessary to set an appropriate initial value to guarantee the algorithm converges and ensure its convergence speed. In this paper, the initial value is determined in the reference frame.

Solving nonlinear equations by Newton's method is an approximation algorithm for linearizing the nonlinear equations. The equation is expanded into Taylor series (TS) at the initial value, and we can get an iterative relation by letting linear part of TS be zero if the derivative of the equation is not equal to zero. The method utilizes the derivative, and the direction of each iteration is the direction in which the value of the current point of the function decreases.

In order to iteratively estimate the node position, we define a measurement vector

$$\mathbf{F} = \left[\boldsymbol{\omega}^T \mathbf{d}^T \right]^T, \tag{4}$$

where $\boldsymbol{\omega} = \left[\alpha_{1,x}, \ldots, \alpha_{K,x}, \beta_{1,z}, \ldots, \beta_{K,z} \right]^T + \left[\upsilon_{1,x}, \ldots, \upsilon_{K,x}, \upsilon_{1,z}, \ldots, \upsilon_{K,z} \right]^T$ containing DOA observations with Gaussian noise and $\mathbf{d}$ is the true value measured from the known position of wireless nodes without noise. The noise distribution of DOA observations is $\mathcal{N}(0, \sigma^2)$. These measurements of wireless nodes in RBL are expressed in (2). Expanding nonlinear equations (2) at the initial value by TS until the expansions are nonlinear, the initial value in this paper is the positions of wireless nodes in the reference frame $\mathbf{C}$, and we obtain

$$\mathbf{F} \approx \mathbf{F}(\text{vec}(\mathbf{C})) + \mathbf{G} \cdot (\text{vec}(\mathbf{S}) - \text{vec}(\mathbf{C})), \tag{5}$$

where $\text{vec}(\mathbf{C}) = \left[\mathbf{c}_1^T, \ldots, \mathbf{c}_K^T \right]^T$, $\text{vec}(\mathbf{S}) = \left[\mathbf{s}_1^T, \ldots, \mathbf{s}_K^T \right]^T$ and $\mathbf{G}$ is the Jacobian matrix of $\mathbf{F}$ which partially derived with respect to the position of wireless nodes in the current frames $\mathbf{S}$ and defined as

$$\mathbf{G} = \begin{bmatrix} \frac{\partial \boldsymbol{\omega}^T}{\partial \text{vec}(\mathbf{S})} |_{\mathbf{S}=\mathbf{C}} \\ \frac{\partial \mathbf{d}^T}{\partial \text{vec}(\mathbf{S})} |_{\mathbf{S}=\mathbf{C}} \end{bmatrix}, \tag{6}$$

where $\frac{\partial \boldsymbol{\omega}^T}{\partial \text{vec}(\mathbf{S})}$ is the partial derivate of $\boldsymbol{\omega}$ with respect to $\mathbf{S}$ and is a matrix of $2K \times 3K$, $\frac{\partial \mathbf{d}^T}{\partial \text{vec}(\mathbf{S})}$ is the partial derivate of $\mathbf{d}$ with respect to $\mathbf{S}$ and is a matrix of $\frac{(K-1)K}{2} \times 3K$. The expressions of $\frac{\partial \boldsymbol{\omega}^T}{\partial \text{vec}(\mathbf{S})}$ and $\frac{\partial \mathbf{d}^T}{\partial \text{vec}(\mathbf{S})}$ are as follows respectively:

$$\frac{\partial \boldsymbol{\omega}^T}{\partial \text{vec}(\mathbf{S})} = \begin{bmatrix} \frac{\partial \alpha_1}{\partial x_1} & \frac{\partial \alpha_1}{\partial y_1} & \frac{\partial \alpha_1}{\partial z_1} & \cdots & \frac{\partial \alpha_1}{\partial x_K} & \frac{\partial \alpha_1}{\partial y_K} & \frac{\partial \alpha_1}{\partial z_K} \\ & \vdots & & \ddots & & \vdots & \\ \frac{\partial \alpha_K}{\partial x_1} & \frac{\partial \alpha_K}{\partial y_1} & \frac{\partial \alpha_K}{\partial z_1} & \cdots & \frac{\partial \alpha_K}{\partial x_K} & \frac{\partial \alpha_K}{\partial y_K} & \frac{\partial \alpha_K}{\partial z_K} \\ \frac{\partial \beta_1}{\partial x_1} & \frac{\partial \beta_1}{\partial y_1} & \frac{\partial \beta_1}{\partial z_1} & \cdots & \frac{\partial \beta_1}{\partial x_K} & \frac{\partial \beta_1}{\partial y_K} & \frac{\partial \beta_1}{\partial z_K} \\ & \vdots & & \ddots & & \vdots & \\ \frac{\partial \beta_K}{\partial x_1} & \frac{\partial \beta_K}{\partial y_1} & \frac{\partial \beta_K}{\partial z_1} & \cdots & \frac{\partial \beta_K}{\partial x_K} & \frac{\partial \beta_K}{\partial y_K} & \frac{\partial \beta_K}{\partial z_K} \end{bmatrix}, \tag{7}$$

$$\frac{\partial \mathbf{d}^T}{\partial \text{vec}(\mathbf{S})} = \begin{bmatrix} \frac{\partial d_{1,2}}{\partial x_1} & \frac{\partial d_{1,2}}{\partial y_1} & \frac{\partial d_{1,2}}{\partial z_1} & \cdots & \frac{\partial d_{1,2}}{\partial x_K} & \frac{\partial d_{1,2}}{\partial y_K} & \frac{\partial d_{1,2}}{\partial z_K} \\ & \vdots & & & & \vdots & \\ \frac{\partial d_{(K-1),K}}{\partial x_1} & \frac{\partial d_{(K-1),K}}{\partial y_1} & \frac{\partial d_{(K-1),K}}{\partial z_1} & \cdots & \frac{\partial d_{(K-1),K}}{\partial x_K} & \frac{\partial d_{(K-1),K}}{\partial y_K} & \frac{\partial d_{(K-1),K}}{\partial z_K} \end{bmatrix}. \tag{8}$$

According to the conditions of Newton's method, we are still need the formula that arrives at its next value from the previous value of the variable, i.e., the iterative relation, which can be shown to be given by

$$\boldsymbol{\delta} = \text{vec}(\mathbf{S}) - \text{vec}(\mathbf{C}) = \mathbf{F}/\mathbf{G}, \tag{9}$$

We can update the iterated value by replacing $\mathbf{C}$ with $\mathbf{C}+\boldsymbol{\delta}$ and obtain the final estimated value by repeating the above update progress until $\boldsymbol{\delta}$ is sufficiently small which means the solutions convergence or a maximum number of iterations has been reached during execution.

The solution of the nonlinear equations can be found by constantly iterating, and it is the position coordinates of wireless nodes in the current frame. Now the positions of the wireless nodes in the reference frame and current frame are known, it is equivalent that in the transformation formula (1), $\mathbf{S}$ and $\mathbf{C}$ both have been known. And the rotation matrix $\mathbf{R}$ and the translation vector $\mathbf{t}$ can be obtained by all known information next.

3.2 The Unit Quaternion Method

There are many ways to express rotation, such as Euler angle, shaft angle and the UQ, etc. [9] In this paper, the UQ method is used to solve the rotation matrix and the translation vector. The UQ method uses a vector to represent the rotation axis and an angular component to represent the angle of rotation around this axis. The UQ is defined as

$$\mathbf{q} = \left[\cos\frac{\theta}{2}, l \cdot \sin\frac{\theta}{2}, m \cdot \sin\frac{\theta}{2}, n \cdot \sin\frac{\theta}{2}\right], \tag{10}$$

where θ is the rotation angle, and 3-D vector (l, m, n) which meet $l^2 + m^2 + n^2 = 1$ is the rotation axis. And the rotation matrix $\mathbf{R}$ can be derived from Rodrigues formula:

$$\mathbf{R} = \mathbf{I} + 2\mathbf{U} \cdot \sin\frac{\theta}{2} \cdot \cos\frac{\theta}{2} + 2\sin^2\frac{\theta}{2} \cdot \mathbf{U}^2$$

$$= \begin{bmatrix} 1 - 2(m^2 + n^2) \cdot \sin^2\frac{\theta}{2} & 2lm \cdot \sin^2\frac{\theta}{2} - 2n \cdot \sin\frac{\theta}{2} \cdot \cos\frac{\theta}{2} & 2ln \cdot \sin^2\frac{\theta}{2} + 2m \cdot \sin\frac{\theta}{2} \cdot \cos\frac{\theta}{2} \\ 2lm \cdot \sin^2\frac{\theta}{2} + 2n \cdot \sin\frac{\theta}{2} \cdot \cos\frac{\theta}{2} & 1 - 2(l^2 + n^2) \cdot \sin^2\frac{\theta}{2} & 2mn \cdot \sin^2\frac{\theta}{2} + 2l \cdot \sin\frac{\theta}{2} \cdot \cos\frac{\theta}{2} \\ 2ln \cdot \sin^2\frac{\theta}{2} - 2m \cdot \sin\frac{\theta}{2} \cdot \cos\frac{\theta}{2} & 2mn \cdot \sin^2\frac{\theta}{2} + 2l \cdot \sin\frac{\theta}{2} \cdot \cos\frac{\theta}{2} & 1 - 2(l^2 + m^2 \cdot \sin^2\frac{\theta}{2}) \end{bmatrix},$$

$$(11)$$

where $\mathbf{I}$ is the unit matrix of size 3, $\mathbf{U} = \begin{bmatrix} 0 & -n & m \\ n & 0 & -l \\ -m & l & 0 \end{bmatrix}$ is the Cross Product matrix of rotary axis (l, m, n), substituting the UQ $\mathbf{q}$ to the equation and we can get rotation matrix:

$$\mathbf{R} = \begin{bmatrix} q_0^2 + q_1^2 - q_2^2 - q_3^2 & 2(q_1 q_2 - q_0 q_3) & 2(q_0 q_2 + q_1 q_3) \\ 2(q_0 q_3 + q_1 q_2) & q_0^2 - q_1^2 + q_2^2 - q_3^2 & 2(q_2 q_3 - q_0 q_1) \\ 2(q_1 q_3 - q_0 q_2) & 2(q_0 q_1 + q_2 q_3) & q_0^2 - q_1^2 - q_2^2 + q_3^2 \end{bmatrix} \quad (12)$$

The UQ $\mathbf{q}$ is the solution which minimums the least square error:

$$\varepsilon^2 = \sum_{i=1}^{N} \|\mathbf{s}_i - \mathbf{R}\mathbf{c}_i + \mathbf{t}\|^2 = \sum_{i=1}^{N} \|\mathbf{s}_{ri} - \mathbf{R}\mathbf{c}_{ri}\|^2 = \sum_{i=1}^{N} (\mathbf{s}_{ri}^T \mathbf{s}_{ri} + \mathbf{c}_{ri}^T \mathbf{c}_{ri} - 2\mathbf{s}_{ri}^T \mathbf{R}\mathbf{c}_{ri})$$

$$(13)$$

where $\mathbf{s}_{ri} = \mathbf{s}_i - \bar{\mathbf{s}}$, $\mathbf{c}_{ri} = \mathbf{c}_i - \bar{\mathbf{c}}$, and $\bar{\mathbf{s}}$, $\bar{\mathbf{c}}$ are mean of $\mathbf{s}_i$ and $\mathbf{c}_i$ respectively. The least square error can be rewritten as $\varepsilon = \mathbf{q}^T \mathbf{P} \mathbf{q}$ according to the attributes of quaternion, and $\mathbf{P}$ is a matrix of 4×4:

$$\mathbf{p} = \begin{bmatrix} H_{xx} + H_{yy} + H_{zz} & H_{yz} - H_{zy} & H_{zx} - H_{xz} & H_{xy} - H_{yx} \\ H_{yz} - H_{zy} & H_{xx} - H_{yy} - H_{zz} & H_{xy} + H_{yx} & H_{zx} + H_{xz} \\ H_{zx} - H_{xz} & H_{xy} + H_{yx} & H_{yy} - H_{xx} - H_{zz} & H_{yz} + H_{zy} \\ H_{xy} - H_{yx} & H_{zx} + H_{xz} & H_{yz} + H_{zy} & H_{zz} - H_{xx} - H_{yy} \end{bmatrix}$$

$$(14)$$

where $H_{ab} = \sum_{i=1}^{N} s_{ri_a} c_{ri_b}$, the UQ $\mathbf{q}$ is the feature vector corresponding to the largest eigenvalue of matrix $\mathbf{P}$. Finally, the rotation matrix $\mathbf{R}$ can be obtained from (10) with the known quaternion $\mathbf{q}$, and the translation vector $\mathbf{t}$ can be obtained from transformation formula (1).

4 Performance Evaluation

In the DOA-based RBL with a single BS, we consider $K = 4$ wireless nodes mounted on a rigid object. The single BS is fixed at the origin and the wireless nodes are distributed as a four-sided pyramid with a bottom of equilateral triangle and three sides of isosceles right triangle with side length of 3 m. According to wireless nodes distribution, the reference frame is

$$\mathbf{C} = \begin{bmatrix} 0 & 3 & 0 & 0 \\ 0 & 0 & 3 & 0 \\ 0 & 0 & 0 & 3 \end{bmatrix}. \tag{15}$$

In the DOA measurements, the noise of the DOA measurement $\boldsymbol{\omega}$ from wireless nodes in the current frame to the single BS are independent, zero-meaning, additive white gaussian noise, with the standard deviation of σ. There are several different values of the Gaussian noise tried in the simulation. The rigid object transforms the angle in the direction of the rotation matrix and moves with a translation vector in the 3-D space.

In the simulation experiment, the rotation angles are set as $[0, 0, 0]^T$, implying that the rigid object does not change direction when moving, and the translation vector is set as $\mathbf{t} = \begin{bmatrix} 5 & 5 & 3 \end{bmatrix}^T$, meaning that the rigid target moves $\sqrt{59}$ m from the reference frame. The simulations are counted average over $N = 1000$ independent Monte Carlo iterations.

The performance of the proposed method is shown in terms of the root mean squared error (RMSE) of the estimates, success rate and running speed of the simulation experiment. RMSE of the estimates of $\mathbf{R}$ and $\mathbf{t}$ are computed by

$$\mathrm{RMSE}(\mathbf{R}) = \sqrt{\frac{1}{N} \sum_{n=1}^{N} \left\| \mathbf{R} - \widehat{\mathbf{R}}_n \right\|}, \tag{16}$$

$$\mathrm{RMSE}(\mathbf{t}) = \sqrt{\frac{1}{N} \sum_{n=1}^{N} \left\| \mathbf{t} - \widehat{\mathbf{t}}_n \right\|}, \tag{17}$$

where $\widehat{\mathbf{R}}_n$ and $\widehat{\mathbf{t}}_n$ mean the estimates in the nth Monte Carlo iteration. As shown in Fig. 2, CCRBs [10] of the DOA-based RBL framework and the RMSEs of the estimates of $\mathbf{R}$ and $\mathbf{t}$ basing on the NIA and UQ algorithms are compared under different noise magnitudes. As can be seen from the figure, the estimation RMSE curves of both rotation matrix and the translation vector are close to their CCRB, which means that the estimates almost reach the optimal value in theory. From the trend of the curve in the figure, as we expected, the RMSE of estimates decreased as the noise level of DOA reduced.

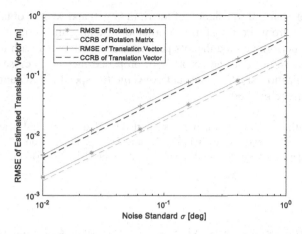

Fig. 2. RMSEs of the RBL estimation vs CCRB of rotation matrix and translation vector

The optimization performance of proposed NIA algorithm is compared with existing heuristic methods including the PSO [11] and PSA methods [10]. Simulation shows that the iteration number of the NIA method for convergence process is around 10 times, when we set the initial solution as the initial frame **C** (it is reasonable since the initial frame is known information). As shown in Table 1, the NIA method for 3-D position estimation of the wireless nodes in current frame are obviously shorten (ms-level) than the heuristic methods while guaranteeing the success rate.

Table 1. The optimization performance comparison of NIA, PSA and PSO methods

σ [deg]	10^{-2}	10^{-1}	10^{0}
PSO [s/%][a]	7.9/100	7.3/95	10.4/51
PSA [s/%]	5.3/100	5.9/100	8.9/70
NIA [s/%]	1.1×10^{-3}/100	0.9×10^{-3}/100	1.8×10^{-3}/76

[a] optimization performance is evaluated in terms of convergence time [s] and success rate [%]

5   Conclusions

In this paper, a framework was proposed to solve the DOA-based RBL problem for joint position and orientation estimation with a single BS. Several wireless nodes were mounted on the rigid object and the topology of these wireless nodes is known. Combining the topology information and the DOA measurements, we obtained the nonlinear model about the position of the wireless nodes. We optimized the model and find the 3-D position of the nodes in the current frame using Newton's method. Then the moving and rotating information of the rigid target with respect to reference frame, which is determined by a translation vector and a rotation matrix respectively, can be determined by the UQ method. The rotation and translation of wireless nodes represents the rotation and translation of the rigid target, and we can obtain the position of the rigid target from the transform information. Finally, the simulation of the proposed method is performed, and then its performance is compared with the CCRB. The simulation results shows that the accuracy of proposed method is close to the CCRB, besides, it optimization success rate and convergence speed significantly outperform the existing heuristic methods.

Funding Information:. This work is partly supported by National Natural Science Foundation of China (No. 61703185 and No. 61701197), Natural Science Foundation of Jiangsu Province (No. BK20180597), China Postdoctoral Science Foundation (No. 2018M641354).

References

1. Chaturvedi, N.A., Sanyal, A.K., McClamroch, N.H.: Rigid-body attitude control. IEEE Control Syst. Mag. **31**(3), 30–51 (2011)
2. Mahony, R., Hamel, T.: Visual servoing using linear features for under-actuated rigid body dynamics. In: IEEE/RSJ International Conference on Intelligent Robots & Systems, Maui, HI, USA, vol. 2, pp. 1153–1158. IEEE (2001)
3. Boukerche, A., Oliveira, H.A., Nakumura, E.F., Loureiro, A.A.: Localization systems for wireless sensor networks. IEEE Wirel. Commun. **14**(6), 6–12 (2007)
4. Chepuri, S.P., Leus, G., van der Veen, A.: Rigid body localization using node networks. IEEE Trans. Signal Process. **62**(18), 4911–4924 (2014)
5. Chepuri, S.P., Leus, G., van der Veen, A.: Joint localization and clock synchronization for wireless sensor networks. In: Conference Record of the Forty Sixth Asilomar Conference on Signals, Systems and Computers (ASILOMAR) 2012, pp. 1432–1436. Pacific Grove, CA. IEEE (2012)
6. Namin, P.H., Tinati, M.A.: Node localization using particle swarm optimization. In: Seventh International Conference on Intelligent Sensors, Sensor Networks and Information Processing 2011, Adelaide, SA, Australia, pp. 288–293. IEEE (2011)
7. Liu, Y.L., Gomide, F.: A participatory search algorithm. Evol. Intell. **10**(1–2), 23–43 (2017)
8. Eggert, D.W., Lorusso, A., Fisher, R.B.: Estimating 3-D rigid body transformations: a comparison of four major algorithms. Mach. Vis. Appl. **9**(5–6), 272–290 (1997)
9. Diebel, J.: Representing attitude: euler angles, unit quaternions, and rotation vectors. Matrix **58**(15), 1–35 (2006)
10. Stoica, P., Ng, B.C.: On the Cramer-Rao bound under parametric constraints. IEEE Signal Process. Lett. **5**(7), 177–179 (2002)
11. Zhou, B., et al.: Accurate rigid body localization using DoA measurements from a single base station. Electronics **8**(6), 622 (2019)
12. Zhou, B., Ai, L., Dong, X., Yang, L.: DoA-based rigid body localization adopting single base station. IEEE Commun. Lett. **23**(3), 494–497 (2019)

Design and Mobile Tracking Performance of a Retro-Directive Array (RDA) Antenna System

Myunggi Kim$^{(\boxtimes)}$, Taebum Gu, and Heung-Gyoon Ryu

Department of Electronics and Engineering, Chungbuk National University,
Cheongju, Chungbuk 28644, South Korea
ecomm@cbu.ac.kr

Abstract. Beamforming is one of the most important technologies for wireless communication systems. A beamforming antenna system can control the radiation beam pattern and thus can reduce power consumption, compared with an omni-direction antenna system. In general, the digital beamforming technology requires a complex control system. However, a digital RDA (retro-directive array) antenna system has very small calculation load and its configuration is quite simple as it transmits to a receiving direction without prior information, and simply needs to estimate the phase from an incident. Thus, a RDA antenna system can reduce the system complexity and power consumption, and improve system performance. In this paper, we describe the structure of a digital RDA system and investigate the beam tracking performance of a digital RDA system. It is shown through simulation results that a digital RDA system can effectively improve the beam tracking performance when a target receiver is moving. The mean beam tracking error can reach 1.9° when the SNR is 10 dB and 0.6° when the SNR is 20 dB.

Keywords: Retro-directive array · RDA · Beam tracking

1 Introduction

With the emergence of many moving-terminal applications, such as an unmanned aerial vehicle (UAV) cellular system [1], there is an increasing demand for tracking high-speed signals between a transmitter and a receiver. Beamforming is an effective technology for controlling the propagation direction and the receipt of RF signals. A beamforming antenna system can control the radiation beam pattern and thus can reduce power consumption, compared with an omni-direction antenna system. In general, the digital beamforming technology requires a complex control system. However, a digital RDA (retro-directive array) antenna system has very small calculation load and its configuration is quite simple as it transmits to a receiving direction without prior information, and simply needs to estimate the phase from an incident. Thus, an RDA antenna system can reduce the system complexity and power consumption, and improve system performance [2, 3]. Beamforming techniques can be divided into digital beamforming antenna techniques and analog beamforming antenna techniques. In general, digital beamforming can reduce the synchronization and power

© ICST Institute for Computer Sciences, Social Informatics and Telecommunications Engineering 2019
Published by Springer Nature Switzerland AG 2019. All Rights Reserved
J. Zheng et al. (Eds.): ADHOCNETS 2019, LNICST 306, pp. 231–237, 2019.
https://doi.org/10.1007/978-3-030-37262-0_19

consumption problems and thus has received more attention [4, 5]. In this paper, we investigate the beam tracking performance of a digital RDA system based on simulation experiments. Through simulation results, we show that a digital RDA system can effectively improve the beam tracking performance when a target receiver is moving in terms of the mean beam tracking error.

The remainder of this paper is organized as follows. In Sect. 2, we introduce the structure of a digital RDA system. In Sect. 3, we describe the system model used in the simulation experiments. In Sect. 4, we show simulation results. In Sect. 5, we conclude this paper.

2   Digital RDA

An RDA (retro-directive array) system is based on a transmission technique that transmits a signal in a receiving direction with an incident angle without any prior direction information, which is quite different from the conventional beamforming techniques. Thus, an RDA system can have faster response with low latency than an omni-direction antenna, and has many other advantages, including battery life extension and so on.

Figure 1 shows an RDA element array. In the array, each antenna element transmits and receives a signal independently [6]. If each antenna transmits an incident signal that has an incident angle θ, the phase delay of the received signal will show $\Delta\varphi$. Thus, $\Delta\varphi$ can be written as

$$\Delta\phi = \frac{2\pi f d \sin\theta}{c} \tag{1}$$

where f denotes the frequency, θ denotes the angle of incidence, d denotes the distance between the antenna and another antenna, and c denotes the speed of light.

In an RDA system, random data are first generated and modulated. After modulation, data are divided into two antenna arrays and are transmitted. Then, the signal passes through an AWGN channel and adds phase delay by the angle of incidence and

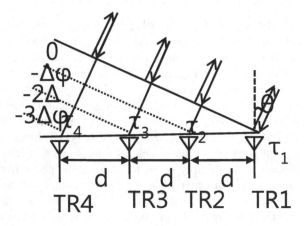

Fig. 1. Illustration of a retro-directive array antenna.

the distance between the antennas. After passing the channel, the phase detector estimates the phase delay and compensates the difference of the phase delay from the received signal. The estimated phase information is stabilized by digital PLL (phase lock loop).

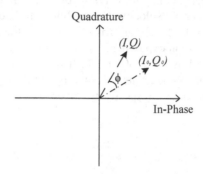

Fig. 2. Phase difference of a reference symbol and the received symbol.

When using the array antenna, the received phase delay is different for each array each antenna. A reverse directional antenna system is a system that returns to the original signal by 180° rotation of the phase delay by calculating the phase delay. Figure 2 illustrates how to handle the phase estimator to determine (I_0, Q_0) of a standard signal that is received the first element. The standard signal estimates the phase difference compared with the input signal. When using a modulation signal of 4-QAM or QPSK, the magnitude of the standard signal is 1.414 and can be expressed as

$$e^{j\varphi} = \cos\varphi + j\sin\varphi = e^{j(\varphi' - \varphi_0)}$$

$$= \frac{e^{j\varphi'}}{e^{j\varphi_0}} = \frac{\sqrt{I_0^2 + Q_0^2}}{\sqrt{I^2 + Q^2}} \cdot \frac{I + jQ}{I_0 + jQ_0} \qquad (2)$$

$$= \frac{\sqrt{2}}{\sqrt{I^2 + Q^2}} \cdot \frac{II_0 + QQ_0 + j(I_0Q - IQ_0)}{2}$$

Generally, due to $|\varphi| \leq 20°$, φ can be approximated as follows

$$\varphi \approx \sin\varphi = \frac{1}{\sqrt{2(I^2 + Q^2)}} \cdot (I_0Q - IQ_0) \qquad (3)$$

where $\frac{1}{\sqrt{2(I^2 + Q^2)}}$ can compensate using AGC (Auto Gain Control). Thus, the phase delay can be approximated as

$$\varphi = I_0Q - IQ_0 \qquad (4)$$

3 System Model for Simulation

To evaluate the beam tracking performance of a digital RDA system, we perform simulation experiments using a Simulink System.

Figure 3 shows the beamforming for a mobile user in a circle track and a line track, respectively, where V is constant velocity, L is the linear distance between a transmitter and a receiver, and θ is AOA (angle of arrival), which is the directivity angle of the bean in space. In the simulation experiments, with reference to the speed of the fastest high-speed train in Korea, V is set to 300 km/h. It is an environment which considers the Doppler frequency. The angle changes for the beamforming to a target user in the circle track and the line track are, respectively, given by

$$\theta = (\frac{360}{2\pi L} Vt) \tag{5}$$

$$\theta = \tan(\frac{Vt}{L} - \tan \theta_0) \tag{6}$$

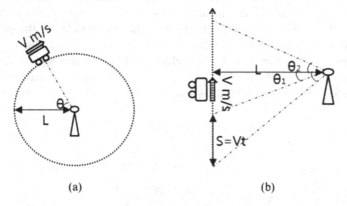

(a)   (b)

Fig. 3. Beamforming for a mobile user in circle and line tracks.

Figure 4 shows a block diagram constructed on the basis of the Simulink simulator software. The theta box, AOA changes along the moving path is generated from the Tracking model box, which determines the phase delay of the receiving antenna. RDA system configuration, and this time, insert it in the channel Doppler frequency is considered. At this time, to compare or track better AOA generated in the tracking model, the phase and RDA system is tracked.

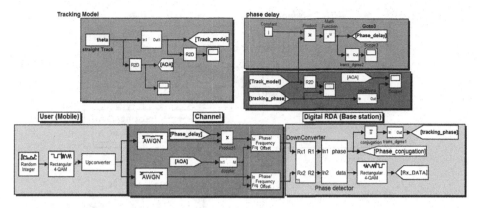

Fig. 4. The block diagram on the basis of the Simulink simulator software.

4 Simulation Results

In the experiments, it is assumed that fast-moving objects move in a straight line. In this case, when a mobile user moves in a straight line track, the expression changes can be each AOA to arrive or each of the received signals of θ.

Figures 5 and 6 show the beam tracking performance of the digital RDA system at each SNR 10 dB and 20 dB, respectively. It is seen that the mean beam tracking error is 1.9° when SNR is 10 dB and 0.6° when SNR is 20 dB.

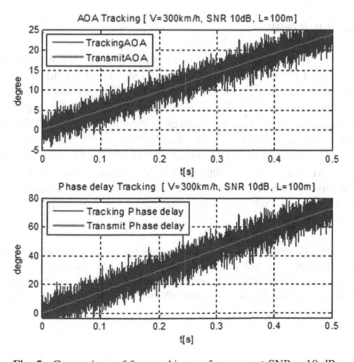

Fig. 5. Comparison of fast tracking performance at SNR = 10 dB.

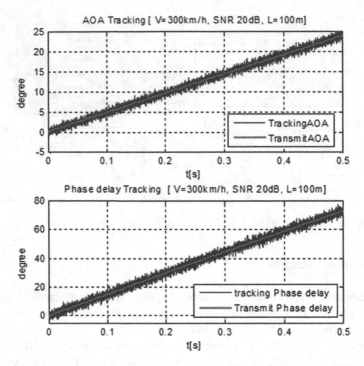

Fig. 6. Comparison of fast tracking performance in multipath environment at SNR = 20 dB.

5   Simulation Results

In this paper, we investigated the high-speed beam tracking performance of a digital RDA system based on simulation experiments. Depending on the number of array antennas and SNR requirement, the range of an error changes and is adjustable to the tolerable limit. It is shown that a digital RDA system can effectively improve the beam tracking performance when a target receiver is moving in terms of the mean beam tracking error. The error of AOA is 0.6° when SNR is 20 dB and the number of array antenna is 8. Even though these are the simulation results by Simulink, we can observe that the digital RDA system is of high-speed tracking performance in real time with acceptable accuracy tolerance. Moreover, an RDA system may become an promising technology in future high capacity communication and high speed mobile communication.

Acknowledgment. This work is a result of the study on the "Leaders in Industry-university Cooperation +" Project, supported by the Ministry of Education and National Research Foundation of Korea. Also, this work was supported by the National Research Foundation of Korea (NRF) grant funded by the Korea government (Ministry of Education) (No. 2016R1D1A1B 01008046).

References

1. Xiao, Z., Xia, P., Xia, X.G.: Enabling UAV cellular with millimeter-wave communication: potentials and approaches. IEEE Commun. Mag. **54**(5), 66–73 (2016)
2. Miyamoto, R.Y., Qian, Y., Itoh, T.: Retrodirective arrays for wireless communication. IEEE Microwave Mag. **3**(1), 71–79 (2002)
3. Kim, S.R., Ryu, H.G.: Phase tracking settling time and BER performance evaluation in the digital retrodirective array antenna system. J. Korean Inst. Electromagn. Eng. Sci. **24**(1), 55–63 (2013)
4. Dylan, G., Loadman, C., Chen, Z.: Retrodirective antenna systems for wireless communications. CNSR **2003**, 20–23 (2003)
5. Coccioli, R., Deal, W.R., Itoh, T.: Radiation characteristics of a patch antenna on a thin PBG substrate. In: IEEE Antennas and Propagation Society International Symposium. 1998 Digest. Antennas: Gateways to the Global Network. Held in conjunction with: USNC/URSI National Radio Science Meeting. Cat. No.98CH36, Atlanta, GA, vol. 2, pp. 656–659 (1998)
6. Qu, D., Shafai, L.: The performance of microstrip patch antennas over high impedance EBG substrates within and outside its bandgap. In: 2005 IEEE International Symposium on Microwave, Antenna, Propagation and EMC Technologies for Wireless Communications, Beijing, vol. 1, pp. 423–426 (2005)

Miscellaneous Topics in Ad Hoc Networks

The Effects of Non-line of Sight (NLOS) Channel on a User with Varying Device Orientations

Shakir Ullah[(⊠)], Saeed Ur Rehman, and Peter Han Joo Chong

Department of Electrical and Electronic Engineering,
Auckland University of Technology, Auckland, New Zealand
{shakir.ullah,saeed.rehman,peter.chong}@aut.ac.nz

Abstract. Recently, there has been a growing interest in visible light communications (VLC) for indoor communication to meet the ever-increasing data demands. Most of the studies have considered the line-of-sight (LOS) channel for VLC communication. However, the LOS gain is constrained as the user moves away from the transmitter (Tx) or his device experiences orientation changes. It is observed in practice, the gain from reflections along the defused/NLOS channels can also contribute to optical gain. This research work, therefore, analytical model the NLOS channels and user's device orientation and analyze its effect on the user's SNR. For simulations, analytical models are integrated into ns3. Our results show that SNR slightly improves, which can be utilized to keep the communication alive during the high mobility scenario that could arise due to device orientation.

Keywords: VLC · NLOS · VLC channel · Mobile VLC

1 Introduction

In recent years the visible light communication (VLC) (operates in the frequency range 430 to 750 THz) has been explored as a complementary interference-free spectrum to RF spectrum for providing data communication. VLC offers a broad spectrum and, therefore, can meet the growing spectrum demand with high data rates to the end-users [1]. Apart from the additional spectrum, the VLC has the added advantage of having a readily available infrastructure in the form of light-emitting diodes (LEDs) at homes and other indoor establishments, making it cost-effective. The VLC uses unlicensed frequency band, and thus, there are no current legal restrictions involving bandwidth allocation. Also, VLC is inherently secure as light cannot penetrate walls, and hence, its communication can be restricted to a specific area which allows it to be used for secure communication in the indoor environment. In recent research articles, the VLC system is looked upon as a potential candidate for the beyond 5G and 6G communication system [2, 3].

The VLC offers many advantages in the context of indoor communication; however, most of its optical gain comes from the LOS channel. In the LOS arrangement the transmitter (Tx) and the receiver (Rx) are required to be directed at each other, and thus

© ICST Institute for Computer Sciences, Social Informatics and Telecommunications Engineering 2019
Published by Springer Nature Switzerland AG 2019. All Rights Reserved
J. Zheng et al. (Eds.): ADHOCNETS 2019, LNICST 306, pp. 241–251, 2019.
https://doi.org/10.1007/978-3-030-37262-0_20

the channel gain depends on the angle of emission (AOE) of the Tx, the angle of incidence (AOI) at the Rx, and the Rx field of view (FOV). Of all these factors, AOI is of critical importance as it depends on the user device orientation and can be a constraining factor on received gain. If the user device is in LOS with Tx, that is its photodetector (PD) is facing in the direction of Tx; the AOI is not a limiting factor and the received gain in maximum. However, in practical scenarios, the receiver orientation changes and as a result, it varies its AOI, which in turn cause variations in the SNR performance.

Although most of the VLC gain is from the LOS channel, however, in reality, the light emitted from Tx does not travel in a perfect beam, but instead many of its rays get scattered in different directions across the room. These rays are reflected to the user device after striking the defused surfaces such as walls, ceilings, or other objects in the room, thus forming a defused or non-line of sight (NLOS) channel. These NLOS/defused channels contribute to the optical gain at the receiver, which can be useful for a mobile user.

The presence of NLOS channels necessitates its modeling and the analysis of its effects on VLC users. In the context of indoor VLC research, the channel modeling and optimization of SNR performance is of significant interests. In [4], VLC's LOS and NLOS channels are modeled using neural networks and based on the proposed model; practical experiments are performed to determine the number of taps required for the channel. The intended model use as input parameters such as reflection coefficients of different materials, noise levels, the Rx gain, and the distance between Tx and Rx. This work considers mobile user only in terms of movement inside the room while the user device orientation changes and its effects on Rx gain are not taken into considerations. Similarly, Miramirkhani et al., in [5], have modeled VLC channel for a mobile user, and based on the proposed model, the power profile as well as the delay spread, are determined at different positions for a random mobile user. This work is, however, not taking into considerations the effect of the NLOS channels on mobile users.

User mobility is mostly considered only in terms of user movement, ignoring changes in device orientation. In [6], experimental work is carried out for multi-input and multi-output (MIMO) VLC systems to increase user data rates. In [7], the authors have implemented the theoretical concepts of VLC in MATLAB for short-range 4x4 MIMO systems. However, MIMO systems are evaluated for LOS arrangement of static users. The user device orientation changes and its effect on the received optical gain have attracted some research. In [8], an access point (AP) selection algorithm is developed, which uses the signal strength and user data rates as an input parameter. This approach considers the user device orientation and its effect on data rates. This study examines both the LOS and NLOS channels; however, the impact of different reflections on mobile user performance is not studied. In [9], authors have optimized bit error rate (BER) performance for different SNR scenario by adjusting the tilting mobile user plane. In [10], the BER and outage probability relationship is derived for a mobile user from the statistical distribution of VLC downlink. In [11], the effects of random receiver orientation (for polar and azimuth variations) on LOS channel gain is studied. However, these works have not considered the NLOS channel during the VLC system modeling. NLOS channel can provide an increase optical gain, which can of help during the device tilting.

Most of the existing work has considered the LOS channel for static users. In some of the studies, the user's device orientation is also taken into considerations. However, these studies do not report the effects of NLOS communication on the user's devices, particularly for orientation changes. In this research work, we analytically model the NLOS channels and orientation changes and then analyze the gain from the defused reflections on mobile users. To evaluate these models, we have developed an ns3 simulation tool based on the VLC open-source module [12].

In Sect. 2, we analytical model the VLC channel. In Sect. 3, we model the user device orientation for arbitrary rotations. In Sect. 4, we discuss the performance evaluation metrics. In Sect. 5, we discuss the simulation setup. The results from the experiments are discussed in Sect. 6, and Sect. 7 concludes the paper.

2 Analytical Modeling of VLC Systems

In the VLC systems, as shown in Fig. 1, the current generated from the LED/laser diode (LD) in the Tx is modulated by the information signal I(t), which varies the intensity of the source optical signal $x(t)$. At the Rx, the photodetector (PD) generates photocurrent directly proportional to the incident optical signal on it.

The transmitted VLC signal travels through the VLC channel, modeled as a linear system according to Eq. (1) [13].

$$y(t) = Rx(t) \oplus h(t) + n(t) \tag{1}$$

Where $y(t)$ represents the output photocurrent, R is the PD's responsivity, $h(t)$ is the channel impulse response, and $n(t)$, represents the noise. The noise sources are the result of interference from the shot and the thermal noise. The channel response can be divided into LOS and NLOS gains, discussed later in details.

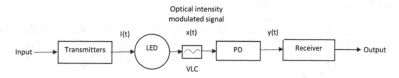

Fig. 1. VLC system main components [13]

2.1 LOS Channel Modeling

In the VLC systems, the photocurrent and incident (instantaneous) optical signal are in direct proportions, and thus it represents a power signal. For this reason, two constraints are imposed on the transmitted signal: (1) the signal must be non-negative, and (2) the transmitted power must be in the range to meet the eye safety as well as minimum illumination requirements. These constraints demand that power must be limited to some constant factor P_{MAX} and by implications the x(t).

The transmitted signals in VLC are real and positive, and thus, the relationship between them can be easily derived with direct current (DC) gain from the VLC channels as below in Eq. (2).

$$P_{Rx} = (H(0) + H(0)_{NLOS})P_{Tx} \tag{2}$$

where P_{Rx} is the power received at Rx, P_{Tx} is the transmitted signal power, the $H(0)$ and $H(0)_{NLOS}$, represents the DC gain from the LOS and NLOS channel (discussed later in Sect. 2.2), respectively. The LOS channel gain can be expressed using Eq. (3) [18] as represented in Fig. 2.

$$H(0) = \frac{(m_l + 1)A}{2\pi d^2} cos^{m_l}(\emptyset)T_s g(\psi) \cos(\psi) \tag{3}$$

Where A is the PD area (m^2), d is the distance between Tx and Rx, and T_s, is the Tx gain. The m_l represents the Lambertian order given as $-ln(2)/ln(2)\cos(\Phi_{1/2})$, where $\Phi_{1/2}$, represents the Tx semi angle at half transmit power. The $g(\psi)$, represents the optical concentrator gain, which can be calculated according to Eq. (3.13) [13], and $\emptyset$ represents the angle of emission at Tx, which, in most of the studies, is considered fixed on the ceiling. The cos (ψ) represents the gain from AOI at the Rx. As we consider user device to experience orientation changes and, therefore, change the AOI which can in turn vary the Rx gain. The AOI gain can be given in Eq. (4) as the ratio of the dot product of the Tx and Rx, the distance d, with the device normal n_r, and the distance norm, $||d||$.

$$\cos \psi = \frac{d.n_r}{||d||} \tag{4}$$

2.2   Non-LOS Channel Modeling

In addition to the parameters from Eq. (3), the NLOS gain calculations needs the room dimensions, walls and ceilings surface areas, the colour of material surfaces, and positioning of the Tx as well as Rx. The Rx power is defined in Eq. (5) [13, 14] (Fig. 2 shows the LOS and NLOS channel model):

$$P_{r-NLOS} = \left(\sum_R H_{NLOS}(0) \right) P_t \tag{5}$$

Where P_{r-NLOS} is the received power from all the NLOS channels and is calculated by integrating all the components after reaching Rx. The reflected light can undergo different orders of reflections, and as a result, could cover different distances. This phenomenon can lead to broadening of the pulse, which can ultimately result in a reduction of signal bandwidth.

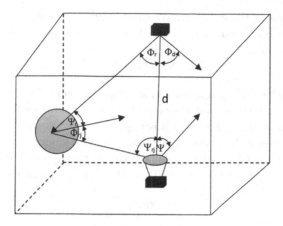

Fig. 2. VLC channel model including LOS and NLOS channels

However, the higher-order reflections contribute less to the optical gain because of larger distance covered and are thus the dominant factor in broadening the pulse. On the other hand, the first-order reflections are dominant contributors to the optical gain and cover less distance while arriving simultaneously. The authors in [15] have used the same observations and considered only first-order reflections in an additive manner with the LOS gain. To measure the effects of first-order reflections, the walls of the room are divided into R reflecting elements; each one has area ΔA. Further, each NLOS channel can be divided into two components. The first component is from transmitting source to a point on the wall (or any other object in the room), acting as a point receiver. The second component is from the point on the walls (acting as a point source) reflecting light, using the Lambertian emission pattern, to the receiver device scaled by walls reflectivity coefficient, p. Using this understanding the impulse response of NLOS channel can thus be represented as below in Eq. (6):

$$H_{NLOS} = \sum_{j=1}^{R} \frac{(m_l + 1)p\Delta A}{2\pi d_{S,j}^2 d_{R,j}^2} cos^{m_l}\left(Q_{Sj}\right) cos\left(\Psi_{Sj}\right) cos\left(\Psi_{Rj}\right) \tag{6}$$

Where $d_{S,j}$ is the distance from the Tx to the wall point, $d_{R,j}$, represents the distance point source to the Rx, and R represents the number of reflectance sources. The values for these parameters are specified in Table 1.

3   Receiver Orientation Modelling

In most studies, the user device's PD is considered static in a LOS arrangement, which gives maximum gain. However, in practical scenarios, mobile devices change their orientation frequently, which affects the SNR from the LOS channels, and consequently affects the data rates, and quality of service (QoS). Modern mobile devices are equipped with components such as gyroscope, and accelerometer, to measure their motion and rotations in 3D. A 3D rotation about an arbitrary point is composed of three rotations, along with x,y and z coordinates [16], represented as in Eq. (7):

$$R = R_x(\alpha)R_y(\beta)R_z(\gamma) \tag{7}$$

These rotations are yaw, pitch, and roll angles, represented by α, β, γ, respectively. The α represents rotation around z-axis, and it can take values from 0 to 360°; β, represents rotation around x-axis, which is tipping device towards and away, and can gain value from −180 to 180°; and γ, represents rotation around y-axis and represents device rotation from left to right and can take values from −90 to 90°. When the user device is static, the normal vector of the PD, n_r [0; 0; 1] ^{T}, is given below in Eq. (8) [8].

$$n_r = R(\alpha, \beta, \gamma) \tag{8}$$

However, after the rotation of the device, the unit normal vector experience rotation changes as given by Eq. (9) [8]:

$$n_r' = \begin{bmatrix} \sin\alpha\sin\beta\cos\gamma + \cos\alpha\sin\gamma \\ \sin\alpha\sin\gamma - \cos\alpha\sin\gamma\cos\beta \\ \cos\beta\cos\gamma \end{bmatrix} \tag{9}$$

After filling this value in Eq. (4), we get the angle of incidence angle at receiver.

4   Performance Evaluation Metric

The proposed VLC system performance is measured in terms of SNR, which is proportional to the square of the received optical power signal. The Eq. (10) expresses the relationship between SNR, the Rx power, and the total noise. We consider noise only from ambient light sources and thermal noise in the Tx and Rx.

$$SNR = \frac{(P_r R)^2}{\sigma_{total}^2} \tag{10}$$

Where P_r denotes the average received optical power of the signal,   is the responsivity of the photodetector and σ_{total}^2 is the total noise variance. In VLC the overall noise is the sum of shot and thermal noise Eq. (11) [12]:

$$\sigma_{total}^2 = \sigma_{shot}^2 + \sigma_{thermal}^2 \tag{11}$$

Based on [12, 17], the shot and thermal noise can be calculated in Eqs. (12) and (13):

$$\sigma_{shot}^2 = 2_q PRB + 2_q I_2 I_b B \tag{12}$$

$$\sigma_{thermal}^2 = \frac{8\pi k T_k}{G_{ol}} C_{pd} A I_2 B^2 + \frac{16\pi^2 k T_k n}{g_n} C_{pd}^2 A^2 I_3 B^3 \tag{13}$$

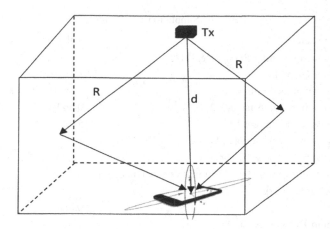

Fig. 3. Simulation setup for ns3 simulator

Where B is the bandwidth of PD, k is the Boltzmann's constant, I_b is the photocurrent due to background radiations, G_{ol} is the voltage gain, T_k is the absolute temperature, C_{pd} is the capacitance per unit area, I_2 and I_3, represents the noise bandwidth factor values. The values used for simulation is provided in Table 1.

5   Simulation Results

To evaluate our proposed model, we have created a scenario in ns3, which consists of a Tx and an Rx, in a room of 5 × 5 × 5 dimensions, as shown in Fig. 3. The Tx is fixed in the roof facing downwards, and Rx is a user device with orientation changes, modeled as discussed in Sect. 3. Further, the walls of the room are considered of plaster, with reflectivity 0.8 [13]. We have used static routing to enforce packets flow in the network, simulated with 1 Mbps of data, where each packet is of 1040 size. We have carried out three types of simulations for evaluating the effects of NLOS channels on VLC user's performance.

In the first scenario, the LOS channel is simulated for a static user according to the parameters shown in Table 1. In the second scenario, the gains from NLOS channels are added to the LOS channel, and the combined channel is evaluated for a user with static device orientation. In the third simulation scenario, the LOS and NLOS channels are combined for a dynamic user, which experiences device orientation changes. In our simulations, we have kept alpha α at 0 and beta (β) varies between −180 to 180. These two parameters show rotation around z-axis and y-axis. The rotation around x is represented by gamma (γ) and varies from −90 to 90. The results are arranged according to the reflectance factor of the wall materials [13]. The parameters for simulations are listed in Table 1 based on [13] and [12].

Table 1. Simulation parameters

Parameter	Value
Lambertian Order Semiangle, Φ1/2	70°
Filter Gain, Ts	1
Boltzmann's constant, k	1.3806e−23 J/K
Noise bandwidth factor, I2	0.562
Background current IB	5100−6 A
Open-loop voltage gain, Gol	10
Fixed capacitance of photo, Cpd	112pF/cm2
Field-effect transistor (FET) transconductance (gm)	30 ms
electronic charge, q	1.60217e−19 C
I3	0.0868
Photo Detector Area, A	1.0e−4 m2
Refractive Index, n	1.5
field of view, ψcon	70○
Transmitter coordinate	(0.0,0.0,50.0)
Receiver coordinate	(0.0,0.0, dist)
α	0.85,0.60
Bandwidth factor, B	10
Distance, d	50 m
Absolute temperature, Tk	295
Reflectance coefficient	0.8
Reflectance Areas	0.28
Dimensions	5,5,5
Temperature, T	5000
FET channel noise factor, Γ	1.5
Modulation Scheme	OOK

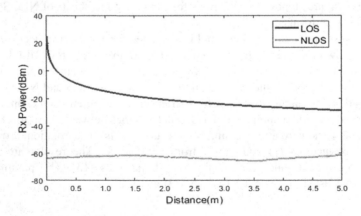

Fig. 4. Received power from LOS only, and combined LOS and NLOS combined channels

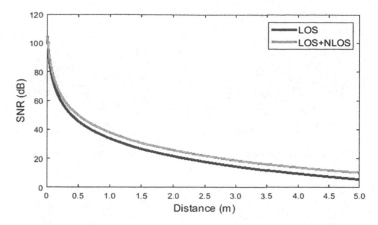

Fig. 5. SNR from LOS only, and combined LOS and NLOS channels when the user device orientation is static

6 Results Discussion

The Rx optical gain, as a function of the distance between Tx and Rx, from the LOS and NLOS channel is shown in Fig. 4. The results show, the gain from the LOS channel is high, but it decreases as the user moves away from Tx, and for NLOS channels, the gain is less but consistent. In Fig. 5, the SNR for combined LOS and NLOS shows improvement over the LOS only channel.

Apart from the above simulations where Rx moves away from the Tx with static device orientation, we have also carried simulations for scenarios where user device experiences orientation changes. The user device orientation is modeled according to Sect. 3. Figure 6 shows a slight improvement of SNR of combined channel over LOS only, specifically when the distance from the Tx increases

From these simulations, it can be observed that user device gets optimum gain from LOS channel up to a certain distance from Tx, and with static orientation. However, when user device moves away from Tx or experiences orientation changes, the VLC SNR performance starts to degrade. On the other hand, when we combine both the channels, the SNR improves. This is very important as in most practical scenarios the user devices are away from Tx and can experience low optical gain from the LOS channel. Similarly, when the user device experience orientation changes the LOS gain suffer as shown Fig. 6, and the VLC gain improves.

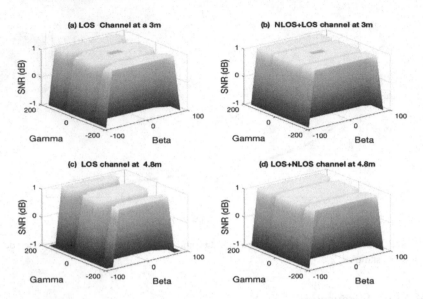

Fig. 6. SNR for LOS and NLOS channel for user device experiencing orientation changes

7   Conclusions

The VLC is coined as a new physical medium for future generation wireless network i.e., beyond 5G and 6G. Existing literature mostly focused on the LOS channel for data communication due to the physics of LED light. However, when the user moves away from Tx or his device orientation changes the receiver gain is drastically affected due to the user movement or orientation changes. This makes the gain from the NLOS/defused channels more critical. Based on our simulation for LOS and combined channel, we have demonstrated that NLOS gain can have a positive effect on the SNR performance and could be a source of communication during the mobile scenario either due to user movement or change in orientation. Building on the existing analysis, our future work would consider the full channel implementation (LOS and NLOS alike) to model the BER and goodput for a mobile scenario and developing algorithms to consider the changes in the handover in a heterogenous environment.

References

1. Turan, B., Narmanlioglu, O., Ergen, S.C., Uysal, M.: Physical layer implementation of standard compliant vehicular VLC. In: Vehicular Technology Conference (VTC-Fall) IEEE 84th, pp. 1–5. IEEE (2016)
2. Strinati, E., Barbarossa, S., Luis Gonzalez-Jimenez, J., Ktenas, D., Cassiau, N., Dehos, C.: 6G: The Next Frontier (2019)
3. Syed, J.N., Sharma, S.K., Wync, S., Patwary, M., Asaduzzaman, M.: Quantum machine learning for 6G communication networks: State-of-the-Art and vision for the future, pp. 46317–46350 (2019)

4. Dong, Z., Shang, T., Gao, Y., Li, Q.: Study on VLC channel modeling under random shadowing. IEEE Photonics J. **9**(6), 1–16 (2017)
5. Miramirkhani, F., Narmanlioglu, O., Uysal, M., Panayirci, E.: A mobile channel model for VLC and application to adaptive system design. IEEE Commun. Lett. **21**(5), 1035–1038 (2017)
6. Rajbhandari, S., et al.: Neural network-based joint spatial and temporal equalization for MIMO-VLC system. IEEE Photonics Technol. Lett. **31**(11), 821–824 (2019)
7. Amsdon, T., Sibley, M.J.: Theoretical concepts and matlab modelling of VLC based MIMO systems, University of Huddersfield (2013)
8. Soltani, M.D., Wu, X., Safari, M., Haas, H.: Access point selection in Li-Fi cellular networks with arbitrary receiver orientation. In: 2016 IEEE 27th Annual International Symposium on Personal, Indoor, and Mobile Radio Communications (PIMRC), pp. 1–6 (2016)
9. Wang, J., et al.: Improvement of BER performance by tilting receiver plane for indoor visible light communications with input-dependent noise. In: 2017 IEEE International Conference on Communications (ICC), pp. 1–6 (2017)
10. Eroglu, Y., Yapici, Y., Guvenc, I.: Impact of random receiver orientation on visible light communications channel. IEEE Trans. Commun. **67**(2), 1313–1325 (2017)
11. Dehghani Soltani, M., Andi Purwita, A., Tavakkolnia, I., Haas, H., Safari, M.: Impact of device orientation on error performance of LiFi systems. IEEE Access **7**, 41690–41701 (2018)
12. Aldalbahi, A., et al.: Extending ns3 to simulate visible light communication at network-level. In: 2016 23rd International Conference on Telecommunications (ICT), pp. 1–6. IEEE (2016)
13. Ghassemlooy, Z., Popoola, W., Rajbhandari, S.: Optical Wireless Communications: System and Channel Modelling with MATLAB (2012)
14. Kahn, J.M., Barry, J.R.: Wireless infrared communication **85**(2), 265–298 (1997)
15. Wu, X., Safari, M., Haas, H.: Access point selection for hybrid Li-Fi and Wi-Fi networks. IEEE Trans. Commun. **65**(12), 5375–5385 (2017)
16. Huynh, D.Q.: Metrics for 3D rotations: Comparison and analysis. J. Math. Imaging Vis. **35**(2), 155–164 (2009)
17. Dimitrov, S., Haas, H.: Principles of LED Light Communications: Towards Networked Li-Fi. Cambridge University Press, Cambridge (2015)

Multiobjective Collaborative Beamforming for a Distributed Satellite Cluster via NSGA-II

Bo Xi[1,2], Tao Hong[1,2(✉)], and Gengxin Zhang[1,2]

[1] National Engineering Research Center, Nanjing University of Posts
and Telecommunications, Nanjing 210003, China
hongt@njupt.edu.cn
[2] Key Lab of Broadband Wireless Communication and Sensor Network
Technology, Ministry of Education, Nanjing University of Posts
and Telecommunications, Nanjing 210003, China

Abstract. In this paper, a distributed satellite cooperative beamforming algorithm is proposed for the satellite cluster formed by multiple distributed formation flying satellites in the space information network. The average pattern function of distributed formation satellites is derived based on random antenna array theory. On this basis, a multiobjective optimization is formulated to enhance the transmit signal in the desired direction while suppress the interference in the undesired direction via nondominated sorting genetic algorithm II (NSGA-II). The simulation results show that the proposed method extends the distributed and cooperative beamforming technology to the research field of space information network and enhances the electromagnetic wave transceiver capability of resource-constrained satellite systems.

Keywords: Space information network · Distributed satellite cluster · Collaborative beamforming · Random arrays · NSGA-II

1 Introduction

Satellite communication has become one of the key technologies in 5G mobile communication network to meet the requirement of the global coverage [1]. Compared with the wireless link of the terrestrial cellular system, the satellite link has the characteristics of large attenuation because of the long distance transmission. Furthermore, the total power of a satellite transponder and antenna aperture is limited due to the satellite launch cost. It is difficult to improve the transmission performance and channel capacity of a satellite link. Therefore, how to improve the electromagnetic wave transceiver capability of resource-constrained satellite systems has become a hot research topic in the field of space information network [2].

Distributed and collaborative beamforming (DCBF) technique is proposed in wireless sensor networks (WSNs) to enhance the transmission performance of the sensor nodes [3]. The solid initial works on the random antenna array paved way to the statistical analysis of collaborative beamforming was presented by Ochiai et al. [4]. On this basis, Ahmedin in [5] investigated the performances of DCBF when the location information of sensor nodes follows the uniformly and Gaussian probability density

J. Zheng et al. (Eds.): ADHOCNETS 2019, LNICST 306, pp. 252–261, 2019.
https://doi.org/10.1007/978-3-030-37262-0_21

function (pdf), and summarized the advantage of 3 dB mainlobe width with uniformly pdf and sidelobe performance with Gaussian pdf, respectively. However, these results based on a particular pdf for a WSNs may not be true for the practical WSNs model. In [6], Huang proposed a novel unified method based on non-parametric kernel to evaluate DCBF performance for various node distributions. In [7], Buchanan extended the WSNs model from 2-dimensional model to 3-dimensional motion-dynamic model, such as unpiloted air vehicle (UAV) clusters scenario.

Compared with the sensor nodes with random distribution characteristic in a certain area, the location information of the distributed formation flying satellites in a space information network has two properties: one is the orbit-project location information with fixed characteristic; the other is the perturbation information, caused by non-spherical of earth, light pressure, lunisolar gravitational and so on, with random distribution characteristic. Thus, the fixed and random characteristics are co-existence for the location information of a distributed formation flying satellites. To enhance the electromagnetic wave transceiver capability of a distributed formation flying satellites, we proposed a cooperative beamforming algorithm to fit the location information characteristic of a distributed formation flying satellites. We derive the average far-field beampattern based on random antenna array theory. Furthermore, a multiobjective optimization is formulated to enhance the transmit signal in the desired direction while suppress the interference in the undesired direction via nondominated sorting genetic algorithm II (NSGA-II) Simulation results showed that the proposed method can obtain a optimal formation of a distributed formation flying satellites for a fixed electro-magnetic wave transceiver task.

2 Average Beampattern of the Proposed Collaborative Beamforming

The system model for a distributed formation flying cluster with N satellites is shown in Fig. 1. The fixed location information for nth satellite is $P_n(r_n, \theta_n, \phi_n)$, where $\theta_n \in [0, \pi]$ and $\phi_n \in [0, 2\pi)$. We assume that the instantaneous actual location information $P'_n(r'_n, \theta'_n, \phi'_n)$, off of the fixed location information caused by the satellite perturbation, for nth satellite is random located in a spherical volume of radius B. The desired direction is denoted by $P_0(r, \theta_0, \phi_0)$.

The following practical considerations and mathematical assumptions arise in this context: (1) the synchronization amongst satellites is assumed sufficient for high-fidelity phase control or time delay with negligible degradation from frequency offsets or phase jitter, (2) all satellites have equal power and all signals experience equal path losses, and (3) the channels between satellites and the target are all ideal. Thus, there are no multipath fading and shadowing.

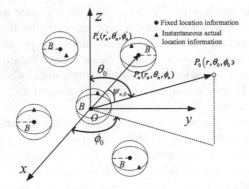

Fig. 1. System model for a distributed formation flying cluster

According to the system model in Fig. 1, the manifold vector is written as:

$$A_n(\theta, \phi) = \overbrace{e^{j\cdot\frac{2\pi}{\lambda}r'_n\left(\cos\psi'_n - \cos\psi'_{n,0}\right)}}^{\text{random term}} \cdot \overbrace{e^{j\cdot\frac{2\pi}{\lambda}r_n\cos\psi_n}}^{\text{fixed term}} \tag{1}$$

$$= e^{j\cdot\frac{2\pi}{\lambda}\left[r'_n\left(\cos\psi'_n - \cos\psi'_{n,0}\right) + r_n\cos\psi_n\right]}, n = 1, 2, \cdots, N$$

where:

$$\cos\psi_n = \sin\theta\sin\theta_n\cos(\phi - \phi_n) + \cos\theta\cos\theta_n \tag{2a}$$

$$\cos\psi'_n = \sin\theta\sin\theta'_n\cos(\phi - \phi'_n) + \cos\theta\cos\theta'_n \tag{2b}$$

$$\cos\psi'_{n,0} = \sin\theta_0\sin\theta'_n\cos(\phi_0 - \phi'_n) + \cos\theta_0\cos\theta'_n \tag{2c}$$

for the sake of analysis the manifold vector $A_n(\theta, \phi)$, we define the following variables as:

$$\rho_0 = \sqrt{(\sin\theta\cos\phi - \sin\theta_0\cos\phi_0)^2 + (\sin\theta\sin\phi - \sin\theta_0\sin\phi_0)^2} \tag{3a}$$

$$\cos\delta = \rho_0^{-1}(\sin\theta\cos\phi - \sin\theta_0\cos\phi_0) \tag{3b}$$

$$\sin\delta = \rho_0^{-1}(\sin\theta\sin\phi - \sin\theta_0\sin\phi_0) \tag{3c}$$

$$\delta = \tan^{-1}\left[\frac{\sin\theta\sin\phi - \sin\theta_0\sin\phi_0}{\sin\theta\cos\phi - \sin\theta_0\cos\phi_0}\right] \tag{3d}$$

$$\cos\gamma = \rho_0^{-1}(\cos\theta - \cos\theta_0) \tag{3e}$$

Substitute (3) into (1), the manifold vector can be also presented as follows:

$$A_n(\theta, \phi) = e^{j \cdot \frac{2\pi}{\lambda} \{r'_n \rho_0 [\sin \theta'_n \cos(\phi'_n - \delta) + \cos \theta'_n \cos \gamma] + r_n \cos \psi_n\}} \tag{4}$$

We also define the following variables simplify the express as:

$$I_n = R_n \sin \theta'_n \cos(\phi'_n - \delta), -1 \leq I_n \leq 1 \tag{5a}$$

$$Q(\theta, \phi) = 2\pi\beta\rho_0 \tag{5b}$$

$$T_n = R_n \cos \theta'_n, -1 \leq T_n \leq 1 \tag{6a}$$

$$G(\theta) = 2\pi\beta\rho_0 \cos \gamma \tag{6b}$$

$$L_n = \frac{r_n}{\lambda} \tag{7}$$

where $R_n = r'_n/B$, $\beta = B/\lambda$ denotes the normalized perturbation radius, L_n is the normalized distance between the nth satellite and the center of coordinate system. Substitute (5)–(7) into (4), we obtain as follows:

$$A_n(\theta, \phi) = e^{j \cdot \{[I_n Q(\theta, \phi) + T_n G(\theta)] + 2\pi L_n \cos \psi_n\}} \tag{8}$$

To obtain the statistical average of the manifold vector $A_n(\theta, \phi)$, we introduce a variable $U_n(-1 \leq U_n \leq 1)$, satisfied with $U_n^2 + I_n^2 + T_n^2 \leq 1$. Without loss of generality, we consider the instantaneous actual location information with the uniformly pdf represented by $f_{r',\phi',\theta'}$ (for the practical perturbation model, the pdf can be obtained by the proposed algorithm in [7]). Therefore, we can derive the pdf for (r', θ', ϕ') as follows:

$$\int_0^1 f_{r'} r'^2 dr' = 1 \rightarrow f_{r'} = 3 \tag{9a}$$

$$\int_0^\pi f_{\theta'} \sin \theta' d\theta' = 1 \rightarrow f_{\theta'} = \frac{1}{2} \tag{9b}$$

$$\int_0^{2\pi} f_{\phi'} d\phi' = 1 \rightarrow f_{\phi'} = \frac{1}{2\pi} \tag{9c}$$

The joint probability density function of U_n, I_n, and T_n satisfies as:

$$\int_0^1 \int_0^{2\pi} \int_0^\pi f_{U_n, I_n, T_n} r'^2 dr' \sin \theta' d\theta' d\phi' = 1 \rightarrow f_{U_n, I_n, T_n} = \frac{3}{4\pi} \tag{10}$$

The joint probability density function of I_n and T_n satisfies as:

$$f_{I_n,T_n} = \int_{-\sqrt{1-T_n^2-I_n^2}}^{\sqrt{1-T_n^2-I_n^2}} f_{U_n,I_n,T_n} dU_n = \frac{3}{2\pi}\sqrt{1-T_n^2-I_n^2} \qquad (11)$$

thus, the average manifold vector can be written as:

$$\bar{A}_n(\theta,\phi) = \int_{-1}^{1}\int_{-\sqrt{1-I_n^2}}^{\sqrt{1-I_n^2}} A_n(\theta,\phi) f_{I_n,T_n} dT_n dI_n$$

$$= 6tinc(Q(\theta,\phi))jinc(G(\theta))e^{j\cdot2\pi L_n(\sin\theta\sin\theta_n\cos(\phi-\phi_n)+\cos\theta\cos\theta_n)} \qquad (12)$$

where $tinc(x) = J_1(x)/x$, $jinc(x) = j_1(x)/x$, $J_1(x)$ denotes the first spherical Bessel function of the first order, and $j_1(x)$ denotes the first Bessel function of the first order. Without loss of generality, we consider the direction $(\theta_0,\phi_0) = (90°,0°)$ as the desired direction and the beampattern in azimuth plane $(\theta = 90°)$ in the following sections. Thus, the variables Q and G satisfied with $Q(\theta,\phi) = 4\pi\beta\sin(\phi/2)$ and $G(\theta) = 0$. Thus, the average manifold vector can be rewritten as:

$$\bar{A}_n(\phi) = 3tinc(\alpha(\phi))e^{j\cdot2\pi L_n\sin\theta_n\cos(\phi-\phi_n)} \qquad (13)$$

where $\alpha(\phi) = 4\pi\beta\sin(\phi/2)$. The average beampattern is presented as:

$$F(\phi) = \frac{1}{N}\sum_{n=1}^{N} 3tinc(\alpha(\phi))e^{j\cdot2\pi L_n\sin\theta_n\cos(\phi-\phi_n)}\cdot w_n \qquad (14)$$

where $w_n \in C$ denotes the weighted value for nth satellite, C denotes the complex field, and $w = [w_1,w_2,\cdots,w_n]^T$ is the weighted vector for the array. The average power pattern can be written as:

$$S(\phi) = |F(\phi)|^2 = \frac{1}{N^2}|\sum_{n=1}^{N} 3tinc(\alpha(\phi))e^{j\cdot2\pi L_n\sin\theta_n\cos(\phi-\phi_n)}\cdot w_n|^2 \qquad (15)$$

We also define the following variables simplify the express as:

$$K(\phi) = \left||F_s(\phi)|^2-|F(\phi)|^2\right| = \frac{1}{N^2}\left|\left|\sum_{n=1}^{N} w_n\cdot A_n(\phi)\right|^2 - \left|\sum_{n=1}^{N} w_n\cdot \bar{A}_n(\phi)\right|^2\right| \qquad (16)$$

similar to the peak-to-average ratio of OFDM signal, we use the complementary cumulative distribution function (CCDF) to evaluate this beampattern difference as:

$$C_{K(\phi)}(z) = P(K(\phi) > z) = 1 - P(K(\phi) \leq z) \qquad (17)$$

3 Optimization Algorithm Design

The NSGA-II algorithm is based on Pareto theory. The multi-objective optimization problem is related to the fast sorting of non-dominated solution sets, which makes the population approach the Pareto front quickly. At the same time, it introduces the Crowding degree coefficient, and abandons the artificially designated parameters of the shared radius in the previous generation algorithm, which better guarantees the diversity of the population. At the same time, an elite strategy was introduced to prevent the loss of the superior solution [8].

Algorithm Framework of the Optimization

Initially generating the initial population of N individuals
Define the largest evolutionary algebra *MaxGen*;
While *gen < MaxGen* **do**
    For $i = 1$ to N **do**
        Fast non-dominated sorting:
        Calculate three objective function values according to formula (18);
        the same layer of individuals have the same non-dominated sorting(i_{rank});
        Crowding degree coefficient:
        Sort by f_1. f_2. f_3 ;
        Marginal individual $= \infty$;

$$i_d = \sum\nolimits_{j=0}^{3}(|f_j^{i+1} - f_j^{i-1}|)$$

        Preserve quality individuals:
        If $i_{rank} < j_{rank}$ **or** $i_{rank} = j_{rank}$ **and** $i_d > j_d$
            Preserve i;
        End
    End
    Crossover, mutation, generate the next generation population;
End

---

4 Simulation Results

Faced with complex spatial network environments, it is necessary to generate corresponding null in strong signal interference sources. Under the condition of $N = 10$, $\beta = 15, L_n = 303$, the desired direction is $\phi_0 = 0°$, and the undesired direction interval is: $\phi \in [0.3°, 0.32°]$, which is intended to produce null in this interval. At the same time, the peak sidelobe level (PSL) is also suppressed to eliminate complex signal interference in the spatial network. The independent variables are: the elevation angle of the nth satellite: $\theta_n \in [0, \pi]$, the azimuth angle of the nth satellite: $\phi_n \in [0, 2\pi)$, and the weight phase $\alpha_n \in [-\pi, \pi]$, and the optimization target is established according to the scene requirements. The function is described by a mathematical formula as:

$$\begin{cases} \min_{\phi_n,\theta_n,\alpha_n} & f_1 = 20\log_{10}|F_{av}(\phi_{ML})| \\[2mm] \min_{\phi_n,\theta_n,\alpha_n} & f_2 = 20\log_{10}\left|\dfrac{\max|F_{av}(\phi_{SL})|}{F_{av}(\phi_{ML})}\right| \\[2mm] \min_{\phi_n,\theta_n,\alpha_n} & f_3 = 20\log_{10}\left|\dfrac{\max|F_{av}(\phi_k)|}{F_{av}(\phi_{ML})}\right|, \;\phi_k \in [0.3°,0.32°] \\[2mm] s.t. & w_n^H w_n = 1, \quad n = 1,2,\ldots,N \end{cases} \quad (18)$$

where ϕ_{SL} is the angle of the sidelobe during the optimization process, and ϕ_{ML} is the angle of the mainlobe. $\phi_k \in [0.3°, 0.32°]$ is the null of the beampattern.

Figure 2 shows that the relationship between mainlobe and PSL/null. We can get better PSL or null by properly sacrificing the performance of the mainlobe.

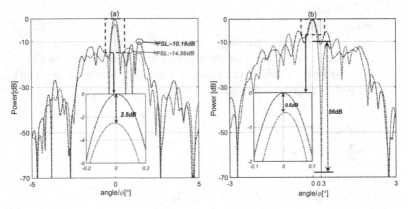

Fig. 2. (a) Relationship between mainlobe and PSL (b) Relationship between mainlobe and null

Figure 3 shows that when the mainlobe power tends to the maximum value, the PSL is also gradually increased. Furthermore, it is a pair of nonlinear contradictory parameters, and we can use this property according to the specific task requirements.

Through the formation of Fig. 4 we can get the beampattern shown in Fig. 5, the desired source azimuth angle: 0°, the maximum power of the array is obtained. The strong signal interference source: (0.3°, 0.32°) forms a null, which can reach about −40 dB. At the same time, the PSL is controlled at −9 dB, which meets the needs of the task.

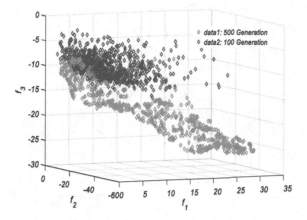

Fig. 3. Pareto frontier solution cluster

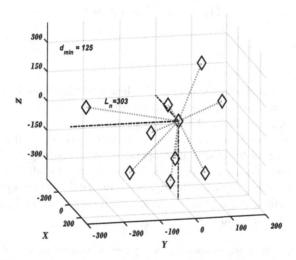

Fig. 4. Satellite cluster formation

The CCDF shows the probability that the average power pattern approaches the instantaneous beampattern. It can be seen that as the threshold power increases, the probability decreases continuously, and the probability of the average power pattern jitter of 4 dB is less than 1%.

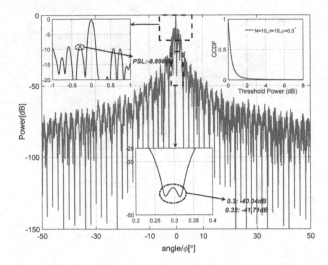

Fig. 5. Array power pattern

5   Conclusion

In this paper, a distributed satellite cooperative beamforming algorithm for the satellite cluster formed by multiple distributed formation flying satellites in space information network is proposed to enhance the electromagnetic wave transceiver capability of a resource-constrained satellite system. Simulation results show that the proposed method extends the distributed and cooperative beamforming technology to the research field of space information network. The issues to be studied in the future such as adaptive beamforming algorithm in high dynamic environment, optimal formation for a electromagnetic wave transceiver task, synchronized methods of a distributed satellites formation flying and so on.

Achnowledgement. The work presented in this paper is partially supported by the National Science Foundation of China (No. 91738201, No. 61801445, No. 61971440). However, any opinion, finding, and conclusions or recommendations expressed in this material; are those of the author and do not necessarily reflect the views of the National Science Foundation.

References

1. Boero, L., Bruschi, R., Davoli, F.: Satellite networking integration in the 5G ecosystem: research trends and open challenges. IEEE Netw. **32**(5), 9–15 (2018)
2. Yu, Q.Y., Meng, W.X., Yang, M.C.: Virtual multi-beamforming for distributed satellite clusters in space information networks. IEEE Wirel. Commun. **23**(1), 95–101 (2016)
3. Jayaprakasam, S., Rahim, S.K.A., Leow, C.Y.: Distributed and collaborative beamforming in wireless sensor networks: classifications, trends and research directions. IEEE Commun. Surv. Tutorials. **19**(4), 2092–2116 (2017)

4. Ochiai, H., Mitran, P., Poor, H.V.: Collaborative beamforming for distributed wireless ad hoc sensor networks. IEEE Trans. Signal Process. **53**(11), 4110–4124 (2005)
5. Ahmed, M.F.A., Vorobyov, S.A.: Collaborative beamforming for wireless sensor networks with gaussian distributed sensor nodes. IEEE Trans. Wirel. Commun. **8**(2), 638–643 (2009)
6. Huang, J., Wang, P., Wan, Q.: Collaborative beamforming for wireless sensor networks with arbitrary distributed sensors. IEEE Commun. Lett. **16**(7), 1118–1120 (2012)
7. Buchanan, K., Huff, G.H.: A stochastic mathematical framework for the analysis of spherically-bound random arrays. IEEE Trans. Antennas Propag. **62**(6), 3002–3011 (2014)
8. Deb, K., Pratap, A., Agarwal, S.: A fast and elitist multiobjective genetic algorithm: NSGA-II. IEEE Trans. Evol. Comput. **6**(2), 1–197 (2002)

AMP Inspired Antenna Activity and Signal Detection Algorithm for Generalized Spatial Modulated NOMA

Xiang Li, Yang Huang, Wei Heng[✉], Jing Wu, Ke Wang,
Gang Wang, and Yuan Zhang

National Mobile Communications Research Laboratory, Southeast University,
Nanjing 210096, People's Republic of China
{230159390, 213151630, wheng, 230169362, 230179413,
wanggang, 101010681}@seu.edu.cn

Abstract. The non-orthogonal multiple access technology has been considered as one of potential technologies for the next generation wireless network. Spatial modulation, which improves both spectral and energy efficiency at the same time, has found its potentials in NOMA system. Spatial modulation, together with multiple-input multiple-output technique, could maintain massive connections and provide low latency at the same time. But it also puts forward challenges for multi-user and signal detection. By exploiting the sparsity nature of generalized spatial modulation system, we formulate the active antenna and user signal detection into a general sparse linear-inverse problem. An approximate message passing based algorithm is proposed to detect the antenna activity and transmitted signal simultaneously in the uplink grant-free NOMA scenario. Expect maximum algorithm is utilized to learn the parameters of activity level and noise variance. Simulation results show that proposed scheme outperforms the CS based schemes over a wide range of SNR and sparsity level. Moreover, proposed algorithm achieves convergency in 15 iterations which makes it very practical.

Keywords: Spatial modulation · NOMA · Approximate message passing · Compressive sensing

1 Introduction

Next generation wireless network is expected to provide low latency and support massive connectivity with a large number of devices. To address these challenges, nonorthogonal multiple access (NOMA), which was proposed to deal with these challenges by efficiently using finite available bandwidth, has been regarded as one of the most promising technologies for the 5G network [1].

In NOMA system, nonorthogonal resources are allocated to different users rather than orthogonal resources distribution in conventional orthogonal multiple access. Therefore, the base station is able to support much more users in resource limited uplink scenario. So far, several NOMA schemes have been investigated. The power domain NOMA utilizes superposition coding at the transmitter and successive

J. Zheng et al. (Eds.): ADHOCNETS 2019, LNICST 306, pp. 262–275, 2019.
https://doi.org/10.1007/978-3-030-37262-0_22

interference cancellation at the receiver [2]. The code domain NOMA takes the forms of low-density spreading CDMA (LDS-CDMA) [3], sparse code multiple access (SCMA) [4] and so on. In order to reduce the control signaling overhead and latency, the grant-free NOMA system where active users transmit data at synchronized time slot without a complex request-grant procedure is investigated here.

Multiple-input multiple-output (MIMO) technology is getting increasing interests by using antennas on the terminals to achieve a better performance. However, a key challenge of future mobile communication network is to strike a compromise between spectral efficiency (SE) and energy efficiency (EE). Fueled by this consideration, the spatial modulation (SM) [5], which uses the spatial constellation to meet the demand of SE and EE, has been established as a promising transmission concept [6]. Figure 1 shows the configuration of different multi-antenna systems. The main distinguishing feature of SM is that it maps additional information on the SM constellation diagram. The generalized SM is a generalization of SM by taking advantage of the whole antenna array without the RF chain limitation. Therefore, the generalized SM fully uses the available antennas to improve SE and EE [7]. This unique characteristic allows the coexistence of high-rate devices and massive connections. Recent analytical and simulation studies have shown that SM outperforms many state-of-art MIMO schemes [8].

According to the statistics, the number of active users is usually much smaller than the number of supported users even in rush hours [9]. This coincides with the sparsity hypothesis of user activity in the NOMA system. Due to the sparsity nature of the SM signals, compressive sensing (CS) based detectors [10, 11] become competitive solutions with low complexity especially in the large-scale scenario.

Recently, approximate message passing (AMP) algorithm [12] was proposed by Donoho to solve CS problems. Despite its low complexity, AMP performs exactly the same as l_1 − norm minimization and it admits rigorous analysis based on the state evolution [13]. AMP has been extended to general linear mixing problems and widely used in various scenarios [14, 15].

Starting from the analysis of generalized spatial modulation system, we develop an AMP-based algorithm to detect the active antennas and the data modulated on each active antenna. To learn the unknown parameters, we present a detailed derivation of the expectation maximization (EM) algorithm iteratively. The simulation results show the effectiveness of proposed algorithm and it performs better than existing CS approaches and converges in 15 iterations.

Notation: Bold lower and upper-case symbols represent vectors and matrices, respectively. The superscript $(\cdot)^{\mathrm{T}}$ denotes the transpose operation and $\mathcal{N}(x; \theta, \phi)$ denotes that x is Gaussian distributed with mean θ and variance ϕ.

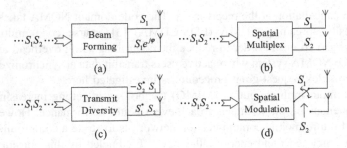

Fig. 1. Illustration of multiple antenna configurations: (a) beam forming (b) spatial multiplex (c) transmit diversity (d) spatial modulation

2 System Model

Here we consider an uplink grant-free NOMA system with one base station and K users of which S are active within one transmission slot. As shown in Fig. 2, the base station is equipped with M antennas and all antennas are set to spatial modulation mode. For simplicity, we assume each user has n_t antennas, however, our algorithm can be easily extended to a more general case. Then the total antenna at the user side is $N = K \times n_t$. The uplink NOMA system can be modelled as

$$y = \sum_{k=1}^{K} G_k x_k + w \tag{1}$$

where $y \in \mathbb{C}^{M \times 1}$ is the receive signal at the base station and $G_k \in \mathbb{C}^{M \times n_t}$ is the channel response matrix of user k. Here we assume the channel is quasi-static, i.e., the coefficients keep constant during one transmission slot. $x_k \in \mathbb{C}^{M \times 1}$ represents the transmitted symbols of user k. Additive white gaussian noise (AWGN) vector $w \in \mathbb{C}^{M \times V} \sim \mathcal{CN}(0, \sigma^2 I_M)$ with I_M being the identity matrix of size $M \times M$. Then Eq. (1) can be rewritten as

$$y = Hx + w \tag{2}$$

where $H = [G_1 \quad G_1 \ldots G_K]$ denotes the equivalent channel matrix. In the generalized spatial modulated NOMA scenario, transmitted signal x is generated by users and their antennas, which is defined as

$$x = [x_1 \quad x_2 \ldots x_K]^T \tag{3}$$

Generally, not all the antennas are active at the same time. We assume $n_a \in [0, n_t]$ antennas are activated randomly at one time slot, then x_i can be expressed as

$$x_i = [0, x_{p_1}, 0, \ldots, x_{p_{n_a}}, \ldots, 0] \tag{4}$$

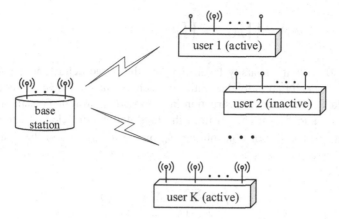

Fig. 2. Generalized spatial modulation in grant-free uplink NOMA system

where $p_j \in [1, n_t]$ is the index of active antenna and $j \in [1, n_a]$. x_{p_j} represents the symbol transmitted on the p_j th antenna which is chosen from a constellation set $\Theta = \{\Theta_1, \Theta_2, \ldots, \Theta_Q\}$, such as PSK or QAM. Then the sum rate is defined as bit per user.

$$R = \log_2 \binom{n_t}{n_a} + n_a \times \log_2 \|\Theta\|_0 \tag{5}$$

According to [9], only a small number of users are active simultaneously and their antennas are activated randomly during transmission. We denote 0 for the antenna which is inactive. Then **x** takes the following form

$$\mathbf{x} = \left[\ldots, \underbrace{0, \ldots, 0}_{\text{inactive user}}, \ldots, \underbrace{x_{p_1}, 0, \ldots, x_{p_{n_a}}}_{\text{active user}}, \ldots \right]^{\mathrm{T}} \tag{6}$$

For a more general case, users have different number of antennas and the number of active antennas is different for each user. Apart from that fact, users may change their spatial constellations between each transmission, so block-sparse hypothesis will not always hold. Active entries are not clustered either, so nearest neighbor sparsity methods do not work well. Therefore, the problem should be modeled as the typical sparse linear inverse problem naturally.

In the uplink grant-free NOMA, BS needs to know the antenna activity before decoding. Therefore, our goal is to estimate the support and value of nonzero element of **x** from **y**. The sparsity level of each antenna is also unknown a prior. Without loss of generality, we assume the prior on each antenna is i.i.d, i.e., having the following marginal pdf

$$p(\mathbf{x}) = \prod_{n=1}^{N} p(x_n) = \prod_{n=1}^{N} [(1 - \lambda_n)\delta(x_n) + \lambda_n f(x_n)] \tag{7}$$

where $\lambda_n \in (0, 1)$ is the sparsity level, $\delta(x_n)$ is the Dirac delta function. It is worth noting that we specify an individual ratio for each antenna rather than a common one. This is one key feature for reconstruction in proposed algorithm. Transmitted symbols on each active antenna are chosen from the modulation constellation set Θ. Let $p_{n,q}$ represents the probability of transmitting Θ_q of the nth user, then the distribution of nonzero entries can be written as

$$f(x_n) = \sum_{q=1}^{Q} p_{n,q}\delta(x_n - \Theta_q) \tag{8}$$

The system considered here is assumed to be well synchronized in each transmission slot and inter-symbol interference is ignored.

3 Proposed Algorithm

3.1 AMP Algorithm

Inspired by approximate message passing algorithms and MAP inference, we detail the proposed detection in Algorithm I. Based on message passing algorithm, we decouple the estimation problem in Eq. (2) into scalar problems:

$$\begin{cases} \mathbf{y} = \mathbf{z} + \mathbf{w} \\ \mathbf{z} = \mathbf{Hx} \end{cases} \rightarrow \begin{cases} \gamma_1 = x_1 + w_1 \\ \cdots \\ \gamma_N = x_N + w_N \end{cases} \tag{9}$$

where the equivalent noise w_n asymptotically follows $\mathcal{CN}(w_n; 0, \phi_n)$. The value of γ_1 and ϕ_n are updated in each iteration. The posterior distribution of x_n is defined as

$$p(x_n|\gamma_n, \phi_n) = \frac{1}{Z(\gamma_n, \phi_n)} p(x_n)\mathcal{CN}(x_n; \gamma_n, \phi_n) \tag{10}$$

where

$$Z(\gamma_n, \phi_n) = \sum_{x_n \in \{\Theta, 0\}} p(x_n)\mathcal{CN}(x_n; \gamma_n, \phi_n) \tag{11}$$

is the normalizing factor and

$$p(x_n) = (1 - \lambda_n)\delta(x_n) + \lambda_n \sum_{q=1}^{Q} p_{n,q}\delta(x_n - \Theta_q) \tag{12}$$

Algorithm I   AMP based detection algorithm

---

(1) initialization

$$\lambda_n^0 = \lambda_0, \hat{x}_n^0 = \lambda_0 \sum_{q=1}^{Q} p_{n,q} \Theta_q, \upsilon_n^0 = \lambda_0 \sum_{q=1}^{Q} p_{n,q} \left|\Theta_q\right|^2 - \left|\hat{x}_n^0\right|^2$$

$$Z_m^0 = y_m, V_m^0 = 0$$

(2) main iteration

for $t = 1 \ldots T$

    for $m = 1:M$ (decoupling step)

$$V_m^t = \sum_{n=1}^{N} \left|H_{m,n}\right|^2 \upsilon_n^t$$

$$Z_m^t = \sum_{n=1}^{N} H_{m,n} \hat{x}_n^t - V_m^t \frac{y_m - Z_m^{t-1}}{\sigma^2 + V_m^{t-1}}$$

    for $n = 1:N$ (denoising step)

$$\phi_n^t = \left(\sum_{m=1}^{M} \frac{\left|H_{m,n}\right|^2}{\sigma^2 + V_m^{t-1}} \right)^{-1}$$

$$\gamma_n^t = \hat{x}_n^t + \phi_n^t \sum_{m=1}^{M} \frac{H_{m,n}^* \left(y_m - Z_m^t\right)}{\sigma^2 + V_m^t}$$

    cal $p\left(x_n^t \middle| \gamma_n^t, \phi_n^t\right)$ using (12)

$$\hat{x}_n^t = \sum_{x_n^t \in \{\Theta, 0\}} x_n^t p\left(x_n^t \middle| \gamma_n^t, \phi_n^t\right)$$

$$\upsilon_n^t = \sum_{x_n^t \in \{\Theta, 0\}} \left|x_n^t\right|^2 p\left(x_n^t \middle| \gamma_n^t, \phi_n^t\right) - \left|\hat{x}_n^t\right|^2$$

    update λ_k and σ^2 using (18) and (24)

finally $\mathbf{r} = \left[\gamma_1^T, \gamma_2^T, \ldots, \gamma_n^T\right]$

(3) select the active antenna using antenna detection rule
in sectiong III-D

(4) decode symbols on each active antenna

From above, the estimates of mean and variance of x_n are

$$\hat{x}_n = \sum_{x_n \in \{\Theta, 0\}} x_n p(x_n | \gamma_n, \phi_n)$$

$$v_n = \sum_{x_n \in \{\Theta, 0\}} |x_n|^2 p(x_n | \gamma_n, \phi_n) - |\hat{x}_n|^2 \tag{13}$$

The term $V_m^t \frac{y_m - Z_m^{t-1}}{\sigma^2 + V_m^{t-1}}$ in decoupling step is known as the *Onsager correction* which is the heart of the AMP [12]. Under large i.i.d. sub-Gaussian channel matrix configuration, Onsager correction ensures that the input of the denoiser can be modeled as

$$\mathbf{Z} = \mathbf{x} + \mathbf{n}, \text{ where } \mathbf{n} \sim \mathcal{CN}\left(\mathbf{0}, \frac{\mathbf{I}_N}{M} \|\mathbf{V}\|_2^2\right) \tag{14}$$

The gaussian distribution enables the denoiser to work efficiently.

From the detail implement of AMP, full knowledge of prior distribution and noise variance are needed, which is an impractical assumption. Therefore, we resort to EM algorithm to learn the unknown parameters. The EM algorithm we adopt here is an increment update rule [16], i.e., updating one element at a time while others remain fixed. EM increases the likelihood probability at each iteration, guaranteeing convergence to at least local maximum of the likelihood function $p(\mathbf{y}|\lambda_k, \sigma^2)$.

3.2 λ_k Update

Now we resort to EM algorithm to learn the user activity λ_n. Since user may change their spatial modulation at each transmission slot, we estimate λ_n element-wisely. Denoting the estimate parameters by λ_n^t at t^{th} iteration, EM updates can be expressed as

$$\lambda_k^{t+1} = \arg\max_{\lambda_k^k \in [0,1]} \mathrm{E}\left\{\ln p\left(x_n^t|\lambda_n^t\right)|\mathbf{y}\right\} \tag{15}$$

where $\mathrm{E}\{\cdot\}$ denotes expectation conditioned on observation $\mathbf{y}$ and parameter λ_k^t. In order to obtain the maximum value, we differentiate Eq. (15) with respect to λ_k^t. and set it to zero:

$$\sum_{x_n\{\Theta,0\}} p\left(x_n^t|\mathbf{y}\right) \frac{\mathrm{d}}{\mathrm{d}\lambda_n^t} \ln p\left(x_n^t|\lambda_n^t\right) \tag{16}$$

where

$$p\left(x_n^t|\mathbf{y}\right) = p\left(x_n^t|\gamma_n^t, \phi_n^t\right)$$

$$\frac{\mathrm{d}}{\mathrm{d}\lambda_n^t} \ln p\left(x_n^t|\lambda_n^t\right) = \frac{\sum_{q=1}^{Q} p_{n,q}\delta\left(x_n^t - \Theta_q\right) - \delta\left(x_n^t\right)}{(1-\lambda_n^t)\delta\left(x_n^t\right) + \lambda_t^t \sum_{q=1}^{Q} p_{n,q}\delta\left(x_n^t - \Theta_q\right)}$$

$$= \begin{cases} \frac{1}{\lambda_n^t - 1} & x_n^t \notin \Theta \\ \frac{1}{\lambda_n^t} & x_n^t \in \Theta \end{cases} \tag{17}$$

Then λ_n^{t+1} can be obtained in a direct form

$$\lambda_n^{t+1} = \sum_{x_n \in \Theta} p(x_n^t | \gamma_n^t, \phi_n^t) \tag{18}$$

3.3 σ^2 Update

Then we derive the update rule for σ^2 given previous parameters. Note that $\mathbf{w}$ is independent of $\mathbf{x}$ and i.i.d, the joint pdf decouples into

$$p(\mathbf{x}, \mathbf{w}) = \prod_{n=1}^{N} p(w_m; \sigma^2) \tag{19}$$

so

$$(\sigma^2)^{t+1} = \arg\max_{\sigma^2 > 0} \sum_{n=1}^{N} \mathrm{E}\{\ln p(w_m; \sigma^2) | \mathbf{y}; \boldsymbol{\theta}^t\} \tag{20}$$

The maximizing value of σ^2 can be obtained by zeroing the derivative, i.e.,

$$\sum_{n=1}^{N} \int_{\sigma^2} p(\sigma^2 | \mathbf{y}; \boldsymbol{\theta}^t) \frac{\mathrm{d}}{\mathrm{d}\sigma^2} \ln p(w_m; \sigma^2) = 0 \tag{21}$$

where

$$\frac{\mathrm{d}}{\mathrm{d}\sigma^2} \ln p(w_m; \sigma^2) = \frac{1}{2}\left(\frac{(w_m)^2}{(\sigma^2)^2} - \frac{1}{\sigma^2}\right) \tag{22}$$

From (21) and (22), we have

$$(\sigma^2)^{t+1} = \frac{1}{N} \sum_{n=1}^{N} \int_{w_m} |w_m|^2 p(\sigma^2 | \mathbf{y}; \boldsymbol{\theta}^t) \tag{23}$$

since $w_m = y_m - z_m$, we have

$$\begin{aligned}
(\sigma^2)^{t+1} &= \frac{1}{N} \sum_{n=1}^{N} \int_{w_m} |y_n - \hat{z}_n|^2 p(\sigma^2 | \mathbf{y}; \boldsymbol{\theta}^t) \\
&= \frac{1}{N} \sum_{n=1}^{N} \left(|y_n - \hat{z}_n|^2 - \mu_{zm}\right)
\end{aligned} \tag{24}$$

Above $\hat{z}_n$ and μ_{2m} are the posterior mean and variance, which can be calculated by

$$
\begin{aligned}
z_m &= \sum_{n=1}^{N} H_{mn} x_n \mu_{zm} \\
&= \sum_{n=1}^{N} |H_{mn}|^2 \gamma_n
\end{aligned}
\tag{25}
$$

3.4 CFAR Threshold

After several iterations, based on the estimated mean and variance, we design an adaptable threshold x_{TH} to detect the support of $\mathbf{r}$ with constant false alarm rate (CFAR)η. Support detection can be seen as the final layer. From Eq. (2) we have

$$
\mathbf{r} = \mathbf{x} + \mathbf{w}
\tag{26}
$$

where $\mathbf{w} \sim \mathcal{CN}\left(\mathbf{0}, \gamma_{1T}^{-1}\mathbf{I}\right)$, and $\mathbf{r} \sim \mathcal{CV}\left(\mathbf{x}, \gamma_{1T}^{-1}\mathbf{I}\right)$. For a given CFAR η, x_{TH} can be derived as

$$
x_{TH} = \sqrt{\gamma_{1T}}\, \Phi^{-1}\left(\frac{\eta+1}{2}\right)
\tag{27}
$$

where $\Phi^{-1}(\cdot)$ is the probit function of the standard normal distribution. Based on this threshold, missing detection can be calculated

$$
\Pr(x_{TH}) = \int_{-x_{TH}}^{x_{TH}} p(x_n|\mathbf{r})dx \approx \lambda \int_{-x_{TH}}^{x_{TH}} \mathcal{N}(x; \theta, \mathbf{\Phi})dx
\tag{28}
$$

Once the threshold is selected, the support is detected for $|\mathbf{r}| \geq x_{TH}$. Then the original symbol pair is restored by applying MAP detection:

$$
\begin{aligned}
x_n &= \arg\max_{x_e \in \Theta} p\left(\Theta_q | x_n\right) \\
&= \arg\max_{x_x \in \Theta} \frac{p\left(x_n | \Theta_q\right) p\left(\Theta_q\right)}{\sum_{x_e \in \Theta} p\left(x_n | \Theta_q\right) p\left(\Theta_q\right)} = \arg\max_{x_x = \Theta} p\left(x_n | \Theta_q\right)
\end{aligned}
\tag{29}
$$

3.5 Parameter Initialization

Since EM algorithm may converge into a local maximum or a saddle point, proper initialization of unknown parameters is essential. The sparsity level is initialized as $\lambda_0 = \frac{M}{N}\rho_{Prc}$ where ρ_{PTC} is the sparsity ratio achieved by Lasso PTC

$$\rho_{PTC} = \max_{a > 0} \frac{1 - 2N/M[(1 + a^2)\Phi(a) - a\phi(a)]}{1 - a^2 - 2[(1 + a^2)\Phi(a) - a\phi(a)]} \tag{30}$$

Due to the fact that the active pdf is symmetric, the active mean is initialized as 0. Then σ^2 is initialized as $(\text{sNR} + 1)\|y\|^2/M$ and SNR is set to 100 if there is no extra knowledge.

3.6   Computational Complexity

The computational complexity is evaluated in terms of floating-point operations (FPOs). The multiplication of a real number and a complex number require 2 FPOs and the multiplication of two complex numbers requires 6 FPOs. The value from operation $\mathcal{CN}(\cdot)$ is implemented by look-up table. In the main iteration of proposed algorithm, the computation of inner decoupling step requires $(10\,N + 2)$ FPOs and these computations need M iterations. The computation of denoising step needs $N(22M + 16\|\Theta\|_0 + 9)$ FPOs. Equations (18) and (24) require $N\|\Theta\|_0$ and $(8\,M + 10)\,(N - 1) + 9$ FPOs, respectively. Therefore, the total computation required by proposed algorithm is $T\big(40MN - 6M + 19N + 17N\|\Theta\|_0 - 1\big)$ FPOs. Modulation order is a factor that affect the computation burden especially when high-order modulations are used.

The computational complexity of proposed algorithm is dominated by matrix-vector multiplications in each iteration, i.e., $\mathcal{O}(MN)$. The number of iterations required to guarantee convergence is not large. From the simulation result shown in Sect. 4, it takes 15 layers to achieve its error floor. Therefore, this linear complexity of proposed algorithm is suitable for large scale antenna MIMO configurations which are encountered in next generation wireless communication system.

4   Performance Evaluation

In this section, we present the simulation results of proposed detection scheme. The base station is equipped with $M = 100$ receive antennas. The number of total supported antennas N is set to 250, thus the overload factor is 250%. The symbols transmitted on the active antenna are QPSK modulated. The channel is modeled as Rayleigh flat fading channel and the elements of channel matrix $\mathbf{H}$ are i.i.d, i.e., $H_{m,n} \sim \mathcal{CN}(0, 1)$. CS based schemes, OMP, SP and CoSaMP are implemented as reference. The performance of user detection and SM demodulation. User detection performance is measured by antenna detection error which is defined as active antenna being detected as inactive. Symbol detection error rate is used to measure signal detection performance.

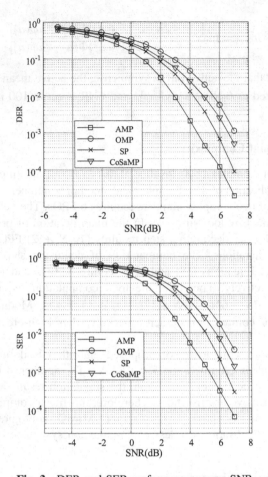

Fig. 3. DER and SER performance versus SNR

The detection error rate (DER) and symbol error rate (SER) of different algorithms is depicted as functions of SNR in Fig. 3. The number of active antennas is set to 10. When measuring the SER, the active antennas is assumed to be known. The proposed detector outperforms SP 1 dB in terms of SER and DER. It is worth mentioning that SP and CoSaMP based methods need the information of the number of active antennas as prior information which is learned iteratively in proposed method.

Figure 4 shows the SER and DER performance versus the sparsity level. It considers the case SNR equals 3 dB and 9 dB. In both configurations, proposed algorithm can achieve a better performance than other methods over a wide range of sparsity level. With up to 15 active antennas, proposed detector still has a 10^{-3} SER and 10^{-4} DER at 9 dB. This means proposed algorithm is robust to a changing number of active antennas. Another interesting observation is that, in low SNR case CoSaMP perform better than OMP, but in high SNR case, OMP is about 1 dB outperform CoSaMP.

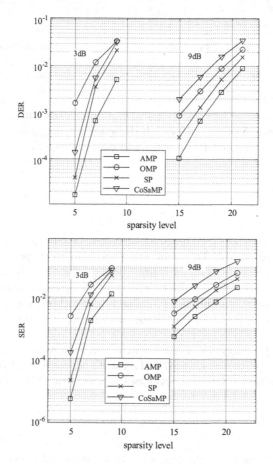

Fig. 4. DER and SER performance versus sparsity level

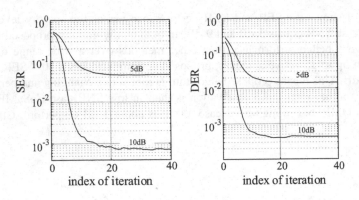

Fig. 5. Convergency performance versus iterations

Figure 5 shows the performance versus iteration indexes with sparsity level being 17 when SNR equals 5 dB and 10 dB. It demonstrates that, proposed detector converges much faster in the first 10 iterations and does not significantly improve after 15 iterations.

5 Conclusion

In this paper, we present an AMP based antenna activity and signal detection algorithm for spatial modulated NOMA. This solution shows an improved performance compared to previous CS approaches. This is mainly because Onsager correction ensures the denoiser input is an AWGN corrupt version of the ground truth. Another major advantage of proposed algorithm lies in the fact that it achieves its convergency in 15 iterations and its linear computational complexity makes it very practical.

Acknowledgment. This work was sponsored by the National Nature Science Foundation of China (NSFC) projects (61771132, 61571111) and the Research Fund of National Mobile Communications Research Laboratory, Southeast University (No. 2019A02).

References

1. Wu, Z., Lu, K., Jiang, C., Shao, X.: Comprehensive study and comparison on 5G NOMA schemes. IEEE Access **6**, 18511–18519 (2018)
2. Islam, S.M.R., Avazov, N., Dobre, O.A., Kwak, K.S.: Power-domain non-orthogonal multiple access (NOMA) in 5G systems: potentials and challenges. IEEE Commun. Surv. Tutor. **12**(2), 721–742 (2016)
3. Hoshyar, R., Wathan, F.P., Tafazolli, R.: Novel low-density signature for synchronous CDMA systems over AWGN channel. IEEE Trans. Signal Proc. **56**(4), 1616–1626 (2008)
4. Nikopour, H., Baligh, H.: Sparse code multiple access. In: Proceedings of the IEEE International Symposium on Personal, Indoor, and Mobile Radio Communications (PIMRC), London, UK, pp. 332–336, September 2013

5. Di Renzo, M., Haas, H., Ghrayeb, A., Sugiura, S., Hanzo, L.: Spatial modulation for generalized MIMO: challenges, opportunities, and implementation. Proc. IEEE **102**(1), 56–103 (2014)
6. Marzetta, T.: Noncooperative cellular wireless with unlimited numbers of base station antennas. IEEE Trans. Wirel. Commun. **9**(11), 3590–3600 (2010)
7. Wang, T., Liu, S., Yang, F., Wang, J., Song, J., Han, Z.: Block-sparse compressive sensing based multi-user and signal detection for generalized spatial modulation in NOMA. In: Proceedings of the IWCMC, Valencia, Spain, pp. 1992–1997, June 2017
8. Di Renzo, M., Haas, H.: On transmit-diversity for spatial modulation MIMO: impact of spatial-constellation diagram and shaping filters at the transmitter. IEEE Trans. Veh. Technol. **62**(6), 2507–2531 (2013)
9. Hong, J.P., Choi, W., Rao, B.D.: Sparsity controlled random multiple access with compressed sensing. IEEE Trans. Wirel. Commun. **14**(2), 998–1010 (2015)
10. Han, Z., Li, H., Yin, W.: Compressive Sensing for Wireless Networks. Cambridge University Press, Cambridge (2013)
11. Gao, Z., Dai, L., Qi, C., Yuen, C., Wang, Z.: Near-optimal signal detector based on structured compressive sensing for massive SM-MIMO. IEEE Trans. Veh. Technol. **66**(2), 1860–1865 (2017)
12. Donoho, D.L., Maliki, A., Montanari, A.: Message-passing algorithms for compressed sensing. Proc. Nat. Acad. Sci. **106**(45), 18914–18919 (2009)
13. Bayati, M., Montanari, A.: The dynamics of message passing on dense graphs, with applications to compressed sensing. IEEE Trans. Inf. Theory **57**(2), 764–785 (2011)
14. Rangan, S.: Generalized approximate message passing for estimation with random linear mixing. In: Proceedings of the IEEE International Symposium on Information Theory (ISIT), pp. 2168–2172, August 2011
15. Schniter, P.: A message-passing receiver for BICM-OFDM over unknown clustered-sparse channels. IEEE J. Sel. Top. Signal Process. **5**(8), 1462–1474 (2011)
16. Neal, R.M., Hinton, G.E.: A view of the EM algorithm that justifies incremental, sparse, and other variants. In: Learning in Graphical Models, vol. 89, pp. 355–368. MIT Press, Cambridge (1998)

A Filtering Dimension Reduction Decoding Algorithm for Underwater Acoustic Networks

Lijuan Wang[1,2], Xiujuan Du[1,2(✉)], Chong Li[1,2], Duoliang Han[1,2],
and Jianlian Zhu[1,2]

[1] School of Computer, Qinghai Normal University, Xining 810008, China
1041517271@qq.com, dxj@qhnu.edu.cn
[2] Key Laboratory of IoT of Qinghai Province, Xining, China

Abstract. Underwater acoustic channels are fragile. Reliable data transmission in underwater acoustic networks (UANs) faces tough challenges. Digital Fountain Code (DFC) is an efficient rateless error-correcting coding technique, in which the redundancy is not fixed and can be decided on the fly as the channel evolves. Thus, DFC is considered near-optimal for underwater acoustic channels. A recursive LT (RLT) code is a DFC tailored for underwater acoustic networks, which allows for lightweight implementation of an encoder and a decoder. Based on the analysis of the RLT algorithm, this paper proposes a filtering dimension reduction (FDR) decoding algorithm for underwater acoustic networks. The FDR decoding algorithm executes XOR operations on the encoded packets in a strict short ring of a generating a matrix to reduce the dimensions of the encoded packets, or generate 1-degree encoded packets. As a result, the FDR algorithm can increase the number of 1-degree encoded packets and reduce the decoding complexity. Moreover, the FDR algorithm can eliminate the waiting time for a traditional decoding algorithm to receive the 1-degree packets, and achieve fast decoding. Simulation results based on NS3 show that the decoding success rate of the FDR algorithm is higher than that of the RLT algorithm.

Keywords: Underwater acoustic network · Reliable transmission · Digital fountain code · Recursive LT · Filtering dimension reduction

1 Introduction

With the development of the wireless sensor network technology and people's increasing attention to underwater resources, marine environment, marine rights and interests, underwater acoustic networks (UANs) have attracted more and more research attention in recent years [1–5]. UANs use acoustic communication, and an acoustic channel is characterized by low bandwidth, long propagation delay, high error probability, Doppler effect and spatiotemporal variation, which make traditional transmission mechanisms inapplicable or inefficient in UANs. Therefore, UANs face great challenges for reliable transmission and call for new reliable transmission mechanisms. Digital fountain code (DFC) is of great significance to achieve reliable transmission in UANs [6–9].

© ICST Institute for Computer Sciences, Social Informatics and Telecommunications Engineering 2019
Published by Springer Nature Switzerland AG 2019. All Rights Reserved
J. Zheng et al. (Eds.): ADHOCNETS 2019, LNICST 306, pp. 276–287, 2019.
https://doi.org/10.1007/978-3-030-37262-0_23

DFC is an efficient rateless error-correcting coding technique. The redundancy of DFC is not fixed and can be decided on the fly as the channel evolves. Thus, DFC is considered near-optimal for underwater acoustic channels. A recursive LT (RLT) code is a DFC tailored for underwater acoustic networks, which allows for lightweight implementation of an encoder and a decoder [10]. Based on the analysis of the encoding characteristics and shortcomings of the RLT algorithm, this paper proposes a filtering dimension reduction (FDR) decoding algorithm, which can reduce the decoding complexity, and eliminate the waiting time for a traditional decoding algorithm to receive the 1-degree packets. Simulation results based on NS3 show that the decoding success rate of the FDR algorithm is higher than that of the RLT algorithm.

The remainder of the paper is organized as follows. Related work is introduced in Sect. 2. An FDR filtering dimension reduction decoding algorithm is presented in Sect. 3. Simulation results are shown and analyzed in Sect. 4. Finally, the paper is concluded in Sect. 5.

2 Related Work

Existing reliable transmission mechanisms for UANs can be divided into three categories: retransmission-based, forward error correction code (FEC)-based, and hybrid approach-based. Digital fountain coding is a reliable coding technique based on forward error correction coding. Early reliable coding techniques based on FEC usually adopted network coding with multipath routing, as proposed by Guo et al. in [11]. However, multipath routing usually brings about collision and retransmission. In [12], Liu and Garcin proposed a packet-level FEC reliable transmission mechanism. In a packet-level FEC-based transmission mechanism, the redundancy transmitted is fixed prior to transmission, which is not applicable in UANs. In [13] Peng et al. proposed a reliable transmission mechanism SDRT for piecewise data. SDRT protocol adopts SVT code to improve encoding/decoding efficiency. Nevertheless, after pumping the packets within the window quickly into the channel, the sender sends the packets outside the window at a very slow rate until receiving a positive feedback from the receiver, which reduces channel utilization. The original ADELIN was proposed in [14], which determines the appropriate FEC assemblage according to the distance between nodes, and realizes reliable transmission for underwater data. In [15], Mo et al. put forward a coding-based multi-hop coordinated reliable transmission mechanism. However, the encoding vectors are generated randomly, and thus the success probability of recovering data packets from encoded packets cannot be guaranteed, and its decoding complexity is higher than other sparse codes. Furthermore, the multihop coordination mechanism requires time synchronization and is restricted in a string topology, where there is a single sender and a single receiver. In [10], Du et al. proposed a RLT (recursive LT) code, which is applicable to dynamic UANs with limited transmission time between two nodes. RLT reduces the overhead of encoding and decoding. An RLT code is a DFC tailored for underwater acoustic networks, which allows for lightweight implementation of an encoder and a decoder. In this paper, an FDR decoding algorithm is proposed to overcome the shortcomings of the RLT algorithm. Next we introduce the RLT algorithm in detail.

For a given parameter $(k, d, \Omega(d))$ of an RLT algorithm, k is the number of original packets, $d(d \in \{1, 2, 3, 4, k\})$ denotes the degree value of an encoded packet, $\Omega(d)$ is the degree distribution. The input packet is represented as $\{S_1, S_2, \ldots, S_k\}$, k input packets composes a set D. The sequence of encoded packets is represented as $\{Y_1, Y_2, \ldots, Y_j, \ldots, Y_n\} (n > k)$. The RLT coding process is described as follows.

(1) From the set D, successively XOR the k input packets to generate one encoded packet with degree k, and then duplicate the encoded packet to obtain $\lceil 1/(1 - p_p) \rceil$ copies. Here, p_p denotes the error probability of a packet.

(2) From the set D, select $\lceil m/(1 - p_p) \rceil$ distinct packets randomly to constitute a seed set U_1 and generate $\lceil m/(1 - p_p) \rceil$ encoded packets with degree 1. Here, m is the expected number of encoded packets received successfully with degree 1. In reality, we can set $1 \leq m \leq \max(\lfloor k/4 \rfloor, 1)$.

(3) Let $U_2 = I - U_1$. From the set U_2, select uniformly $\lceil k/(2(1 - p_p)) \rceil$ input packets at random, and do XOR operation respectively with one packet selected randomly from the set U_1. Thus, generate $\lceil k/(2(1 - p_p)) \rceil$ encoded packets with degree 2.

(4) Let $U_3 = I - U_1 - U_2$. If $|U_3| > \lceil k/(6(1 - p_p)) \rceil$, select $\lceil k/(6(1 - p_p)) \rceil$ input packets at random from the set U_3; otherwise, from the set D, do XOR operation, respectively, with one packet from the set U_2 and another from the set U_1 to generate $\lceil k/(6(1 - p_p)) \rceil$ encoded packets with degree 3.

(5) Let $U_4 = I - U_1 - U_2 - U_3$. If $|U_4| > \lceil (\xi + k/3 - m - 1)/(1 - p_p) \rceil$, select randomly $\lceil (\xi + k/3 - m - 1)/(1 - p_p) \rceil$ input packets from the set U_4; otherwise, from the set D, do XOR operation, respectively, with three packets from U_1, U_2, U_3 respectively, to generate $\lceil (\xi + k/3 - m - 1)/(1 - p_p) \rceil$ encoded packets with degree 4.

3   FDR Decoding Algorithm

3.1   Analysis of RLT Coding

Consider a set of input (original) packets with each having the same number of bits. The RLT encoder takes input packets and generates a potentially infinite sequence of encoded packets. Each encoded packet is computed independent of others. More precisely, given k input packets $\{S_1, S_2, \ldots, S_k\}$, a sequence of encoded packets $\{Y_1, Y_2, \ldots, Y_j, \ldots, Y_n\}$ are generated, where $n > k$.

The generating matrix G_{kn} is a $k \times n - order$ binary matrix. Let $G_{kn} = [g_1, g_2, g_3, \ldots]$ be the generating matrix with n column vectors, $g_m = [g_{1m}, g_{2m}, \ldots, g_{km}]^T$, $m = 1, 2, 3, \ldots n$. The value of each vector member is 0 and 1. Thus, G_{kn} is expressed as

$$
\begin{array}{c}
\begin{array}{c} S_1 \\ S_2 \\ S_3 \\ S_4 \\ S_5 \\ \cdots \\ S_{k-1} \\ S_k \end{array}
\left[
\begin{array}{ccccccccc}
1 & 0 & 1 & 1 & 0 & 0 & 1 & \cdots & 0 & 1 \\
0 & 0 & 1 & 1 & 1 & 1 & 0 & \cdots & 1 & 1 \\
0 & 1 & 0 & 0 & 1 & 0 & 1 & \cdots & 0 & 0 \\
1 & 1 & 0 & 1 & 0 & 0 & 1 & \cdots & 0 & 1 \\
0 & 0 & 1 & 0 & 1 & 1 & 0 & \cdots & 1 & 1 \\
\cdots & \cdots & \cdots & \cdots & \cdots & \cdots & \cdots & \cdots & \cdots & \cdots \\
1 & 1 & 0 & 0 & 1 & 0 & 1 & \cdots & 1 & 0 \\
1 & 0 & 1 & 1 & 1 & 1 & 0 & \cdots & 0 & 0
\end{array}
\right] \\
\;\;\; Y_1 \;\; Y_2 \;\; Y_3 \;\; Y_4 \;\; Y_5 \;\; Y_6 \;\; Y_7 \;\cdots\; Y_{n-1} \; Y_n
\end{array}
$$

There may exist some "short rings" in the generating matrix of the RLT encoded packets. The definition and properties of a "short ring" are given below.

Definition 1. In the generating matrix, if there are two or more columns, of which the values of corresponding two or more rows are all "1", then the elements with value "1" in these rows and corresponding columns constitute a closed ring, which is called "short ring".

If the number of rows satisfying the definition of a "short ring" is two, then the short ring formed by these two rows is called $4 - memberd$ ring. If the number of such rows is three, then the short ring is a $6 - membered$ ring, and so on. Assuming that the number of rows satisfying the definition of a "short ring" is $k'\left(2 \leq k' < k\right)$, the short rings formed by them are $2k' - membered$ ring. Here, the definition of "short ring" is introduced to explain the phenomenon of decoding termination existed in the RLT algorithm, which is shown in Fig. 1.

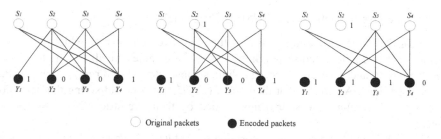

Fig. 1. Decoding termination of RLT code

In Fig. 1, it is seen that $Y_1 = S_2$, $Y_2 = S_2 \oplus S_3 \oplus S_4$, $Y_3 = S_1 \oplus S_2 \oplus S_3$, and $Y_4 = S_1 \oplus S_2 \oplus S_3 \oplus S_4$. According to the RLT decoding rules, we firstly find out the 1-degree encoded packet Y_1, then decode it to obtain S_2. Thus the line connecting Y_1 and S_2 can be removed. Next XOR operations for $\{Y_2, Y_3, Y_4\}$ and S_2 are performed. After that, the lines connecting $\{Y_2, Y_3, Y_4\}$ and S_2 are removed respectively. At this moment, the degree values of the remaining encoded packets Y_2, Y_3, Y_4 are 2, 2, 3. Without any 1-degree encoded packet, the decoding process of RLT is forced to terminate. The corresponding generating matrix of Y_2, Y_3, Y_4 is shown in Fig. 2.

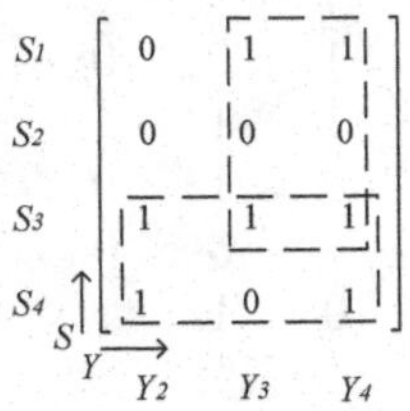

$$
\begin{array}{c}
S_1 \\
S_2 \\
S_3 \\
S_4
\end{array}
\begin{bmatrix}
0 & 1 & 1 \\
0 & 0 & 0 \\
1 & 1 & 1 \\
1 & 0 & 1
\end{bmatrix}
$$

$$
\begin{array}{cccc}
 & Y_2 & Y_3 & Y_4
\end{array}
$$

Fig. 2. An example of short rings

In Fig. 2, the generating matrix contains two $4 - memberd$ short rings. The values of both Y_3 and Y_4 columns are "1" in the first row as well as the third row. Similarly, the values of both Y_2 and Y_4 columns are "1" in the third row as well as the fourth row. Given (n, k, Ω_x) of RLT, k is the number of original packets, n denotes the number of encoded packets. The proportion of column vectors with weight i of the generating matrix $k \times n - order$ G to the total column vectors is Ω_i. Thus, the probability of a column vector with weight i in G can be calculated as

$$
P_i = \Omega_i / \binom{k}{i} \tag{1}
$$

The probability that a column vector with weight j and a column vector with weight i constitute a $4 - memberd$ short ring is given by

$$
P_{r\cdot 4}(i,j) = \Omega_i \Omega_j \binom{k-2}{j-2} / \left(\binom{k}{k-j} \binom{k}{j} \right) \tag{2}
$$

Next we give the definition of a "strict short ring".

Definition 2. In the generating matrix, if there are two columns, of which the values are all "1" in two or more corresponding rows, and the values are all "0" in other rows, then these rows and the corresponding columns constitute a closed ring, which is called "strict short ring". Assuming that there are $k'(2 \leq k' < k)$ rows satisfying the definition of a "strict short ring", the short rings formed by them are strict $(2k') - membered$ rings.

The probability that a column vector with weight $j(j > 2)$ and a column vector with weight 2 constitute a strict $4 - membered$ short ring can be calculated as

$$
P_{strict(r\cdot 4)}(2,j) = \Omega_2 \Omega_j \binom{k-2}{j-2} / \left(\binom{k}{k-j} \binom{k}{2} \right) \tag{3}
$$

Accordingly, the probability that a column vector with weight j and a column vector with weight $m(m < j)$ constitute a strict $2m - membered$ short ring can be calculated as

$$P_{strict(r \cdot 2m)}(m, j) = \Omega_m \Omega_j \binom{k-m}{j-m} / \left(\binom{k}{k-j} \binom{k}{m} \right) \tag{4}$$

Then the probability of a strict $4 - memberd$ short ring in the order-generating matrix is given by

$$P_{strict(r \cdot 4)} = \binom{n}{2} \sum_{j=2}^{\Omega_k} \Omega_2 \Omega_j \binom{k-2}{j-2} / \binom{k}{k-j} \binom{k}{2} \tag{5}$$

Accordingly, the probability of a strict $2m - memberd$ short ring in the generating matrix can be approximately expressed as

$$P_{strict(r \cdot 2m)} = \binom{n}{2} \sum_{m=2}^{\Omega_{k-1}} \sum_{j=3}^{\Omega_k} \Omega_m \Omega_j \binom{k-m}{j-m} / \left(\binom{k}{k-j} \binom{k}{m} \right) \tag{6}$$

3.2   FDR Decoding Algorithm

In Fig. 1, the generating matrix contains two $4 - memberd$ strict short rings. Accordingly, we analyze the original packet set. The set of the original packets corresponding to Y_2 is $\{S_3, S_4\}$. The set of the original packets corresponding to Y_3 is $\{S_1, S_3\}$. The set of the original packets corresponding to Y_4 is $\{S_1, S_3, S_4\}$. The above three sets have the following inclusion relationships: $\{S_3, S_4\} \subsetneq \{S_1, S_3, S_4\}$ and $\{S_1, S_3\} \subsetneq \{S_1, S_3, S_4\}$. Here, $S_1 = Y_2 \oplus Y_4$ can be obtained by XOR operation of Y_2 and Y_4. S_4 can be obtained by XOR operation of Y_3 and Y_4. S_3 can be obtained by XOR operation of Y_3 and S_1. According to the RLT decoding rules, decoding operations of S_2 is $C_{S2} = 1$, while the decoding operations of S_1, S_3, S_4 is infinite, which can be defined as $C_{S1}, C_{S3}, C_{S4} \to \infty$. Therefore, the decoding operations of all original packets are $C_{all} = C_{S1} + C_{S2} + C_{S3} + C_{S4} \to \infty$. But through XOR operations between the decoded packets S_1, S_3, S_4 can be decoded. The decoding operations of S_1, S_2, S_3, S_4 are $C'_{S1} = 1$, $C'_{S2} = 1$, $C'_{S3} = 2$, $C'_{S4} = 1$. The decoding operations of all original packets are $C'_{all} = C'_{S1} + C'_{S2} + C'_{S3} + C'_{S4} = 5 \ll C_{all}$.

A strict short-ring seems to be worthless for the traditional decoding technique. However, if the decoding algorithm is changed, the strict short-ring can play an active role in the decoding process and the contribution of a strict short-ring would not be ignored. What's more, a strict short-ring may even become the key to decoding the remaining packets in the "stop set".

Conclusion 1. If the two columns constituting a short ring have different degrees, and the values of the column with a smaller degree in other rows are all "0", then the two encoded packets corresponding to the short-ring can be XOR operated, and the generated encoded packet, which is called quadratic encoded packet, has a degree equal to the degree-difference of the two packets involving XOR operation. Thus, the degrees of packets are filtered and reduced by FDR decoding. If the degree-difference is 1, the degree of quadratic encoded packets is 1 and an original packet is recovered.

In RLT, a receiving node starts a decoding process after receiving a certain number of encoded packets. FDR eliminates the waiting time of the RLT algorithm, and thus achieves fast decoding. After encoding, the 1-degree encoded packets are sent first, and the FDR decoder starts immediately the decoding process upon receiving a packet no matter whether the degree value of the encoded packet is 1 or not. As in Fig. 1, after receiving two encoded packets, Y_4 and Y_3, the receiver compares the original packet ID sets. If one set is another set's subset, the receiver also starts the decoding process and decodes the two encoded packets. Therefore, we obtain the following conclusion.

Conclusion 2. When an FDR receiver receives encoded packets, it can start the decoding process as long as there exists a true inclusion relationship between the two sets of original packets. It does not have to wait for the encoded packet with 1-degree, which reduces the decoding time to some extent.

Based on the above two conclusions, this paper proposes a filtering dimension reduction decoding algorithm (FDR), and introduces the design and decoding process of the FDR decoder. Firstly, we define some parameters used in the FDR decoding algorithm.

Definition 3. The encoder takes k original packets $S : S = \{S_1, S_2, \ldots, S_k\}$ and generates n encoded packets $Y: Y = \{Y_1, Y_2, \ldots, Y_i \ldots, Y_n\}$. k original packets are encoded into n encoded packets Y. The degree of encoded packet Y_i is defined as $d(Y_i)$. The FDR algorithm divides the encoded packets into two types, the encoded packets generated by the sender and the quadratic packets generated by XOR operations between encoded packets. Quadratic packets is defined as $Y_{sec}.T$ represents the set of original packets that generate an encoded packet.

According to the degree of encoded packets, we adopt the idea of layering to design the decoder. There are five degree values of the encoded packets, which are $d = 1$, $d = 2$, $d = 3$, $d = 4$, $d = k$. Respectively, the decoder is designed into five layers, l_1, l_2, l_3, l_4, l_k which is illustrated in Fig. 3.

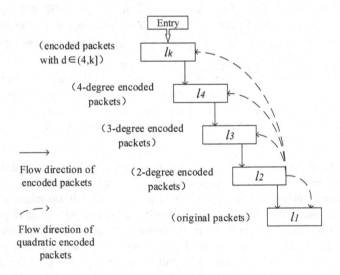

Fig. 3. Design of decoder

Each layer of the decoder stores encoded packets with a degree value equal to the value of the layer. It should be noted that the encoded packets at the layer include not only the encoded packets from the senders, but also the quadratic encoded packets generated by XOR operation from the decoder of the receiving node. For example, l_2 stores all 2-degree encoded packets. One packet in l_2 may be the 2-degree encoded packets received from the sender, or a 2-degree quadratic packet generated by the XOR operation at a higher layer. In addition, it should be noted that l_k stores all encoded packets with d-degree value, where $d \in (4, k]$. The encoded packets are stored in the form of $key - value$. key represents the set T, the IDs of input packets, and $value$ corresponds to the encoded packet. For example, $Y_i = S_1 \oplus S_2 \oplus S_3$, and the ID of S_1, S_2, S_3 are known to be $\{0, 1, 2\} - Y_i$. Therefore, the $key - value$ stored is as $\{0, 1, 2\} - Y_i$. The encoded packets go downstairs through the decoder. Once it satisfies the XOR condition with a certain packet at one of the layers, or in other words, once all the original packets that participate in the lower-degree encoded packet are also involved in the higher-degree encoded packet, they do XOR operations. In this way, the encoded packet with a higher degree value is updated to the quadratic packet, and its degree value is reduced. By filtering high-degree encoded packets and reducing their degree values, FDR speeds up the decoding process to a certain extent. It is not difficult to imagine that the encoded packets with higher or lower degree values have a higher probability to do XOR operations with other encoded packets. Theoretically, it is impossible for the key value of each layer to have a true inclusion relationship with one key value at the lower layer except l_1. The FDR decoder is in the decoding state from the receipt of the first encoded packet until the l_1 layer contains all the original packets.

4 Numerical Results

In this section, we evaluate the performance of the FDR decoding algorithm through numerical results. In order to eliminate the impact of packet loss and packet collision on the decoding success probability as much as possible, we focus on single-hop communication between a source node and a destination node. Through NS3 simulations and MATLAB experiments, we compare the FDR algorithm and the RLT algorithm in terms of the successful decoding probability, and demonstrate the stability of the FDR algorithm.

4.1 Simulation Settings and Parameters

In this section, we evaluate the performance of the FDR decoding algorithm through simulation experiments. All simulations are performed using Network Simulator 3, and a two-dimensional regular hexagonal topology of seven nodes is used, as shown in Fig. 4.

In Fig. 4, six nodes are located at the vertex of hexagonal network topology as source nodes. The remaining one is located at the center of the network as a sink node. The direction of data flow is from a source node to the sink node. The communication between a source node and the sink node is single-hop and the transmission range is r. In order to eliminate the packet collision, we control the six source nodes to send packets to the sink node at different time by setting different packet interval.

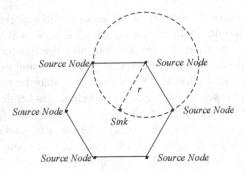

Fig. 4. Hexagonal network topology

The parameters used in the simulation experiment have a big impact on the experimental results. The values of parameters such as "simulation time, bandwidth, transmission power and receiving power" are given in Table 1. The data generated at the application layer by a source node is divided into several blocks, each block composed of about k data packets (here $k = 60$). Each data packet consists of three parts: head fields, load and FCS check.

Table 1. Experimental parameters.

Parameters	Value
Simulation time/s	6000
Size of data block/B	2975–8955
Length of load/B	200
Bandwidth/kbps	10
Route protocol	LB-AGR
MAC protocol	RCHF
Transmitting power/W	2
Receiving power/W	0.75
Range/m	1500

4.2 Simulation Results

The successful decoding probability is defined in formula (7), where $N_{total-trans}$ represents the total number of times that a source node sends data packets to the sink node, and $N_{retrans}$ denotes the number of times that the sink node restores the original data packets successfully. The difference between $N_{total-trans}$ and $N_{retrans}$ is $N_{one-time-succ}$, which represents the number of times that the sink node decodes successfully at the first time. The successful decoding probability of one single hop is defined as $N_{one-time-succ}$ divided by $N_{total-trans}$.

$$P_{Dec-succ-hop} = \frac{N_{Total-trans} - N_{retrans}}{N_{Total-trans}} = \frac{N_{one-time-succ}}{N_{Total-trans}} \qquad (7)$$

The simulation results are shown in Fig. 5. The horizontal axis of Fig. 5 represents the number of encoded packets sent out by a source node each time, and the vertical axis represents the successful decoding probability of one transmission. In the experiment, 4×4 sets of experimental data using the FDR algorithm with different k values are also counted in $N_{total-trans}$ and $N_{retrans}$, as shown in Fig. 6(a), (b), (c), and (d). Figure 5 shows the successful decoding probability of one transmission with the FDR algorithm and the RLT algorithm, respectively.

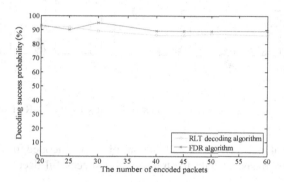

Fig. 5. Comparison in terms of the successful decoding probability

It can be seen that the successful decoding probability with the FDR algorithm is generally higher than that with the RLT algorithm. When the number of encoded packets is small, such as n = 20, the successful decoding probability with the two decoding algorithms is almost equal, e.g., RLT reaches 92% and FDR can reach 93%. The mutation occurs at n = 25, where the successful decoding probability with FDR is 90%, slightly lower than that with RLT, which is 92%. When n = 30, the performance of the FDR algorithm is significantly better than that of RLT, i.e., the former is 95% and the latter 89%. When the number of encoded packets exceeds 40, the successful decoding probability with the RLT algorithm is basically 86%, while that with the FDR algorithm is about 89%. Generally speaking, the performance of the FDR algorithm is better than that of the RLT algorithm.

Figure 6(a) shows four groups of experimental data when the number of original packets k is 25 and the number of encoded packets n is 32. Take group 3 experiment as an example. The total number of times that a source node sends data packets to the sink node is 143, but only 10 of them are the number of times with secondary successful decoding.

Figure 6(b) shows four groups of experimental data when the number of original packets is 30 and the number of encoded packets is 38. Figure 6(c) shows four groups of experimental data when the number of original packets is 35 and the number of encoded packets is 44. Figure 6(d) shows four groups of experimental data when the

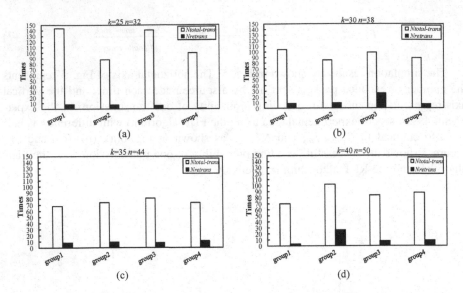

Fig. 6. $N_{total-trans}$ and $N_{retrans}$ under different k by the FDR algorithm

number of original packets is 40 and the number of encoded packets is 50. The statistical data are consistent with the trend of the successful decoding probability in Fig. 5.

5 Conclusions

In this paper, we proposed a filtering dimension reduction (FDR) decoding algorithm for underwater acoustic networks (UANs), which is more suitable for reliable transmission of underwater communication. The FDR algorithm executes XOR operations on the encoded packets to reduce the dimensions of the encoded packets or directly generate some 1-degree packets. As a result, the FDR algorithm can increase the number of 1-degree encoded packets and reduce the decoding complexity. Moreover, the FDR algorithm can eliminate the waiting time for a traditional decoding algorithm to receive the 1-degree packets, and achieve fast decoding. The simulation results show that the successful decoding probability with the FDR algorithms is higher than that with the FDR algorithm.

Acknowledgment. This work is supported by the National Natural Science Foundation of China (Grant No. 61962052), the IoT Innovation Team Foundation of Qinghai Office of Science and Technology, the Key Lab of IoT of Qinghai, the Hebei IoT Monitoring Center (No. 3142016020) and Key Projects of Hebei Province (Grant No. 19270318D).

References

1. Hao, K., Jin, Z.G., Shen, H.F.: An efficient and reliable geographic routing protocol based on partial network coding for underwater sensor networks. Sensors **15**(6), 12720–12735 (2015)
2. Du, X.J., Huang, K.J., Lan, S.L., Feng, Z.X., Liu, F.: LB-AGR: level-based adaptive geo-routing for underwater sensor network. J. China Univ. Posts Telecommun. **21**(1), 54–59 (2014)
3. Wang, Y., Li, Q., Zhang, G.P., Liang, G.L., Ma, S.L.: Phase-difference ambiguity resolution for USBL underwater acoustic positioning systems. Acta Electron. Sin. **45**(11), 2787–2794 (2017)
4. Du, X.J., Peng, C.Y., Liu, X.X.: Hierarchical code assignment algorithm and state-based CDMA protocol for UWSN. China Commun. **12**(3), 50–61 (2015)
5. Jiang, P., Feng, Y., Wu, F.: Fruit fly inspired underwater sensor network deployment algorithn. Acta Electron. Sin. **45**(6), 1403–1407 (2017)
6. Zhang, X., Chang, Y., Song, K., Li, C.G., Yang, L.X.: A novel parameter estimation algorithm for underwater acoustic channels. Acta Electron. Sin. **47**(2), 509–512 (2019)
7. Liu, K.N., Zhao, Z.H., Wang, Y.: AdaCode: adaptive codes in IEEE 802.11n wireless long-distance links. Acta Electron. Sin. **46**(12), 2942–2949 (2018)
8. Ma, H.Y., Fan, X.K., Wang, S.M., Dong, Y.M.: Secure hierarchical hybrid encryption communication protocol based on quantum teleportation for underwater sensor networks. J. Softw. **25**(1), 39–46 (2014)
9. Zhu, J., Liu, J., Zhao, H., Xu, Y.: Research on reliable protocol based on randon-walk model in UWSN. Chin. J. Comput. **39**(5), 1007–1020 (2016)
10. Du, X., Li, K., Liu, X.: RLT code based handshake-free reliable MAC protocol for underwater sensor networks. J. Sens. **15**, 12720–12735 (2016)
11. Guo, Z., Xie, P., Cui, J.H., Wang, B.: On applying network coding to underwater sensor networks. In: Proceedings of the 1st ACM International Workshop on Underwater Networks, Los Angeles, CA, USA, p. 109 (2006)
12. Liu, B., Garcin, F., Ren, F.: A study of forward error correction schemes for reliable transport in underwater sensor networks. In: Proceedings of IEEE Communications Society Conference on Sensor, Mesh and Ad Hoc Communications and Networks, pp. 197–205 (2008)
13. Xie, P., Zhou, Z., Peng, Z., Cui, J.H., Shi, Z.: SDRT: a reliable data transport protocol for underwater sensor networks. Ad Hoc Netw. **8**(7), 708–722 (2010)
14. Liu, B., Chen, H., Lei, X., Ren, F., Sezaki, K.: Internode distance-based redundancy reliable transport in underwater sensor networks. EURASIP J. Wirel. Commun. Netw. **2010**, 1–16 (2010)
15. Mo, H., Peng, Z., Zhou, Z., Zuba, M.: Coding based multi-hop coordinated reliable data transfer for underwater acoustic networks: design, implementation and tests. In: Globecom Workshops (2013)

A Homology Based Coverage Optimization Algorithm for Wireless Sensor Networks

Lei Xiang[1], Feng Yan[1(✉)], Yaping Zhu[1], Weiwei Xia[1], Fei Shen[2],
Song Xing[3], Yi Wu[4], and Lianfeng Shen[1]

[1] National Mobile Communications Research Laboratory,
Southeast University, Nanjing, China
{220160868, feng.yan, xyzzyp, wwxia, lfshen}@seu.edu.cn
[2] Shanghai Institute of Microsystem and Information Technology,
Chinese Academy of Sciences, Shanghai, China
fei.shen@wico.sh
[3] Department of Information Systems, California State University,
Los Angeles, CA 90032, USA
sxing@exchange.calstatela.edu
[4] Key Laboratory of OptoElectronic Science and Technology for Medicine
of Ministry of Education, Fujian Provincial Key Laboratory of Photonics
Technology, Fujian Normal University, Fuzhou, China
wuyi@fjnu.edu.cn

Abstract. Simplicial complex provides a precise and tractable representation of the topology of wireless sensor networks. In this paper, a coverage optimization algorithm based on Rips complex is given for the purpose of energy conservation of wireless sensor networks. Considering an area of interest which is covered by sensor nodes completely and even superfluously, our algorithm is performed to turn off redundant sensor nodes effectively in the network while maintaining the coverage consistently. Simulation results show that this distributed algorithm can remove more than 70% internal sensor nodes, and complexity analysis for our algorithm is given.

Keywords: Coverage optimization · Homology · Wireless sensor networks

1 Introduction

Coverage of target fields provides a metric of quality of service of wireless sensor networks (WSNs). Sensor nodes in WSNs are capable of collecting, storing and processing environmental information, and communicating with neighboring nodes. So

---

This work is supported in part by the National Natural Science Foundation of China (No. 61601122, 61871370 and U1805262), the Open Project of Key Laboratory of Wireless Sensor Network & Communication, Shanghai Institute of Microsystem and Information Technology, Chinese Academy of Sciences (No. 20190907), the Fundamental Research Funds for the Central Universities (No. 2242019K40188), the Natural Science Foundation of Shanghai, China under grant No. 18ZR1437500, the Hundred Talent Program of Chinese Academy of Sciences under grant No. Y86BRA1001.

J. Zheng et al. (Eds.): ADHOCNETS 2019, LNICST 306, pp. 288–301, 2019.
https://doi.org/10.1007/978-3-030-37262-0_24

sensor nodes are responsible for monitoring the area of interest. However, these nodes are supported by limited energy. Power conservation is focused on to prolong the lifetime of WSNs. The aim of coverage optimization in this paper is to turn off redundant sensor nodes as many as possible to save energy while maintaining the coverage of a network.

There are a number of researches concerning the coverage problem of WSNs [1]. One type of approaches is based on location of sensor nodes, in which some computational geometry tools are used, such as Voronoi diagrams or Delaunay triangulation [2–4]. Such location-based approaches require too much knowledge of the target field and the pattern of deployment of sensor nodes. Moreover, they suffer from the weakness that they can be too expensive to compute in real-time. Distance-based approaches are another kind of solutions to the coverage issues of WSNs [5, 6]. Location of sensor nodes may not be the necessity to the algorithms of this kind. Instead, they require to measure the distance between sensor nodes and obtain the precise geometry of target field, which is gained at high expense in practice. The third type of approaches is based on connectivity information between nodes in WSNs. By means of algebraic tools, homology theory more specifically, the topology of network is prone to building and analyzing [7]. Structure of the network is modeled by Rips complex in [8] to propose a sufficient coverage criterion. However, the work in [7] and [8] does not solve the problem about how to place sensor nodes to maximize the coverage. The distributed version of the ideas proposed in [7] and [8] is firstly implemented in [9]. By means of combinatorial Laplacians, coverage holes are localized by computing the sparse generator of the first homologous class and redundancies in the sensor network are reduced by finding a sparse cover of the region. A centralized reduction algorithm is proposed in [10] to remove superfluous vertexes to make simplicial complex as planar as possible while maintaining connectivity and coverage of a network. But the computation complexity analyzed of it is explosive as the dimension of simplicial complex increases. Extending this idea further, two homology based algorithms, a simulated annealing one and a robust one, are introduced in [11] for the sake of power conservation, but they are still accomplished at high expenses when constructing the complex and performing these algorithms. Simple-connectedness graph and fundamental group perservering transformation are posed in [12] to do the skeleton extraction of network in distributed fashion. Research in [13] develops this approach to propose a homology preserving transformation to delete redundant vertexes and edges to make simplicial complex more planar. According to a strong collapse approach, a reduction algorithm for abstract simplicial complex is proposed in [14] to simplifying the topology of network.

This paper presents a coverage optimization algorithm for WSNs in a 2-dimensional plane through reduction of simplicial complex in a distributed way with low complexity. We firstly construct the simplicial complex, specifically Rips complex [7], corresponding to the connectivity graph of network; then weight of all vertexes are computed after the definition of weight information; lastly, those superfluous vertexes and edges are identified and removed recurrently based on our complex expansion algorithm to make the Rips complex as planar as possible. Meanwhile, the first two homology of the complex is maintained during this process. Simulation results imply an excellent performance on the coverage optimization of the network.

The rest of the paper is organized as follows. Section 2 gives necessary assumptions of sensor nodes and network, together with some knowledge of mathematical basis; detailed description of our coverage optimization algorithm is presented in Sect. 3; then simulation results and discussion are given in Sect. 4 and conclusion is in Sect. 5 of this paper.

2 Models and Preliminaries

2.1 Network Models and Assumptions

In this connectivity-based algorithm, sensor nodes are capable to sense their neighborhood within a circle of radius R_s and communicate with neighbors within a circle of radius R_c for the construction of Rips complexes, where all the vertexes are modeled from sensor nodes in the WSN. Different from directional sensor networks, e.g. in [15], sensors in this paper are assumed to be omni-directional, that is they sense in all directions. As for the boundary of target field, it is covered by fence nodes and its coverage is required to be consistent, which implies that fence nodes should be retained. All the other sensor nodes in the network are internal ones, whose responsibility is keeping the inner area of network covered.

2.2 Mathematical Preliminaries

Simplicial complexes give a representation of higher order relations than graphs with respect to the topology of WSNs. Given a set of points V, a k-simplex $(k \in Z)$ is an unordered k-tuples $[v_0, v_1, \ldots, v_k]$ where $v_i \in V$ and $v_i \neq v_j$ for all $0 \leq i \neq j \leq k$. For example, a 0-simplex is a vertex, a 1-simplex is an edge, a 2-simplex is a triangle with its interior included, and a 3-simplex is a solid tetrahedron. The faces of a k-simplex include all the $(k\text{-}1)$-simplexes in form of unordered subset $[v_0, v_{i-1}, v_{i+1}, \ldots, v_k]$ for $0 \leq i \leq k$. So there are $k + 1$ faces in a k-simplex. An abstract simplicial complex is a finite collection of simplexes that is closed with regard to inclusion of faces of all the simplexes in it, and its dimension is the highest dimension of all the simplexes in it. For example, a geometric realization of abstract simplicial complex is depicted in Fig. 1, which consists of one 2-simplex and four 1-simplexes.

Fig. 1. An example of abstract simplicial complex

In this paper, Rips complex is adopted to represent the topology of networks. Definition of Rips complex is presented below. The construction of the Rips complex is not difficult to understand: a k-simplex $[v_0, v_1, \ldots, v_k]$ is included in $\mathcal{R}_\in(S)$ when the Euclidean distance between every two vertexes v_l and v_m is no longer than the fixed radius $\in$, that is $\| v_l - v_m \| \leq \in$ for all $0 \leq l \neq m \leq k$.

Definition 1 (Rips Complex). *Given a finite set of points S in $\mathbb{R}^n$ and a fixed radius $\in$, the Rips complex of S, $\mathcal{R}_\in(S)$, is the abstract simplicial complex whose k-simplexes correspond to unordered $(k + 1)$-tuples of points in S that are pairwise within Euclidean distance $\in$ of each other.*

Now, the theoretical basis of simplicial homology is to be presented. The r-chain group $C_r(K)$ of a simplicial complex K is a free Abelian group generated by the oriented r-simplexes of K. Let $\sigma_r(p_0, \ldots, p_r)(r > 0)$ be an oriented r-simplex. The boundary $\partial_r \sigma_r$ of σ_r is an $(r\text{-}1)$-chain defined by $\partial_r \sigma_r \equiv \sum_0^r (-1)^r (p_0 p_1 \ldots \hat{p_i} \ldots p_r)$, where $\hat{p_i}$ means point p_l is omitted. If $c \in C_r(K)$ satisfies $\partial_r c = 0$, c is called a r-cycle. The set of r-cycle $Z_r(K)$ is a subgroup of $C_r(K)$ and is called the r-cycle group. If there exists an element $d \in C_{r+1}(K)$ such that $c = \partial_{r+1} d$ then c is called a r-boundary of d. The set of r-boundaries $B_r(K)$ is a subgroup of $C_r(K)$ and is called the r-boundaries group. The rth homology group $H_r(K), 0 \leq r \leq n$, associated with K is defined by $H_r(K) \equiv Z_r(K)/B_r(K)$. Homology is topological invariants. According to the knowledge of homology group, two r-cycles z and z' are in one homology class if and only if $z - z' \in B_r(K)$, in which case z is said to be homologous to z'. More detailed information may turn to [16].

3 Algorithm Descriptions

3.1 Model Construction and Weight Computation

The neighboring set of any vertex v_i in the Rips complex is denoted by $N(v_i)$ in this paper. The definition of the neighboring set of any k-simplex is given as follow.

Definition 2 (Neighboring Set of k-simplex). *For a certain k-simplex $s_k = [v_{k0}, v_{k1}, \ldots, v_{kk}]$, the neighboring set of s_k $N(s_k)$ is the intersection of neighboring sets of all vertexes in s_k, that is, $N(s_k) = \bigcap_{i=0}^{k} N(v_{ki})$.*

The concept of weight is introduced here to serve as a measure of proximity redundancy of vertexes. The weight w_v of an internal vertex v reflects the density of neighbors in the surrounding area. There are two kinds of internal vertexes: redundant and crucial vertexes. The former are referred to as ones whose all the 2-simplexes have at least one neighbor individually, which implies that they are vertexes of higher dimension simplexes than 2-simplex and thus are candidates of redundant vertexes. While the latter are referred to as ones at least one of whose 2-simplexes has no neighbor. In addition, fence vertexes are required to keep active all the time as mentioned before. All these idea is reflected in the weight information computed according to algorithm 1 given below. A simple example of redundant vertex is any one of the vertexes of a tetrahedron, because any vertex is superfluous to the other three ones in the plain.

Because the attention of this paper is focused on planar plane, the dimension of simplicial complex here is 2, which reduces the complexity of constructing Rips complex corresponding to the network. For the convenience of representation, $T(v)$ is used to denote the set of all 2-simplexes of which vertex v is a part. For any 2-simplex $t \in T(v)$, $n(t)$ denotes the neighboring set of t. Then the weight computation of vertexes is given as follow:

Algorithm 1. Weight Computation

Begin

1:    **for** any fence vertex v
2:        $w_v = 0$
3:    **end for**
4:    **for** any internal vertex v
5:        **if** $\exists t \in T(v)$, $n(t)$ is empty **then**
6:            $w_v = 0$
7:        **else**
8:            $w_v = 2$
9:        **end if**
10:   **end for**

End

3.2   Complex Expansion

Homological invariance is inspected in some previous papers from the metric of Betti numbers [17]. However, the cost of computing Betti numbers is expensive. Complex expansion algorithm given here reduces the simplicial complex corresponding to the WSN while maintaining the homology in much lower complexity.

There is no 1-dimensional or 2-dimensional coverage holes in the neighboring graph of an internal redundant vertex or edge. The aim of complex expansion algorithm is to identify them. Take an internal vertex v as an example. For two different vertex v_i and v_j in the neighboring set $N(v)$, if there is at least one path between them, they are connected to each other. If any two vertexes in the neighboring set are connected, the neighboring graph is connected accordingly. No 1-dimensional coverage holes means there is only one connected component in the neighboring graph, that is, the neighboring graph is connected. While no 2-dimensional coverage holes in the neighboring graph implies all the area of target field is within the union of covering range of all sensor nodes. It is the same case with internal redundant edges.

Obviously, there is no 1-dimensional and 2-dimensional coverage hole in the interior of a 2-simplex. In addition, ideally reduced Rips complex should remain as planar as possible, which is the source of our idea. Considering a 2-simplex t in $N(v)$ as the origin of complex expansion, denoted by R_{cov}. According to the knowledge given above, another 2-simplex t_1 in $N(v)$ is able to bond with R_{cov} exactly when the intersection of them is a 1-simplex, namely a common edge of them. As shown in Fig. 2, the 2-simplex t, that is R_{cov}, and t_1 form a new sub Rips complex R_{cov1} which is in the same homologous class with R_{cov} because the difference between the boundaries of them is the boundary of t_1. Therefore, the expansion from R_{cov} to R_{cov1} maintains the homology. Then update R_{cov} with R_{cov1} and continue to search for 2-simplex in $N(v)$ that is able to bond with R_{cov} exactly. Repeat the above steps until no more 2-simplex in $N(v)$ can join R_{cov}. Now, if all the vertexes in R_{cov} are the same to $N(v)$, the vertex v is proved as superfluous and can be swept off. All internal vertexes and edges are subjected to the process of complex expansion above independently. If a vertex or an edge, along with its some neighbors, is determined concurrently to be redundant, then the one with the least id among them has the priority to be removed. Thus, no two internal neighboring vertexes or edges will be removed simultaneously. All the neighbors of the removed vertex or edge will eliminate it from their neighboring sets respectively and continue to perform the next round decision.

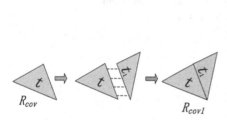

Fig. 2. Bonding of two 2-simplexes

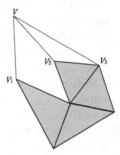

Fig. 3. Example of illegitimate vertex in complex expansion

During the process of complex expansion, the 2-simplex t_1 sharing a common edge e_{com} with any 2-simplex in R_{cov} can join it. Therefore, search of t_1 is actually the search of $N(e_{com})$ in the remaining vertexes of $N(v)$. That is, the complex expansion is proceeded by adding legitimate vertexes to R_{cov} formed by the subset of neighboring set $N(v)$. A legitimate vertex v' is required to meet the following two conditions: (1) v' has at least two neighbors in R_{cov}; (2) these neighbors of v' are one-hop connected. As shown in Fig. 3, vertex v cannot join R_{cov} because the neighbors of it in R_{cov}, v_1, v_2 and v_3, fail to satisfy pairwise one-hop connectivity, which would cause the difference between the boundaries of R'_{cov} and the original R_{cov} is not a boundary. An example of complex expansion for a vertex is presented in Fig. 4. Vertex 1 in Fig. 4(a) is the candidate to investigate, and the sub-complex incident to its neighboring graph is shown. Beginning by the 2-simplex in (b), the process of expansion is carried out with the addition of legitimate vertexes to the current sub-complex within neighboring set of vertex 1, as shown in (c) and (d). This expansion is successful since the set of vertexes in final sub-complex in (d) is exactly the neighboring set of vertex 1 and thus it is proved to be redundant. Details of complex expansion are presented in algorithm 2.

Algorithm 2. Complex Expansion

Begin

1:    construct Rips sub-complex in active neighbors set *Neighb*

2:    **for** every 2-simplex *tri* **do**

3:        get the vertexes set *vert_set* of *tri* and set *rest_vert* of rest vertexes in *Neighb*

4:        **while** *rest_vert* is not empty **do**

5:            **for** every vertex *v* in *rest_vert* **do**

6:                **if** vertex *v* is legitimate **then**

7:                    add *v* to *vert_set* and update the *vert_set*

8:                **end if**

9:            **end for**

10:           remove common vertexes shared by *rest_vert* and *vert_set* from *rest_vert*

11:           **if** *rest_vert* is not changed after this removal **then**

12:               ex_flag = 1

13:               break

14:           **end if**

15:       **end while**

16:       **if** *ex_flag* == 1 **then**

17:           continue

18:       **end if**

19:       **if** *rest_vert* is empty **then**

20:           c_flag = 1;

21:           return;

22:       **end if**

23:   **end for**

End

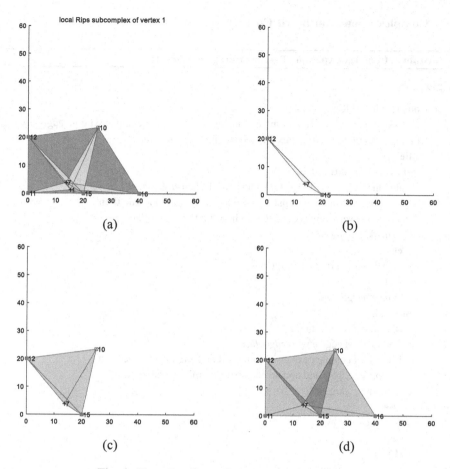

Fig. 4. Example of complex expansion for vertex 1

3.3   Complex Expansion Based Coverage Optimization

Algorithm 3. Complex Expansion Based Coverage Optimization

Begin

1:    Construct initial Rips complex
2:    Get 1-skeleton of initial Rips complex, flag every edge and get the maximum *edge_flag*
3:    Compute weight of every vertex and the maximum *weight_max*
4:    **while** *ve_flag* == 0 **do**
5:       **while** *weight_max* > 0 **do**
6:          find the vertex *p* with least ID whose wight is *weight_max*
7:          **if** result of complex expansion operated on *Neighb_p* is true **then**
8:             remove vertex *p* and update weight of vertexes in *Neighb_p*
9:             mark *ve_flag* as 1
10:          **else**
11:             weight of vertex *p* is set to 0
12:          **end if**
13:          update *weight_max*
14:       **end while**
15:       **while** *edge_flag* > 0 **do**
16:          find the first edge *e* with *edge_flag*
17:          **if** result of complex expansion operated on *Neighb_e* is true **then**
18:             remove edge *e* and update neighbor sets of two endpoints of *e*
19:             mark *ve_flag* as 1
20:          **else**
21:             flag edge *e* by 0
22:          **end if**
23:       **end while**
24:       **if** *ve_flag* == 1 **then**
25:          update the weights of those vertexes with weight 0
26:          update the flags of those edges with flag 0 to 1
27:          *ve_flag* = 0
28:       **end if**
29:    **end while**

End

Based on the complex expansion algorithm described above, coverage optimization algorithm proposed here delete redundant vertexes and edges recurrently to make the Rips complex as planar as possible. Before every round of identification, weight information is updated. Then the determination for every candidate vertex and edge is performed in distributed way. Once a vertex or an edge is recognized as redundant, it will be removed with its simplexes. And the neighboring set of its neighbors are required to update. While if it is recognized as critical, it will not be identified in the current round and will remain critical in the following rounds till the end of the algorithm. At the end of every round, if there are some vertexes or edges deleted, the algorithm will proceed to next round; otherwise, it means there is no more redundancy in the complex and the algorithm comes to an end. The whole reduction algorithm for simplicial complex is given in algorithm 3 above.

4 Simulation and Performance Analysis

4.1 Simulation Discussion

The results of our algorithm are simulated with MATLAB R2017b. We deploy the set of vertexes randomly using Poisson point process in the given area. It can be seen in Fig. 5 that one implementation of Complex Expansion algorithm on the Rips complex with parameter $\in = 30$ is presented within a square of side length $a = 60$. Internal vertexes are distributed randomly within the area with their average number μ subject to Poisson point process, while fence vertexes are fixed along the boundary, with covering radius $r = 15$ of them all, as shown in Fig. 5(a). Corresponding initial Rips complex is shown in Fig. 5(b). Internal vertexes are starred while fence vertexes are squared and starred.

Vertex 14 in Fig. 5(b) is squared indicating that it is crucial according to weight computation, and it remains crucial during the whole process of our algorithm. Now, vertex deletion and edge deletion of first round are performed. From Fig. 5(c) and (d), it is not difficult to find vertex 4, 8 and 16 are removed and so is the case with 64 edges. The remaining vertexes are marked with red square to imply that they are crucial in this round. So it is necessary to update the weight information for the continuation of our algorithm. What follows is similar to the first round. After the second round, 6 vertexes and their simplexes are deleted shown in Fig. 5(e). Then after 5 rounds of execution, the Rips complex is reduced as much as possible and remains stable. As shown in Fig. 5(f) and (g), the snapshots after round 4 and round 6 are chosen to present the redundancy of the current Rips complex. Due to the deletion of 3 internal vertexes and their simplexes, the Rips complex after 4 rounds is more planar with 6 internal vertexes. While another 2 rounds of iteration takes more 2 redundant internal vertexes away and the Rips complex in Fig. 5(g) is the most planar one that our algorithm are able to give. It is obvious that only 4 internal vertexes exist in the final reduced Rips complex and all of them are squared indicating that they are essential for the coverage of internal area, which is proved in the corresponding covering discs presented in Fig. 5(h). The ratio of removed internal vertexes to all the internal vertexes is 77.78% this time, which is excellent.

With a series of parameters chosen to ensure coverage, the mean values of 1000 simulation results in different vertex density are collected and the corresponding ratios of removed internal vertexes to all internal vertexes after the execution of our algorithm and Reduction Algorithm in [10] respectively are shown in Fig. 6 and runtime of them is shown in Fig. 7. From Fig. 6, the ratio increases with the increase of vertex density, which is reflected by average number μ of internal vertexes. Furthermore, the performance of Complex Expansion Algorithm is closer to that of Reduction Algorithm when

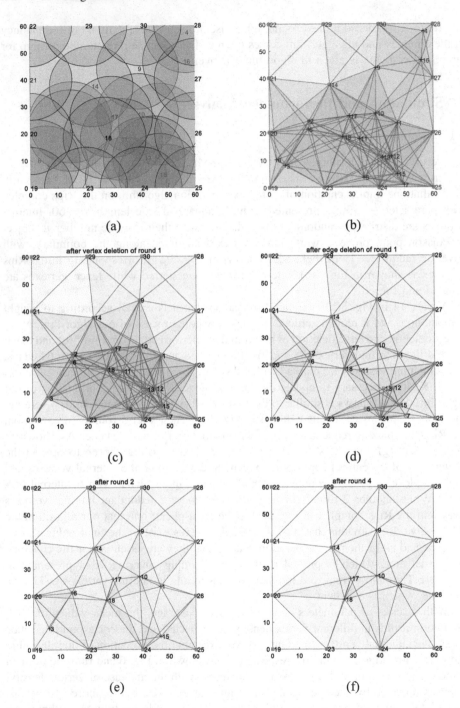

Fig. 5. Process of complex expansion based coverage optimization algorithm. (a) Initial covering discs. (b) Initial Rips complex. (c) After vertex deletion of round 1. (d) After edge deletion of round 1. (e)–(g) Reduced Rips complex after round 2, 4, 6. (h) Final covering discs

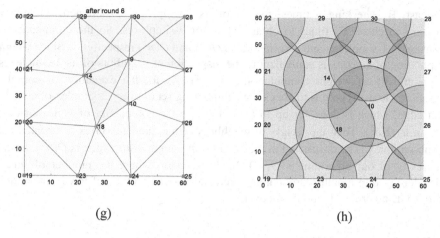

(g)   (h)

Fig. 5. (*continued*)

there are more and more internal vertexes in the initial Rips complex. For example, when μ is chosen as 16, ratio of removed internal vertexes to all internal vertexes for RA and CE algorithms is 73.80% and 70.55% respectively; while that of them is 80.60% and 80.00% respectively when μ is 26.

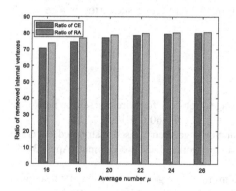

Fig. 6. Ratio of removed internal vertexes to all internal vertexes of algorithm CE and RA

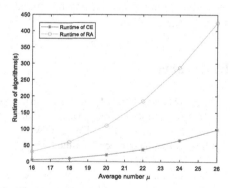

Fig. 7. Runtime of algorithm CE and RA

4.2 Complexity Analysis

As shown in Fig. 7, the computational complexity between them is remarkable. Complexity of Reduction Algorithm in [10] increases exponentially with the number of vertexes of the Rips complex, which has been analyzed in detail. Let n denote the average number of neighbors of individual vertexes in the Rips complex in CE algorithm. As for construction of 1-simplexes and 2-simplexes, each vertex needs to obtain its neighboring set and its neighbors' sets, which is achieved by two rounds of broadcast. By checking n times, the set of its 1-simplexes is obtained; while it is necessary to check C_n^2 times to obtain its set of 2-simplexes. So the complexity of constructing 1-simplexes and 2-simplexes is $O(n)$ and $O(n^2)$ respectively. Since weight computation of a vertex is equivalent to the inspection of neighbors of its 2-simplexes, the complexity of weight computation is $O(n^2)$. As for the execution of complex expansion, the worst case is to check the neighboring set of every 2-simplex of a vertex or an edge, which is done for up to nC_n^2 times, so the complexity of vertex or edge deletion is $O(n^3)$. Then the weight of neighbors of a redundant vertex is updated and the sub-complex is reconstructed in the neighboring graph of it, which is $O(n^2)$. So the complexity of our algorithm is $O(n^3)$. In the scenario where the number of sensor nodes deployed to monitor target area is tremendous, the runtime of RA is unbearable and our CE algorithm is more practical.

5 Conclusion and Future

In this paper, a homology based coverage optimization algorithm is proposed to simplify the wireless sensor network when it gives superfluous coverage to the target field. Different from most existing homological approaches, our algorithm performs redundant sensor nodes deletion from the perspective of connectivity of the neighboring graph of internal sensor nodes. Moreover, the complexity of this algorithm is much lower. Yet, our algorithm is constrained in full coverage situation and suitable for two-dimensional plane. Applying this algorithm to k-coverage scenarios is a research direction in the future.

References

1. Elhabyan, R., Shi, W., St-Hilaire, M.: Coverage protocols for wireless sensor networks: review and future directions. J. Commun. Netw. **21**(1), 45–60 (2019)
2. Ma, H.C., Sahoo, P.K., Chen, Y.W.: Computational geometry based distributed coverage hole detection protocol for the wireless sensor networks. J. Netw. Comput. Appl. **34**(5), 1743–1756 (2011)
3. Soundarya, A., Santhi, V.: An efficient algorithm for coverage hole detection and healing in wireless sensor networks. In: Proceedings of the 1st International Conference on Electronics, Materials Engineering and Nano-Technology, pp. 1–5. IEEE, Kolkata (2017)
4. Rachid, B., Amar, L.: Boundary and holes recognition in wireless sensor networks. J. Innovation Digital Ecosyst. **3**(1), 1–14 (2016)
5. Novella, B., Tiziana, C., Tom, F.L.P., Simone, S.: Autonomous deployment of heterogeneous mobile sensors. IEEE Trans. Mobile Comput. **10**(6), 753–766 (2011)
6. Zhang, Y., Zhang, X., Fu, W., Wang, Z., Liu, H.: HDRE: coverage hole detection with residual energy in wireless sensor networks. J. Commun. Netw. **16**(5), 493–501 (2016)
7. Ghrist, R., Muhammad, A.: Coverage and hole-detection in sensor networks via homology. In: Proceedings of the 4th International Conference on Information Processing in Sensor Networks, pp. 254–260. IEEE, Boise (2005)
8. Silva, V.D., Ghrist, R.: Coordinate-free coverage in sensor networks with controlled boundaries via homology. Int. J. Robot. Res. **25**(12), 1205–1222 (2006)

9. Tahbaz-Salehi, A., Jadbabaie, A.: Distributed coverage verification in sensor networks without location information. IEEE Trans. Autom. Control **55**(8), 1837–1849 (2008)
10. Vergne, A., Decreusefond, L., Martins, P.: Reduction algorithm for simplicial complexes. In: 2013 Proceedings of IEEE INFOCOM, pp. 475–479. IEEE, Turin (2013)
11. Le, N.-K., Martins, P., Decreusefond, L., Vergne, A.: Simplicial homology based energy saving algorithms for wireless networks. In: 2015 IEEE International Conference on Communication Workshop (ICCW), pp. 166–172. IEEE, London (2015)
12. Dong, D., Liu, Y., Liao, X.,: Fine-grained boundary recognition in wireless ad hoc and sensor networks by topological methods. In: Proceedings of the 10th ACM International Symposium on Mobile Ad Hoc Networking and Computing, pp. 135–144. MobiHoc, New Orleans (2009)
13. Yan, F., Vergne, A., Martins, P., Decreusefond, L.: Homology-based distributed coverage hole detection in wireless sensor networks. IEEE/ACM Trans. Netw. **23**(6), 1705–1718 (2015)
14. Ma, W., Yan, F., Zuo, X., Hu, J., Xia, W., Shen, L.: Simplicial complex reduction algorithm for simplifying WSN's topology. In: Zheng, J., Xiang, W., Lorenz, P., Mao, S., Yan, F. (eds.) ADHOCNETS 2018. LNICST, vol. 258, pp. 25–35. Springer, Cham (2019). https://doi.org/10.1007/978-3-030-05888-3_3
15. Guvensan, M.A., Yavuz, A.G.: On coverage issues in directional sensor networks: a survey. Ad Hoc Netw. **9**(7), 1238–1255 (2011)
16. Munkres, J.R.: Elements of Algebraic Topology, 2nd edn. Addison-Wesley, New Jersey (1993)
17. Edelsbrunner, H., Parsa, S.: On the computational complexity of betti numbers: reductions from matrix rank. In: Proceedings of the Twenty-Fifth Annual ACM-SIAM Symposium on Discrete Algorithms, pp. 152–160. SIAM, Portland (2014)

Rail Vehicle Fire Warning System Based on Gas Vapor Sensor Network

Min Ai[1] and Rui Tian[2(✉)]

[1] China Railway Signal & Communication Shanghai Engineering Bureau
Group Co., Ltd., Shanghai 200436, China
Min.ai_cn@hotmail.com
[2] Beijing Engineering Research Center for IoT Software and Systems,
Information Department, Beijing University of Technology,
Beijing 100124, China
Rui.tian@bjut.edu.cn

Abstract. Fire accidents in rail vehicles often cause unpredictable catastrophic losses due to high population density and closed environment. At present, existing smart fire prevention schemes are mostly based on the emergency treatments after the fire. Since it takes time for firefighters arriving at the fire, the fire may already become disastrous at that time. This paper proposes a detection framework and also detailed sensing and data processing technologies, in order to detect volatile flammable liquid in closed spaces such as rail vehicle carriages. The proposed mechanism is designed to eliminate potential fire disaster based on gas vapor sensor network. Experiment results shows the proposed surveillant system can detect gasoline vapor components in small space with high sensitivity while maintaining very low false detection rates to external interferences.

Keywords: Fire alarming · Sensor network · Gas vapor · Outlier detection

1 Introduction

Among common public safety accidents, fire disasters always lead to catastrophic consequences, especially when fire accidents happen in closed spaces such as rail vehicle carriages. Recently, IoT (Internet of things) technologies have been widely adopted for indoor surveillances, such as monitoring home, office buildings, warehouses and so on. These IoT systems are generally based on intrusion detection or video surveillance [1]. For fire prevention in closed public places such as rail vehicle carriages, traditional means detect fire through discovering flame or combustion products in the environment. Since it takes time for firefighters arriving at the places where fire broke out, fast spreading fire may already become disastrous.

In order to meet requirements of preventing fire in closed public places like rail vehicle carriages, this paper proposes detection mechanism for flammable and explosive liquids detection. At present, in various industries, there are many monitoring systems and sensing technologies for such detection requirements. Such as liquid component detection based on infrared or ultrasonic absorption, measurement of gas production based on high-precision combustible gas meters. However, these methods

J. Zheng et al. (Eds.): ADHOCNETS 2019, LNICST 306, pp. 302–313, 2019.
https://doi.org/10.1007/978-3-030-37262-0_25

generally require specialized environments, and often rely on expensive equipment, which causes high system construction costs. However, for fire preventing in common small public areas, it is impossible to customize surveillance environment for each scene. This paper proposes the fire detection mechanism in small space based on sensor network, which has low implementation cost as well as high scalability.

We make following contributions in this paper: (1) Extensive experiments have been carried out to verify the feasibility of detecting gasoline volatiles using commercial combustible gas sensor probes; (2) We proposed a judgment logic of anomalous gasoline gas diffusion based on temporal and spatial correlation analysis; (3) This paper presents a framework for the detection of gasoline volatile and data processing based on sensor networks; (4) Extensive experiments have been carried out to verify the effectiveness of the detection system.

This rest of this paper is organized as follows: Sect. 2 puts forward the design motivations of this paper. Section 3 introduces the basic principle of the proposed detection mechanism. Section 4 introduces the framework and detail mechanisms of gas detection. Section 5 verifies the detection performance of the system through real experiments. Section 6 concludes the whole paper.

2   Related Work and Motivations

At present, much work has been done in automatic fire alarm systems [2], of which the most common applications include residential area fire prevention [3], forest fire prevention [4], and coal mine fire prevention [5] and so on. This paper targets at fire detection for small public places, which has the similar design goals as residential fire prevention.

The work on automatic fire prevention for residential areas started very early. Since the 1990s, a series of research results have been published, such as selecting specific sensor sets to form a sensor array, designing a self-learning electronic nose to realize fire signs [6]. With the rapid development of wireless sensor network (WSN) technology in recent years, a considerable part of the work began to design networked automatic fire detection systems. As described in [7], an early fire detection system was developed, which was suitable for fire prevention in open spaces such as rural areas and urban areas. They incorporated temperature sensors and maximum likelihood algorithm to fuse sensory information. In [8], a WSN system for preventing fire accident on the running train was proposed. They monitored the temperature of the coaches to determine the fire. When the ambient temperature exceeds the critical temperature, all the drivers and passengers will be alarmed, the drivers can then manually stop the train and open water sprinkles all over the coaches. In [9], a fire-alarming system for indoor environment was proposed, which is capable of assisting firefighting activities including fire alarming, fire rescuing and firefighter orientation. Since fire usually spread quickly in small indoor environment, fire alarm based on detecting combustion products in the air will largely shorten the emergency response time. Focusing on detecting the flammable and explosive liquid in small public places, this paper tries to trigger fire alarm through detecting fire conditions and is an early warning system.

Since flammable liquids are generally volatile, we propose to detect flammable liquids in small spaces through monitoring the concentrations of target liquid vapors. Combustible gas monitoring is common in petrochemical's production and transportation [10]. In these applications, usually high-precision gas sensors are needed to accurately measure the concentration of certain type gas in the air. Such sensors usually cost high and only have limited detection ranges [11]. And further, to make these sensors work, usually calibration routines is required, such as calibrating the sensor's measurement data by venting a volume of standard sample gas (such as hydrogen, isobutene, etc.) in a standard closed space [12]. If we carried out the above calibration operation in a public place, the maintenance cost is unbearable.

Considering above characteristics, we propose the design objectives of this paper as: (1) High abnormal event reporting rate and very low abnormal event false alarm rate; (2) The ability to tolerate a variety of external disturbances such as airflow, temperature and humidity fluctuation, crowd movements in the monitoring spaces; (3) Do not need frequent calibration and maintenance, easy to deploy, and has a relative long working life time.

3   Gas Vapor Diffusion Model

We have tested several combustible gas sensors for their detection capabilities of unknown type of combustible vapor gas, and we choose to use TGS2602 for system implementation.

Gas detection mechanism aims to discover the abnormal gasoline vapor diffusion in the surveilling space as soon as possible. Gas sensors measure nearby gas concentrations, and gas diffusion law determines spacial distribution of gas concentration.

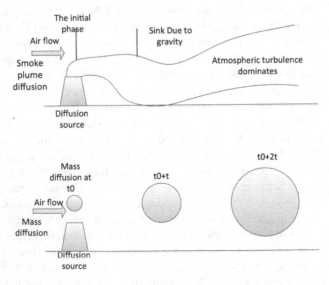

Fig. 1. Smoke plume diffusion and mass diffusion model

When gasoline is stored in a closed gasoline barrel, or when petrol barrel is open without shaking, gas diffusion process is dominated by smoke plume diffusion. As contrast, when gasoline is suddenly exposed to the air, much gas vapor will spread in short time, and lead to a hybrid diffusion process of mass diffusion and smoke plume diffusion. Figure 1 illustrates smoke plume diffusion process as well as mass diffusion process respectively. Under the smoke plume diffusion model, gas concentration has a relatively stable spatial distribution. Therefore, gas diffusion behavior can be conjectured by analyzing correlations between measurements of the sensors located at different positions. Under mass diffusion model, gas concentration at specific location is time varying.

To further explore sensor network's ability of detecting gasoline diffusion process, we deployed a layered sensor array at the height of 50 cm, and on the ground. As shown in Fig. 2, three groups of six sensor nodes were deployed. The distances between two adjacent groups is 100 cm. In this experiment, air flows from right to left as shown in the figure.

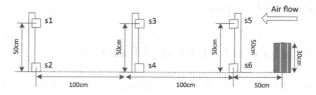

Fig. 2. Detection of gas diffusion process

We collected measurements of the sensor groups after opening the petrol barrel, in an enclosed space and an open space respectively. The measurements are plotted in Figs. 3 and 4.

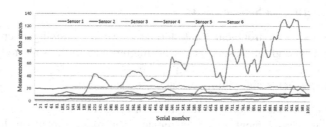

Fig. 3. Measurement curves of sensors in an enclosed space

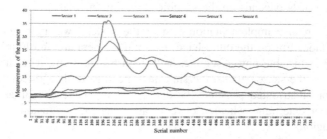

Fig. 4. Measurement curves of sensors in an open space

From Fig. 3 we can see that, when air circulation is poor, due to continuous evaporation of gasoline gas in the air, the concentration of gasoline gas appears an upward trend. At the same time, due to air circulation, the gas concentration appears fluctuations. Whereas when the air circulation is good, in the early diffusion stage, the relative gas concentration will significantly increase due to mass diffusion, and then continued to decrease over time. At last, the smoke plume diffusion dominates the diffusion process, and each sensor node presents a stable relative concentration distribution according to its position.

Based on above observations, we conclude typical characteristics of sensor measurements in a gas vapor diffusion process as following: (1) **Periodicity**: Due to air turbulence, the measurement time series show fluctuations according to time. (2) **Correlation:** Under the smoke plume diffusion model, the sensors near to each other show certain correlation in the measurements, especially for those deployed between upper and lower layers. (3) **Localness:** Fluctuations in sensor measurements due to gasoline vapor diffusions are generally limited to a small range without a consistent change in global sensor nodes.

4 Data Acquisition and Alarming Mechanism

From above observations, we define system flows as two parts: (1) The sensor nodes detect local gas concentrations and send them to the sink node after filtering noises. (2) The sink node maintains multiple threads for every sensor node, performs online outlier detection for time series of each sensor node, and then jointly analyzes measurements from multi sensor nodes to judge outlier events.

This section will introduce specific techniques adopted at each stage.

4.1 Data Filtering on Sensor Nodes

In order to remove environmental interferences, we use moving average filter to sampling raw data, and let sensors only send filtered data to the sink node for further processing.

The moving average algorithm work as follows:

(a) Maintaining a time window of length N on each sensor node;
(b) When new measurement arrives, it replaces the measurement on the tail of the time window, and then the arithmetic average of the N measurements in the time window is took as the sampled value after filtering;
(c) The value of N depends on the specific sampling interval.

In order to reduce implementation cost of the system, we try to avoid frequent sensor calibration. But on the other hand, external temperature and humidity fluctuations, as well as instable power supplies will disturb measurement readings. So after data filtering on the sensor nodes, the sink node need to further process the received data flow from distributed sensors. By distinguishing the cause of abnormal data changes, it can determine whether there is abnormal gas diffusion in the current monitoring region.

We use periodicity, correlation and localness characteristics to determine whether there is an exception event by analyzing the temporal and spatial correlation between measurements of different sensors deployed in the monitoring region. We analyze the correlation of different measurements by quantifying time series similarity. For more accurate quantization calculation, it is first needed to extract time series sub-segment from the original time series for matching. In this paper, we use time-series segmentation through extracting important points.

Considering the periodic characteristics of volatile gas concentration variation, we want to choose complete measurement fluctuation period series for analysis. Therefore, we use local extreme points of time series as the key point.

Suppose the measurement time-series of sensor X is represented as $X = \{x(t_i)\}_{i=1}^{n}$, wherein $[x_i, \ldots, x_{(i+a)}]$ is a subset of the time series. If there is a minimum value x_{min} or a maximum value x_{max} in the subset, then these two elements are referred as local minimum and maximum points. The local maximum/minimum point extraction algorithm is as follows:

Algorithm 1: Extreme point extraction algorithm for time series

Input : Time interval a , measurement series X

Output : Local extreme points set

Function : Find out the local extreme points in X

Algorithm :

(1) x_{min}=x1, x_{max}=x1
(2)   for j in 1 to m :
(3)   for i in j to j+a :
(4)   if $x_i > x_{max}$
(5) x_{max}=x_i, t_{max}=t_i
(6)   else if $x_i < x_{min}$
(7) x_{min}=x_i, t_{min}=t_i
(8)   end if
(9)   end for
(10)   return $(x_{min}, t_i), (x_{max}, t_i)$

Through Algorithm 1, the maximum and minimum points can be extracted to form a new time series $y(t_i)$ $i \in \{1, \ldots, n\}$, $t_i \in \{1, \ldots, m\}$, wherein n is the number of the original sequence elements, m is the number of important points, and a is a configurable parameter to control the number of output extreme points.

4.2 Quantifying Similarities Between Time Series

Although the sensor nodes with different distances from the diffusion source have different fluctuation amplitudes in the measured gas concentration curves, they have similar varying patterns. For this feature, we choose to use dynamic time warping distance (DTW) to quantify the morphological similarity between different measurement sequences.

Suppose there are two time series of length m, n respectively:

$$q[1 : m] = \{q_1, q_2, \ldots, q_m\} \tag{1}$$

$$c[1 : n] = \{c_1, c_2, \ldots, c_n\} \tag{2}$$

DTW distance for q, c can be calculated by constructing a distance matrix of size $m \times n$, called bending matrix, as shown in Fig. 5.

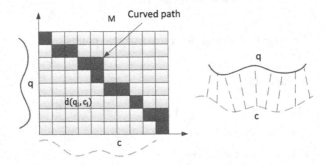

Fig. 5. Bending matrix to calculate DTW

From bending matrix, the matching between q and c points is transformed into a curved path in the bending matrix from the square(1, 1) to the square(m, n):

$$W = w_1, w_2, \ldots, w_l(\max(m, n) \leq l \leq m + n) \tag{3}$$

We define a mapping function $f_w : (q, c) \rightarrow W$ that maps the (q, c) point pairs in the curved path to a square in the curved path:

$$w_k = f_w(q_i, c_j), \ 1 \leq i \leq m, 1 \leq j \leq n, \ 1 \leq k \leq l \tag{4}$$

Then the problem of calculating DTW distance between q and c is transformed into figuring out a curved path which has the smallest distance in the bending matrix W:

$$\text{DTW}(q,\ c) = \arg\min_{w}\left(\sum_{i=1}^{c} w_i\right) \qquad (5)$$

4.3 Gas Vapor Source Detection

Figure 6 shows outlier detection flow chart of our system. When two time series are normalized, they are considered related if their DTW distance is less than a specified value. If a sensor node reports abnormal time series which are related to other sensor's reported time series, a potential gas vapor source will be considered in the surveillant carriage by the sink node. If there is no correlation between different sensors' reports, the sink node will continue observing whether the reporting sensor node will continuous send other abnormal time series pieces. If so, a gas vapor source is also considered near the reporting sensor node is. If a sensor node and the nearby sensor nodes simultaneously appear abnormal fluctuation of the measured value, it is deemed that there is a gas vapor source nearby.

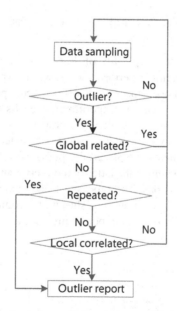

Fig. 6. The flow chart of abnormal gas diffusion judgment

5 Evaluation

We set up an experimental environment as shown in Fig. 7 to test gas vapor diffusion detecting capability. In the experiment, 12 sensor nodes were deployed in two layers in a closed room. Sensors A0, B0, C0, D0, E0 and F0 are deployed on the ground, while sensors A1, B1, C1, D1, E1 and F1 are deployed at the height of 50 cm. The distance between sensors was 2 m in x-axis direction and 2 m in y-axis direction. In the figure, two positions are marked. At position 1, vapor diffusion source (gasoline drum) is 1 m from both the x-axis and the y-axis. At position 2, vapor diffusion source is 1 m from the node C0 and the node D0. The diffusion source is a 5L petrol barrel with a 10 cm diameter lid and 35 cm height.

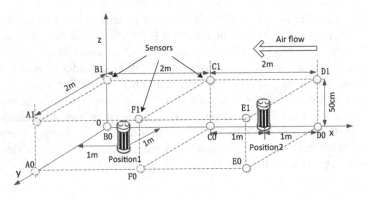

Fig. 7. Experimental environment

Firstly, we test the system's capability of detecting gas vapor diffusion, and then, we examine its anti-false alarming performance towards typical external turbulences. We tested closed oil drum in open space and closed space, open oil drum in open space and closed space respectively, the four experimental results are as shown respectively in Figs. 8, 9, 10 and 11. Then we circulate air, change the ambient temperature, and shake sensor nodes to see how the system responds to external interferences.

For the first four experiments, we placed the petrol barrel at positions 1 and 2, and opened the barrel lid immediately in the latter two experiments, recorded the alarm time of the system to above operations. The process of each experiment lasted 2 min, and repeated 20 times. Figures 8, 9, 10, and 11 shows the cumulative distribution of the alarm delay of the first four groups of experiments. In these graphs, we treat the time out reports as failure detections.

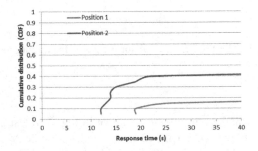

Fig. 8. Closed gasoline barrel in the open space

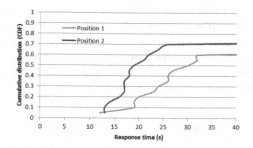

Fig. 9. Closed gasoline barrel in the enclosed space

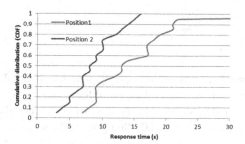

Fig. 10. Open gasoline barrel in the open space

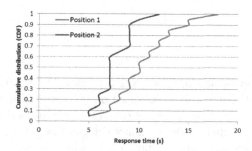

Fig. 11. Open gasoline barrel in the enclosed space

From the above experimental results, it can be seen that, when the gasoline barrel is at position 1, the system has a higher detection delay than that at position 2. This is because the diffusion source is farther away from sensor nodes, hence the fluctuations in the sensor measurements become subtle. Think node requires more data to determine if there are abnormal gas vapor diffusions. In the experiments with sealed petrol barrels, slight amount of gas leakage can lead significant reduction in event detection rates. Especially in the first group of experiments, when we place the closed petrol barrel in the open space, the detection ratio always lies under 40%. We can also see that, the detection rate will significantly increase when the distance between diffusion source and monitoring sensors decreases. As in the first experiment, the system had a 25%

improvement in detection rate when we move the gasoline barrel from position 2 to position 1, and also about 10% improvement in the second experiment.

At last, we test the sensor network system's tolerance towards external interferences. We force air circulation, then change the room temperature, and sway sensor nodes to disturb measurements. Each action is repeated 20 times, and then we record the alarm times of the system as shown in Table 1.

Table 1. System alarm performance

Events	Correct alarm times	False alarm times	False alarm rate
Force air flow	19	1	5%
Change ambient temperature	20	0	0%
Shake sensors	17	3	15%
Total	**56**	**4**	**6.7%**

In the case of forced air circulation, the system has one false judgement in 20 attempts, the false alarm rate is 5%. In the case of forced ambient temperature changes, all the judgements are made correctly. In the case of artificially shaking sensor nodes, the system has 3 false judgements in 20 attempts, the false alarm rate is 15%. In this experiment, since we are using very tense external interference, especially the air flow intensity and the amplitude of artificial sensors are higher than the general situations, the overall false alarm rate is controlled under 7%, indicating good anti-jamming capability.

6   Conclusion

In this paper, a gas vapor detection framework is proposed to detect fire hazard in small public places like rail vehicle carriages. Based on the gas diffusion model and experimental results under typical small space scenario, we proposed sensor deployment scheme, as well as detection logic for abnormal gasoline vapor diffusion. We also implemented data sampling and filtering mechanisms, as well as outlier decision schemes based on DTW distance quantization.

The experimental results show that, our system can detect the gasoline barrel in the room (small space) in short time in most cases, while maintaining very low false alarm rates to typical external interferences.

References

1. Amewornu, E.M.: Design of wireless home security alarm system. Afr. J. Appl. Res. (AJAR) **1**(1), 397–412 (2016)
2. Gaur, A., Singh, A., Kumar, A., Kulkarni, K.S.: Fire sensing technologies: a review. IEEE Sens. J. **19**(9), 3191–3202 (2019)

3. Rao, S., Nithya, G.K. Rakesh, K.: Development of a wireless sensor network for detecting fire and Gas leaks in a collapsing building. In: Proceedings of the 5th International Conference on Computing, Communications and Networking Technologies (ICCCNT), Hefei, pp. 1–7. IEEE (2014)
4. Sudha, P., Murugan, A.: Detection of forest fire using Dezert-Smarandache theory in wireless sensor networks. In: Proceedings of the IEEE International Conference on Power, Control, Signals and Instrumentation Engineering (ICPCSI), Chennai, pp. 2274–2079 (2017)
5. Bhattacharjee, S., Roy, P., Ghosh, S., Misra, S., Obaidat, M.S.: Wireless sensor network-based fire detection, alarming, monitoring and prevention system for Bord-and-Pillar coal mines. J. Syst. Softw. **85**(3), 571–581 (2012)
6. Bahrepour, M., Meratnia, N., Havinga, P.J.M.: Use of AI techniques for residential fire detection in wireless sensor networks. In: Proceedings of the 5th Artificial Intelligence Applications and Innovations (AIAI) Workshop, Greece, pp. 311–321 (2009)
7. Zervas, E., Sekkas, O., Hadjieftymiades, S., Anagnostopoulos, C.: Fire detection in the urban rural interface through fusion techniques. In: Proceedings of the IEEE International Conference on Mobile Adhoc and Sensor Systems (MASS 2007), Pisa, pp. 1–6 (2007)
8. Ramasamy, R.P., et al.: Avoidance of fire accident on running train using zigbee wireless sensor network. Int. J. Inf. Comput. Technol. **3**(6), 583–592 (2013)
9. Ghosh, P., Dhar, P.K.: GSM based low-cost gas leakage, explosion and fire alert system with advanced security. In: Proceedings of the International Conference on Electrical, Computer and Communication Engineering (ECCE), Cox's Bazar, Bangladesh, pp. 1–5 (2019)
10. Chang, J.I., Lin, C.C.: A study of storage tank accidents. J. Loss Prev. Process Ind. **19**(1), 51–59 (2006)
11. Campo, O.D.: Modular compressed natural gas (CNG) station and method for avoiding fire in such station. U.S. Patent No. 6,732,769 (2004)
12. Berndt, D.J., Clifford, J.: Finding patterns in time series: a dynamic programming approach. In: Advances in Knowledge Discovery and Data Mining, pp. 229–248. The MIT Press, Portland (1996)

Guessing Intrinsic Forwarding Trustworthiness of Wireless Ad Hoc Network Nodes

Jerzy Konorski$^{(\boxtimes)}$ and Karol Rydzewski

Faculty of Electronics, Telecommunications and Informatics, Gdansk University of Technology, ul. Narutowicza 11/12, 80-233 Gdansk, Poland
jekon@eti.pg.edu.pl

Abstract. A novel node misbehavior detection system called GIFTED is proposed for a multihop wireless ad hoc network (WAHN) whose nodes may selfishly refuse to forward transit packets. The system guesses the nodes' intrinsic forwarding trustworthiness (IFT) by analyzing end-to-end path performance rather than utilizing unreliable and incentive incompatible low-layer mechanisms. It can work with occasional IFT jumps, directional antennae, multichannel transmission, end-to-end encrypted packets, any single-path source routing protocol, and any number of selfish nodes; this makes it a valuable alternative to existing misbehavior detection schemes. GIFTED relies on approximate decomposition of a path equation system arising from successive performance reports from source nodes. The ability to near-perfectly guess IFT in the presence of various perturbations is demonstrated through Monte Carlo and time-true simulations, and compared with an existing weighted path trust scheme.

Keywords: WAHN · Modeling · Reputation · Selfish behavior · Path equations

1 Introduction

Nodes of multihop wireless ad hoc networks (WAHNs) are often modeled as autonomous selfish entities. To conserve its power and bandwidth resources, a selfish node may drop some or all offered transit packets instead of forwarding them towards destination. Such misbehavior affects the perception of benefits at other nodes and may instill similar behavior in them. To incentivize cooperative forwarding behavior on the part of selfish nodes, credit-based (micropayment) schemes [1] create a rudimentary market where funds earned for forwarding packets can buy other nodes' forwarding services, and game-theoretic solutions [2] arrange a noncooperative game whose Nash equilibrium entails cooperative forwarding behavior. In the reputation system approach [3], network nodes offer forwarding services in pursuit of high reputation. The underlying (often tacit) premise is that a node's forwarding behavior can be conceptualized as a private information-type and quantifiable disposition toward forwarding transit packets, which we call here *intrinsic forwarding trustworthiness* (IFT).

J. Zheng et al. (Eds.): ADHOCNETS 2019, LNICST 306, pp. 314–331, 2019.
https://doi.org/10.1007/978-3-030-37262-0_26

The main functions of a reputation system are: (1) guessing the network nodes' IFT from some observable performance characteristics, and quantitatively expressing the guesses as *reputation levels*, and (2) enforcing nodal cooperation, e.g., through elimination of nodes with low reputation levels (the pathrater approach [4]), or refusal to forward such nodes' source traffic (the indirect reciprocity approach [5]). We focus on function 1, which after nearly two decades of active research still poses a major challenge. To perform this function, a number of works, e.g., [4, 6–8] exploit the *watchdog* mechanism, known to be unreliable, incentive incompatible, and prone to inter-node collusion. Other low-layer schemes attempt direct location of misbehaving nodes on paths, e.g., Two-ACK [9], node auditing [10], or flow conservation checking [11]. They too lack incentive compatibility and mostly fail to systematically address the problem of guessing individual IFT from collective service of multiple nodes [12]; an exception is the solution in [10], where, however, a huge price is paid in terms of communication and processing complexity. In [13], a neighbor node X's IFT is guessed by counting packets received from X whose source addresses are not X.

We propose an algorithm called $\underline{G}$uessing $\underline{IFT}$ from $\underline{E}$nd-to-end $\underline{D}$elivery (GIFTED) to perform function 1 based on observed end-to-end packet delivery ratio (PDR). GIFTED can work with directional antennae, multichannel transmission, end-to-end encrypted packets, any single-path source routing protocol, e.g., Dynamic Source Routing (DSR) [14], any number of misbehaving nodes, and independently of the low-layer communication mechanisms. PDR is derived by a source node from end-to-end feedback information such as TCP ACKs or quality of experience (QoE) assessment (shown to be closely related to PDR [15]), and subsequently reported to the reputation system. Such an approach only relies on reports from source nodes, which have natural incentives for truthful PDR reporting. Reports from the source nodes of successive paths used during the network operation give rise to a system of path equations where the observed PDRs are regarded as products of the respective transit nodes' unknown IFTs (cf. [16]). In theory, guessing IFTs amounts to solving path equations [17], but proceeding directly in this way one is unable to cover any realistic network scenarios, in which the IFTs and PDRs suffer from various perturbations. In this paper, we account for such perturbations by constructing linear programs with random requirements. Unfortunately, known solutions of such linear programs only yield reputation levels as point estimates of the nodes' individual IFTs [18, 19]. This drawback calls for a revised approach to yield reputation intervals as well, and so to provide a measure of confidence about the guessed IFT. The proposed GIFTED algorithm achieves this through approximate decomposition of the arising path equation systems.

So far, few schemes based solely on end-to-end on path performance have been studied, cf. [20, 21]. The scheme in [20] is close in spirit to ours in that it uses a similar WAHN model. It singles out transit nodes that appear on multiple low-trust paths, where a path trust level is inferred from end-to-end PDR and delay via fuzzy reasoning. Nodal reputation is a point estimate of IFT, derived as a weighted sum of incident paths' trust values (thus we later refer to the scheme as *weighted path trust*, WPT). Contrary to GIFTED, it sets strong requirements as to the percentage of misbehaving nodes in the network and in particular along each path. Also, perturbations of IFTs and PDRs are not addressed. Finally, the fuzzy reasoning leading to paths' trust levels inevitably introduces a degree of arbitrariness through the defined membership functions, whereas GIFTED defines path performance directly as the observed end-to-end PDR.

We formalize our WAHN model in Sect. 2, and in Sect. 3 explain the idea of path equations and perturbations of PDRs. GIFTED operation is presented in Sect. 4. In Sect. 5, using several introduced metrics of interest, we evaluate GIFTED via Monte Carlo and time-true simulation, and briefly compare with WPT. Finally, Sect. 6 discusses the viability of GIFTED and outlines future work.

2 WAHN Model

A WAHN topology is an undirected graph $(\mathbf{N}, \mathbf{E})$, where $\mathbf{N}$ is the set of nodes able to transmit and receive data, and $\mathbf{E} \subseteq \mathbf{N} \times \mathbf{N}$ is the set of node pairs within each other's reception range. The network nodes are uniquely identifiable, as ensured by a separate identity management system. The traffic pattern is represented by a set $\mathbf{K}$ of feasible source-destination paths over which data packets are transferred in successive user sessions. For a path $k \in \mathbf{K}$, let $S_k, D_k \in \mathbf{N}$ denote the source and destination nodes, and $\mathbf{X}_k \subseteq \mathbf{N} \setminus \{S_k, D_k\}$ the set of transit nodes (whose order on path is irrelevant).

Transit nodes in $\mathbf{X}_k$ may selfishly drop transit packets offered during a user session. S_k keeps track of the end-to-end PDR[1], e.g., by means of TCP ACKs for successive packets in the case of data traffic sessions, or by exploiting tight correlation between PDR and the perceived QoE in real-time traffic sessions [15]. The network employs a reputation system whose task is to guess each node's IFT from observed PDR and disseminate the resulting reputation data among all the nodes. For ease of exposition we conceptually assign this task to a single trusted third party called *reputation server* (RS).[2] RS operates in time *rounds* $t = 1, 2, \ldots$, the end of round t being marked by reception of a PDR report $\langle PDR_{k_t}, \mathbf{X}_{k_t} \rangle$ from the source node S_{k_t} of a path $k_t \in \mathbf{K}$ upon termination of a user session. Denote by $\mathbf{SPD}_t$ the current *stored path database* (SPD) at RS, i.e., the set of all PDR reports received up to round t. Based on SPD and using GIFTED, RS calculates and disseminates among all the nodes each node's reputation level. Hence, watchdogs or other low-layer mechanisms are dispensed with and guessing forwarding behaviors of transit nodes from reported PDR is the main challenge. Note that source nodes are naturally interested in truthful PDR reporting, whereas transit nodes are interested in reliable transfer of end-to-end feedback (ACK- or QoE-related).

With regard to a node $X \in \mathbf{N}$ in round t, we introduce two quantities. One, denoted $g_{X,t}$, is its IFT, the percentage of offered transit packets it intends to forward towards destination. This is a ground truth-type quantity, known only to node X itself. An IFT-based decision related to an offered transit packet can be construed as forward with

---

[1] To keep the presentation simple, we disregard other observable end-to-end characteristics, such as packet delay, sequencing or jitter.

[2] While such a centralized approach permits to abstract from the details of report collection and reputation data dissemination, nothing prevents deployment of a distributed version of the proposed scheme, e.g., with multiple RSs (possibly located at all source nodes), as no inter-RS synchronization would be needed.

probability $g_{X,t}$ and drop with probability $1 - g_{X,t}$. The other quantity, denoted $r_{X,t}$, is node X's current reputation level, i.e., IFT guessed by GIFTED from observed end-to-end on path performance, and later disseminated among all the nodes. We assume that $g_{X,t} \in [0, 1]$ and $r_{X,t} \in [0, 1]$, where 0 signifies a complete lack of cooperation (no packet forwarding) and 1 signifies fully cooperative behavior (no packet dropping). Ideally, $r_{X,t} = g_{X,t}$ for all X and t, but in reality these quantities may differ due to possible perturbations as described below. Maintaining $r_{X,t}$ close to $g_{X,t}$ is the goal of the reputation system's function 1 mentioned in Sect. 1.

The adopted WAHN model subsumes the following assumptions:

(i) an a priori trust relationship exists between the source and destination of each path [21], enabling mutual authentication and preventing end-to-end ACK forgery,

(ii) the employed routing protocol reveals $\mathbf{X}_k$ to S_k (e.g., in an RREP message of the DSR protocol),

(iii) all packets within a user session follow the same path (i.e., single-path routing is employed),

(iv) the forward/drop decisions at transit nodes are statistically independent and not path selective.[3]

Figure 1 provides an illustration and summary of notation. Clearly, assumptions (ii) and (iii) restrict the volatility of the WAHN topology—static or quasi-static topologies are allowed, also characteristic of wireless mesh or sensor networks. Note that our focus on IFT guessing rather than cooperation enforcement allows to regard $\mathbf{K}$ and $g_{X,t}$ as exogenous input to the model.

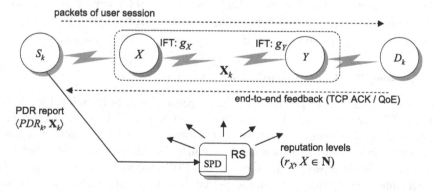

Fig. 1. Path layout, nodal IFT, and RS operation.

---

[3] Path selective IFT implies malice towards specific source nodes or a clever strategy of confusing RS, whose benefits are not always clear [17]. Modifications of GIFTED to deal with it are possible.

3 Path Equations

In light of assumptions (iii) and (iv), the probability of a packet delivery on path $k_t \in$ **K** in round t is:

$$p_{k_t} = \begin{cases} \prod_{X \in \mathbf{X}_{k_t}} g_{X,t}, & \mathbf{X}_k \neq \emptyset, \\ 1, & \mathbf{X}_k = \emptyset, \end{cases} \tag{1}$$

where the latter part stems from the fact that neither the source nor the destination node is ever interested in dropping an on-path packet.

3.1 Guessing IFT from PDR

In the idealized model where $g_{X,t} = const.$ for $t = 1, 2, \ldots$ and $PDR_{k_t} = p_{k_t}$, guessing nodal IFT based on end-to-end PDR is straightforward. The idea is to calculate the *reputation intervals* $(r_{X,t}^{\text{low}}, r_{X,t}^{\text{high}})$ admitted by the path equations derived from **SPD**$_t$, i.e., the escribed cuboid of the region of feasible solutions of the path equation system. These intervals are nonempty, and eventually become singletons as SPD size grows over time. Formally, RS solves a set of optimization problems:

$$\begin{aligned} & \text{find } r_{X,t}^{\text{low}} = \min g_{X,t}, \ r_{X,t}^{\text{high}} = \max g_{X,t} \\ & \text{over } (g_{Y,t}, Y \in \mathbf{N} \backslash \{X\}) \text{ with } 0 \leq g_{Y,t} \leq 1 \\ & \text{s.t. path equations } \prod_{Y \in \mathbf{X}_k} g_{Y,t} = PDR_k, \ \langle PDR_k, \mathbf{X}_k \rangle \in \mathbf{SPD}_t. \end{aligned} \tag{2}$$

Upon a logarithmic transformation, (2) becomes a set of linear programs. Node X's current reputation level (guessed IFT) is taken as $r_{X,t} = (r_{X,t}^{\text{low}} + r_{X,t}^{\text{high}})/2$. In particular, when nothing can be stated except that $g_{X,t} \in [0, 1]$, $r_{X,t} = 0.5$ is guessed.

3.2 Guessing IFT Under Perturbations

The above idealized model precludes stochastic perturbations or intentional variability of nodal IFTs, or inaccurate PDR reporting; yet in reality all these can occur. Poor wireless propagation, access delays, buffer overflow and sampling errors may cause actual forwarding behavior of a node to fluctuate between rounds and differ from intended IFT; the same pertains to the end-to-end PDR observed at the source node. On a larger timescale, changing attitudes caused by exogenous factors (e.g., power shortage or surge in handled traffic), as well as a node's cooperation strategy, may cause occasional significant IFT jumps. Finally, end-to-end feedback information may be lost before reaching RS. As a result, the path equation system (2) may become inconsistent over time: in different rounds, unknowns $g_{X,t}$ pertaining to the same node X will differ in values, and/or path equations pertaining to the same set of transit nodes $\mathbf{X}_{k_t}$ will differ in their right-hand sides. We aggregate all such perturbations into the reported PDR:

$$PDR_{k_t} = p_{k_t} + z_t \tag{3}$$

where p_k is given by (1) and z_t is a discrete-time biased white noise with moving average $\bar{z}_t$, referred to as *network bias*. The latter is a parameter of a realistic network model (in the idealized model, $\bar{z}_t = 0$). We assume that $\bar{z}_t$ is path independent and can be estimated by RS in each round, e.g., through smoothening of successive estimates $\bar{z}_t = PDR_{k_t} - \prod_{X \in \mathbf{X}_{k_t}} r_{X,t}$, $t = 1, 2, \ldots$

4 GIFTED Operation

An inconsistent system (2) (or its equivalent system of linear programs) can be approximately solved via least squares minimization [18] or probabilistic analysis under random requirements [16]. A downside of such methods is that they yield for each node a single reputation level and not an interval, hence no confidence information on the guessed IFT; in addition, specific probabilistic characteristics of z_t and/or arbitrary penalty functions sometimes have to be assumed. To obtain reputation intervals, we adopt a heuristic approximation combining modification and decomposition of (2).

A single execution of linear programs equivalent of (2) in round t produces a set of current reputation interval endpoints $\{(r_{X,t}^{\text{low}}, r_{X,t}^{\text{high}}), X \in \mathbf{N}\}$, later disseminated among all the network nodes; initially, $(r_{X,0}^{\text{low}}, r_{X,0}^{\text{high}}) = (0, 1)$. For the idealized model ($\bar{z}_t = 0$ and static IFT), **SPD**$_t$ eventually yields enough independent path equations and the reputation intervals narrow down to singletons: $r_{X,t}^{\text{low}} = r_{X,t}^{\text{high}}$ for all $X \in \mathbf{N}$ (*perfect accuracy* is perceived). Stored paths can then be removed from **SPD**$_t$ as long as perfect accuracy is still perceived, to limit the size of SPD and so to simplify the optimization problems (2). For the realistic model, when **SPD**$_t$ grows too large, the system (2) becomes inconsistent, which RS easily detects. RS can then remove stored path equations until the system becomes consistent, usually producing non-singleton reputation intervals. Consequently, perfect accuracy will be perceived rarely and perhaps wrongly, as $r_{X,t}^{\text{low}} = r_{X,t}^{\text{high}} \neq g_{X,t}$ is in principle possible.

Some modifications of (2) and design decisions are necessary to keep both the accuracy and the SPD size reasonable. To account for perturbations of PDR, a path equation in (2) is turned into a pair of inequalities:

$$PDR_k \leq \prod_{Y \in \mathbf{X}_k} g_{Y,t} \leq PDR_k - 2\bar{z}_t. \tag{4}$$

Next, we define ε, the accuracy/inconsistency tolerance, helpful in quantifying a less rigid perception of ε-*inconsistency* and ε-*perfect* accuracy, defined below, and c, the critical SPD size. GIFTED removes stored paths (starting from the oldest one) either upon finding (2) ε-inconsistent, until ε-consistency is obtained, or upon perception of ε-perfect accuracy in the presence of c stored paths, as long as ε-perfect accuracy holds. The latter provision is a greedy heuristic (clearly, a hypothetical optimal path removal policy might retain some redundant path equations to prevent a forthcoming inconsistency).

To define ε-inconsistency and ε-perfect accuracy, suppose the system (2) subject to (3) and (4) is found inconsistent in round t. Still, it is possible to decompose it into consistent subsystems with disjoint subsets of path equations; for a given $X \in \mathbf{N}$, each subsystem i produces a local reputation interval $(r_{X,t}^{low}(i), r_{X,t}^{high}(i))$. Because of the original inconsistency it must be that $\max_i r_{X,t}^{low}(i) > \min_i r_{X,t}^{high}(i)$ for some $X \in \mathbf{N}$, and the difference between $m_{X,t}^{low} = \max_i r_{X,t}^{low}(i)$ and $m_{X,t}^{high} = \min_i r_{X,t}^{high}(i)$ measures the degree of inconsistency. As the reputation interval we take the narrowest local reputation interval. We will call (2) ε-inconsistent if $m_{X,t}^{low} - m_{X,t}^{high} > \varepsilon$ for some $X \in \mathbf{N}$, and ε-consistent otherwise. For simplicity, the same value ε is used to define ε-perfect accuracy as $\left| r_{X,t}^{high} - r_{X,t}^{low} \right| \leq \varepsilon$ for all $X \in \mathbf{N}$.

Solving (2) in the above way might be computationally hard due to the large number of subsystems to be examined. Instead, a heuristic approximate decomposition procedure GIFTED-AD, specified in Fig. 2, is proposed. Based on input $\bar{z}_t$ and $\mathbf{SPD}_t$ it calculates the $m_{X,t}^{low}$ and $m_{X,t}^{high}$ as the reputation interval endpoints obtained from a subsystem of (2) whose equations are picked at random as long as ε-consistency is preserved. Note that besides reputation intervals (i.e., guessed IFT), the output of GIFTED-AD is detection of ε-inconsistency (if the while loop stops before exhausting $\mathbf{SPD}_t$) and of ε-perfect accuracy. Using GIFTED-AD as a building block, Fig. 3 summarizes the operation of GIFTED.

5 Evaluation

5.1 Metrics of Interest

We are primarily interested in metrics of ε-perfect accuracy of the reputation levels produced by GIFTED, namely:

- *%Accuracy*—the proportion of time where ε-perfect accuracy extends at least to *lookahead* nodes, defined as transit nodes on paths to be discovered in "near future". Let L be the number of "near future" rounds. Then *%Accuracy* is incremented in round t if for all $l = 1,...,L$ and $X \in \mathbf{X}_{k_{t+l}}$, $|r_{X,t+l}^{low} - g_{X,t+l}| < \varepsilon$ and $|r_{X,t+l}^{high} - g_{X,t+l}| < \varepsilon$.

- *%ApproxAccuracy*—approximate ε-perfect accuracy, the proportion of time where the $r_{X,t}$ are nearly accurate: for all $l = 1,...,L$ and $X \in \mathbf{X}_{k_{t+l}}$, $|r_{X,t+l} - g_{X,t+l}| < \varepsilon$. This may hold even when RS is recovering from the inconsistency of (2) after path removal and ε-perfect accuracy does not hold, so *%ApproxAccuracy* $\geq$ *%Accuracy*.

Both these accuracy metrics are calculated after a warm-up period, starting in the initial round with $\mathbf{SPD}_0 = \varnothing$ until ε-perfect accuracy is first reached, i.e., for $t \geq TTA = \min\{t \geq 1 \text{ such that } \forall_{X \in \mathbf{N}} |r_{X,t}^{low} - g_{X,t}| < \varepsilon \wedge |r_{X,t}^{high} - g_{X,t}| < \varepsilon \}$.

Repeatedly solving (2), perhaps multiple times per round if path removal from SPD is necessary, requires a computational effort depending on $|\mathbf{SPD}_t|$. Hence, another metric of interest is:

- mean SPD size, which should be finite, while the instantaneous value of $|\mathbf{SPD}_t|$ can fluctuate over time.

foreach $X \in \mathbf{N}$

$\quad (r_{X,t}^{\text{low}}, r_{X,t}^{\text{high}}) \leftarrow (0,1);$

$\quad (m_{X,t}^{\text{low}}, m_{X,t}^{\text{high}}) \leftarrow (-\infty, \infty);$

$\quad (q_{X,t}^{\text{low}}; q_{X,t}^{\text{high}}) \leftarrow (-1, 2);$ //auxiliary variables

while $\left(\exists_{X \in \mathbf{N}} (r_{X,t}^{\text{low}}, r_{X,t}^{\text{high}}) \neq (q_{X,t}^{\text{low}}, q_{X,t}^{\text{high}}) \right) \wedge \left(\forall_{X \in \mathbf{N}} m_{X,t}^{\text{low}} - m_{X,t}^{\text{high}} \leq \varepsilon \right)$

$\quad (q_{X,t}^{\text{low}}, q_{X,t}^{\text{high}}) \leftarrow (r_{X,t}^{\text{low}}, r_{X,t}^{\text{high}});$

$\quad$ pick a random $\langle PDR_{k_t}, \mathbf{X}_{k_t} \rangle \in \mathbf{SPD}_t$ not picked before;

$\quad$ **if** $PDR_{k_t} > 0$ **then foreach** $X \in \mathbf{X}_{k_t}$

$\qquad m_{X,t}^{\text{low}} \leftarrow \max\{m_{X,t}^{\text{low}}, PDR_{k_t} / \prod_{Y \in \mathbf{X}_{k_t} \backslash \{X\}} q_{Y,t}^{\text{high}}\};$

$\qquad m_{X,t}^{\text{high}} \leftarrow \min\{m_{X,t}^{\text{high}}, (PDR_{k_t} - 2\bar{z}_t) / \prod_{Y \in \mathbf{X}_{k_t} \backslash \{X\}} q_{Y,t}^{\text{low}}\};$

$\quad$ **foreach** $X \in \mathbf{N}$

$\qquad (r_{X,t}^{\text{low}}, r_{X,t}^{\text{high}}) \leftarrow (\min\{r_{X,t}^{\text{low}}, m_{X,t}^{\text{low}}\}, \max\{r_{X,t}^{\text{high}}, m_{X,t}^{\text{high}}\})$

$\qquad\qquad\qquad$ //ensures low endpoint $\leq$ high endpoint

Fig. 2. GIFTED-AD heuristic for approximate reputation intervals.

upon reception of a PDR report in round t

$\quad$ add received PDR report to $\mathbf{SPD}_t$;

$\quad$ **repeat**

$\quad\quad$ GIFTED-AD($\mathbf{SPD}_t$, $\bar{z}_t$);

$\quad\quad$ **if** ε-inconsistency detected **then**

$\quad\quad\quad$ remove oldest PDR report from $\mathbf{SPD}_t$;

$\quad\quad$ **until** ε-consistency detected;

$\quad$ **if** $|\mathbf{SPD}_t| \geq c$ **then while** ε-perfect accuracy detected

$\quad\quad$ remove oldest PDR report from $\mathbf{SPD}_t$;

$\quad$ GIFTED-AD($\mathbf{SPD}_t$, $\bar{z}_t$);

$\quad$ update reputation intervals;

$\quad \bar{z}_t \leftarrow ((t-1)\bar{z}_{t-1} + \tilde{z}_t)/t$ // $\tilde{z}_t$ defined at end of Section 3

Fig. 3. Summary of GIFTED operation.

5.2 Monte Carlo Simulations

Monte Carlo simulations of GIFTED were conducted under several additional modeling assumptions: (v) for all $X \in \mathbf{N}$, $g_{X,t} \in [g^{\min}, 1]$ with a predefined $g^{\min} > 0$,

(i)   nodal IFT is quasi-static over time, initialized to a random value and in each round re-initialized (i.e., exhibiting a significant jump) with a fixed probability $1/\tau_1$,

(ii) no nodes are preferred during path discovery, hence the set of transit nodes of a discovered path looks as if it were selected at random,

(iii) perturbations of PDR are modeled according to (3) using artificial discrete-time biased white noise with a fixed $\bar{z}_t$.

Assumption (v) stems from the ability of GIFTED to quickly and fairly accurately guess nodes' IFT under typical traffic conditions (the observed *TTA* were on order of a few dozen). If a source node refuses to set up a path containing transit nodes with $r_{X,t}^{high} < g^{\min}$ (a rudimentary pathrater) then such transit nodes cease to appear in subsequent path equations and can be neglected without loss of generality. In assumption (vi), one expects $\tau_1 >> 1$: consistent forwarding behavior is to be noted by RS and bring about desired reputation with knock-on benefits. Note that $\tau = \tau_1/|\mathbf{N}|$ is a parameter measuring the network-wide IFT variability (mean number of rounds with constant IFTs at all the nodes); $\tau = \infty$ corresponds to static IFT. Assumption (vii) models a volatile network topology (topology changes being, however, rare enough as to mostly allow the same path for all session packets) and presents a worst-case scenario for RS, should it attempt to confine its computation effort to a small subset of the most popular transit nodes. Assumption (viii) is necessary since real-world causes of perturbations, like transmission corruption or buffer overflow, would be difficult to reflect in Monte Carlo modeling. Table 1 specifies the simulation setup.

Table 1. Monte Carlo simulation setup.

Symbol	Meaning	Value
$|\mathbf{N}|$	Number of nodes	16
$g^{\min}$	Minimum nodal IFT	0.5
$|\mathbf{X}_k|$	Path length (no. of transit nodes)	Uniform(1..5)
τ	Network-wide IFT variability	50..∞
$\bar{z}_t$	Network bias	$-0.03..0$
c	Critical SPD size	100
ε	Accuracy/inconsistency tolerance	0.05
L	No. of "near future" rounds	4

For $\bar{z}_t = 0$, $r_{X,t}^{low} = r_{X,t}^{high} \neq g_{X,t}$ was never observed and $r_{X,t}^{low} \leq g_{X,t} \leq r_{X,t}^{high}$ held true whenever the system (2) was consistent—GIFTED either correctly bounded IFT from below and above, or detected inconsistencies. With $\bar{z}_t \neq 0$ this was no longer true: GIFTED performed satisfactorily for $\bar{z}_t = -0.01$ (found in time-true simulations to be typical of light/medium traffic, with up to 2 concurrent active paths), but less so for $\bar{z}_t \leq -0.03$ (found typical of extremely heavy traffic with up to 4 concurrent active paths, rather unrealistic in a WAHN environment, as nodal buffers then often incurred offered load of packets and node-RS messages exceeding 100% of the transmitter capacity).

Figure 4 presents the accuracy of the reputation intervals and resulting reputation levels, averaged over **N**, i.e., $\frac{1}{|N|} \sum_{X \in N} (g_{X,t} - r_{X,t}^{low})$, $\frac{1}{|N|} \sum_{X \in N} (r_{X,t}^{high} - g_{X,t})$, and $\frac{1}{|N|} \sum_{X \in N} (r_{X,t} - g_{X,t})$ (ideal plots would lie on the $y = 0$ line). The top plots for static IFT ($\tau = \infty$) illustrate the good accuracy under light/medium traffic (*left*) and the adverse effect of extremely heavy traffic (*right*); yet even in the latter case the $r_{X,t}$ remain fairly accurate, showing that GIFTED manages to keep both endpoints of the reputation intervals equidistant from the ground-truth IFT. Quasi-static IFT with $\tau = 100$ is

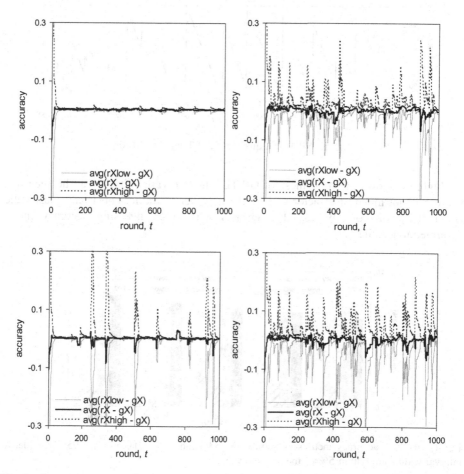

Fig. 4. Average accuracy for Monte Carlo simulations; $\tau = \infty$ (*top*) and $\tau = 100$ (*bottom*), network bias = −0.01 (*left*) and −0.03 (*right*).

assumed in the bottom plots. Under extremely heavy traffic, the picture looks much the same as for $\tau = \infty$. However, under light/medium traffic, ε-perfect and approximate ε-perfect accuracy persist, occasionally disturbed upon path removal due to inconsistency, mostly following a significant jump in some node's IFT. Each such disturbance is recovered from and ε-perfect accuracy is quickly restored, which demonstrates a self-stabilizing property of GIFTED under perturbations.

Figure 5 plots $|\mathbf{SPD}_t|$ for $\tau = 100$, and $\bar{z}_t = -0.01$ (light/medium traffic) and $\bar{z}_t = -0.03$ (extremely heavy traffic). It is visible that c is never reached in the latter case, since path removal following ε-inconsistency of (2) is quite frequent. However, smaller $|\mathbf{SPD}_t|$ (on average 31.7 vs. 47.3 under light/medium traffic) is paid for by worse guessing accuracy. Since $|\mathbf{SPD}_t|$ largely determines the computational complexity of GIFTED, we conclude that the scheme is computationally affordable even for RS with a relatively low-end processor.

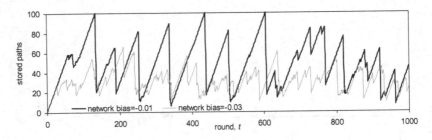

Fig. 5. SPD size, quasi-static IFT with $\tau = 100$.

Figure 6 shows the robustness of GIFTED to IFT variability. It can be seen that while τ is not much of a factor under extremely heavy traffic, consistent quasi-static nodal IFT with roughly $\tau \geq 100$ ensures fairly high guessing accuracy under light/medium traffic.

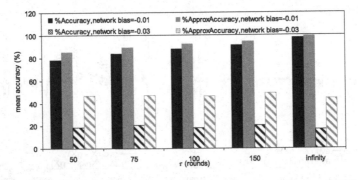

Fig. 6. Average accuracy metrics vs τ after 100 independent simulation runs; 95% confidence interval widths are within 5% of the average values.

5.3   Time-True Simulations

Time-true simulations were performed using Omnet++ v5.0.0 with INET framework v3.4.0 [22]. Assumptions (i) through (vi) remained in force, whereas instead of assumption (vii), a static 16-node WAHN topology in Fig. 7 was assumed. Each successive user session involved a 1 MB file transfer. For user packets, DumbTCP was used, an Omnet++'s TCP implementation with Nagle's algorithm disabled. For node-RS messages (PDR reports and disseminated reputation levels), UDP was used. User sessions were initiated at random instants and over randomly chosen paths. The number of concurrent sessions (active paths) varied up to M, where $M \leq 3$ and $M = 4$ corresponding to light/medium, and extremely heavy traffic conditions, respectively. The input traffic rates varied accordingly from 50 kb/s to 240 kb/s.

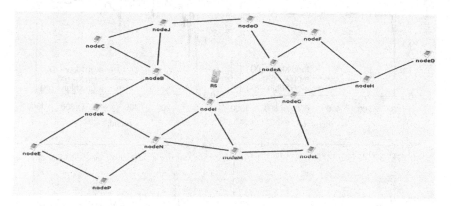

Fig. 7. Simulated 16-node WAHN.

Table 2 presents the simulation setup; other characteristics are as in Table 1 except that $\bar{z}_t$ is now estimated from observed PDRs as explained at the end of Sect. 3.

Table 2. Time-true simulation setup.

Parameter	Value
Nodal transmission power	1 mW
Receiver sensitivity	−90 dBm
Transmission error model	Ieee80211BerTableErrorModel [22]
MAC protocol	9 Mb/s IEEE 802.11 g
Nodal buffer size	50 user packets
Routing protocol	DSR with RREQ period = 1 s
Transport protocols	DumbTCP (between S_k and D_k), UDP (between node and RS)
TCP settings	MSS = 1452 B, window = 65535 B
Concurrent active paths	1..4

Figure 8 presents sample accuracy plots. For the light/medium traffic (left) they are qualitatively similar to those in Fig. 4, except that $\bar{z}_t$ was often a little below –0.01 due to occasional buffer overflow, which made it harder for GIFTED to recover from inconsistencies in (2). For the extremely heavy traffic (right), $\bar{z}_t$ was distinctly below –0.03, which prevented ε-perfect accuracy. Still, the $|r_{X,t} - g_{X,t}|$ remained fairly low on average, with reputation levels slightly overestimating ground-truth IFT. The $|\mathbf{SPD}_t|$ plots, not shown here, were similar to those in Fig. 5.

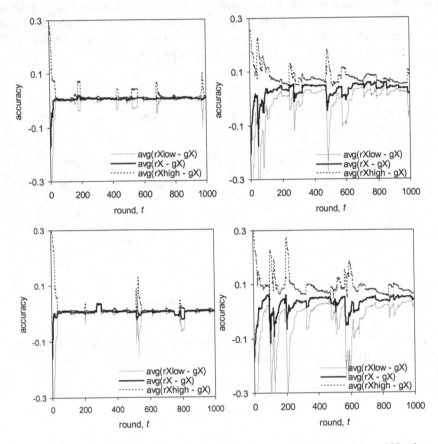

Fig. 8. Average accuracy for time-true simulations; $\tau = \infty$ (*top*) and $\tau = 100$ (*bottom*), light/medium traffic (*left*), heavy traffic (*right*).

5.4   Comparison with WPT

As mentioned in Sect. 1, the WPT scheme of [20] guesses a node's IFT as a weighted sum of incident paths' trust values. The latter are derived via fuzzy reasoning from end-to-end performance metrics such as PDR or average packet delay. For ease of comparison we take a path's trust value to be the observed PDR. Then for each node $X \in \mathbf{N}$:

$$r_{X,t} = \alpha \sum_{k \in \mathbf{K}_{X,t}} \frac{s_k}{\sum_{k \in \mathbf{K}_{X,t}} s_{k'}} PDR_k, \tag{5}$$

where $\mathbf{K}_{X,t}$ is the set of paths in $\mathbf{SPD}_t$ incident on X, i.e., for which $X \in \mathbf{X}_k$, (PDR_k, $k \in \mathbf{K}_{X,t}$) are the corresponding observed PDR values, and s_k is a measure of similarity of PDR_k to other PDR values in $\mathbf{K}_{X,t}$: $s_k = 1/ \sum_{k' \in \mathbf{K}_{X,t}} |PDR_k - PDR_{k'}|$. We have added the correction factor $\alpha > 1$ to account for the presence of other misbehaving transit nodes on the same path. Note that a path's trust value weighs more if it is close to the trust values of the other paths in $\mathbf{K}_{X,t}$; this is to control the impact of outlier paths with an abnormal number of misbehaving transit nodes, and of possible misreporting of PDR by misbehaving source nodes.

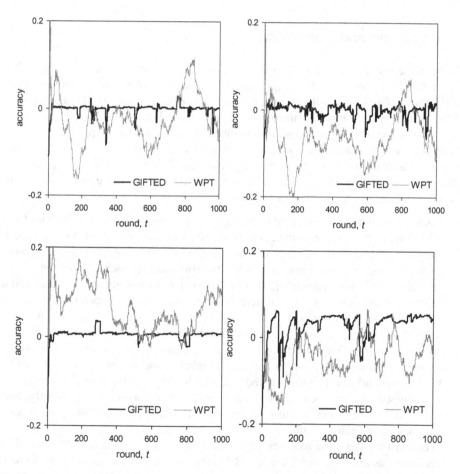

Fig. 9. Comparison of GIFTED and WPT average accuracy of reputation levels for $\tau = 100$; Monte Carlo simulations (*top*), time-true simulations (*bottom*); light/medium traffic (*left*), heavy traffic (*right*).

Figure 9 presents a comparison of GIFTED and WPT in terms of the average accuracy of reputation levels, i.e., $\frac{1}{|N|} \sum_{X \in N} (r_{X,t} - g_{X,t})$, for $\tau = 100$. Other relevant parameters are the same as in Table 1 and Table 2, in particular, the critical SPD size $c = 100$. The correction factor α was set to 2 to ensure that the accuracy plots lie as close as possible to the $y = 0$ line. One sees that for the volatile topology used in the Monte Carlo simulations, GIFTED yields a distinctly better accuracy both under light/medium and heavy traffic, whereas that of WPT tends to be unacceptably poor and varies unpredictably over time, roughly in step with significant IFT jumps. Decreasing c produces an even more erratic behavior of the average accuracy in terms of variability and magnitude. For the static topology used in the time-true simulations, GIFTED clearly outperforms WPT under light/medium traffic; under heavy traffic, GIFTED slightly overestimates ground-truth IFT as was noted earlier, yet even then produces more accurate guesses than WPT.

6 Discussion and Conclusion

In the presented reputation system for WAHNs and its underlying novel algorithm called GIFTED, nodes' IFT are guessed indirectly from observed end-to-end PDR performance. GIFTED is able to recover from perturbations of nodal IFTs and observed PDR, including occasional significant IFT jumps, as well as to work with any single-path source routing protocol, and any number of selfish nodes. It produces interval estimates of IFTs (hence, incorporating estimation credibility), which is a unique feature against the background of existing schemes. This makes GIFTED a valuable alternative to existing misbehavior detection schemes. A few more points are worth stressing regarding the viability of GIFTED:

- much research has been devoted to distinguishing nodes' cooperative behavior from misbehavior, and in case of the latter, to identify its reasons: bad intentions or harsh channel/traffic conditions, with an ultimate goal to eliminate intentionally misbehaving nodes, cf. the sequential probability ratio test approach [23] or the packet loss autocorrelation approach [24]; in contrast, we do not attempt to label nodal behavior in any way, nor do we differentiate treatment (such a "liberal" view echoes that of [21])—our premise is that if a node X exhibits $g_X < 1$, it must have its reasons and should be later avoided or punished regardless of those reasons,
- no cooperation is required from low-layer mechanisms like watchdog or ACKs covering path segments, which are often unreliable and not incentive compatible; PDR reports rely on end-to-end feedback which has to be employed anyway,
- no attempt is made to locate packet losses (hence, misbehaving nodes) directly; thus costly challenge-response based node audit mechanisms or flow conservation analyses are dispensed with,
- in contrast with existing schemes, any number of misbehaving nodes along a path is permitted, as are time-variable nodal IFTs, any source routing protocol, directional antennae, multichannel transmission, and e-t-e encrypted packets,

- an extension to multipath routing and path changing during a session is straight-forward upon a slight modification whereby the destination node appends to end-to-end ACKs information on actual paths followed by individual packets,
- GIFTED is incentive compatible—cooperation is required only from interested parties: transit nodes relay end-to-end ACKs towards the source node to get credit for forwarding session packets (note that collusion among transit nodes is not an issue, as poor path performance would reflect on all of them), and the source node sends truthful PDR reports to RS to help derive accurate reputation levels (which it may use when selecting paths for subsequent sessions); the latter assumption is sometimes questioned, e.g., [20] addresses slander/harboring on the part of source nodes, whereas prevention of spurious end-to-end ACKs and/or PDR reports would require some cryptographic proof of packet forwarding by transit nodes,
- more sophisticated node behavior, e.g., path selective, sleeper or on-off attacks [3] is arguably covered at least in part by the resiliency of GIFTED to limited-frequency significant IFT jumps,
- although RS has been assumed a trusted third party, in real life source nodes may be concerned about the privacy of their PDR reports (in particular, the transit nodes they often use); anonymization of PDR reports thus remains an issue, and
- in the distributed version of GIFTED, sketched in footnote 2, scalability of the path equation systems to be solved by each source node's RS could be ensured by only accepting PDR reports pertaining to a transit node subset of interest, e.g., in the geographical vicinity of the source node.

Since GIFTED involves approximate decomposition of a path equation system, validation through both Monte Carlo and time-true simulations was conducted. For a 16-node WAHN, various parameter configurations were tested to determine the robustness of GIFTED, i.e., the ability to near-perfectly guess the nodes' IFT in the presence of perturbations, as well as the required size of SPD. Overall, GIFTED turned out fairly robust, except when too frequent significant jumps of IFT (one in less than 50 rounds, network-wide) or extremely heavy traffic (more than three active paths at a time) created a network bias below -0.03, in which case both $\left| r_{X,t}^{\text{high}} - r_{X,t}^{\text{low}} \right|$ and $|r_{X,t} - g_{X,t}|$ typically became intolerable. Still, GIFTED was found to compare favorably with the existing WPT scheme [20] in all examined WAHN settings.

Besides the obvious task of specifying a distributed version of GIFTED (possibly including node mobility to extend our results to vehicular and mobile ad hoc networks), which is our planned immediate future work, a serious challenge is to design an IFT guessing scheme able to cooperate with a non-source routing protocol. This will permit to deploy GIFTED-like solutions in volatile WAHN topologies (e.g., featuring highly mobile nodes), where DSR fails due to an explosion of RREQ and RREP messages. Finally, the effectiveness of GIFTED combined with pathrater or indirect reciprocity based cooperation enforcement mechanisms will be investigated.

Acknowledgment. Work funded by the National Science Center, Poland, under Grant UMO-2016/21/B/ST6/03146.

References

1. Buttyan, L., Hubaux, J.-P.: Stimulating cooperation in self-organizing mobile ad hoc networks. ACM J. Mob. Netw. (MONET). Special Issue on Mobile Ad Hoc Networks (2002)
2. Li, Z., Shen, H.: Game-theoretic analysis of cooperation incentive strategies in mobile ad hoc networks. IEEE Trans. Mob. Comput. **11**(8), 1287–1303 (2012)
3. Movahedi, Z., Hosseini, Z., Bayan, F., Pujolle, G.: Trust-distortion resistant trust management frameworks on mobile ad hoc networks: a survey. IEEE Commun. Surv. Tutor. **18**(2), 1287–1309 (2016)
4. Buchegger, S., Le Boudec, J.-Y.: Performance analysis of the CONFIDANT protocol. In: Proceedings of the 3rd ACM International Symposium on Mobile Ad Hoc Networking and Computing, Lausanne, Switzerland, pp. 226–236 (2002)
5. Jaramillo, J.J., Srikant, R.: A game theory based reputation mechanism to incentivize cooperation in wireless ad hoc networks. Ad Hoc Netw. **8**, 416–429 (2010)
6. Michiardi, P., Molva, R.: CORE: a collaborative reputation mechanism to enforce node cooperation in mobile ad hoc networks. In: Proceedings of the 6th IFIP Communications and Multimedia Security Conference, Portoroz, Slovenia, pp. 107–121 (2002)
7. Gupta, S., Kumar, C.: An intelligent efficient secure routing protocol for MANET. Int. J. Futur. Gener. Commun. Netw. **6**(1), 111–131 (2013)
8. Rodriguez-Mayol, A., Gozalvez, J.: Reputation based selfishness prevention techniques for mobile ad-hoc networks. Telecommun. Syst. **57**, 181–195 (2014)
9. Gopalakrishnan, K., Uthariaraj, V.R.: Acknowledgment based reputation mechanism to mitigate the node misbehavior in mobile ad hoc networks. J. Comput. Sci. **7**(8), 1157–1166 (2011)
10. Zhang, Y., Lazos, L., Kozma, W.J.: AMD: audit-based misbehavior detection in wireless ad hoc networks. IEEE Trans. Mob. Comput. **15**(8), 1893–1907 (2016)
11. Graffi, K., Mogre, P.S., Hollick, M., Steinmetz, R.: Detection of colluding misbehaving nodes in mobile ad hoc and wireless mesh networks. In: Proceedings of the IEEE GLOBECOM 2007, Washington DC (2007)
12. Paracha, M.A., Ahmad, S., Akram, A., Anwar, M.W.: Cooperative reputation index based selfish node detection and prevention system for mobile ad hoc networks. Res. J. Appl. Sci., Eng. Technol. **4**(3), 201–205 (2012)
13. Chiejina, E., Hannan Xiao, H., Christianson, B.: A dynamic reputation management system for mobile ad hoc networks. In: Proceedings of the 6th Computer Science and Electronic Engineering Conference, Colchester, UK, pp. 133–138 (2014)
14. Johnson, D., Maltz, D., Broch, J.: DSR: The Dynamic Source Routing Protocol for Multi-Hop Wireless Ad Hoc Networks. Addison-Wesley, Boston MA (2001)
15. Nowicki, K., Uhl, T.: QoS/QoE in the Heterogeneous Internet of Things (IoT). In: Batalla, J. M., Mastorakis, G., Mavromoustakis, C.X., Pallis, E. (eds.) Beyond the Internet of Things. IT, pp. 165–196. Springer, Cham (2017). https://doi.org/10.1007/978-3-319-50758-3_7
16. Liu, K.J.R., Wang, B.: Cognitive Radio Networking and Security A Game-Theoretic View. Cambridge University Press, Cambridge (2011). ch. 11
17. Konorski, J., Rydzewski, K: A centralized reputation system for MANETs based on observed path performance. In: Proceedings of the 8th IFIP Wireless and Mobile Networking Conference, Munich, Germany, pp. 56–63 (2015)
18. Lawson, C.L., Hanson, R.J.: Solving Least Squares Problems. Prentice-Hall, Englewood Cliffs (1974)

19. Kim, N.J.: Linear programming with random requirements. Utah State University reports, paper 272 (1968)
20. Tan, S., Li, X., Dong, Q.: A trust management system for securing data plane of ad-hoc networks. IEEE Trans. Veh. Technol. **65**(9), 7579–7592 (2016)
21. Xue, Y., Nahrstedt, K.: Providing fault-tolerant ad-hoc routing service in adversarial environments. Wirel. Pers. Commun. **29**(3/4), 367–388 (2004)
22. OpenSim Ltd. Homepage. https://omnetpp.org/. Accessed 19 July 2019
23. Refaei, M.T., DaSilva, L.A., Eltoweissy, M., Nadeem, T.: Adaptation of reputation management systems to dynamic network conditions in ad hoc networks. IEEE Trans. Comput. **59**(5), 707–719 (2010)
24. Shu, T., Krunz, M.: Privacy-preserving and truthful detection of packet dropping attacks in wireless ad hoc networks. IEEE Trans. Mob. Comput. **14**(4), 813–828 (2015)

Author Index

Printed in the United States
by Bookmasters

Printed in the United States
By Bookmasters